The Collector's Voice:
Critical Readings in the Practice of Collecting

Perspectives on Collecting
Edited by Susan Pearce
University of Leicester, UK

The Collector's Voice:
Critical Readings in the Practice of Collecting

Volume 2
Early Voices

Edited by
SUSAN PEARCE AND KEN ARNOLD

Ashgate

Aldershot • Burlington USA • Singapore • Sydney

© 2000 Susan Pearce and Ken Arnold

All rights reserved. No part of this publication may be reproduced, stored in a retrieval system, or transmitted in any form or by any means, electronic, mechanical, photocopied, recorded, or otherwise without the prior permission of the publisher.

The authors have asserted their right under the Copyright, Designs and Patents Act, 1988, to be identified as the authors of this work.

Published by

Ashgate Publishing Ltd
Gower House, Croft Road,
Aldershot, Hampshire GU11 3HR
England

Ashgate Publishing Company
131 Main Street
Burlington, Vermont 05401–5600
USA

Ashgate website: http://www.ashgate.com

ISBN 1 85928 418 3

British Library Cataloguing-in-Publication Data
The collector's voice: critical readings in the practice
   of collecting
   Vol. 2: Ancient voices
   1. Antiquities – Collection and preservation – History
   2. Collectibles – History   3. Collectors and collecting in
   literature   4. Europe – Antiquities
   I. Pearce, Susan M. (Susan Mary), 1942–   II. Arnold, Ken
   069.4'094'0903

US Library of Congress Cataloging-in-Publication Data
The collector's voice : critical readings in the practice of collecting / edited by Susan Pearce and Alexandra Bounia and Ken Arnold.
      p.   cm.   Contents: v. 1. Ancient voices — v. 2. Early voices.
      Includes bibliographical references and index.
      1. Collectors and collecting—History.   2. Collectors and collecting—Europe—
   History.   3. Collectors and collecting—Philosophy.   4. Collectors and
   collecting—Social aspects.   I. Pearce, Susan M.   II. Bounia, Alexandra.   III.
   Arnold, Ken
   AM221.C65   2000
   790.1'32—dc21   00–0044169

This volume is printed on acid-free paper.

Typeset by Manton Typesetters, Louth, Lincolnshire, UK.
Printed in Great Britain by MPG Books Ltd, Bodmin, Cornwall.

Undergraduate Lending Library
WITHDRAWN

Contents

III Enlightened voices

IV Antique voices

V   Strange voices

General Preface to Series

The study of collecting is a growth point in cultural studies. Like most exciting developments, it is on the cusp where older studies meet and stimulate each other; but it is also conceived as a study of practice, of the ways in which people make sense of the world by bringing elements together. Because we and our world are material, and our ways of understanding are tied to the physical reality of material, one of the prime ways in which this sense is created is through the accumulation and juxtaposition of material things. Following the seminal publication of Benjamin's essays and Arendt's Introduction to them (1970), a range of studies have been important in the development of our understanding in this field. Some have been in the broader field of material culture (for example Appadurai, 1986; Miller, 1985; Hodder, 1986). Others have contributed to our understanding of museums, as the institution *par excellence* which sustains and is sustained by the practice of collecting (for example Hooper-Greenhill, 1992; Bennett, 1995; Pearce, 1992). Closely related to this has been the whole People's Show Project which brought contemporary collectors into museum galleries and opened up an important range of popular collecting issues (for example Lovatt, 1997). This climate of interest, linked with important studies by Baudrillard (1984), Pomian (1990) and Stewart (1984) have stimulated a number of specialised studies in the collecting field. Elsner and Cardinal have published an important collection of essays on individual collecting topics (1994) and Pearce has produced a broad analysis of collecting practice (1995) and a study of contemporary popular collecting practice (1998), while Martin has published an analysis of the relationship between collecting and social institutions at the end of the twentieth century (1999). Arnold has produced a study of the 'cabinets of curiosity' phenomenon, and Bounia and Thomason have turned their attention to ancient collecting, Bounia of the classical world (1998) and Thomason of the ancient Middle East. Flanders is working on the collecting processes associated with nineteenth-century museums, and a number of similar pieces of work are in progress.

This intellectual realisation has been matched by a flood of popular interest in collectors and collecting. The *Independent, The Times* and the *Guardian* now run regular collecting columns. The BBC sees ever-increasing spin-offs from the *Antiques Roadshow* programme, and the other channels, television and radio, have their own series. A parallel reverberation of the same phenomenon is seen in the extent to which collecting, used in a variety of ways, appears as a recurrent theme in contemporary fiction.

The four volumes of *The Collector's Voice: Critical Readings in the Practice of Collecting* series take the perspective of the long term. The first, *Ancient Voices*, addresses collecting practice in ancient northern Europe, ancient and classical Greece and imperial Rome, and the post-Roman period through the early and high Middle Ages to the beginnings of European early modernism in the fifteenth century. The second, *Early Voices*, covers collecting during the sixteenth and seventeenth centuries, and into the early eighteenth century. The third, *Imperial Voices*, concentrates upon nineteenth- and earlier twentieth-century collectors up to about 1960. The final volume, *Contemporary Voices*, focuses attention upon the nature of collecting in the closing decades of the twentieth century. In all four volumes the written, or sometimes recorded, voices of the collectors themselves are paramount, but it is hoped that the editorial content which surrounds each text will place the quoted material in its appropriate context.

Two issues emerge clearly from what has been said: the definition of 'collecting'; and the idea of a 'European tradition' of collecting, which presupposes that the notion of a continuity of ideas and practices from one generation to another over a period of several millennia within a particular, and relatively limited, geographical area is a valid premise on which to mount investigation. Benjamin in his essay on his library (1970), and Arendt in her Introduction to his essays, both of which stand at the head of the contemporary critique of collecting practice, make the point that 'insofar as the past has been transmitted as tradition, it possesses authority; insofar as authority presents itself historically, it becomes tradition' (Arendt, 1970: 38). But this line of thought undermines the notion of tradition as an essentially valid element in the historical process; it does not break out of the human predicament which means that the only way in which to behave newly or differently is to do so in relation to a past, which is inevitably perceived as a powerful influence upon the present. And, of course, through most generations, people have not particularly wished to break dramatically with the past, but rather to improve upon it.

The generational link is essentially one of perception: individuals in each generation have an idea, by word of mouth or by reading, of what their predecessors did, and make their own use of what comes to them as the traditions of the past; it should be recognised that the capacity to accumulate goods, and to access the traditions of the past, tend to rest with the same restricted class of people, for whom the past as they perceive it is of importance because it provides the legitimisation for their present position. To put the point slightly differently, the fostering of the notion of a broad European tradition has been an important aspect of self-identity among the collecting classes, whatever they have actually made of it, and so it must also do so in a critique of collecting practice.

The definition of 'Europe' emerges within this context as a series of self-fulfilling arguments. These centre on a broadly similar 'heroic' prehistory across Europe susceptible to interpretation along Homeric lines, and a range of shared authors writing in Greek and Latin, beginning with Homer. Christendom follows as the successor to the classical world, defined in opposition to Islam and sharing a Latin culture which endured into the eighteenth century. Thereafter is seen a common Enlightenment, a common focus on imperialist nation states, and a common disillusion as the second millennium AD closes. Outsiders have been variously defined as barbarians, non-citizens, pagans and natives, and as being unenlightened and underdeveloped, but the core area defined in terms of the perceived intellectual tradition of which collecting is a part has remained remarkably stable, historical fluctuations notwithstanding, and concentrates upon north-western Europe and the lands around the northern Mediterranean shore.

Within all this, how can 'collecting' and 'collection' be viewed usefully as an aid to the critique through personal testimony of particular material social practices? Here we have to recognise that collecting is a complex business and that a difficult path must be taken between 'collecting' as narrowly defined in recent decades, and in relation to recent generations (see Pearce, 1995: 39–56 for a summary), and much broader 'accumulation' which contemporaries would not have seen as 'collections' in any meaningful way (although successors might). The view taken in the last three volumes of this series is that 'collectors' are left to be self-defining on the understanding that they will define themselves, of course, according to their perception of their relationship to the European tradition just discussed. The first volume takes a wider view, for reasons which are discussed in its Introduction.

The contemporary interest in collecting practices, referred to earlier, needs the core reference material which is essential to its study, and the present series addresses this need. This formative material is extremely difficult to access because it is widely scattered, exists only patchily in specialist libraries and archives, and sometimes requires translating, usually from Greek or Latin, into English. The editors have endeavoured to bring the most interesting material together, translate it if necessary, and present each piece with an introduction, explanatory notes and bibliographical references. All choice is subjective, and not all will agree with the choices made here; and the editors themselves are aware of much interesting material which has had to be omitted. But we hope that enough is offered to provide material for discussion and to provoke future review of notions about collecting practices in the European tradition.

Susan Pearce, General Editor
August 1999

Acknowledgements

Many people have helped to bring this book into being. Susan Pearce would particularly like to thank the librarians at the Society of Antiquaries, the British Library, the Bodleian Library and the University of Leicester Library. She is also grateful to Professor Aubrey Newman and Chris Albury for help with material, and Ann Sarson for her expert word-processing. Ken Arnold wishes to thank Julie Hochstrasser, and the invaluable assistance of Paul Psoirios for the translation from the Latin of the extract from the work of Samuel à Quiccheberg.

We are both grateful to Rachel Lynch and Cathrin Vaughan at Ashgate Publishing and our best thanks go to our families and friends for encouragement and support. All errors and omissions are, of course, our own responsibility.

Every effort has been made to trace all the copyright holders, but if any have been inadvertently overlooked the publishers will be pleased to make the necessary arrangement at the first opportunity.

Introduction

The title of this, the second volume of the *Collector's Voice* series, was chosen with great care, and the final selection, *Early Voices*, is intended to reflect the notion that between 1500 and 1820 (or thereabouts) the conceptual world of Europe had been transformed from what might be labelled a medieval outlook, to one which clearly has much in common with that of the world we inhabit. The bundle of images, concepts, assumptions and capacities which together make up the mindset of what is often called 'modernism' came together in these centuries, which embrace the earlier phase (roughly 1500–1660) and a middle phase (roughly 1660–1820). The final phase of 'late' or 'mature' modernism (c. 1820–1960) will be the subject of Volume 3. The perceived relationship between humankind and the material world is in many ways at the heart of the transformation, and its collecting aspect is traced here.

This volume is divided into five parts, a division which serves two purposes. It reflects a chronological distinction in which the material discussed in Part I, 'Curious voices', covers broadly 1500–1660, that in Part II, 'Scientific voices', covers 1660–1730, and that in Part III, 'Enlightened voices', 1730–1820. However, the last two chapters parallel what we see happening in the later part of the period: Part IV, 'Antique voices', discusses the siren lure the remains of classical antiquity had for the collectors of the period, and Part V, 'Strange voices', charts the underside of the Enlightenment.

Sixteenth- and early seventeenth-century museums were placed at the very core of an intellectual quest that they helped define: namely the disciplined exploitation of wonder and curiosity. In this period, museums became the unofficial laboratories *cum* public fora for a new empirical and increasingly 'rational' approach to the material world. The manner in which collectors and curators pursued this research agenda was to bring within museum walls a whole series of enquiries and interests which had hitherto been scattered across various disciplines, as well as commercial and social spheres – from the treasure chests of seafaring adventurers to the fashionable studies of *virtuosi* gentlemen, and from alchemists' garrets to apothecaries' storerooms.

A seemingly improbable start for this era in the history of museums is located in a curious wooden structure, stuffed full of images, words and objects, to be found in 1530s Venice – Guilio Camillo Delminio's memory theatre. The contraption, which was meant to present the entire body of the world's knowledge in microcosm to a royal personage, crystallised at least three key elements in the emergent idea of the early modern museum. First, the physical space of Camillo's theatre aimed to impart knowledge in a condensed manner; second, it housed not just words but also images and objects, and third, it strove to focus attention by excluding the outside world of distractions.

The same goal of using a 'cabinet' to capture the world in microcosm was to be found in a work by Samuel á Quiccheberg, held by many to be the first published treatise on modern museums. Buildings and collections of the type Quiccheberg outlined could, by the mid-sixteenth century, already be found in Europe; but his pioneering innovation lay in turning an aristocratic habit into an abstract museological monograph. A third foundational text in this formative period of modern museology came from the pen of Gabriel Kaltermarckt, an itinerant artist who sought employment as royal curator by proposing the establishment of an Italian-style *Kunstkammer* in the city of Dresden.

These theoretical tracts were balanced by the practical activities of many more contemporary collectors. The passage from Ulisse Aldrovandi's work on insects (1602) reveals both some of the physical but also the social skills required of a museum collector and cataloguer. His collection of natural history specimens, and the didactic and disciplinary function to which he put it, also serves to indicate the emergence of an almost separate tradition of collecting alongside the more aristocratic concern for art treasures. His use of specimens in an exhaustive survey of nature in all its specificity turned on its head the dominant medieval concern to descend from theoretical principles to natural examples.

A working principle in Aldrovandi's encyclopaedic enterprise, this concern with empiricism was at the heart of Francis Bacon's scientific, cultural and social philosophy. Though Bacon does not himself seem to have set up a museum, his advice about doing so allows us to call attention to the absolutely central role of Baconian thought in the development of museums in this period. Bacon was in all things a reformer, and his recipe for improving intellectual life was to accumulate vast arrays of factual evidence, from which conjectures inductively and inevitably would follow. Along with libraries, gardens, menageries, chemical laboratories, mechanical workshops and the like, the other innovative institution central to this enormous empirical enquiry was the museum.

Along with empirical enquiry, another endeavour fundamentally crucial to the formation of early modern museums is travel. One looks in vain for a poorly-travelled collector in this period. In England, the importance of travel was twofold, providing both the opportunity to collect new objects but also exposing initially the upper classes to the fashionable Continental habit of collecting. A prime example of how such travel could spawn a lifetime of collecting comes in the figure of Thomas Howard, Earl of Arundel, whose London house had by the late 1630s taken on the appearance of one of the Italian palaces that he had first fallen in love with when on tour twenty years earlier. This aristocratic enthusiasm for collecting was particularly effectively disseminated through works like that of Henry Peacham (himself patronised by the Earl of Arundel), which included collecting coins and antiquities amongst its guidelines for proper gentlemanly conduct, thus creating a new social category: the gentleman-scholar. The social spread of this collecting urge was further aided by the practice of grand collectors employing 'agents'. A notable example of this effect comes in the career of John Tradescant the elder, who as gardener to various members of the aristocracy founded the museum which was to become the Ashmolean Museum in Oxford.

Collectors of both high and low birth were both prone to seeing and using their collections as a source of anecdotes – as, that is, a narrative extension of their own life stories. This intellectual rationale for teasing knowledge out of objects is perfectly illustrated in the preserved notes to the collection of John Bargrave (1610–80), in which his gathered objects are almost exclusively described in terms of anecdotes and narratives that they prompt him to remember. Bargrave's catalogue exemplifies a trend running throughout much seventeenth-century collecting – namely the crucial role played by the collector's or curator's own personal knowledge in the presentation of his curiosities. Though subject to the much more rigorous analysis demanded by the process of turning such anecdotes into a published monograph, this same strategy of using objects to anchor a series of narratives can also be seen in Robert Plot's reliance on objects in compiling his topographical, natural historical surveys of Oxfordshire (1677) and Staffordshire (1686).

An object-type commonly designated at the time as 'artificial' (that is, man-made) and 'exotic' (that is, not from the West) tended to be treated to a rather different form of analysis. Because reliable reports of new or poorly understood overseas lands were hard to come by, the real objects sent back by the likes of the John Winthrops, grandfather and grandson, to the Royal Society in London at the end of the seventeenth century were welcomed as a form of evidence that could reassuringly be contemplated and to some extent tested back home. The huge numbers of new objects that such voyagers brought or sent back to Europe were most commonly assessed in terms of how they compared to familiar objects, with which – either in terms of their form or especially their use – they seemed to bear a striking resemblance. Much of the interest in the material culture of foreign countries was therefore distinctly utilitarian. As a consequence, objects from far-flung cultures tended to be ascribed a categorical character that it was extremely tempting to understand simply in terms of variations within a known category. Limited as this type of analysis clearly was, even impoverished mental exercises suggest the way ahead for what would more than a century later become a museum-based enquiry into non-Western material cultures.

The intellectual strategies employed on the one hand to understanding objects as factual evidence of a collector's anecdotal tales, or on the other, as functional units from a different but comprehensible 'exotic' culture, were both destined to be seen as peripheral to a third more important method of extracting knowledge from objects, which, it was held, allowed objects to 'speak for themselves'. The rudiments of this ultimately dominant methodology can, for example, be seen in the work of James Petiver, a London apothecary who used his shop to accumulate a vast collection of natural history specimens. Derivative rather than original, Petiver's methods sum up the standard practices of many early eighteenth-century collectors, who simply recorded specimens by 'Names, Descriptions and Vertues'.

What Petiver's vague notion of 'vertue' masked was the complex and increasingly absorbing question of how most appropriately to order and organise a collection. As the passage taken from Robert Hooke's writings makes clear, this question had elaborate philosophical implications about the nature of both human minds and the world they perceived. Reaching back to the legacy of Renaissance memory theatres, Hooke conceived of the mind as an ordered space for impressions of material objects, that is, a sort of museum in the mind. Such rather arcane philosophical speculations had their more tangible implications in suggesting that such 'mental repositories' would best be nurtured by well-ordered actual museums.

These abstract philosophical musings were further elaborated by John Wilkins, one of the primary advocates for the new empirical science in England, whose work on reforming language made great claims for the significance of establishing a well-ordered, universally representative museum, in order to yield taxonomic tables on which a new language would be based. Like many of the Royal Society's goals, Wilkins' scheme for the museum was overambitious, but it did give a clear purpose to many of those most closely involved in the society's museum, making their primary concern its rational organisation, and thereafter reorganisation. So that although Nehemiah Grew's 1681 published catalogue of the museum embodied an eclectic survey of other taxonomic schemes, his efforts did nonetheless bear the strong imprint of Wilkins' philosophy.

The enduring impact of the Wilkins' philosophical prescriptions for museums were, however, best seen in the activities of individual collectors like the geologist and earth theorist John Woodward, whose collecting activities were animated by his intention to organise his specimens in a scientifically authoritative manner. What cemented attitudes like Woodward's into a more or less fixed research policy for museums was the conversion of private cabinets into institutional museums. The latter tended to be larger, and they also at least promised greater security and longevity for the collections. However, the real significance of the shift came in the associated ideology that museums should be part of an effort to add to investigative philosophy as a form of public knowledge, rather than just private diversion.

That stated, one Englishman's private collections rivalled the scale of material gathered in any contemporary institutional museum, and he was Hans Sloane. Professionally guided into lucrative medical practice by Thomas Sydenham, Sloane's 'virtuosic' concerns for natural history were encouraged and refined under the guidance of John Ray, Robert Boyle and Joseph de Tournefort. His collecting habit started on youthful botanising trips and flourished with increasing financial security, until in 1753 his collections included hundreds of shells, thousands of vegetable specimens, and tens of thousands of medals. A collection on this scale constituted something of an institution in its own right even before it was formally used as the nucleus for a new national institution (the British Museum), destined to have such a large and lasting impact on the history of museums.

Meanwhile, the collectors of the generation which come to early maturity around 1700 were able, as no predecessors had been, to draw on very large and relatively well-documented collections, especially in the natural history or *naturalia* field. The extract taken from the work of Valentini, in which he lists the major European collections known to him, encapsulates a number of important themes. The big collections, which were, of course, surrounded by a large cloud of smaller ones, were well known, had often produced published catalogues, and were open to visits from suitable persons. As the eighteenth century progressed, hand-lists of collectors and collections were compiled and circulated or published relatively readily (see, for example, the list made by Mendes da Costa published in the *Gentleman's Magazine* 1812, 82: 205; 83: 107).

This meant that contemporary students had a body of material on which to work, and that there was sufficient material available to enable patterns to emerge and broader conclusions about the nature of the natural world to be drawn. It also meant that collecting entered a new phase of self-consciousness and self-confidence which would ultimately feed into the establishment of national museums, and their connection with nationalism.

The career of Carl Linnaeus brings out the significance of the collecting network particularly clearly. Linnaeus himself made a substantial collection of natural history specimens, most of which eventually came to England, but he was also able to work on the material in the collections of Hans Sloane, of the Royal Society, and of other collectors in London.

The classification system which he devised for nature, that is virtually for God himself, with its strongly erotic overtones, and its sense of cosmological order and propriety, had a profound effect on Linnaeus' own and subsequent generations. It took up the early modern notion of the collection as microcosm of the universe and transformed it into a detailed chart of eternal correspondence in which not just singular pieces, but all normal natural elements, had their appointed place. The Linnaean system is an ancient idea expressed in enlightened, scientific terms, and its imaginative effect was correspondingly powerful. Through him, and others like him, the scientists of the eighteenth and nineteenth centuries were able to establish a mode in which God (although not necessarily the Christian God) could be seen as a scientist, and his world as a regulated, orderly place where sensible predictions would produce expected outcomes.

The natural history theme, an area of collecting where Britons were particularly important, continues with the Duchess of Portland, who also had very important classical material, with Joseph Banks whose travels with Captain James Cook gave him a special chance to gather Pacific specimens, and with Mary Anning and Ethelred Bennett, whose interest was aroused by the fossil-rich countryside in which they lived. It is worth noting the significance of these women collectors in a field which is often written of as if it were a male preserve. The cross-links between collectors, and the relation of them all to the growing specimen market, are also very important. A means for publishing the details of finds became necessary, and the *Philosophical Transactions of the Royal Society* carried this kind of information, among other less prestigious publications.

Meanwhile, collections of artwork continued to be made, for reasons in which the desire to impress loomed large. The letter from John Talman to Dr Aldrich concerning the sale of the Resta Collection of drawings combines an idea of how such sales could be managed with details of a collection whose pedigree was supposed to span European art and art appreciation. Similarly, Thomas Martyn's description of English art collections show both how extensive these were by the 1760s, and how much interest there was in gathering together information about them. An effort to be impressive naturally stimulates satire, which was, in any case, a favourite genre of the eighteenth century. One of the most famous and most successful compositions out of much contemporary occasional verse lampooning collectors is given here: Alexander Pope's lines, 'Timon's villa', itself part of a larger work, but we should remember that satire, like the humorous cartoon, only crystallises at the end of a process, when the object of the funny story is a well-established and usually respected social habit.

How established and respected is made very clear by the major efforts directed by European royalty to the development of their art collections. The creation of prestigious princely art collections runs back, of course, to the Medicis and their Italian contemporaries, followed swiftly by various Hapsburg and German princes, and then those of north-western Europe: a high point was reached with the collection of Charles I of England. Gradually, the royal collections were turned by their owners into public museums. The Viennese Royal Collection was moved into the Belvedere Palace in 1776, and here an historical display was conceived, with pictures in schools and periods with uniform frames and labels, and a specially written *Guide* by Christian von Mechel. All this was intended to help public viewers understand what they were seeing, and became the art gallery norm. By the 1760s the Dresden Gallery of the Electors of Saxony was open to the public, and the Florentine Uffizi was donated to the state in 1743. The Munich Glyptothek was built as a public museum for the Bavarian royal collection, and open by 1830. Art was becoming valued not just for its spiritual qualities, but also because it offered a way of linking these virtues with a strengthening national consciousness.

In Britain and France, where national self-consciousness perhaps ran deepest, the emergence of national collections was more tortuous, perhaps because it was more overtly political. In Britain, the British Museum was officially opened in 1759 and was an amalgamation of several private collections, principally that of Sloane. It was originally best endowed with books and manuscripts, especially the collections of Harley, Cotton and King George III. Alone among the great European museums, it was not, and is not, primarily a museum of art (something which overseas visitors still find strange) and it was not until it started accumulating major collections of classical antiquities, beginning with that of Townley in 1805, that it began to acquire what is now seen as its essential character. At the same time, its natural history collection grew, and had eventually to be constituted as a national museum in its own right as the Natural History Museum (the initial decision to divide off the natural history collections was taken in 1878). By the 1820s, it was the grandest statement of the encyclopaedic museum available to the public. Its opening in 1759 had indicated not only the increasing importance that would be placed on the manner in which the visiting public would perceive the collection but also the inherent order of objects and natural specimens that they were encouraged to imbibe.

In France, political upheavals, themselves part of gathering modernism, overtook events. There had been a plan since at least the 1740s to turn the royal collections housed in the old Louvre Palace into a museum with public access. Eventually, after much debate and in radically different circumstances, this was achieved in 1792. At the same time, radical

Revolutionary politics were forced to come to terms with the huge quantity of antiquities and artworks which derived from the *ancien régime* and were therefore ideologically suspect, but which were also recognised as important and as part of the genius of France. The solution was to treat them as belonging to the Republic, to be gathered, catalogued, dispersed and displayed for the edification of the citizens. The same sentiments may have originally animated Napoleon, but his acquisition of Continental artworks for France soon took on the character of trophy hunting and imperial glorification.

The presence of antiquity, so visible in Rome and the Italian countryside, but also open to view across Spain, Austria, France and Britain northwards to Hadrian's Wall, had never dropped from the consciousness of Christendom: the Pope was Bishop of Rome, the Emperor Caesar's successor, and Latin the language of the Western church. We hear throughout the centuries between the political collapse of the western Roman empire around AD 450 and the creation of new interest a little before 1500, sporadic mentions of men who were interested in, and made collections of, the physical remains of Roman culture. We know a little of the activities of men like Wilfred of Northumbria, Henry of Winchester and Master Gregory who maintained the link across the centuries, and probably there were others of whom we do not hear. This interest fed into the efforts of the Medici and others of their contemporaries, who were collectors of the antique, so that by the 1480s it looks as if a collectors' market in classical statuary and architectural fragments had already been established (see Volume 1 of this series).

Interest gathered throughout the sixteenth and seventeenth centuries, with the Earl of Arundel as the premier northern collector, but as the enlightened and scientific views created by the generation which flourished in the last third of the seventeenth century superseded the earlier preoccupation with religious practice, so classical norms of thought and representation were seen as increasingly significant. In the thought of Winckelmann, especially, these were linked with an historical view of art which allowed it to be understood as a succession of 'periods' in which early tentative styles come to full flower, and then degenerate, and also with the new idea that 'art' existed as a spiritual quality in its own right as an object of contemplation. The result was an emphasis on the 'great' period of Greek art – that of Phideias and Praxiteles in the fifth century BC – the works of which were to be seen as the peak of a qualitatively superior human endeavour.

Winckelmann brought the new discoveries (from 1748) at Pompeii and Herculaneum to a wide audience. At much the same time the classical world beyond Italy was beginning to be systematically explored, with Revett and Stuart in Athens, sponsored by the Society of Dilettante, and

Robert Wood in Palmyra, of which he wrote an influential description and art-historical analysis. The result was a powerful impetus to the collection of antique marbles, and in Britain major collections were formed by Charles Townley and Henry Blundell, together with many small accumulations. This activity was part and parcel of the fashion for the Grand Tour which required young men of education, means and fashion to travel to Italy, spending time on the trip visiting historical sites, acquiring cosmopolitan polish, and returning with antiquities with which to furnish their country houses. Richard Worsley is typical of this company, although distinguished by the size and importance of his collection. A generation later, William Hamilton acted in a broadly similar spirit.

Through a cascade effect, natural in a society like Britain's with a thrusting bourgeoisie fuelled by the profits of gathering industrial change and imperial trade, who were anxious to spend money and gain fashion, a consumer market in antiquities and the antique style developed. Plasterwork shops produced and sold a range of domestic fittings in the classical taste, which were collected then and have been ever since. Families like the Albacini sold art-quality plastercasts taken from classical originals which went to build up a range of collections in Britain. As the Tatham–Holland correspondence shows, many collectors were willing to acquire a mixture of genuine classical pieces, copies taken directly from the antique, and contemporary material designed in the antique taste.

This points up a crucial moment in the creation of taste. Winckelmann had never visited Greece, and his knowledge of classical art depended not upon the Greek originals from which that art had developed but upon Italian material, generally either later Roman copies of Greek pieces, or later Roman work executed in what by then, from about AD 100 onwards, had become styles that Winckelmann himself would have reckoned 'degenerate'. The tone of much of this art could be seen as soft in line and often sentimental and cliché-ridden in style. Equally, the middle generations of the eighteenth century were not especially interested in notions of 'the real thing' or 'the original', perhaps because for many of them art was conceived as part of a domestic design (grand or humbler) in which display and collection served the larger story. For these reasons pieces were often recut, like Blundell's Hermaphrodite, to bring them into contemporary narratives.

As a result of this, the generation of around 1800 experienced a profound culture shock when authentic early classical Greek material started to arrive in northern Europe. Royal Navy cruises like that commanded by Beaufort began to bring back improved intelligence of the conditions and contents of Asia Minor, and at about the same time professionals like Cockerell and his colleagues, and diplomats like Elgin, began to excavate major Greek monuments such as the temples of Bassae and

Aegina, and the Athenian Parthenon. When the Parthenon marbles arrived in London, they forced a re-evaluation of what 'classical art' meant, and stimulated the nineteenth-century reappraisal of the art of the antique world and how the integrity of artworks should be judged. It is significant that this change of heart matched the entry into antiquities collecting of the great European museums, as major players. The Aegina marbles went to the Munich Museum, and those of Bassae and Athens to the British Museum, where they were seen to take pride of place in comparison with the earlier, originally private, collections of Arundel, Townley and others, which were also in, or arriving in, the public museums. Their display in these museums, as Ambulator's musing shows us, had become a matter of public comment and criticism.

Meanwhile, different currents in the body social were creating different kinds of collecting. The enlightened rationalism which, when directed towards the outer world produced a view of natural, classifiable order, suggested different ranges of feeling when the gaze was turned inwards. Equally, the dry, somewhat passionless gaze of reason triggered its inevitable opposite. The result was a mode of sentiment, in which emotions were cultivated and personal feeling exalted, a mode which gathered force as the eighteenth century progressed and eventually produced what is usually called the Romantic Movement, and its (slightly older) dark twin, the Gothic. Both produced much writing, especially in the new form of the novel, and two of the most influential Gothic novels of the period, *Vathek* and *The Castle of Otranto*, were written by premier collectors, William Beckford and Horace Walpole. Both also created new forms of collecting in their own right. In both, a view of the past, a vision of the exotic, and an interest in sensation for its own sake were becoming informing motifs.

The new worlds (that is, of course, new to Europeans) which had been opening up ever since the Spanish voyage to America in 1492 and the contemporary Portuguese voyages around Africa, had forced Europeans to realise that ways of life existed that had no reference to the conceptual and social systems, chiefly Christian and Islamic, with which they were familiar. The effort to understand this eventually created the field of study known as anthropology, which, we now see, was as much about defining Western attitudes as it was about understanding anybody else. But in the eighteenth century, this lay in the future. The material culture brought back from distant places was often acquired chiefly as a casual adjunct to the formal collecting of natural specimens, and frequently it was gathered because the men recognised that it would have a financial value back in England. The wealth of India seemed inexhaustible, and was a prime target for this kind of acquisition, in which, sometimes, particular groups of interesting material were kept in collected form.

Objects from the islands of the South Seas, already established in popular view as a paradise on earth, commanded particular attention. Relatively large quantities of such material came back to England from the three voyages led by Captain James Cook and that led by Captain George Vancouver, together with some others of less significance. This material was sold, and subsequently sold on, many times, with the result that tracing it and endeavouring to discover its present whereabouts has become a major scholarly preoccupation. Cook voyage material found its way into the British Museum, and also into the Leverian Museum, and hence to a large number of later eighteenth- and early nineteenth-century collectors, whose own collections ended up in the institutional museums of the later nineteenth century, where they remain. The Vancouver material has had an equally tortuous history.

The museum, in London, of Sir Ashton Lever is pivotal in the construction of the public museum mode and the kind of collections it was desirable to have on display within it. Lever had some spectacular Cook Pacific pieces, which passed to William Bullock when the collections changed hands. Bullock opened a new kind of exhibition in his Piccadilly Egyptian Hall, one which endeavoured to put his preserved animals in 'naturalistic' settings, and displayed his human artefacts in the same room. Both these museums had a serious purpose, although allied to a certain sensationalism and a commercial endeavour. The same generations saw the development of exhibitions which were purely commercial and sensational in intent: these were often put on in inns or local halls and they often travelled around on a touring circuit. The exhibition in York Castle, although static and particularly gruesome, had a good deal in common with these displays.

What we might call the 'higher sensationalism' is evident in the collecting practices of William Beckford, whose architectural and artefactual imagination drew upon fantasies of the Orient and the medieval. His creation at Fontwell Abbey was one of the inspirations behind what we now call 'Victorian Gothic'. Horace Walpole, with his villa and collection at Strawberry Hill, Twickenham, London did something of the same, and so did John Soane, with his house and museum in Lincoln's Inn Fields, London. All these collectors, in their distinctive ways, constructed modes of relating to the material world of the past, itself one of the key ideas of the Romantic disposition.

A desire to grasp the past, particularly the ancient and medieval past of Britain herself, had been gathering momentum, hand in hand with developing national fervour of which it is an important part, since the sixteenth century, and onwards through the seventeenth century. By the early eighteenth century there was interest enough to inspire the founding of what eventually became the Society of Antiquaries of London, whose journal *Archaeologia* became a forum for the recording and discussion of the material remains of the British past. A similar movement was taking place among those concerned with early literary remains, as the history of the manuscript material drawn upon by Bishop Percy for his *Reliques* shows.

This is the background to Walter Scott's preoccupation with the medieval and early modern past of Scotland, and in particular of his own Scottish border country, where, as he saw it, there was played out the clash between older ways of life and the new demands made by an increasingly complex industrial and capitalist society. Scott had an important collection of his own, but he also made the notion of collecting as a way of relating to the past a central idea in one of his novels, *The Antiquary*. The same nexus of interests brought the Newcastle Society of Antiquaries into being, and saw the development of the society's collection of north-eastern regional antiquities.

The point was made at the beginning that in 1500 the mindset of Europe was still essentially medieval, orientated to a cosmology which placed God directly as an interventionist within human affairs, and to a belief which sharply separated men from the natural world. By 1800, God was distanced from his creation in an irreducible network of classificatory principles. Man had been allotted a Linnaean name in the scheme of things, and was viewing nature as of itself sublime. The evidence of collected materials was demonstrating the ordering of the natural world, the relationship of past to present whether of the classical or the British past, and the fragmentation of categories in the search for immediate emotional gratification. It is these themes which the material gathered here is intended to illuminate. Every choice involves rejection, and inevitably much interesting material has had to be omitted. Not all readers will agree with the selections made, but we hope that the material included is sufficiently interesting and varied to make its points.

Arnold has been responsible for Parts I and II and for the section on Gowan Knight in Part 3, and Pearce for Parts III, IV and V; we are jointly responsible for the Introduction. The degree of modernisation of spelling and presentation which should be made to the extracts has proved a difficult question. We have provided some in the interests of helpfulness (for example 'f' has been changed to 's' where appropriate) but have tried to leave sufficient of the original form to give integrity and preserve the period flavour. Similarly, in the bibliographical references to the source of the extracts, we have sacrificed some consistency in order to give helpful details of material published in the early period.

Susan Pearce and Ken Arnold

Part I
Curious Voices

1

Giulio Camillo's magical proto-museum

The memory theatre of Guilio Camillo Delminio (to give him his full name) was so well known in sixteenth-century intellectual circles that its creator was ranked amongst the most famous men of his day. In short, his 'theatre' was a wooden structure, stuffed full of meaningful images and words, which was shown first in Venice and then copied in Paris (Yates, 1966: 130–72).

Camillo was born in about 1480, and for some time taught at Bologna University. Much of his life, however, was spent in working on his extraordinary scheme for a memory theatre – a physical embodiment of a particular approach to the ancient art of memory. Invented by the Greeks, the tradition of this sometimes religious and always magical art was passed on to the Romans and then elaborated upon in medieval Europe. Used by the orators of antiquity, this art was transformed in the Middle Ages into a methodology that could be employed in moral education and disputation. In the hands of Camillo and other later Renaissance interpreters such as Ramon Lull, Giordano Bruno and Robert Fludd, a legacy of this technique was further given a much more occult character. Finally, when taken up by the seventeenth-century philosophers Bacon and Descartes, the tradition was yet again reformed in order to put it to work in the service of the 'new sciences'.

Camillo's theatre took some of its form from the Roman theatre as described by Vitruvius. The use of numerology and astrology was crucial to its construction – seven gangways with seven doors, the seven pillars of Solomon's House of Wisdom, seven tiers representing the spheres of the universe, and so forth. In Camillo's scheme, the normal function of a theatre with an attentive audience spread around a central spectacle was reversed with a single 'spectator' standing where the stage would be, looking out towards the auditorium where images and texts were spread.

The connection between this remarkable construction, inspired as it was by somewhat obscure classical notions of memory and oration, might at first sight seem a rather long way removed from the history of museums. But a number of fundamental principles in the scheme are highly relevant to the evolution of a concept that came to be called (or maybe re-called) a museum. The space of the theatre was defined and created for the purposes of imparting learning and knowledge in a condensed manner; it used a juxtaposition of images which, it was believed, could impart a level of

3

understanding not accessible to learning from words in books alone; and finally, it made a virtue of excluding distractions, so that a spectator's attention was inevitably focused on the collected pictures presented in a predetermined arrangement. These fundamental principles were set to re-emerge during the next century in the shape of repositories and museums of the early modern era.

The following passages come from two letters written in Padua in 1532 by Viglius Zuichemus to Erasmus.

VIGLIUS ZUICHEMUS TO ERASMUS

They say that this man has constructed a certain Amphitheatre, a work of wonderful skill, into which whoever is admitted as spectator will be able to discourse on any subject no less fluently than Cicero.[1] I thought at first that this was a fable until I learned of the thing more fully from Baptista Egnatio. It is said that this Architect has drawn up in certain places whatever about anything is found in Cicero ... Certain orders or grades of figures are disposed ... with stupendous labour and devine skill[2] ...

The work is of wood marked with many images, and full of little boxes; there are various orders and grades in it. He gives a place to each individual figure and ornament, and he showed me such a mass of papers that, though I always heard that Cicero was the fountain of richest eloquence, scarcely would I have thought that one author could contain so much or that so many volumes could be pieced together out of his writings. I wrote to you before the name of the author who is called Julius Camillus. He stammers badly and speaks Latin with difficulty, excusing himself with the pretext that through continually using his pen he has nearly lost the use of speech. He is said however to be good in the vernacular which he has taught at some time at Bologna. When I asked him concerning the meaning of the work, its plan and results – speaking religiously and as though stupefied by the miraculousness of the thing – he threw before me some papers, and recited them so that he expressed the numbers, clauses, and all the artifices of the Italian style, yet slightly unevenly because of the impediment in his speech. The King is said to be urging that he should return to France with the magnificant work.[3] But since the King wishes that all the writing should be translated into French, for which he had tried an interpreter and scribe, he said that he thought that he would defer his journey rather than exhibit an imperfect work. He calls this theatre of his by many names, saying now that it is a built or constructed mind and soul, and now that it is a windowed one. He pretends that all things that the human mind can conceive and which we cannot see with the corporeal eye, after being collected together by diligent meditation may be expressed by certain corporeal signs in such a way that the beholder may at once perceive with his eyes everything that is otherwise hidden in the depths of the human mind. And it is because of this corporeal looking that he calls it a theatre.[4]

When I asked him whether he had written anything in defence of his opinion, since there are many to-day who do not approve of this zeal in imitating Cicero, he replied that he had written much but had as yet published little save a few small things in Italian dedicated to the King. He has in mind to publish his views on the matter when he can have quiet, and the work is perfected to which he is giving all his energies. He says that he has already spent 1,500 ducats on it, though the King has so far only given 500. But he expects ample reward from the king when he has experenced the fruits of the work.

Source

Letters written from Viglius Zuichemus to Erasmus in 1532, reproduced in *Erasmus, Epistelae*, edited by Allen P. S. et al., 9: 479; 10: 29–30, which are quoted in Yates, Frances, 1966, *The art of memory*, London, Routledge & Kegan Paul: 130–32

Notes

1 Marcus Tullius Cicero (106–43 BC) was a Roman consul and writer, re-nowned and revered by many Renaissance scholars for his widely-reputed oratory skills.
2 After having written this, Viglius visited Venice, met Camillo, and was shown the theatre. The next extract is taken from a letter written after this visit.
3 Francis I of France was informed of and became interested in Camillo's theatre, and in 1530 Camillo went to France. The King gave him money to help with the project, and by so doing became the focus of one version of the theatre erected in Paris, which was meant to reveal its treasures to only one person: the King himself (Yates, 1966: 129–30).
4 These mystical links between physical objects and pictures and the mental comprehension resulting from contemplating them within a confined space has ever since provided an abstract philosophical premise for what happens to us in museums and galleries.

Reference

Yates, 1966

2

Samuel á Quiccheberg's 'classes': the first modern museological text

Samuel á Quiccheberg's book is often described as the first published treatise on modern museums. Collections of the type he outlined, and buildings like that in which he recommend they be kept, were already in existence, particularly in Italy. Quiccheberg's reputation lies in his conversion of his knowledge of this existing practice into a museological argument set out in a full-scale monograph. Some commentators have seen in his work the crucial shift from medieval *Schatzkammern* (accidental accumulations of treasures and rarities, which were at best taken stock of in an inventory) to *Wunderkammern* (systematic accumulations of curiosities that were then conceptually organised in catalogues) (Raby, 1985: 251–8; von Schlosser, 1978; Balsiger, 1970).

His work contained both an abundance of practical advice and a detailed classification system. The bulk of the work is organised as a series of ordering principles for the ideal princely curiosity cabinet, and is presented as a comprehensive set of 'inscriptions' divided into five 'classes', with ten or eleven 'inscriptions' per 'class'. He also made the distinction between a *Wunderkammer* (a cabinet of natural specimens) and a *Kunstkammer* (a cabinet of so-called 'artificial' specimens – that is, man-made artefacts).

Quiccheberg's ambitions for the breadth of scope of such a cabinet were typical of the Renaissance in encompassing nothing less than every known object and artefact. Universal in vision, the cabinet was to form the microcosmic condensation of the whole macrocosm, offered up to the central figure of a prince. In this fashion, his scheme bore many philosophical similarities with Camillo's memory theatre, and indeed his use of the term *Theatri* in the title to his work might well be a direct reference to Camillo's title *Idea del Teatro* (see Chapter 1 in this volume).

Quiccheberg was a Flemish doctor, who acted as Albrecht V's adviser on artistic matters. Though this work is not set out in any way as an introduction to Albrecht V's Munich Kunstkammer, many of the desirable characteristics that he prescribed for the museum and its collections were clearly drawn from his knowledge of it (Seelig, 1985: 76–89).

SAMUEL Á QUICCHEBERG'S THIRD AND FOURTH CLASSES
■

THIRD CLASS

First Inscription

Marvellous and rather rare animals:[1] rare birds, animals, fishes, shellfish, which exist in land, sea, rivers, forests, other places; and these may be in pieces or they may be whole, preserved in any manner or condition, and dried out.

Second Inscription

Poured or molded animals: made of metal, plaster, clay and any productive material whatsoever, by whatever technique, which look like they are alive because they have been skilfully fashioned, as for example lizards, snakes, fishes, frogs, crabs, insects, shellfish, and whatever is of that order, and can look real once it is painted.

Third Inscription

Pieces of rather large animals, and of rather small ones as well if there are any worthy of note: and in this section are horns, beaks, teeth, hooves, bones, internal stones, pelts, feathers, claws, skins, and whatever exists among the remaining parts which can offer a little variety.

Fourth Inscription

Different kinds of skeletons: or else bones put together, as for example, of men, women, apes, little pigs, birds, frogs, and other different things. Likewise things fashioned by craftsmanship according to the parts of a man, as for example human eyes, with their membranes, ears, noses, hands, as for example prosthetic devices for people who have been recently mutilated.[2]

Fifth Inscription

Seeds, fruits, legumes, grains, roots that take the place of seeds: and things that are called material to this class, provided that they are suitable for preservation and nice to look at, either for the sake of the variety of their nature or the diversity of their nomenclature, and here maybe you would want to give preference to those which are from foreign countries, or are amazing, or are fragrant.[3]

Sixth Inscription

Herbs, flowers, twigs, boughs, pieces of bark, logs, roots, et cetera. These must be dry, real, and select, laid out according to their classes or else molded by pouring in metal of some sort, or woven in silk or depicted by any modern art. In this group are kept also all classes of wood according to their peculiar divisions.

Seventh Inscription

Metals and metallic substances from mines and true roots of metals, mineral slag formed in a furnace, likewise solid veins of metals of absolute purity, and all these things imitated artificially, and metals which have in various degrees been smelted, some more and some less purified.

Eighth Inscription

Gems and precious stones, for example, diamonds, sapphires, emeralds, rubies, and so forth, likewise gem crystals, some of them in their raw state, some of them polished, and similar glittery substances, and some of these may be lightly set into gold so that they may be fitted into bracelets, or into the ears, things on the foreheads, and necklaces.

Ninth Inscription

Rather remarkable rocks, stones (other than precious stones), as for example remarkable marbles, jaspers, alabaster, et cetera, and so various kinds of marble: porphyrite, donysium, ophiticum, et cetera. These of course are not translucent but very ornate. There are in this class also medicinal rocks which are not clear: hematites, aetites, magnets, et cetera.

Tenth Inscription

Colours and pigments: colours which are poured, crumbled, mineral colours, water colours, oil paints, glass colours, and so forth, for dyeing, painting and colouring metals, gums, wax, sulphurs, wood, ivory, weaving and wool. You can have individual containers of oil paints, as well as others mixed and gummed up with water.

Eleventh Inscription

Substances of the earth, both wet and dry: either in their natural condition or worked on and purified, or clinging to or growing on something:

clods, chalky soil, clay soil, fertile earth and other coloured earths, like-wise vitriols, natural glass, alumina, salts, and terrestrial rocks, and the porous rock of the seacoast. It does well to finish out this heading with substances which are found in dripping hot springs and caves.

FOURTH CLASS

First Inscription

Musical instruments: various kinds of pipes, horns, stringed instruments, hollow ones, rounded ones, clavichords, drums, and many other types which pertain to their own choruses, either ensemble or solo.

Second Inscription

Mathematical instruments: astrolabes, spheres, cylinders, quadrants, clocks, geometers, staffs for measuring land and sea, in war and peacetime. Note here also regular bodies of multiple forms, combined with a beautiful transparency.

Third Inscription

Instruments for writing and drawing or painting: as for example vellum, paper, tablets, pugillares (to prick the vellum to get even lines), reeds, pencils, pens, struck type, printer's inks, compasses, rulers, and many other things of this sort, apportioned into their own little boxes. So also various kinds of containers of great capacity associated with this.[4]

Fourth Inscription

Instruments of force, as for example those used for lifting very heavy weights, for breaking down gates, hinges, locks, implements for hauling in various modes: traction, vection, rolling, dragging, pushing, also im-plements for climbing anywhere, sailing anywhere, swimming anywhere, or for simulating flight.

Fifth Inscription

Instruments of workshops and laboratories: things used in both these two by the more skilled of the artisans: sculptors, turners, goldsmiths, casters, workers in wood, or instruments ultimately of all or any artisans whom this earth on which we live nourishes in our century.

Sixth Inscription

Surgical and anatomical instruments, as for example forceps, saws, sy-
ringes, instruments to cut veins, mirrors, combs, speculae, and anything
the practice of surgery supplies in abundant number and which people in
other professions use as well: barbers (who were also leechers), bath
people, et cetera.

Seventh Inscription

Hunting instruments: and whatever is necessary in the country and in the
keeping of gardens: as for example the ones of use for catching birds and
fish, at least if they be clever of design, as for example snares, traps for
deer, hooks and tridents for fishes, et cetera, but also many other things
for horticulture, planting and transplanting, weeding and hoeing.

Eighth Inscription

Articles for playing with: those which relate to exercise which require
skill and are rather pleasant and which pertain chiefly to physical agility.
Of these types of things are the discus, javelins, pyramids, dice, globes,
short spears, balls, et cetera. And these draw those who are more simple
into admiration of those who gesticulate.

Ninth Inscription

Weapons of foreign races: and other most rare and useful arms as for
example bows, catapults, spears, quivers, et cetera, and whatever is so
unusual that it may seem transferable no less for the purpose of an
admirable theatre than for a well equipped armoury.

Tenth Inscription

Foreign clothing, as for example Indian dress, Arabian dress, Turkish
dress, and even amongst that the more rare of it: and some fashioned of
feathers, some of a web, and of any marvellous manufacture or texture
you like, or even stitched together out of various hides. Likewise miniature clothing of foreign nations as if for dolls, for distinguishing the
clothing worn by unmarried girls, widows, women who are engaged, et
cetera.

Eleventh Inscription

Rather unusual durable clothing: as for example belonging to the early ancestors of any theatre founder. There may possibly be in this category a cloak of a general or emperor, a ducal robe, and any priestly garment whatsoever, et cetera. Likewise other ornaments like necklaces, balls, belts, pockets, crests, et cetera, kept for the sake of some pleasant remembrance.

Source

Samuel á Quiccheberg, *Inscriptiones Vel Tituli Theatri Amplissimi ...*, Munich, 1565 (Copy taken from manuscript translation from the Latin by Julie Hochstrasser with the invaluable assistance of Paul Psoinos).

Notes

1   This interest in the marvellous and rare was one of the hallmarks of the Renaissance cabinet, which continued throughout the early modern, and indeed into the modern period. In an era when mystical resemblances were held to bind micro- and macrocosms, a small selection of objects could be seen as standing in for the rest of the world outside the repository. Later, when the magic of those links came under critical scrutiny, it become much harder to square the continued preferences for marvellous unusual objects with the goal of universal reference, in which surveying the typical made better strategic sense than hoarding the rare.
2   The rapid switch from 'natural' specimens to 'artificial' ones is typical of the frequent links that Quiccheberg draws between the two domains (God and man-made) throughout his work.
3   Quiccheberg's clear interest in the impression of the collection on a potential visitor is one which for much of the seventeenth century became subsumed by a more dominant 'scientific' concern with the knowledge claims that could be made about a collection and its classification.
4   It is interesting that his classification scheme here includes the containers for the objects as a class of object in themselves. Similarly, the history of collecting is elsewhere designated as itself something to be collected.

References

Balsiger, 1970
Raby, 1985
von Schlosser, 1978
Seelig, 1985

3

Gabriel Kaltermackt's advice to princes

Neither birth nor death dates are known for Gabriel Kaltermackt (or Kaldemarck), nor is the nature of his education known. What we do know is that he was a widely travelled artist; and most significantly, that he wrote a detailed report to Elector Christian I of Saxony, in which he proposed the establishment of a *Kunstkammer* of an Italian princely type (dominated by artworks) in Dresden. The guidelines that he produced form a fundamental document in the history of collecting, though, as various parts of the work indicate, his intentions in writing them were, in part, simply an elaborate way of suggesting a possible future employment for himself as 'curator' to the collection (Menzhausen, 1985; Gutfleisch and Menzhausen, 1989).

His scheme stands in marked contrast to Quiccheberg's advice in his 1565 *Inscriptiones vel tituli theatri amplissimi* (see Chapter 2 in this volume), which argued for setting up a Kunstkammer on an encyclopaedic rather than art-dominated basis. Part of Kaltermackt's implicit advice was to dismantle, or at least separate off, the existing collection amassed by Christian I's predecessor Augustus, which included musical and scientific instruments as well as other tools used by goldsmiths, sculptors, cabinetmakers, turners, surgeons and so on – a category that amounted to as many as 8,000 objects from a total of 10,000 in the collection, all of which he derided as merely tools to produce 'works', rather than real 'works' in their own right.

Part of his classic Renaissance argument for why Christian I might want to consider founding such a collection was that other earlier, and indeed contemporary, European sovereigns had gained undying fame through the collection of works of art. But what was original to his argument, though also absolutely necessary within the Lutheran moral and cultural context in which he was working, was his contention that the acts of collecting and then making 'the right use' of art treasures would in themselves constitute an article of the 'true religion'. Paintings (and other iconographic arts such as sculpture and coins) might in particular bring 'delight to the eyes', conjuring up and making real heroes and authors who might then encourage those who saw and admired them to themselves 'do good and avoid evil'. This attitude stood in effect at something of a midway position between a Catholic reverence for the spiritual aspects of art and a Calvinist suspicion of the whole enterprise (Gutfleisch and Menzhausen, 1989: 4). With an eye to the potential cost of such a collection, Kaltermackt also advised the procurement of casts of sculptures, along with printed drawings and contemporary paintings not yet inflated in price by age, a measure further given license to by his philosophical commitment to the idea of art as a source of information rather than spiritual inspiration.

Kaltemarckt's advice did not, in fact, achieve its aims. Christian I died in 1561, four years after the report was penned, and subsequently more rather than less of the typical *Kunstkammer* pieces that Kaltermarckt had despised were added to the collection – that is, antiquities, curiosities and automata. Another hundred years were, in fact, to pass before his ideas were realised in Dresden; and only recently has his work been championed as a classic text in the museological tradition.

COLLECTING, BY KALTERMACKT

Although all sovereignty involves, next to God, good laws and weapons, eminent and highly intelligent sovereigns have always made a great effort to protect their subjects not only through considerable military equipment but also through good books and writings. The libraries and book collections of the two kings Ptolemy Philadelphus in Egypt and Attalus of Pergamum, as well as those of other potentates, bear, as examples worthy of eternal praise, laudable testimony of this. In these present times, the same is seen in some distinguished potentates of the Christian world, among whom the learned many years ago counted the house of the Medici in Florence, and whom many regard as having ascended to princely, indeed almost to kingly majesty, more through collections of good books and through supporting the liberal arts of the burghers than through any other of their praiseworthy deeds.[1]

In addition to such libraries and book collections, illustrious potentates also established picture galleries or art collections (whatever one wants to call them) in order to encounter the events of history and those who through their deeds created them not only in books but also, through drawings and paintings, as a delight to the eye and a strengthening of memory, as a living incitement to do good and avoid evil, and also as a source of study for art-loving youth.[2] What quality of painters and sculptors the school of art of Cosimo and Lorenzo Medici, sovereigns of Florence, has produced is evident from the works of its artists in the many places where they practised. The fact that these arts, as well as music, are the most amiable is generally acknowledged, since music, through hearing, and the visual arts, through sight, arouse man to proper and honest joy, and are nobly given and ordained by God. For this reason, these two arts have always been used, also in church, for the worship of God, and have, therefore, been preferred to all other arts. Although they have often been forced into the use of idolatry and other outrages, as is also true of the Bible itself, this is due neither to the Bible nor to these two arts but rather to their misuse. In all my simplicity, I am certain that just as no people under the sun (except for the orthodox Christian church) has a thorough understanding of God, so too the right use of sculptures and paintings is confined to the true religion. This requires no proof, since it is obvious that the ancient and highly intelligent heathens, the Greeks and the Romans etc. (who admittedly spent a great deal of money on the visual arts), the papists (who are equally liberal in this respect), the Turks and the present zealots and iconoclasts all possess neither true religion nor the right use of the visual arts.[3] The heathens and papists misuse the visual arts for the sake of idolatry while the Turks and the zealots have not the least liking for them. We ought, therefore, to thank God Almighty greatly for his having given to us, in addition to the revelation of his holy and divine Word, the ability to appreciate the right use of the visual arts, and we should, besides such thanksgiving. ask Him that we may fruitfully put into practice this knowledge or insight. ...

The best adornment and treasure of a prince and sovereign includes not only and above all orthodox religion, faithful subjects and sufficient money, but also his possession of magnificent munitions and military equipment, of a glorious library and book collection, of artful sculptures and paintings. In this way he earns immortal praise both from friend and foe, from the learned and the ignorant, from artists and art lovers. His Electoral Grace, beloved master and father Christian has, to his most praiseworthy memory, attained a great name among the potentates of Christianity through a magnificent and widely acclaimed armoury and through a considerable library. His Electoral Grace obviously intends not only to enlarge and to improve these two treatures but also in the best possible way to found the third treasure, an art collection, which, according to reliable report, is still lacking. For this reason (also because of the inclination I have to these arts). I am urged obediently to offer His Electoral Grace my humble, simple yet well-meant considerations on this most princely and praiseworthy intention, considerations about what belongs to an art collection, how it should be arranged and how it can daily be enlarged and improved.[4] ...

What belongs in an art collection

A well equipped art collection ought primarily to contain three things. First, sculptures. Secondly, paintings. Thirdly, curious items from home and abroad made of metals, stone, wood, herbs – whether from above the ground, from within the ground or from the waters and the sea. Next, utensils used for drinking or eating which nature or art has shaped or made out of such materials. Then, antlers, horns, claws, feathers and other things belonging to strange and curious animals, birds or fishes, including the skeletons of their anatomy. I believe there is no need to relate here how and where these are to be found, especially since such things are regularly obtainable in large quantities in Germany and Italy. I will, therefore, leave this aside and address only the two former aspects of art collections.

The other part of the art collection should consist of coins and medals made of copper, brass, silver, gold and other ores, portraying Roman emperors, kings, potentates, their wives and children, also eminent military men, learned men and other famous persons. Much deceitful dealing occurs with such medals, which often takes in even such persons, who pretend to be experts here and call themselves antiquaries. Although these are useful to have for the study of history, there is, I believe, no need to spend excessively on such medallions (like some who pay 70 or more crowns for a single medal). Yet, princes and great masters ought to make an effort to procure original pieces while others should be content with imitations.[5] Many magnificent men have been deceived in this area, have been sold old things at prices exceeding their original value …

An art collection cannot be completed within one, two or even three years but has to grow gradually over the years. Often, learned and other art-loving persons possess excellent works of art, which sometimes their heirs, being ignorant here, carelessly neglect upon the decrease of those who collected them with such industry, effort and expense. Yet, where it is known that great masters are keen to obtain such works of art, these are usually overestimated and overpriced, for which reason it is important to be circumspect here, letting unassuming persons order and buy such things (in this way some expense can sometimes be saved).

At this point ought to follow an account of how the rooms containing art should be prepared, of how the works of art should be arranged in them and of what qualifications the person in charge of them should have. Since, however, this can best be done once a considerable number of such works of art have been collected, I will come to an end here. It only remains to be said that musical, astronomical and geometrical instruments, as well as those of numismatists, goldsmiths, sculptors, carpenters, woodturners and grinders ought to be kept separately from the art collection. Since these are not themselves pieces of art but only means for producing them, they ought to be allocated special places among the liberal arts near the library.[6]

Source

Gabriel Kaltermarckt, 'Bedenken wie eine Kunst-cammer Aufzurichten seyn Möchte' ['Thoughts on how a kunstkammer should be formed']. Transcription and translation by Barbara Gutfleisch in Barbara Gutfleisch and Joachim Menzhausen, 'How a kunstkammer should be formed: Gavriel Kaltemarckt's advice to Christian I of Saxony on the formation of an art collection, 1587', *Journal of the history of collections*, 1 no. 1, 1989: 3–32.

Notes

1   In this reference to the Medicis, Kaltermackt firmly located the potential aspirations that Christian I might have in forming an art collection within the context of the princely ideal of the Italian Renaissance of gaining reflected glory from artistic possessions and commissions.

2   This is the core of Kaltermackt's moral argument – pitched very carefully at a Lutheran Elector – about the value of amassing an art collection.

3   Here Kaltermackt is distancing his argument for the correct use of a picture collection within 'the true religion' of Lutheranism from any similar inclinations that might be found in other religious contexts.

4   This is one of a number of passages in the work, where Kaltermackt is clearly offering himself as a candidate to help form Christian I's prospective art collection.

5   This statement clearly contradicts an argument he makes elsewhere, that the use of casts rather than original sculptures is in fact permissible, since the primary reason for collecting such work is the moral inspiration that comes with contemplating the subjects depicted rather than any reverence for the work itself.

6   This recommendation can be taken as a thinly-veiled criticism of the types of objects collected by Christian I's predecessor Augustus. Kaltermackt was suggesting that Augustus' collections, in being primarily formed of such instruments, might be rehoused in order to make room for the art collection he was advocating.

References

Gutfleisch and Menzhausen, 1989
Menzhausen, 1985

4

Francis Bacon advises how to set up a museum

Though there is no evidence for Francis Bacon himself having been actively involved with a museum or collection, there is no doubt that his philosophical teachings and writings significantly influenced the evolution of early modern museums. As a patriotic philosopher, his purpose was as much to reform the English nation as to reform the system of knowledge he saw around him. In this way, his prescriptions for science – one of his chief intellectual aims – had a distinctly social flavour, with a mass of participatory observation serving as the first level of a pyramid of knowledge, which through the application of inductive logic would lead to unassailable truths (Webster, 1975; Hill, 1965; Browne, 1978: 507–16; Perez-Ramos, 1988).

Bacon's programme for intellectual reform centred on a universal natural history, which was based on the accumulation of vast arrays of factual evidence, stripped clean of theoretical argument. For Bacon, individual facts had to come before conjectures; the latter could only properly follow inductively from the compilation of the former. The implementation of this insistent demand for the accumulation of data ranging from experimental results to circumstantial reports, helped bring about the mid-seventeenth-century transformation of a whole range of empirical studies into geography, geology, chemistry, electricity and magnetism (Kuhn, 1977: 41–52; Daston, 1988).

Within his ardent quest to gather and inspect 'particulars', Bacon developed plans for a number of innovative institutions that would be the workshops of his new scientific enterprise – most famously the imaginary institution 'Solomon's House' as outlined in his *New Atlantis*. Amongst the separate elements of such institutions, museum collections became an indispensable tool, indeed a logical necessity.

Bacon made his most explicit reference to the role of museums in the passage that follows from his revel or play *Gesta Grayorum*. The work, which concerns the court and kingdom of the Prince of Purpoole was presented at Gray's Inn during the Christmas festivities of 1594–95, though only printed in 1688. The performance included dancing and singing and a number of set speeches. Such revels served in part as parties and in part as training grounds in

the manners of the learned and noble. One of the play's characters, the Prince of Purpoole's 'Second Counsellor, advising the
Study of Philosophy', proposes four material aids to benefit philosophical study: a library, a combined garden, zoo and aquarium, a
laboratory or still house and 'a goodly huge cabinet'. As this
passage makes clear, then, museums were, within Baconian philosophy, one of the central places of inquiry and investigation –
factories for the essential production of facts.

FROM GESTA GRAYORUM

The Second Counsellor, advising the Study of Philosophy

It may seem, most excellent Prince, that my Lord which now hath spoken
did never read the just censures of the wisest men, who compared great
conquerors to great rovers and witches, whose power is in destruction
and not in preservation; else would he never have advised your Excellency to become as some comet or blazing star, which should threaten
and portend nothing but death and dearth, combustions and troubles of
the world. And whereas the governing faculties of men are two, force and
reason, whereof the one is brute and the other devine, he wisheth you for
your principal ornament and regality the talons of the eagle to catch the
prey, and not the piercing sight which seeth into the bottom on the sea.
But I contrariwise will wish unto your Highness the exercise of the best
and purest part of the mind, and the most innocent and meriting conquest,
being the conquest of the works of nature; making this proposition, that
you bend the excellency of your spirits to the searching out, inventing
and discovering of all whatsoever is hid and secret in the world;[1] that
your Excellency be not as a lamp that shineth to others and yet seeth not
itself, but as the Eye of the World, that both carrieth and useth light.
Antiquity, that presenteth unto us in dark visions the wisdom of former
times, informeth us that the [governments of] kingdoms have always had
an affinity with the secretes and mysteries of learning. Amongst the
Persians, the kings were attended on by the Magi. The Gymnosophists
had all the government under the princes of Asia; and generally those
kingdoms were accounted most happy, that had rulers most addicted to
philosophy. The Ptolemies in Egypt may be for instance and Salomon
was a man so seen in the universality of nature that he wrote an herbal of
all that was green upon the earth. No conquest of Julius Caesar made him
so remembered as the Calendar. Alexander the Great wrote to Aristotle,
upon the publishing of the Physics, that he esteemed more of excellent
men in knowledge than in empire.[2] And to this purpose I will commend

to your Highness four principle works and monuments of yourself: First, the collecting of a most perfect and general library, wherein whatsoever the wit of man hath heretofore committed to books of worth, be they ancient or modern, printed or manuscript, European or of the other parts, of one or other language, may be made contributory to your wisdom. Next, a spacious, wonderful garden, wherein whatsoever plant the sum of divers climates, out of the earth of divers moulds, either wild or by the culture of man brought forth, may be with that care that appertaineth to the good prospering thereof set and cherished: This garden to be built about with rooms to stable in all rare beasts and to cage in all rare birds; with two lakes adjoining, the one of fresh water the other of salt, for like variety of fishes. And so you may have in small compass a model of universal nature made private.[3] The third, a goodly huge cabinet, wherein whatsoever the hand of man by exquisite art or engine hath made rare in stuff, form, or motion; whatsoever singularity chance and the shuffle of things hath produced; whatsoever Nature hath wrought in things that want like and may be kept; shall be sorted and included. The fourth such a still-house, so furnished with mills, instruments, furnaces, and vessels, as may be a place fit for a philosopher's stone.[4] Thus, when your Excellency shall have added depth of knowledge to the fineness of [your] spirits and greatness of your power, then indeed shall you be a Trismegistus;[5] and then when all other miracles and wonders shall cease by reason that you shall have discovered their natural causes, yourself shall be left the only miracle and wonder of the world.

Source

Spedding, J., Ellis, R. and Heath, D. (eds), 1890, *The Works of Francis Bacon*, Volume 8, London: 334–5

Notes

1   Bacon is almost certainly referring here to the earth's secrets that, like many of his contemporaries, he believed could only be revealed through hermetic studies. The mystical and magical aspects of the new sciences proposed by Bacon and his followers had their significance for the enterprise of setting up museums too, for many of the objects they contained were commonly held to have powers well beyond those which could be apprehended through ordinary studies.

2   As with the principal rival new philosophy of science, Cartesianism, Bacon's prescriptions for erecting a new epistemological structure drew heavily on classical sources while simultaneously preaching the need to completely

break with the past. The empiricism that inspired the founding of many seventeenth-century museums was one of the tools that Bacon held would enable the new age to rise above the limitations of the 'ancients'.

3   This period did, indeed, see significant developments in the provision of university libraries, botanical gardens and zoos.

4   Increasingly stripped of its alchemical associations, this fourth category of 'works and monuments' is what became the chemical and physical laboratory of modern science. All manner of combinations of Bacon's four institutional elements (library, garden and zoo, museum and laboratory) were put into practice. At the Ashmolean Museum in Oxford, for example, the basement of the museum was established with chemical apparatus; while in Leyden, the university museum shared its location with yet another investigative space, not mentioned by Bacon, the anatomy theatre (Simcock, 1984).

5   This is a direct reference to the so-called 'thrice great' Hermes who, until exegetical work published in the seventeenth century revealed otherwise, was believed to be an extremely ancient source of alchemical wisdom.

References

Browne, 1978
Daston, 1988
Hill, 1965
Kuhn, 1977
Perez-Ramos, 1988
Simcock, 1984
Webster, 1975

5

The German traveller Thomas Platter describes the English collection of Walter Cope

Visiting England in 1599, the German traveller Thomas Platter declared that the country's 'most resplendent objects may be seen in and around London'. Platter was impressed with the city's civic pomp, and with the wealth of its merchant population; but, like most Continental visitors, he also spent much of his time viewing the sights. In Southwark, he saw bull and bear baiting; at Hampton Court, furniture and tapestries; at the Royal Palace in Greenwich, he looked at a number of 'splendid objects [that] were gifts to the queen from the great potentates and lords'; at the Tower of London, he admired the animals, cannons, shields and weapons, and also 'three chests full of stuff, such as bed-knobs ... and very costly cushions'; while at Whitehall Palace, 'Besides other curiosities, [he] saw an immense whale rib' (Thomas Platter's *Travels in England*, 1599: 106, 159–60, 170–71, 201–3, 215). One other visit significantly to impress Platter was to the home of a certain Walter Cope who, he reported, 'led us into an apartment, stuffed with queer foreign objects in every corner'.

Used from his European travels to contemporary Continental cabinets, Platter did not find the cabinet in itself all that unusual, though it clearly was of intrinsic interest. Within England, however, the fashion in which Cope filled his rooms with such curiosities as a unicorn's tail, the Queen of England's seal, an Indian canoe and Chinese boxes was certainly exceptional, and possibly even unique. Sir Walter Cope's collection, from which Platter described some fifty or so items or categories of curiosity, seems to be the very first record of an English collection. An acquaintance of Cope's, Sir Robert Bruce Cotton (1570–1631), had another early collection, mostly of antiquities and manuscripts. Clearly, it was Cope's foreign travels, particularly – as Platter stresses – his time spent in the 'Indies', that gave him the opportunity to gather the extraordinary contents of his museum (Mirrless, 1962; Sharpe, 1979; Rigby, 1944; MacGregor, 1985).

It is difficult to overemphasise the importance of the phenomenon of travel to the formation of early modern museums. As Lorraine Daston has declared, 'Travel was the alpha and omega of collecting, being both the source of the bulk of the objects ... and the occasion for inspecting them' (Daston, 1988: 455). And most of those who gathered museum collections were themselves well travelled. Whilst on their travels they were able to pick up items that might on their return be installed in their own cabinets, but travel also gave them an opportunity to compare the collections they knew from home with those they found on their travels. Back home, a traveller's collection enabled him to relive his travels. One travelled then in order to collect, but also one collected in order to travel – at least in one's imagination. In this light, the wording of the epitaph on the family tomb of the pioneer English collectors John Tradescant (father and son) seems especially well chosen: the two men lived, it declared, 'till they had travelled art and nature thro".

THOMAS PLATTER IN LONDON

There are a great many inns, taverns, and beer gardens scattered about the city, where much amusement may be had with eating, drinking, fiddling and the rest, as for instance in our hostelry, which was visited by players almost daily. And what is particularly curious is that the women as well as the men, in fact more often than they, will frequent the taverns or ale-houses for enjoyment. They count it a great honour to be taken there and given wine with sugar to drink; and if one woman only is invited, then she will bring three or four other women along and they gaily toast each other; the husband afterwards thanks him who has given his wife such pleasure, for they deem it a real kindness.

In the ale-houses tobacco or a species of wound-wort are also obtainable for one's money, and the powder is lit in a small pipe, the smoke sucked into the mouth, and the saliva is allowed to run freely, after which a good draught of Spanish wine follows.[1] This they regard as a curious medicine for defluctions, and as a pleasure, and the habit is so common with them, that they always carry the instrument on them, and light up on all occasions, at the play, in the taverns or elsewhere, drinking as well as smoking together, as we sit over wine, and it makes them riotous and merry, and rather drowsy, just as if they were drunk, though the effect soon passes – and they use it so abundantly because of the pleasure it gives, that their preachers cry out on them for their self destruction, and I am told the inside of one man's veins after death was found to be covered in soot just like a chimney. The herb is imported from the Indies in great quantities, and some types are much stronger than others, which difference one can immediately taste; they perform queer antics when they take it.[2] And they first learned of this medicine from the Indians, as Mr. Cope a citizen of London who has spent much time in the Indies, informed me; I visited his collection with Herr Lobelus, a London physician, and saw the following objects.

This same Mr. Cope inhabits a fine house in the Snecgas [sic]; he led us into an apartment, stuffed with queer foreign objects in every corner, and amongst other things I saw there, the following seemed of interest.

1   An African charm made of teeth.
2   Many weapons, arrows and other things made of fishbone.
3   Beautiful Indian plumes, ornaments and clothes from China.
4   A handsome cap made out of goosefoots from China.
5   A curious Javanese costume.
6   A felt cloak from Arabia.
7   Shoes from many strange lands.
8   An Indian stone axe, like a thunder-bolt.
9   Beautiful coats from Arabia.
10   A string instrument with but one string.
11   Another string instrument from Arabia.
12   The horn and tail of a rhinoceros, is a large animal like an elephant.
13   A fan made out of a single leaf.
14   Curious wooden and stone swords.
15   The twisted horn of a bull seal.
16   A round horn which had grown on an English woman's forehead.
17   An embalmed child (Mumia).[3]
18   Leathern weapons.
19   The bauble and bells of Henry VIII's fool.[4]
20   A unicorn's tail.
21   Inscribed paper made of bark.
22   Indian stone shears.
23   A thunder-bolt dug out of a mast which was hit at sea during a storm; resembles the Judas stone.
24   A stone against spleen disorders.
25   Artful little Chinese box.
26   Earthen pitchers from China.
27   Flying rhinoceros.
28   (Caterpillar) Hairy worm, sidopendra.
29.   Flies which glow at night in Virginia instead of lights, since there is often no day there for over a month.
30   A small bone implement used in India for scratching oneself.
31   The Queen of England's seal.
32   Turkish Emperor's golden seal.
33   Porcelain from China.
34   Falcon's head made of fine feathers.
35   Many holy relics from a Spanish ship which he helped to capture.

36   A Madonna made of Indian feathers.
37   A Turkish pitcher and dishes.
38   An Indian chain made of monkey teeth.
39   A sea-halcyon's nest, sign of a calm sea.
40   A pelican's beak, the Egyptian bird that kills its young, and after-
     wards tears open its breast and bathes them in its own blood, until
     they have come to life.
41   A mirror which both reflects and multiplies objects.[5]
42   Crowns made of claws (ungulis).
43   Heathen idols.
44   Saddles from many strange lands; they were placed round the top
     on stands.
45   Two beautifully dyed Indian sheepskins with silken sheen.
46   Remora. A little fish which holds up or hinders boats from sailing
     when it touches them, likewise another species called 'torpedo'
     which petrifies and numbs the crews' hands if it so much as touches
     the oars.
47   A sea mouse (mus marinus).
48   Numerous bone instruments.
49   Reed pipes like those played by Pan.
50   A long narrow Indian canoe, with the oars and sliding planks, hung
     from the ceiling of this room.

He possessed besides many old heathen coins, fine pictures, all kinds of
corals and sea plants in abundance. There are also other people in London interested in curios, but this gentleman is superior to them all for the
strange objects, because of the Indian voyage he carried out with such
zeal. In one house on the Thames bridge I also beheld a large live camel.

Source

Thomas Platter's *Travels in England, 1599 rendered into English from the
    German, and with introductory matter by Clare Williams*, London, 1937:
    170–73.

Notes

1   For travellers and collectors alike, alehouses and, later in the seventeenth
    century, coffee houses, provided extremely convenient places in which to
    meet others with similar interests and, indeed, in which to conduct some of
    the collector's trade. These institutions on occasions themselves made a

show of unusual objects and artefacts; and the tradition of establishments that serve refreshments acting as unofficial museums has, of course, continued until today.

2   Tobacco plants (newly discovered and experimented with in Europe) were items likely to be found in virtually every seventeenth-century museum.

3   Mummies were a highly-prized rarity found in many collections. They tended to be drawn from a medical market where they were bought and sold for the extraordinary healing powers that they were believed to have. Sometimes the bodies of criminals filled with bitumen and baked were substituted for the nobler specimens from ancient sources. The famous French physician Nicholas LeFevre, for example, maintained that 'The Mummy, which is prepared out of the Flesh of Man, is one of the noblest Remedies' (LeFevre, 1670: 135).

4   The personal effects of royalty were also prized items in many a collection. The fairly common idea of the mystical powers adhering to royal personalities gave such items a particular attraction.

5   Mirrors were by no means universally available objects. The magical use of them in spells, charms and experiments also made them more interesting than they have come to appear to later ages.

References

Daston, 1988
LeFevre, 1670
MacGregor, 1985
Mirrless, 1962
Rigby and Rigby, 1944
Sharpe, 1979

6

Ulisse Aldrovandi collects insects

Ulisse Aldrovandi (1522–1605) was professor of natural philosophy at the University of Bologna and director of the botanical
garden there. It was, however, his exploits as a collector and
particularly the extraordinary tale of his incorporation of a dragon
into his collection, that made him, for many educated sixteenth-
century Italians, a household name. Aldrovandi's collection (like
those of Francesco Calceolari in Verona, Michele Mercati in Rome
and Ferrante Imperato in Naples) emerged alongside aristocratic
collections of treasures and artworks, but featured natural history
objects instead. What was particularly notable about Aldrovandi
was the fashion in which he used his collections as a didactic and
professional resource (Findlen, 1996; Olmi, 1985: 5–16; Castellani,
1970).

Aldrovandi's encyclopaedic efforts to produce empirical tables
of the whole natural world were thoroughly indicative of a general
shift in the study of natural history away from traditional inquiries
into 'universal nature' towards a concern with specific instances.
This was a new form of investigation which worked up from the
actual specimens, rather than descending from theoretical principles (Findlen, 1996: 165). Though very much pointing in the
direction of the new science, Aldrovandi nevertheless understood
his own activities in thoroughly Aristotelian and Plinian terms, as
the fruition of a quest in which authority and experience were
harmoniously applied. The fulcrum about which old became new
was the expanded role for observation, much of it based on collections.

By 1595 Aldrovandi's museum contained about 8,000 tempera
illustrations, 14 cupboards of the woodblocks used to illustrate his
books, 11,000 animals, fruits and minerals and 7,000 plant specimens in some fifteen volumes of pressed and preserved examples
(Olmi, 1985: 8). The sheer volume of Aldrovandi's collecting
efforts, as well as his notoriety, ensured his place as one of the
foundational figures both in the establishment of a culture of
natural history in Renaissance Italy and, through his particular
choice of methodology, in the early evolution of the museum as
the institution within which to base natural history research.

Aldrovandi's museum was created as a combined laboratory
and lecture theatre in which nature could first be experimented
upon and then spoken of and argued about. Like many who fol-

lowed him, one of Aldrovandi's principle goals for his museum-based natural history was the reform of materia medica – that is, the range of medicinally effective substances sold and used by a variety of medical practitioners. Differences of opinion were fought out in bitter professional disputes, and the Renaissance museum provided him with both the evidence to shore up an argument and the chamber in which to conduct the debate.

As is indicated in the following passage, the new form of observational natural history was very much launched from a local context. Observation from the ground up often meant that the observer had to become acquainted with the local topography at first hand – hence the birth, or possibly rebirth, of the field trip. Aldrovandi's comments make it clear that it was important for a naturalist to cultivate good relationships with the people in the area where he was doing his collecting. Though botanists were particularly important in reviving and modifying observational procedures, this passage also indicates how the method was extended to other areas of natural history.

THE FIELD TRIP

When I reflect on the many days I have given to this study, and what expenses I have incurred, I cannot but wonder how I have been able to obtain possession of, and to examine, and to describe such a number of minute creatures.[1]

For the obtainment of my object, I was in the habit of going into the country for months during the summer and autumn,[2] not for relaxation, like others; for at these times I employed all my influence, as well as money, to induce the country-people to bring me such insects, whether winged or creeping, as they could procure in the fields or underground, and in the rivers and ponds.[3] When any were brought to me, I made inquiries about its name, habit, locality, etc. I often, too, wandered over the marshes and mountains, accompanied by my draughtsman and amanuenses, he carrying his pencil, and they their notebooks.[4] The former took a drawing if expedient, the latter noted down to my dictation what occurred to me, and in this way we collected a vast variety of specimens.[5]

Source

Ulisse Aldrovandi, 1602 *De animalibus insectis libri septum*, Bologna, quoted from Willy Ley, 1968 *Dawn of Zoology*, Englewood Cliffs, NJ: 158, in Paula Findlen, 1996, *Possessing Nature: Museums, Collecting, and Scientific*

Culture in Early Modern Italy, Berkeley and London, University of California Press: 169–70.

Notes

1   Natural historical work of the scope pursued by Aldrovandi could only be undertaken by someone who could command patronage from royalty, nobility or rich merchants. Humbler trips were mounted by less well-known investigators, while others went no further than territory with which they were confident of having some familiarity. It was not until the seventeenth century that such field trips came regularly to be mounted from institutional bases such as university museums.
2   This seasonal bias inevitably had its consequences on the findings of field-work-based natural histories, so that botanical works, for example, dealt fairly exclusively with blooms, foliage and fruit.
3   Children were not infrequently employed to find out or hunt down specimens.
4   Aldrovandi's trips clearly involved a significant entourage of helpers; scribes, guides, artists and general assistants were all involved in his collaborative trips (Findlen, 1996: 170).
5   The practicalities of such field trips also led to the evolution of equipment, skills and routines specially developed for natural historical investigations in the field. Portable equipment was a necessity, as were the skills of working in the open in a variety of weather conditions. The use of delivery systems to allow material to be sent back to the museum also evolved during the next century or so.

References

Castellani, 1970
Findlen, 1996
Olmi, 1985

7

Henry Peacham's advice to gentleman collectors

Proper guidelines for gentlemanly conduct, which came to include collecting coins and other antiquities, were an early seventeenth-century English obsession. It was the Earl of Arundel (patron to Henry Peacham) who set the most remarkable and ambitious example for those inclined to collect antiquities. Significantly, this was just the time when the phrase 'a scholar and a gentleman' was gaining popular currency. Much of the conduct, including coin collecting, deemed appropriate to a gentleman was directly copied from Continental courtly practice, Peacham declaring in the passage reproduced here that 'The pleasure of them is best knowne to such as have sene them abroad in France, Spaine and Italy, where the Gardens and Galleries of great men are beautified and set forth to admiration with these kinds of ornaments' (Peacham, 1634: 104). A fine collection then could be taken as a sure sign of superior social standing, so that even humbler virtuosi like John Evelyn were eager, albeit on a more modest scale, to pursue the same interests (de Beer, 1955). It was the French writer on the subject, Louis Jobert, who declared that 'If it were with Sciences as it is with Nobility, which draws its principal glory from its Antiquity, the Science of Medals, without dispute, would be the most considerable and esteemed' (Jobert, 1697: 1).

When set in gentlemanly cabinets, coin collections commonly prompted a good deal of almost ritualised activity amongst collectors. Woven throughout these practices, however, was also a certain amount of scholarly learning which could be paraded as a shibboleth of breeding: 'How often, [asked one writer on the theme] hath Breeding proved a better and surer estate than Lands, Riches, and Honours; all these things are subject to losses, chances and revolutions; but Breeding is an unestimable treasure, unseparable from him who hath it' (Gailhard, 1678: 3). It was on this basis that coin collecting fitted so perfectly into what Henry Peacham, the foremost champion of these gentlemanly accomplishments, called a compendium of 'most necessary and commendable Qualities' (Smith Fussner, 1962: 49–51).

It was the 1634 edition of Peacham's *The Compleat Gentleman* that marked something of an official arrival for numismatics in polite English circles; the chapter on antiques, including coins, from which the following extracts are taken, having been absent from earlier editions. As Peacham informed his readers, 'such as are skilled in [it] are by the Italians termed Virtuosi' (Peacham, 1634: 105; Houghton, 1942: 57). Virtuosi collectors were not themselves, however, very often able directly to contribute to the subject. To those that could not, John Evelyn, in his 1697 *Numismata*, suggested that they employ 'some learned and knowing Person' to keep and catalogue the library and museum, thereby ensuring that a virtuosi cabinet would still yield 'something of Use and Advantage to the Republic of Letters'. Such arrangements were, however, much less common in England than, as Evelyn had it, in other more 'Polite and Learned Nations' on the Continent (Evelyn, 1697: 255).

THE COMPLEAT GENTLEMAN: ANTIQUITIES

Out of the Treasury of Storehouse of venerable Antiquities, I have selected these three sorts. *Statues*, *Inscriptions*, and *Coynes*; desiring you to take a short view of them, ere you proceed any further.

The pleasure of them is best knowne to such as have seen them abroad in *France*, *Spaine* and *Italy*; where the Gardens and Galleries of great men are beautified and set forth to admiration with these kinds of ornaments. And indeed the possession of such rarities, by reason of their dead costlinesse, doth properly belong to Princes, or rather to princely minds.[1] But the profitable necessitie of some knowledge in them, will plainly appeare in the handling of each particular. Sure I am, that he that will travell, must both heed them and understand them, if he desire to bee thought ingenious, and to bee welcome to the owners. For next men and manners, there is nothing fairely more delightful, nothing worthier observation, than these Copies and memorials of men and matters of elder times; whole lively presence is able to perswade a man, that he now seeth two thousand yeeres agoe.[2] Such as are skilled in them, are by the *Italians* termed *Virtuosi* as if others that either neglect or despise them, were idiots or rakehels. And to say truth, they are somewhat to be excused, if they have all *Leeshebbers* (as the *Dutch* call them) in so high estimation, for they themselves are so great lovers of them (& *fimilia fimili gandet*) that they purchase them at any rate and lay up mightie treasures of money in them. Witnesse then Exchequer of mettals in the Cabinets of the great Duke of Tuscany, for number and raritie absolutely the best in the world, and not worth so little as 100,000 pound. For proofs whereof, doe but consider the number of those which *Peter do Medicis* lost at *Florence* upon his banisment and departure, thence, namely, a hundred thousand peeces of gold, and silver, and brasse, as *Philip de Commines* reporteth, who mentioneth them as an infinite treasure. And yet *Peter* was but a private man, and not to be, any way compared with the Dukes of his House, that here have beene since, all of them great and diligent gatherers of all manner of Antiquities. And for Statues, the *Diana of Ephesus* in the marble chamber at *Paris, Laocoon* and *Nilus* in *Beluere* at *Rome*, and many more, are peeces of inestimable value; but the matchlesse, and never too much admired *Toro* in Cardinall *Farneses* garden out strippeth all other Statues in the world for greatnesse and workemanship. It comprehendeth a great Bull, and (if my memory faile mee not) seven or eight figures more as great as the life, all of one entire peece of marble, covered with a house made of purpose, and estimated at the wealth of a kingdome, as the *Italians* say, or all other Statues put together ...

I come to the last of our select Antiquities, Coynes. They are much easier to come-by, than either Statues on Inscriptions; first in regard of their numerous quantitie; and secondly, by reason of their small bulke, which make the purchase cheaper, and the carriage lighter: Those I intend to handle, are Hebrew, Greeke and Latine. Of these, divers learned men have treated; chiefly, *Budeus, Agricola, Alciat, Carolus Molineus, Hotomannus, Didacus Covarruvins, Willebrordus Snellius,* and *Edovardus Breremoad*.[3] These Authors treat of the severall Species or kinds of old Coynes, and of their weight and value in moneyes of these times. There are others that have collected and represented the stamps, that is, the Figures and Inscriptions of all the individuall or severall peeces that ever they saw or read of. Such are *Goltzius* for Greeke pieces, *Fulvius Vrsinus* for Consulars, *Occo* for Imperials. And for the rates at which they are now bought and sold in Germany, *Halsius*. To these I add *Savot* his Discourse *des Medailles*, which excels for the materiall part or mettle of old Coynes. And for any thing omitted by the rest I will deliver the summe of what these have of the severall species of these old moneys, but the study of individuals, I will leave to your owne reading and handling.[4]

Source

Peacham, Henry, 1634, *The compleat gentleman. Fashioning him absolut, in the most necessary and commendable qualities concerning minde or body that may be required in a noble gentleman*, London: 104–6, 112–13.

Notes

1   Collecting antiquities was most definitely a socially restrictive activity. In a highly status-conscious society, having the wherewithal as well as the learn-

ing and leisure to pursue such an attribute of gentlemanly conduct turned coin collecting into as much a game of one-upmanship as a pursuit governed by intrinsic values.

2   It was a frequently stated attribute of coin collecting that because they provided some tangible material contact with ancient people, the collection and study of coins gave some special insight into the lives and times of people so far removed from themselves.

3   As Peacham's list indicates, there was already by the early seventeenth century a considerable literature devoted to coins, medals and their collection.

4   Studying coins provided a number of rewards for their collectors and admirers. One could, as Peacham says, seek to understand the pictures and icons used on their faces, as well as the inscriptions they bore. One could also see them as providing evidence for the history of ancient finance and commerce. While for those with proto-archaeological inclinations (and these tended to be scholarly numismatists supported by a university, rather than gentlemen collectors), coins were also treated as objects whose physical attributes, and even the physical contexts in which they were found, could all be used to tell a story about the people who had originally held and used them.

References

de Beer, 1955
Evelyn, 1697
Gailhard, 1678
Houghton, 1942
Jobert, 1697
Peacham, 1634
Smith Fussner, 1962

8

The Earl of Arundel views the King of Bohemia's collection

The formation of cabinets and museums on English soil had to wait for the habit of Continental travel to become common, at least amongst the gentry. The early seventeenth-century princes Henry and Charles in fact tended not to travel, but members of their aristocracy did. Chief amongst them was undoubtedly Thomas Howard, Earl of Arundel, who first voyaged abroad in 1612, ostensibly to search out a cure for his incipient consumption. A year later he set off again, this time in the company of his wife and the architect Inigo Jones, and proceeded to tour the Continent with great thoroughness (Haynes, 1975; Howarth, 1985; Hale, 1963; Stove, 1952; Hibbert, 1969; Trease, 1967).

It was during these travels that Arundel both gained a profound admiration for Italian culture, and set about acquiring as much of it as he could. Indeed, his appetite soon outgrew his own abilities to collect, so that his chaplain, his son's tutor and a number of friends all came to act as his agents. As a result, by the late 1630s Arundel's homestead had been converted into a worthy imitation of an Italian palace and garden, adorned with vast arrays of statues, busts, inscriptions, paintings, manuscripts, coins and gems.

In 1636 Arundel went on a diplomatic mission to visit Emperor Ferdinand II in Linz, Germany. Diplomatically, the trip was a failure, but in terms of his interests as an art-lover and connoisseur, the journey was richly rewarding. The job of recording all the events on this journey was given to a young man called William Crowne, whose record is preserved in his *A True Relation of all the Remarkable Places and Passages observed in the Travels of ... Thomas Lord Howard* (Springell, 1963: 44–5). The following passage is taken from his account of their visit to the 'Ketschin' (Hradschin) castle in Prague on 6 July 1636.

HRADSCHIN CASTLE, PRAGUE

Early next morning, on July 6, we left for PRAGUE, some five Dutch miles away, for the early part of our journey through pleasant plains and meadows until, nearing the city, we came into a rocky and hilly countryside, in which the city is engulfed. The hills are planted with vines, which surround its three towns, NEWSTADT, OLDSTADT, and the SLOSTADT.

We entered NEWSTADT by a fine gateway and passed through to His Excellency's lodging in OLDSTADT which is inhabited chiefly by Jews, who have four synagogues there. In one of them I saw a rabbi circumcise a child.[1] Arrived here, we were told how the terrible thunderstorm and lightning, previously mentioned, had ruined the crop of corn and the vineyards in the more distant parts of the country – there had been hailstones as big as one's fist and many cattle had been killed.

Between where we were and the SLOSTADT runs a pleasant river called the MULDOW, bridged by a fine stone bridge as long as London Bridge. His Excellency crossed this bridge on his way to visit the castle of Ketschin, where the King of Bohemia lived. This castle is a large imposing fortress built on a high hill within the SLOSTADT and, passing a guard of soldiers at one of the gates, we entered it through three fine courtyards in one of which there is a bronze statue of ST GEORGE on horseback, and also a fountain. From here we stepped into a spacious hall containing many fine niches and resembling Westminster, with the difference that their Courts of Judicature are in other rooms hereby. Ascending some stairs, we passed through many fine rooms well furnished with pictures and tapestries, and with one particular room hung with English pictures of our own nobility which the King of Bohemia was obliged to leave behind.

We went on until we came to their Council Chamber on the third storey, the scene of the rebellion in which the members of the Chamber hurled three of the Emperor's representatives through the window on to the ground fifty-five feet below, where now three gilt crosses stand to mark the spot. Though pistols were discharged at them as they lay below, not one was killed and in fact two of the three are still alive.

From the Council Chambers we went down to a stately room with fine central pillars and bronze statues beside them, and with pictures of Indian horses hanging on the walls.[2] In the dining room adjoining was a table of mosaic work whence, by some means, came music; while at one end of the room was a collection of choice armour, together with a gun which, without the use of gunpowder, could fire a bullet.

Next we visited the SCHANT ROOM, where the treasury was housed and where there was also the most wonderful collection belonging to the Emperor RODOLPHUS.[3]

In the first room were cupboards set in the walls on our right hand.
The first cupboard exhibited a collection of coral;
the second, porcelain;
the third, mother-of-pearl;

the fourth, a collection of quaint engravings on copper plates;

the fifth and sixth contained mathematical instruments;

the seventh, basins, ewers and cups all made of amber;[4]

the eighth, cups made of agates, gold and crystal;

the ninth, of rocks;

the tenth, of mosaic work in stone;

the eleventh, cups made of ivory, and also a great UNICORN'S horn, one yard long;

the twelfth showed embossing work;

the thirteenth, engravings;

the fourteenth, antiques in silver;

the fifteenth, cabinets of Bohemian diamonds and small chests of Bohemian pearls;

the sixteenth was devoted to astronomical instruments;

the seventeenth and eighteenth, to INDIAN work;

the nineteenth, to work from the East (Turkey Work);

the twentieth displayed a life-like statue of a woman, covered with taffeta.

In the middle of the room were clocks of all kinds: one shaped like a globe was a musical block; a second, surrounded by small pillars, had a metal ball running round in a groove, and from it hung two thin cords which, when pulled, caused sweet music to sound, though we could not discern whence it came.[5] A third clock, with a gaily coloured face and dial that stood out boldly, gave out the sound of singing, how we could not tell. A fourth, beside which was a beautiful table in mosaic work, was an enclosed clock, and a fifth, possessing pillars arranged to form four separate ascents, had a metal ball running round in a groove right up to the top and was also musical. A sixth clock was in the form of a globe and against the background of gold on its face, coloured green to resemble a field, a buck ran in and out while pursuing hounds gave tongue; in the lower section of this clock, quaint figures danced and music sounded. A seventh clock showed a globe.

On the wall opposite, antiques and pictures were displayed and there was also an intricately-wrought iron chair of fine craftsmanship.

In another little room we inspected cabinets that contained presents given to the Emperor, for instance gilt helmets, head-pieces and statues.

Along the walls of the third room were four cupboards full of rare pictures, while in the middle of the room were unusual things such as a boar in roughcast, done to the life, also a life-like statue of a brawny Amazon and in addition a cupboard of ancient books.

In the fourth room were three cupboards filled with anatomies of several rarities such as cockatrices, and fishes partly resembling men. A fourth cupboard contained large rare shells of all kinds and a library with one enormous Folio, the work of a friar imprisoned in a dungeon for some heinous crime. After forty years of imprisonment, this man was discovered by some brother friars who, in passing the place where he was incarcerated, heard his cries, made investigations, and found this poor fellow who showed them this book, containing the Old and New Testaments, together with many strange histories, which – with the assistance of the Devil, as he imagined – he has spent all those years in writing. He died, however, very soon after being rescued from his dungeon.

From here, after viewing the skins of those Indian horses whose pictures were hanging in the 'masking room', we entered a large church in the middle of the Castle, noting the beautiful wood-carvings of the choir stalls and the tomb of JOHN NEPOMEWS, the Queen's confessor, put to death in 1383 by order of Wenceslaus, the fourth King of Bohemia, after being cruelly tortured to reveal Her Majesty's confession.

From hence, His Excellency went to see a garden behind the Castle, which contained a covered arbour half a mile long, at the end of which we had a delightful view over the whole city.

Source

Crowne, William, 1937, *A True Relation of all the Remarkable Places and Passages observed in the Travels of ... Thomas Lord Howard* London, reproduced in Francis C. Springell, *Connoisseur & Diplomat*, London, Maggs Brothers, 1963: 70–73.

Notes

1 The ceremony of circumcision was witnessed and described frequently by English travellers on the Continent. The establishment of a separate Jewish quarter and community within Prague dated from the tenth and eleventh centuries and survived until the Nazi period.
2 The term 'Indian' was very widely employed, often simply designating an object's 'exotic' origins.
3 As a collector and patron, Emperor Rudolph II was the German counterpart of the Earl of Arundel, though a generation younger. While Arundel tended to be more selective in his tastes, both men shared a keen passion for the works of Albrecht Dürer. Rudolph was well educated in mathematics, astronomy and science; he spoke six languages fluently, drew and painted well, and also had a considerable knowledge of things antiquarian (Springell, 1963: 118).
4 Like many minerals used in jewellery, amber was at this time widely held to

possess magical qualities, which naturally added to the collectors' interest in acquiring examples of it.

5 Collections of clockwork items were also very prevalent in princely cabinets of this sort, craftsmen not infrequently being employed to manufacture pieces specifically for collections. Again, the mysterious, even 'magical', overtones of their mechanisms made them especially collectable.

References

Hale, 1963
Haynes, 1975
Hibbert, 1969
Howarth, 1985
Springell, 1963
Stove, 1952
Trease, 1967

9

John Evelyn records in his diary the collections he has seen in Florence

Evelyn was principally an arboriculturist and horticulturist. He studied anatomy and physiology in Padua in 1645–46. His *Sylva* (mostly a practical and encyclopaedic work on trees) was the first work published by order of the Royal Society. Evelyn was also extensively involved in the setting up and early running of the Royal Society. Like many virtuosi of his day, Evelyn's interests were extremely broad and eclectic: another of his works, *Numismata*, was a book of advice on collecting coins and medals. Though not himself an especially notable collector (a curiosity cabinet of his can still be seen at the Geffrey Museum in London), the idea of collecting was central to all his work; following the Italian fashion, Evelyn's writings on gardens also bore a strong imprint of the 'cabinet' mentality (Hunt, 1985). For today's historian of museums, a principal interest in Evelyn lies in his familiarity with virtually all the major collections of his day across the whole of Europe.

John Evelyn spent a good part of his life either looking at the collections of others, or amassing his own. Almost every page of his diary, especially those covering his Continental travels during the mid-1640s, reveals some store of rarities and curiosities in which he delighted – the cabinet at the Palais de Luxembourg, the pavilion and fountains at St-Germain-en-Laye, the college in Pisa, Signor Septalla's curiosities in Milan, the Duke of Guize's collection in Aix en Provence, and so on and so forth. And his correspondence, again particularly from this period of intense travel, only adds to the impression of a man driven by an insatiable thirst for the rare and the curious (Vale, 1977: 73; Hale, 1963: 13–22, 30–36; Stoye, 1952: 449).

However, as an incident that occurred in October 1644 clearly shows, inquisitiveness could, if his purse strings allowed, quickly be followed by acquisitiveness. For having examined many such pieces in the cabinets of others, Evelyn decided to 'purchas[e] the Pietra Comm[e]ssa Pieces for my Cabinet; [and later to] collect some Prints & drawings [before going] ... to see the renouned Church, Chapell & Library of St Laurences' (de Beer, 1955: 198). The copious records of Evelyn's extensive travels provide our most monumental record of the fashion for collecting while travelling abroad in a period of English culture dominated by the lure

and fame of a more sophisticated Continental taste and connoisseur-
ship. In the following extract, Evelyn describes his impressions of
a range of sites in Florence, as he reports to find them at the end of
October 1644. However, as the notes make clear, it is debatable
how much of this account is based on his own eyewitness reporting and how much on a compilation of printed sources.

FLORENCE, 1644

Hence to another of the Dukes Palaces cal'd Palazzo Vecchio[1] before
which is the statue of David, & Hercules killing of Cacus, the worke of
Baccio Bandinelli, the other of Michael Angelo. The quadrangle about
this is of the Corinthian order, & in the halls many rare marbles; as those
of Leo the tenth, and Clements the VIIth, both Popes of the Medicean
family; also the Acts of Cosimo in rare Painting. In the Chapell is conserv'd
(as they would make us believe) the Original Gospel of St. John, writen
with his owne hand; together with the so famous Florentine Pandects;
here are likewise divers precious stones; & neere it another pendent
towre (like that at Pisa) always threatning ruine: Hence we goe to the
Publique Court of Justice, under which is a stately Arcade for men to
walke in; & over that the shops of divers rare Artists, who continualy
worke for the Greate Duke; and above this that so renowned *Ceimeliarcha*[2]
or Repository where in are divers hundreds of admirable Antiquities,
Statues or Marble and Mettal, Vasas of Porphyrie &c but amongst the
statues none so famous as the S[c]ipio, the boare &c: the Idol of Apollo
brought from the Delphic Temple, & two triumphant Columnes: Over
these hang the Pictures to the life of the famous Persons[3] & Illustrious
men, whither excelling in Arts or Armes to the number of 300, taken out
of the Musaeum of Paulus Jovius; Then they lead us into a large Square
roome, in the middle whereoff stood a Cabinet of an octangular forme so
adornd and furnish'd with Christals, Achat, Sculptures &c as certainely
exceedes any description.[4] Upon it is a globe of Ivory rarely carv'd,
Hercules his Labours in Massy Silver, & many imcomparable Pictures in
small; Likewise another which had about it eight oriental Columns of
Alabaster, on each whereof was plac'd an head of a Caesar, cover'd with
a Canopy so richly beset with precious Stones, that they resembled a
firmament of Starrs: This Cabinet was valued at 2 hundred thousand
crownes; Within was our Saviours Passion, and 12 Apostles of incomparable Amber. In another with Calcidon Pillars was a Series of Golden
Medaills. [In this Cabinet is call'd the *Tribuna*, in which is a pearle as big
as an haizel nut: The Cabinet is of Ebonie, Lazuli & Jasper: Over the
doore a round of *M: Angelo*, on the Cabinet Leo the tenth with other

paintings of Raphaels, *del Sartos, Perugino & Coregio* viz. a *St. John*, a *Virgin*, a *boy*, two Apostles & two heads of *Durer*, rar[e]ly carved.[5] Here is also another rich Ebony Cabinet, Cupola'd with a tortois shell and containing a Collection of gold Medails esteemd worth 50000 crounes,[6] a wreathed Pillar of Oriental Alabaster, divers Paintings of *da Vinci, Pontorno, del Sarto*, an Ecce homo of Titian, a *boy* of *Bronzini &c*:

They also shew us a branch of Corall fix'd on the rock which they affirme dos still grow.]

In another roome is kept the Tabernacle appointed for the Chapel of St. Laurence, about which are placed divers small statues of Saints of precious materials, a piece of that Art & Cost, as having been these 40 yeares in perfecting, is certainely one of the most curious & rare things in the World.

Here were divers incomparable tables of Pietra Commessa,[7] which is a marble ground inlayd with severall sorts of marbles & stones of divers colours, in the shapes of flowers, trees, beasts, birds & Landskips like the natural: In one is represented the Towne of Ligorne, by the same hand who inlays the Altar of St. Laurence, Domenico Benotti of whom I purchas'd nineteen pieces of the same worke for a Cabinet.[8] In a Presse neere these they shew'd us an Iron-naile, one halfe whereof being converted into gold by one Thurnheuser a German Chymist, is look'd on as a greate rarity [but it plainly appears to have ben but sother'd:][9] There is a curious Watch, a monstrous Turcois as big as an Egge, on which is engraven an Emperors head: From hence we went into the Armory, where is conserved many antique habits, as that of the Chineze Kings, the Sword of *Charlemain*: an Italian lock for their wanton Wives or jealous Husbands: Hanibals headpiece, & a [huge] Load-stone [of a yard long] of that Vertue as it beares up 86 pounds weight very well [in a chaine of 17 links, such as the slaves are tied to].[10] In the Presse of another roome they shew'd us such rare tourneries in Ivory, as are not to be describ'd for their curiosity: likewise faire Pillar of Oriental Alabaster, and 12 vast & compleate Services of Silver plate, & one of Gold; all of them of [incomparable] workmanship; besides a rich embrodred Saddle [of pearls] sent by the Emp: to this Duke [& here is that embrodred chaire set with precious stones, that he sits in when on St. *Johns* day he receives the Tribute of the Citties:][11]

Source

de Beer, E.S. (ed.), 1955, *The diary of John Evelyn*, Vol. 2, Oxford, Clarendon Press: 188–93.

Notes

1 Evelyn's description of the Palazzo Vecchio was taken from the author Pflaumern. Interestingly, a good number of his accounts were embellished if not directly copied from contemporary source-books and guidebooks (de Beer, 1955: 188–93).

2 Meaning treasure houses. The variety of nomenclature applied to the various types of collections held at this time is rarely consistent. 'Repository', 'museum' or 'musaeum', 'collection' and 'cabinet' were commonly used interchangeably.

3 A number of these pieces can still be seen in either the Uffizi or the archaeological museum in Florence.

4 Evelyn appears to have misread or mistranslated his sources here and has confused a description of the room in which the cabinet stood with the cabinet itself. The word 'cabinet' was at the time used to refer both to a room and to a piece of furniture.

5 A number of these pieces are also still to be found in museums and palaces in Florence. Though here, again, Evelyn has become confused in some of his descriptions, for example implying that the Durer portraits are sculptures.

6 This astounding valuation provides some indication of the enormous values attached to collections of coins and medals in particular.

7 Florentine mosaic.

8 Here again is evidence of how, given the means, admiration could then inspire acquisition.

9 That is, gold-plated.

10 That is, a naturally occurring magnetic ore which could hold that weight of the type of chain that would have held galley slaves.

11 This refers to the St John's Day ceremony, the most important in the Florentine year.

References

de Beer, 1955
Hale, 1963
Stoye, 1952
Vale, 1977

10

The collection of King Charles I of England

While medieval collections tended to consist of precious items, some objects of great curiosity (for example unicorns' horns) and armoury, Renaissance collectors were instead more concerned with the arts (a gallery of pictures was commonly taken as a badge of princely worth) and with a wider range of collectibles: coins and medals, antiquities, some mathematical and musical instruments, gems, cameos and so on. Drawing its spiritual inspiration and many of its physical artefacts from Italy, Charles I's collections marked something of a culmination in European princely collecting (Lightbown, 1989: 53).

England's Renaissance court was focused on the royal presence, and the removal of Charles I's head in 1649 inescapably marked the court's summary extinction (Herrmann, 1972; Haskell and Penny, 1981; Millar, 1960). By 20 July of the same year, most of the fine art and other collections, the furniture, the tableware, regalia, clothing and other belongings of the royal family – that is, the charmed fabric that had been symbolically so important to the regime – were ready to be sold by an Act of Parliament. The text that follows forms part of the 'true and perfect Inventories' made by appointed trustees in an attempt to quantify and evaluate the late King's assets (Millar, 1972: xi–xxv).

Elsewhere in England, the interregnum similarly signalled to a number of collectors the need, temporarily at least, to abandon ship. Styling himself a 'sworn servant to his Majesty', Robert Hubert, for example, withdrew his collections from England and exhibited them in Leipzig and Hamburg, only bringing them back to London after the Restoration (Hunter, 1989; Murray, 1904: 127). Overall, the general effect on museums of the disruptions surrounding the Civil War was merely a temporary suspension of collecting activity at the very highest social level, and amongst any others politically aligned with it. However, this social revolution did, in England at least, mark a permanent change in the dominant character of collecting. Crudely stated, collecting before the Civil War was prominently conducted in the areas of fine art, jewellery, numismatics and antiquities, and by the aristocracy and upper nobility; after the war, natural history collecting came to dominate, this time being undertaken by more of the mercantile and artisanal classes – broadly speaking by more of the 'middling sort'.

ASSETS OF THE LATE KING

An Inventory of severall things
received from some Genlemen
in whose Custody there were, and now
remayning in Somersett house
Clossett, in M[r.] Brownes Charge.[1]

		li	s	d
[1]	A Garter of blue Velvett sets with 412 small Diamonds formerly in Captaine Prestons Custody and now in the Clossett at Somersett house valued at	0160	00	00

        Sold to Ireton 3 Jan. 1949/50 for £205.

		li	s	d
[2]	One Coller of Esses of gould formerly in Collonell Harrisons Custody and now being in the said Clossett p oz 33 oz 1/2 valued at 3[li] per Ounce	0106	10	00

        Delivered to the Mint.

		li	s	d
[3]	The handle of a rodd formerly in the Custody of the Kings Sadler[2] and now remayning in the said Clossett p oz 4 Ounces ½ ⅛, being gould sett with small Rubies and Diamonds valued at	0018	00	00
		0284	10	00

[*Soc. of Antiq. MS., f. 19*]

		li	s	d
[4]	The Gould and silver belonging to an old Cross being all wood underneath, and sett with Counterfeit stones formerly in the Custody of M[r] Hunt, an Officer of the Hon[ble] House of Comons, the gould weighing 13 Ounces 1/2 and the silver 31 oz the gould valued at 3[li] per Ounce and the silver at 5[s] per Ounce	0048	05	00

[5] A Silver Seale Calld y[e] Queenes
Seale[3] formerly in the Custody of the
said Mr. Hunt p 0z 32 Ounces at 5[s]
per Ounce[4]   0008   00   00

                                               0056   05   00
                                               0284   10   00
To[ts] of this last parcell   0341   05   00

The Totall of the whole   li   s   d
Duplicate amounts to   14221: 15: 04:

A Mildemay
John: Foche
David Powell
Ph: Carteret.
MLempriere.

Source

Millar, O. (ed.), 1972, *The Inventories and Valuations of the King's Goods 1649–1651*, Vol. 43, Walpole Society, 1970–72, Glasgow, University Press: 52–3.

Notes

1 The Royal goods and collections were an essential part of the fabric of pre-revolution courtly society, largely run according to nuanced rules of giving gifts and receiving favours. The lively exchange in these items meant that they not infrequently changed hands.
2 The King's Saddler was a certain Charles Tennant (Millar, 1972: 52).
3 Other copies of the inventory described this piece as 'the Dutchy Seal' (Millar, 1972: 52).
4 This particular section of the inventory is dominated by items of jewellery. Other sections dealt with plate (that is, silverware) kept at Whitehall and in the Tower, statues kept at Somerset House and at Greenwich, pictures at Whitehall, Greenwich and Hampton Court, and what are referred to as 'goods' gathered from a wide variety of royal properties.

References

Haskell and Penny, 1981

Herrmann, 1972
Hunter, 1989
Lightbown, 1989
Millar, 1960
Millar, 1972
Murray, 1904

11

John Dury advocates school museums

In the first half of the seventeenth century in England, the ferment of reforming ideas associated with the teachings of Francis Bacon encouraged a fundamental re-evaluation of many aspects of society and culture. The heady, idealistic, millennarian outlook, most famously embodied in the writings of John Milton, had its more pragmatic foundations in various practical reforming projects (Webster, 1978; Sharp, 1977). And, as the publisher's note accompanying John Dury's *The Reformed School* declared, 'The readiest way to Reform both Church and Commonwealth, is to reform the schools of Education therein' (Dury, 1650: 'Publisher to the Reader').

The pressure for these reforms came from a variety of sources: an increasingly powerful mercantile and artisanal population demanding new educational services, the growing taste amongst the gentry for grooming themselves on new standards of virtuosity, and the requirement for new lay administrators and professionals to fill the gap created by the demise of the clerical monopoly on culture, all played their part. An ardent band of reformers responded to these pressures with a vast range of suggested changes. The level of their enterprise is hinted at in the fact that the two decades after 1640 saw in England the publication of no less than fifty separate works on educational reform (Stone, 1964: 41–80; Watson, 1909).

Amongst the range of reforms proposed for all levels of education and concerning everything from pedagogical methods and curricula to diet and exercise, the most significant in terms of the history of museums was that relating to language instruction. Although attracting a great deal of attention on English soil, many of these ideas were in fact originally developed by men who were educated, and often born, overseas in Protestant Europe, the most influential amongst whom was Johan Amos Comenius. It was Comenius who argued that language instruction should be taught 'truely and demonstrate[d] ... solidly, that it may thoroughly appear ... as the firme foundations of things themselves' (Comenius, 1938: 4). For young students, this could best be achieved by the use of pictures, or better still objects. For as John Dury stated: 'the teaching of words is no further usefull than the things signified therby are familiar to the imagination'. And for this reason, the school should 'indeed become a School of things obvious to the senses' (Comenius, 1664: 'The Translator'). It is a scheme along these lines, in which for the purposes of language teaching the schoolroom was to take on the additional characteristics of a theatre and a museum (a *Musaeum ormianum* or school reposi-tory, as Cyprian Kinner, another educational reformer, described it), that Dury elaborated in the text that is to follow (Kinner, 1648; Turnbull, 1947; Young, 1932: 32–50; Webster, 1970).

There is little evidence that schools along the lines suggested by Comenius, Dury, Hartlib, Kinner, Hoole and the like made much of a lasting impression on the English educational scene. However, Hoole's activities as a working teacher – one passion-ately committed to the need for 'object lessons' in which 'sensual objects be rightly presented to the senses' – include what might well be the first ever recorded visits by school classes to a mu-seum. '[O]f all place I know in England', he declared, London was the 'best for the full improvement of children in their educa-tion, because of the variety of objects which daily present them-selves to them, or may easily be seen once a year, by walking to Mr. John Tradescants, [i.e. the Tradescant museum in Lambeth,] or like houses or gardens, where rarities are kept' (Hoole, 1913: 284–5).

THE REFORMED SCHOOL

Concerning the Means and Instruments which are to be had in a readinesse, and ordered for use, that these Tasks may thus be prosecuted on all hands.

The things necessary to be made use of for bringing all this to passe,[1] are 1. a convenient House fitted with rooms, wherein the Scholars may be at their exercises. 2. the scholasticall Furniture, and dressing of those rooms, 3. the Books and other Implements, which the Ushers[2] and Schollers must have at hand.

The House, where this course of education should be intended, must not be within the City, but should be near unto it, in a good air, large and spacious; and as it were in the Countrey, with large gardens and orchards, near the places of tillage and of pasturage, that the Countrey may afford unto the Scholars the aspect and observation of all Naturall things, wherein they are to be taught, and the City may afford them the sight of all Artificial things; of all Trades and Manufactures, wherewith they are to be made acquainted.[3]

The Rooms wherein the Scholars should be at the exercises, should be foure: Three lesser ones, for each Usher and his peculiar Scholars one, and one large one; or rather a Galley which should be for common use unto all.

The Scholasticall furniture and dressing of these rooms ought to be this.

The large common room ought to be furnished with all manner of Mathematicall, Naturall, Philosophicall, Historicall, Medicinall, Hiero-glyphicall and other sort of pictures, maps, globes, instruments, models, engines, and whatsoever is an object of sense in reference to any Art or Science, these things are to be set in their order, according as they are subordinate unto severall Sciences; that at the times appointed, the Ush-ers may leade their Scholars into it; to receive the lessons which they shall give them; upon the ocular inspection of the Things, which shall be shewed unto them.[4]

The lesser rooms each ought to be furnished with a high seat for the Ushers; that he may overlook all his Scholars, and wish twentie distinct places, so ordered for the Scholars to sit or stand in; that their faces may be all towards him: and each in his place may have his own desk, to keep all his papers and other things to be used in good order. In each of those rooms there should be an iron fornace or stove to keep it warm in the winter.

The Books which the Scholars shall have in the School shall be none but such as their Usher shall put in their hands. In the second Period of Institution, they shall have no books but their Latine, Greek and Hebrew *Janua's*, and the Bible of the Old and New Testaments in these Tongues, and in their Mother-tongue. In the third Period, besides these books, they shall have from time to time, such as their Usher by the Governours direction shall furnish them withall, and none other; not any longer then be thinks fit.

The Instruments besides pen, ink and paper, shall be a pen or stick with black lead; a pen-knife, a pair of compasses, a ruler, a slate, and some other impelements which from time to time shall be put in their hands and taught to make use of according to the degree of their profi-ciency.[5]

Source

John Dury, 1650, *The Reformed School*, London, A Scolar Press Facsimile, Menston, England, Scolar Press, Ashgate, 1972: 74–6.

Notes

1 Dury here refers to the proper method of education that has been laid out in his book thus far.
2 The 'ushers' are the school teachers.
3 Dury seems here to be suggesting the type of 'field trips' – both into the country to observe nature and to cities to observe the man-made world – that a number of the other education reformers envisioned and indeed practised with their pupils.
4 In short, what Dury is calling for is that the largest of the school's four rooms be set up as a museum for a form of teaching based on 'the ocular inspection of the Things'.
5 The range of 'instruments' that Dury is suggesting these pupils be instructed in handling indicates another common feature of these educational reforms, namely a focus on practical as well as scholarly abilities.

References

Comenius, 1938
Comenius, 1664
Dury (or Durie), 1650
Hoole, 1913
Kinner, 1648
Sharp, 1977
Stone, 1964
Turnbull, 1947
Watson, 1909
Webster, 1970
Webster, 1978
Young (ed.), 1932

12

The catalogue of the Tradescant collection: England's first substantial museum

Much of the collecting that went on in early modern Europe was a princely and aristocratic affair. The grand collectors, however, often employed 'agents' drawn from other social classes to gather material for them by proxy; and as a result, many an agent gained the taste and enthusiasm to admire and then acquire themselves. Possibly the most notable English example of this effect came in the career of John Tradescant the elder, who founded the most important English collection of the first half of the seventeenth century – a collection which, in the hands of Elias Ashmole, later became the core of the Ashmolean Museum in Oxford.

Acting successively as head gardener for Robert Cecil (the first Earl of Salisbury), his son William, Edward Lord Wooton, the Duke of Buckingham, and finally, Charles I's wife Henrietta Maria, John Tradescant showed little reticence about using his position to procure items for his own garden and museum, often from duplicates or unwanted remainders of gifts or bribes initially intended for loftier hands. Much of the contents of his museum, then, arrived as leftovers from the excesses of courtly consumption. Not just the collections, but even the site in Lambeth where he set about housing his treasures, together with the garden that surrounded it, was also obtained through courtly favours, this time from the Duke of Buckingham.

These aristocratic connections continued to flourish after he was settled in Lambeth, with the 'Ark' (as the museum was commonly termed) soon becoming established as a popular resort for visits by the mighty and wealthy, many of whom were subsequently recorded as benefactors to the Tradescant museum. In Tradescant's mind grew the assumption that he somehow belonged in the elevated circles in which he moved, and this led him to adopt a spurious coat of arms, which he erected on his house and used to seal his will (Leith-Ross, 1983: 28–44, 79–84; MacGregor, 1983: 3–8; Allan, 1964; Hadfield, 1960: 79).

The social benefits that Tradescant gained from collecting indicate how the process of building a museum collection gradually came to be not only the preserve of a narrow elite, but also a potential means of advancement for a much broader segment of society. Though by no means pursued exclusively for these ends, a significant number of English collectors did emerge from the lower nobility and upper ranks of the 'middling sort' during the seventeenth century, many of whom gathered their specimens and rarities in the spirit of learned enquiry. The Tradescant collection was typical in being gathered partly for reasons of family aggrandisement, and partly for the sake of learning and the accumulation of knowledge about the material world. Elements of both motivations can be found in the lasting record of their efforts, the printed catalogue from which the following extract is taken.

THE TRADESCANT COLLECTION CATALOGUE

To *John Tradescant* the younger,
surviving.

Anagr:

JOHN TRADESCANT.

Cannot hide Arts

Heire of my Fathers goods, and his good parts,
Which both preservest, and augment'st his store,
Tracing th' ingenuous steps he trod before:
Proceed as thou begin'st, and win those hearts,
With gentle curt'sie, which admir'd his Arts.
Whilst thou conceal'st thine own, and do'st deplore
Thy want, compar'd with his, thou shew'st them more.
Modesty clouds not worth, but hate diverts,
And shames base envy, ARTS he CANNOT HIDE
That has them, Light through every chink is spy'd.

On *John Tradescante* the elder,
deceased.

Anagr:

JOHN TRADESCANTE.

Had inocent Artes.
Can honest Art die?
Artes cannot die.[1]

Nor court, nor shop-crafts, were thine ARTES,[2] but those
    Which *Adam* studied ere he did transgresse:
    The Wonders of the Creatures, and to dresse
The worlds great Garden. Sure the Sun ne're rose
Nor couch'd but blush'd to see thy roofe enclose;
    More dainties than his orb,[3] CAN Death oppress
    Such HONEST ART as this, or make it less?
No: Fame shall still record it, and expose
    Industrious care to all eternity.
    The body may, and must: ARTES CANNOT DIE.

To the Ingenious
READER

For some *reasons* I apprehend my self engaged to give an *account* of *two*
things, that refer to the ensuing *piece*: The one, for not *publishing* this
Catalogue untill now: The other, of the *mode & manner* thereof, being
partly *Latine* and partly *English*.

About three years agoe (by the perswasion of some *friends*) I was
resolved to take a *Catalogue* of those *Rarities* and *Curiosities* which my
Father had scedulously *collected*, and my *selfe* with continued diligence
have *augmented*, & hitherto preserved together: They then pressed me
with that Argument, *That the enumeration of these Rarities, (being more*
for variety than any one place known in Europe *could afford) would be*
an honour to our Nation, and a benefit to such ingenious persons as
would become further enquirers into the various modes of Natures admi-
rable workes, and the curious Imitators thereof:[3] I readily yeilded to the
thing so urged, and with the assistance of two worthy *friends* (well
acquainted with my design,) we then began it, and many *examinations* of
the *materialls* themselves, & their *agreements* with severall Authors *com-*
pared, a *Draught* was made, which they gave into my hands to examine

over. Presently thereupon my *onely Sonne dyed*, one of *my Friends* fell very *sick* for about *a yeare*, and my *other Friend* by unhappy *Law-suits* much disturbed. Upon these accidents that *first Draught* lay neglected in *my hands* another year. Afterwards my said Friends call again upon me, and the designe of *Printing*, a new *contrived*, onely the prefixed *Pictures* were not ready, and I found my kinde friend *Mr. Hollar* then engaged for about tenne Moneths, for whose hand to finish the *Plates*, I was necessarily constrained to stay untill this time.

Now for the *materialls* themselves I reduce them unto two sorts; one *Naturall*, of which some are more familiarly known & named amongst us, as divers sorts of Birds, foure-footed Beasts and Fishes, to whom I have given usual English names. Others are lesse familiar, and as yet unfitted with apt *English* termes, as the shell-Creatures, Insects, Mineralls, Outlandish-Fruits, and the like, which are part of the *Materia Medica*; (Encroachers upon that faculty, may try how they can crack such shels).[4] The other sort is *Artificialls*, as Vtensills, Householdstuffe, Habits, Instruments of VVarre used by several Nations, rare curiosities of Art, &c.[5] These are also expressed in *English*, (saving the Coynes, which would vary but little if Translated) for the ready satisfying whomsoever may desire a view thereof. The *Catalogue* of my *Garden* I have also added in the Conclusion (and given the names of the *Plants* both in *Latine* and *English*) that nothing may be wanting which at present comes within view, and might bee expected from-

Your ready friend
JOHN TRADESCANT.

A view of the whole.

1 Birds with their eggs, beaks, feathers, clawes, spurres.
2 Fourfooted beasts with some of their hides, hornes and hoofs.
3 Divers sorts of strange Fishes.
4 Shell-creatures, whereof some are called *Mollia*, some *Crustacea*, others *Testacea*, of these, are both *univalvia*, and *bivalvia*.
5 Severall sorts of Insects, terrestriall – *anelytra, coleoptera, aptera, apoda*.
6 Mineralls, and those of neare nature with them, as Earths, Coralls, Salts, Bitumens, Petrified things, choicer Stones, Gemmes.
7 Outlandish Fruits from both the *Indies*, with Seeds, Gummes, Roots, Woods, and divers Ingredients Medicinall, and for the Art of Dying.[6]
8 Mechanicks, choice pieces in Carvings, Turnings, Paintings.
9 Other variety of Rarities.

10   Warlike Instruments, European, Indian &c.
11   Garments, Habits, Vests, Ornaments.
12   Utensils, and Householdstuffe.
13   *Numismata*, Coynes antient and modern, both gold, silver and cop-
      per, Hebrew, Greeke, Roman – both Imperiall and Consular.
14   Medalls, gold, silver, copper, and lead.

Hortus Tradescantianus.

15   An enumeration of his Plants, Shrubs, and Trees both in English
      and Latine.
16   A *Catalogue* of his Benefactors.

Musaeum

TRADESCANTIANUM

Some kinds of Birds *their Egges, Beaks, Feathers, Clawes, and Spurres.*

1. EGGES

Cassawary, or Emeu, *vide Aldrov:*
   Harveum, G.A.
Crocodiles, Estridges,
Soland-goose, Squeedes (from *Scotland*).

Divers sorts of Egges from *Turkie:*
   one given for a Dragons egge.
Easter Egges of the Patriarchs of
   Jerusalem.

2. BEAKS, or HEADS

Cassawary, or Emeu, Griffin, Pellican,
   Shoveler, and thirty other severall
   forrain sorts, not found in any Author.
Aracari of *Brasil*, his beak four inches
   long, almost two thick, like a Turkes
   sword.
Ardeola *Brasil*: his beak three inches
long, described, *Margrav: 5. 13.*[7]

Guara of *Marahoon Brasil:* his beak like
   a *Poland* sword.
Jabira, *Brasil*: beak eleven inches long.
Macucagua, *Brasil: Margrav: 5. 13.*
Soco, Brasil: Margrava. 5. 5.
Tamatia, *Brasil: Margrav: 5. 10.*
Sixteen severall strange beaks of Birds
   from the East India's.

3. FEATHERS

Divers curious and beautiful coloured
   feathers of Birds from the West India's.
The breast of a Peacock from the West
   India's.
A white Plume.
Two feathers of the Phoenix tayle.

Tops of the white and black Herne, black
   and milke-white Herne.
Feathers of divers curious and strange
   forraign Birds.[8]
Many several sorts of Hernes and
   Estridges feathers.

4. CLAWES

The claw of the bird Rock; who, as Authors report, is able to trusse an Elephant.

Eagles clawes.

Cock spurrs three inches long.

A legge and claw of the Cassawary or Emeu that dyed at *S. James's, Westminster*[9]

Twenty severall sorts of clawes of other strange birds, not found described by Authors.

5.   Whole BIRDS

Kings-fisher from the *West India's*.

Divers Humming Birds, three sorts whereof are from *Virginia*.

Matuitui, the bigness of a Thrush, short neck and legges.

Bitterns two sorts, Batts – Red and blew Bird (from *Virginia*).

Penguin, which never flies for want of wings.

Puffin.

Pellican.

Shoveler.

Tropick bird.

Apous.

Fulica.

Tropick bird.

Dodar, from the Island *Mauritius*, it is not able to flie being so big.[11]

White Partridge.

Spanish Partridge

Wood-Pecker from the *West India's*.

A black bird with red shoulders and pinions, from *Virginia*.[10]

Birds of Paradise, or Manucodiata: whereof divers sorts, some with, some without leggs.

Birds of Paradise from the Mount of *Moret*, described by *Hacluite*.

A small Grayish bird from the *East India's*.

A white Ousle, or white Black-bird.

The Gorara or Colymbus from *Muscovy*: And another taken upon the *Thames* and given by *Elias Ashmole*, Esq.

Many rare and beautifull Indian birds, not found described in Authors.

Barnacles, four sorts.

Solon Goose.

Squeede from the Basse in *Scotland*.

The Bustard as big as a Turky, usually taken by Greyhounds on *Newmarket-heath*.

Divers sorts of Birds-nests of various forms.

Source

Tradescant, John, 1656, *Musaeum Tradescantianum or a collection of rarities preserved at South-Lambeth neer London* London, reproduced in Leith-Ross, P., 1984, *The John Tradescants*, Bristol, P. Owen: 229–34.

Notes

1   The early seventeenth century was a period obsessed with potentially meaningful anagrams.

2   By implication at least, Tradescant's life of gardening for the nobility and simultaneously gathering a famous museum about himself, is here used to

locate his social position as somewhere between the court and ordinary commerce.

3   In other words, Tradescant had managed to transplant the world's entire material diversity under his own roof.

4   This issue of nomenclature has always been a crucial one in the formation of museum catalogues. The intellectual ferment of seventeenth-century Europe very much hinged on a progressive move away from the exclusive use of classical languages in books of learning towards a greater exploitation of the vernacular. Tradescant's compromise of employing English names for the commoner items and Latin for those less familiar was a frequent, if sometimes less explicitly stated, ploy. One significant consequence of such a decision was the relative positioning of material in catalogues, which were commonly listed alphabetically.

5   This division of 'artificial' and 'natural' items (man-made and God-made, as it were) had by the seventeenth century become virtually ubiquitous in such catalogues. However, especially in the cases of some 'exotic' arte-facts, deciding what category to assign a given object was not always an easy matter.

6   This is self-evidently the transitional section where 'natural' objects be-come 'artificial', for though many medicines (materia medica) and dye-stuffs were used in the state they were found, they clearly shared some characteristics with man-made objects by virtue of their identification and categorisation according to their use.

7   This reference to a named author, and an earlier comment about some thirty birds' beaks 'not found in any Author' clearly indicates that in Tradescant's mind the learned context for his catalogue was the increasingly large genre of natural historical literature.

8   The use of such an extraordinarily vague and general description is typical of catalogues of this period.

9   Such references to the centres of English power are scattered throughout the catalogue. They are indicative of the source of material, but also reflect Tradescant's eagerness to make allusions to his frequent contacts with the 'great' of the land.

10 This could well have been picked up by the younger Tradescant, who travelled to America.

11 Part of this specimen of that infamous extinct bird has been preserved and can still be seen in the present Ashmolean Museum, having been removed from the rest of the bird that was destroyed by fire.

References

Allan, 1964
Hadfield, 1960
Leith-Ross, 1983
MacGregor, 1983

13

John Bargrave gives an account of his museum collection

John Bargrave (1610–80) was a traveller and collector, a Fellow of Peterhouse College, Cambridge and a Canon of Canterbury Cathedral. During some 'four journeys from London to Rome and Naples ... often seeing' a variety of rarities and curiosities, he was himself 'likewise put into a humour of curiosity', with the result that he gathered quite a sizeable collection of his own, which he stored 'in a cabinet in [his] study at [his] canonical house ... [in] Canterbury' (Bann, 1994; Bargrave, 1968: 115–16; Sturdy and Henig, n.d.).

The following passage is taken from Bargrave's catalogue of his collection, and consists entirely of an elaborate description of one of its items, a piece of obelisk. The account, notable for the fashion in which information and anecdotes are spun about the nucleus of a single museum object, provides a colourful example of a crucial facet of many seventeenth-century collections – namely, the inseparable bond between the collector and what he or she had collected. Bargrave gave a similar treatment to any number of other collected treasures described in his catalogue (Bargrave, 1968: 115–40).

What is so striking about the approach to gaining knowledge from objects that this example from Bargrave's catalogue exemplifies, is the place given to the collector's or curator's own personal knowledge. For this type of account is full of insights that could only have been gained by individuals in the presence of the object itself – by those who had bought, found, owned or lived with it; with the result that, just as the collector or curator and the storyteller were one and the same, so the individual object became inseparable from what was known about it. Far from 'speaking for themselves', then, the objects presented in catalogues of the type compiled by Bargrave – a style of presentation repeated both in a genre of county-based topographical literature and in many numismatical texts – were instead ones that existed within a narrative web constructed about the objects by a person who had worked or even lived with it.

This curatorial methodology can be characterised as one in which objects were used both to generate and validate a varied, sometimes seemingly random collection of facts, observations, insights and conjectures. On one occasion at least, the metaphorical picture of an object 'issuing a story' was turned into a physical reality. For the great collector Hans Sloane had in his collection a bone spoon from New England, on the surface of which Sloane had gone so far as to inscribe a report of the circumstances under which the spoon had been made and acquired – an account that elsewhere was repeated as entry number 1730 in his catalogue of 'Miscelanies' [sic]. Sloane's emphatic gesture with an inked quill was the concrete extension of the abstract idea that an object's story should somehow adhere to the object itself. Bargrave's more orthodox approach was, instead, to scribble his account on paper; but the manuscript catalogue was kept in close proximity with his collection, actually within the cabinet, as, perhaps, a sort of song sheet from which his objects could at any moment be expected to break into voice.

DR BARGRAVE'S MUSEUM

(18)   A Roman aegle, in brass; modern.

(19)   A piece of a kind of jasper stone, almost like a heart, polished,[1] being a piece of that famous obelisk that now standeth in the chiefest place of Rome, called Piazza Navona, *olim Circus Agonalis*, set up there on a most magnificent fabrick, like a rock, out of which floweth 4 fountains, very large, signifying by the figures of colossean statues of the 4 rivers of Europe, Asia, Africa and America, by the hand of Cavalier Bernino, that famous architect, my neighbour and friendly acquaintance, – Pope Innocent the 10th being at that vast expense.

When I was at Rome, 1646, this obelisk lay broken in 4 or 5 pieces, with the fall of it, in the Circle of the Emperor Caralla, near St. Sebastian and Metella's Tomb, now a noble antiquity, and called *Capo di Bove*. I took another stone and with it broke off of the butt end of it this piece and as much more, and had this polished. The obelisk, as it lay then and as it is now, is full of Egyptian hyerogliifficks, of which Father Kercherius, that eminent Jesuit, and of my acquaintance, hath writt a large folio. All the other guglios, or obeliscs, at Rome seem to be all of the same sort of stone, and are stupendious to imagine how they could possibly be hewn in that bigness and hight out of any rock, though it may be they might afterward be hewn into that pyramidical proportion and shape that they now bear. All full of Egyptian hyroglificks, that largest of all before St. Peter at the Vatican excepted, which is one intyre precious stone – at least, better than marbel, and I think (by my piece) a jasper; and yet is esteemed to be higher by 3 or 4 foot than the maypole in the Strand at London. Another is dexterously placed on the Via Flaminia, at the Porto dell Populo, in a poynt to be seen from 3 of the great streets of Rome.

Another dispute is, how it was possible to transport so vastly weighty things from Egypt to Rome as one of those stones are, they having then no such ships as we have now, their byremes and tryremes being but pittiful boats, yet sufficient to make them masters of the seas in those times. There are several treatises on this subject,[2] and the most probable that I find is, that they were brought upon warffs or raffts of many pines and firs, fastened by art together, and, the stones being laid upon them, they, with a stearer or two or three at the end of those raffts, came *terra*, *terra*, *terra* (as the Italians term it) along the coast, or, at least, from promontory to promontory, until they came to Ostia and so 10 miles up the Tyber to Rome. Many long and large warfes or rafts of these firs and pine trees I have found troublesome to our boats on the Danube, the Rone or Rhodanus, on the Rhine, and Elve, down which rivers an infinite abundance of that tymber passeth daily thus fastened together, and on some of them they build 2 or 3 little hutts or cabans and dress their meat. Thus as to these pyramids' transport.

Another of these vast stones layeth all along full of hyerogliphics, in that which is now Prince Ludovicio's formerly Sallust's garden. And, to see how Rome layeth under its own ashes, one walketh in the streets over one of these famous Egyptian obelisks every day, in a little by passage of a narrow descent that is between Antonina's famous pillar and the Rotunda. I could go directly to it if I were there, but I have forgotten the name of the place.[3] There one day an antiquarian had me down a poor man's cellar and there showed me 4 or 5 yards of one of these pyramids. How far it runneth under ground they know not. It was full of hieroglyphics, and it pittied me to see how the stone was cut and mangled for the convenience to set wine vessels on it. The poor man getteth his rent by showing of it to strangers that are curious – as I confess I always was, and would wish every gentleman traveller to be so.

Source

'Catalogue of Dr. [John] Bargrave's Museum' (1676), reproduced in *Pope Alexander the Seventh and the College of Cardinals* by *John Bargrave* ..., Edited by James C. Robertson, printed for the Camden Society, Vol. 92, London, 1968: 117–19.

Notes

1   David Sturdy and Martin Henig have described the object as a 'polished heart-shaped plaque of green stone. L: 6 cms' (Sturdy and Henig, n.d.). The

object, along with most of the other material from his cabinet, as well as the cabinet itself, can still be viewed by prior permission in the library of Canterbury Cathedral.

2   Bargrave makes clear here another part of the methodology for constructing narratives vouchsafed by the material existence of an object – namely research into the object type and its circumstances. This often took a variety of forms ranging from physical and chemical experiments to, as here, recourse to scholarly sources for the current thinking on a particular subject. The whole scholarly apparatus of providing references with page numbers and so on was also at this time just becoming an established intellectual routine.

3   In this delightfully conversational remark one gets the clearest indication of the tone in which Bargrave's accounts were delivered – sounding for all the world as if it were a transcribed record of his response to a casual question put directly to him about one of his treasures.

References

Bann, 1994
Bargrave, 1968
Sturdy and Henig [n.d.]

Part II
Scientific Voices

14

John Wilkins experiments with a philosophical museum language

During his lifetime, John Wilkins was widely regarded as one of the chief promoters of the new science in England, and one of his more extraordinary schemes was to invent an entirely new philosophical language, which would foster the spread of natural knowledge and true religion. Within the fairly widespread movement for language reform, his scheme was unquestionably the most ambitious and accomplished (Aarsleff, 1976). Wilkins' *An essay towards a real character and philosophical language* was an impressive 500-folio tome, presented in four main parts: a 'prolegomena' generally discussing the nature of and faults within existing languages; a 'Universal Philosophy', that is 'a regular enumeration and description of all those things and notions, to which marks or names ought to be assigned according to their respective natures'; the 'philosophical grammar', by the rules of which sentences and speeches were to be constructed; and finally, a section in which the written script and spoken sounds of the language were detailed.

It was the second and by far the longest of these sections, involving the encyclopaedic categorisation and classification of the universe, that embodied the task for empirical science. To this end, what Wilkins quickly settled upon was the need for taxonomic tables in which objects and ideas could first be isolated and identified by their distinctive features, and then related by definable 'differences' initially to other similar things, and eventually to the whole of reality. It was here that museums played their role.

In his capacity as one of its leading members, Wilkins was eager to ensure that the young Royal Society be furnished with all the materials it needed to promote philosophical enquiry. Thus, in November 1663, he 'presented the society with several things for their repository': some seventeen objects in all, including a windgun, an ostrich egg and a lodestone (Birch, 1756, Vol.1: 324; Hunter, 1989). The accumulation of a sizeable, well-ordered museum was generally held to be a high priority for the society. Thomas Sprat, in his history *cum* apology for the group, had it that 'one of the Principal Intentions they props'd to accomplish, was a general Collection of all the Effects of Arts, and the Common, or Monstrous Works of Nature' (Sprat, 1667: 251). With his language scheme in mind, and in particular the job of constructing the taxonomic tables detailing nothing short of the world's entire contents, Wilkins thought that the collection might become 'in a very short space ... the most useful Repository in the world' (Wilkins, 1668: 'Epistle Dedicatory').

THE EPISTLE

I am not so vain as to think that I have here completely finished this great undertaking, with all the advantages of which such a design is capable. Nor on the other hand, am I so diffident of this Essay, as not to believe it sufficient for the business to which it pretends namely the distinct expression of all things and notions that fall under discourse.

I am sensible of sundry defects in the severall parts of this Book: And therefore would make it my humble motion to your Lordship and this Society, that you would by your Order appoint some of our number, thoroughly to examin & consider the whole, and to offer their thoughts concerning what they judge fit to be amended in it.[1] Particularly in those Tables that concern the species of *Natural bodies*; which, if they were (so far as they are yet known and discovered) distinctly reduced and described. This would very much promote and facilitate the knowledge of Nature, which is one great end of your Institution.[2] And besides, the ranging of these things into such an order as the Society shall approve, would afford a very good method for your *Repository*, both for the disposal of what you have already, and the supplying of what you want, towards the compleating of that Collection, so generously begun of late, by the bounty of *Mr. Daniel Collwal*, a worthy Member of this *Society*. And by this means, I should not doubt, but that in a very short space, you would have the most useful *Repository* in the World.[3]

Is it no easie undertaking to *Enumerate* all such matters as are to be provided for in such a design; But the business of *Defining*, being amongst all others the most nice and difficult, must needs render it a very hard task for any one to attempt the doing of this, for all kinde of *Things*, *Notions*, and *Words*, which yet is necessary to the design here proposed.

Upon which account I may be excused for being so sollicitous about the assistance of others in these matters, because of their great difficulty and importance. The compleating of such a design, being rather the work of a *College* and an *Age*, then of any single Person: I mean, the combined Studies of many Students, amongst whom, the severall shares of such a Work, should be distributed; And that for so long a course of time, wherein sufficient experiments might be made of it by practice.

It has been sayd concerning that famous *Italian* Academy styled *de la Crusca*, consisting of many choice Men of great Learning, that they bestowed forty years in finishing their *Vocabulary*. And 'tis well enough known, that those great Wits of the *French* Academy, did begin their *Dictionary* in the year 1639. And for the hastning of the Work, did distribute the parts of it amongst severall Committees; and yet that undertaking is (for ought I can understand) far enough from being finished.

Now if those famous Assemblies consisting of the great Wits of the Age and *Nations*, did judge this Work of *Dictionary-making*, for the polishing of their Language, worthy of their united labour and studies; Ceertainly then, the Design here proposed, ought not to be thought unworthy of such assistance; it being as much to be preferred before that, as *things* are better then *words*, as *real knowledge* is beyond *elegancy of speech*, as the *general good of mankind*, is beyond that of any particular *Countrey* or *Nation*.[4]

I am very sensible that the most usefull inventions do at their first appearance, make but a very slow progress in the World, unless helped forward by some particular advantage. *Logarithms* were an Invention of excellent Art and usefulness; And yet it was a considerable time, before the Learned Men in other parts, did so farr take notice of them, as to bring them into use. The Art of *Shorthand*, is in its kind an Ingenious device, and of considerable usefulness, applicable to any Language, much wondered at by Travailers, that have seen the experience of it in *England*: And yet though it be above Three-score years, since it was first Invented, 'tis not to this day (for ought I can learn) brought into common practice in any other Nation. And there is reason enough to expect the like Fate for the design here proposed.

The only expedient I can think of against it, is, That it be sent abroad into the World, with the reputation of having bin considered and approved of, by such a *Society* as this; which may provoke, at least, the Learned part of the World, to take notice of it, and to give it such encouragement, as it shall appear to deserve.

And if upon such an amendment and recommendation by this Society, the design here proposed, should happen to come into common use, It would require the Honour you bestow upon it, with abundant Interest. The being Instrumental in any such discovery as does tend to the Universal good of Mankind, being sufficient not only to make the *Authors* of it famous, but also the *Times* and *Places wherein they live*.[5]

Source

Wilkins, John, 1668, *An essay towards a real character and philosophical language*, London: The epistle dedicatory.

Notes

1   An undertaking of this grandeur was always going to have to be collabora-
    tive in nature. Wilkins was assisted in his efforts by the likes of Samuel
    Pepys, Francis Lodwick, William Petty, Seth Ward, George Dalgarno, Robert
    Hooke, William Lloyd, Francis Willughby and John Ray.
2   Wilkins' methodology for categorising the contents of nothing less than the
    entire universe in truth never strayed far from the basic Aristotelian tree of
    knowledge. By this means he arrived at some forty genera and 4,000 items.
    The inadequacies of these numbers fairly quickly became apparent, and
    Wilkins was himself forced to admit that there were some 'things which may
    seem to be less conveniently disposed of in' his own tables.
3   The construction of Wilkins' taxonomic tables in principle rested on the use
    of the Royal Society's repository. Certainly, John Ray and Francis Willughby's
    classification of animals and plants which did end up in Wilkins' new lan-
    guage scheme were derived in part from work on the collections. The influ-
    ence exerted by Wilkins' philosophical language on Ray's search for a
    'rational' order in the natural specimens he examined was profound; but
    even Ray soon found it impossible not to deviate from the scheme as laid out
    by Wilkins.
4   This paragraph presented the philosophical and indeed moral argument for
    Wilkins's proposed work: namely, that it would replace the 'elegancy of
    speech' with 'real knowledge', which in turn would bring a 'general good of
    mankind' where previously there had been strife and war caused by the
    'curse of confusion' that surrounded the ambiguities of language. The areas
    of life that this scheme would enhance also, he believed, included commerce
    and religion.
5   In fact, the practical application of Wilkins' language seems to have been
    extremely limited, though Robert Hooke did write his *Description of
    helioscopes* (1676) in Wilkins' character. More damning still, there is little
    or no evidence for Wilkins' scheme being used when it came to organising
    the Society's own repository. Certainly, Grew's catalogue bears no signs of
    the specific as opposed to general influence of Wilkins' scheme (Salmon,
    1979: 192–5; Knowlson, 1975: 103–5; Gunther, 1931: 151; Hunter, 1989).

References

Aarsleff, 1976
Birch, 1756
Gunther, 1931
Hunter, 1989
Knowlson, 1975
Salmon, 1979
Sprat, 1667
Wilkins, 1668

15

John Winthrop reports upon some American curiosities

More than just pleasant curiosities, objects brought back from travel to far-off lands came to serve as a type of evidence, whose reliability many felt was sadly lacking in other forms of reporting on foreign lands. Ben Jonson, for one, thought that voyagers were in the habit of quite simply lying about what they had seen. John Lawson's attitude was only marginally less critical: he believed that the poor standard of reporting resulted from the type of people who went on voyages: namely, 'the meaner Sort, and generally of a very slender Education'. And John Winthrop, as he declared in the following letter to Henry Oldenburg, was particularly suspicious of 'matters reported by Indians, [which needed, he explained,] … good examinations and further enquiry'. Theophilus Lavender spoke for many when he declared that 'One eie witnesse is worth more then ten ear witnesses' (Hodgen, 1971; Lawson, 1709: preface; Lavender, 1609: 'To the reader').

Reliable reports from foreign adventurers were thus highly prized. And in this respect, the John Winthrops, grandfather and grandson, served as some of the Royal Society's most fruitful colonial adventurers and settlers. The former sent it a number of gifts starting with a hoard of plants, ores, minerals and shells in 1669; while the latter donated a collection of eight 'natural Curiosities he had made in New England and New York' in January of 1726, and another much larger collection of some 364 items in June of 1734 (Stearns, 1970: 95–117, 247–52; Stearns, 1952–56: 206–32).

Much of the interest in the material culture of foreign countries was distinctly utilitarian; the core question commonly asked was: Of what possible use could the material be when brought home? This was seemingly the motivation behind Hans Sloane's descriptions of the manufacture of sugar, the 'manner of propagating, gathering & curing ye Granaor Cochineel' and the operation of the 'Ginn Cotton' included in his report of a voyage to the West Indies (Sloane, 1707: Vol. 1: lxi, xlvi; Vol. 2: 68). It was also unmistakable in John Winthrop's remarks in the passage that follows, where he stated that he was sending 'as much as I could for this season procure, of the silke downe', and 'some eares of Indian corne … [which] may be likely to ripen in England if planted in April'. Interestingly, Winthrop elsewhere referred to another gift, 'the nest of a very small bird, w'ch we call an humming bird' – an object without any obvious use – as a 'trifle' (Hall and Hall, 1966: 201).

The other principle issue faced by those involved in sending back material from foreign cultures was that of nomenclature. The use of a native name often indicated that an object had not been immediately recognised – the intention being that the native word could be learned as shorthand for the explanatory description needed to identify it. Thus the 'Canoo' was a 'sort of Boat' very fully described by Nehemiah Grew in the catalogue to the Royal Society's repository, and the 'Tamahauke', a 'Brasilian Fighting-CLUB'; while the strange shell money used on the American coast was, as John Lawson explained, called 'Peak or Wampum'; and their houses built of bark: 'Wigwams' (Grew, 1685: 364, 367; Lawson, 1709: 173, 178).

WINTHROP TO OLDENBURG
26 AUGUST 1670A
FROM THE ORIGINAL IN ROYAL SOCIETY MS. W 3, NO. 23

Boston in New-England
Aug: 26: 1670

Sr

I have received yours of Mar: 26: last together wth those new bookes, and the Phylosophicall transactions of the last yeare, for wch I returne my humble thankes, esteeming them all very highly and so doe such other persons heere, who know the worth of them, to whom I am communicating them as I have such former, wch came to my hands, to their great delight & satisfaction; I have indeavoured about that stellar fish according to those particulars of inquiry directed in your letter, but can yet meet wth none (though I have asked of many fishermen, both before it was sent away, and since I had your letter) who have to their remembrance seene the like: but am in hope shortly to speake wth that very person a fisherman, who brought it from sea, he is master of a Vessell, & is now out at sea upon a fishing voyage, but he is shortly expected. I have now sent a few more such things as these parts affoard: they are in 2 round boxes and an other small long box,[1] they are put aboard a ship of wch Capt: — Peirce is master: and are directed to Mr. Adam Winthrop for the Royall Society;[2] they are marked on one of the tops as in the marg Be pleased to present my humble duty to the President & Royall Society to whose commands I am alwaies obliged & ready to obey: For that perticular you are pleased to intimate about a naturall history of this country: although I am often observing and collecting and have some fragments of what hath come to hand yet I thinke it may be too soone to undertake that worke, there having beene but little tyme of experience since our beginnings heere and the remote Inland partes little discovered, matters reported by Indians many tymes uncertaine and need good examination & further inquiry: but a little tyme may give more advantage for some beginning, at least of such an adventure: there is yet no certainty, of what is underground, there are some appearances upon the surface in some places of lead & other mineralls, but there have yet none wrought upon but Ironston, wch hath beene also mostly of that sort wch is called the Bog mine, wch is found only in low grounds not deepe nor of any great thicknesse; the hinderances, and difficulties of further discoveries of subterraneall productions were mentioned formerly in other letters. some other things I expect hither shortly, wch are intended for the Repositiory of the Royall Society, wch I directed to be brought hither before I came from Connecticutt, wch I hope may be sent by some other ship and then you may also expect other letters from

your affectionate servant

J Winthrop

Be pleased to present my humble service to Sr. Robert Moray, and acquaint him that I am very mindful of his commands by your letter about the Silkepodds, but the season is not yet, they are not yet ripe, and when they are ripe they must be withered awhile before they can be putt up.

I am not unmindfull about those cranburies for your selfe, but the season is not yet for them (as I am informed) nor for their transportation I hope to have a fitt oportunity, in the sutable tyme, and if I should be gone hence before I intend to leave order wth some freind for the procuring & shipping of them.

I should be glad to be informed whether you had a letter of the yeare 1668: wherin was a large letter to Mr. Haake they were sent with a pecquet to mr Henry Ashurst (as I remember) but I have not heard whether received by mr Haake or your selfe.[3]

In the biggest of those boxes now sent there are two skinnes of those snakes wch they call heere rattle snakes; from the rattle yt is upon the taile they have that denomination: they are stuffed wth something to the proportion of their bignesse, when they were alive: they are not of the largest size, I had formerly sent over much bigger, but they came not to you. I could at this tyme procure no other: one of them hath its rattles whole upon the other I doubt have some broken off, except it be very young. But it is the Indian brought it: Its said their age is knowne by the number of those partitions upon the rattle, and that every yeare is added another of those fibers to the rest the snake usually makes a noise, by shaking that rattle upon its taile when it seeth any come towards it, and at other tymes. and by that meanes is often warning of the danger, before one cometh neer them but sometymes they are asleepe, or lye still wch is dangerous to such as walke in the woods, & to horse & other cattle.[4]

There is also some of the roote of that herbe wch is called the Virginia snakeweed, of wch there is both of that wch grow in Virginia and of the like sort wch groweth in the more Westerly parts of New England & Long Island. but I have seene nor heard of any in these Easterly parts it is used as a certaine meanes of cure to those who are bitten by that snake the cure is by chewing a little of it, and swallowing some of the Juice of it, and applying some, of that wch was chewed, to the place:

There is in the other round box some eares of Indian corne of such a kind yt it wilbe ripe heere as soone as the other sort though planted much later, this grew in the same ground after turnep seed had been ripe & gathered the same spring yt it was planted, it may be likely to ripen in England If planted in Aprill. In that manner they traie their corne to hang up, & so it will keepe long, although hung abroad It is put up so that their manner of tracing may be seene one halfe of the traice was cutt of before it was put up. the planter desirous to reserve some to be planted again having but little of the seed of that kind: In the same box is also in a bag some nuts like wallnutts wch are usually called butternutts, & by some oylenutts. The Indians make an oyle of them: there are also hazell nutts wch being of the naturall growth of his country, & not of plants or nutts brought out of England, are put in to fill up the box.

In the long box are some of the dwarfe oakes, wch were gathered Early at the beginning of the budding of the acornes, that they might not fall off as the riper acornes doe they were prepared to be sent before I had intelligence of the former received & being ready put up I thought fitt to send them; and in the same box are a few branches of ye butternut tree.

There is also a small long fish taken here in the salt water I know no name for it nor have seene of them before, It is in a paper wthin a peice of a caule. There is also a fish wch they call an Horn fish, but I thinke it is not of these seas, but brought from about Jamaica, or some part of the West Indies:

In one of the round boxes is also a small stone like chrystall wch An Indian (from whom I had it) affirmed fell wth thunder & they call them thunderstones, & the Indians all agree to their relation of them that such fall downe with thunder.[5]

ADDRESS
    For my worthy freind
    Mr Henry Oldenburg

Secretary to the
    Royall Society
      In
        London

Source

Letter from John Winthrope to Henry Oldenburg, written from 'Boston in New-England' on 26 August 1670. Reproduced in *Correspondence of Henry Oldenburg*, ed. and transl. Hall, A. R. and Hall, M. B., 1970, Vol. 7, Madison, University of Wisconsin Press: 142–5.

Notes

1 A meeting of the Royal Society on 27 October 1670 was duly shown the material Winthrop refers to.
2. Adam Winthrop was John's nephew. He had gone to England in the winter of 1669–70, after graduating from Harvard College and settled as a merchant in Bristol.
3 The difficulty of sending anything (letters or specimens) across such distances cannot be overestimated.
4 This appears to be a retelling of some knowledge about rattlesnakes passed on by Indian contacts. Nehemiah Grew's catalogue of the Royal Society's repository duly did describe some rattlesnake skins.
5 The amount of knowledge of Indian practices and customs, and even beliefs, that Winthrop was able to pass back along with his specimens was rare indeed.

References

Grew, 1685
Hall and Hall, 1966
Hall and Hall, 1970
Hodgen, 1971
Lavender, 1609
Lawson, 1709
Sloane, 1707
Stearns, 1952–6
Stearns, 1970

16

Robert Plot surveys the natural history of Oxfordshire

Robert Plot's chief intellectual legacy lies in his two county-based natural histories of Oxfordshire (1677) and Staffordshire (1688). Entries in both books carry unmistakable evidence of the influence exerted by collections of objects on his work. In the first place, they show his widespread use of the numerous private as well as institutional collections he came across in his travels: for example, the arteries of 'an ancient person ... to be seen in the custody of Mr. Pointer', the fish 'taken in the river Tame ... by Goodyer Holt Free-Mason ... who presented it to Colonell Comberford ... who ... placed it in his Hall', and a toucan 'whose beak is near as big as its whole body' that was to be seen in 'the Repository in the Medicine-School [that is, Oxford University's Anatomy School] (Plot, 1677: 178, 211–12; Plot, 1686: 240).

Plot was also involved with the Ashmolean Museum in a number of ways: it was the Oxford scholar Humphrey Prideaux's opinion that Plot's work on his natural history of Oxfordshire was of primary importance in the museum's establishment (Ovenell, 1986; MacGregor and Turner, 1986). By the time his natural history of Staffordshire had been published, Plot had become firmly established in the roles of, as its title page proudly declared, 'Keeper of the Ashmolean Museum and Professor of Chymistry in the University of Oxford'. The foundation of the museum thus added another readily available source of material culture evidence for his natural histories. Plot also gathered a collection of curiosities for himself, items like 'the redstones found in Tene brock', described in Staffordshire, of which he kept 'a very large one in my Staffordshire Cabinet' (Plot, 1686: 165).

Drawing on all these collections of curiosities, Plot's natural histories amounted to something of a selective material analysis of two counties in the English nation. The information he presented was both accurately distributed on detailed maps and securely bonded to actual physical objects. For Plot, text, map and museum collection formed a closely aligned trinity. And, just as the map gave to the written information a geographical and social reality, so the curiosities and rarities provided material support. The validity of his work was, in Plot's mind, partly vouchsafed by the 'approbation of the most knowing in these matters, such as the

Honorable Robert Boyle Esq., Dr. Willis, Dr. Wallis ... etc.', but even more compellingly by the fact that most of the 'Curiosities, whether of Art, Nature or Antiquities ... are so certain truths, that as many as were portable, or could be procured, are in the hands of the Author' (Plot, 1677: 'Epistle Dedicatory').

In addition to his curatorial duties at the Ashmolean Museum, Plot was also responsible for making it foundational to the activities of one of the intellectual groups so important in the scientific culture of late seventeenth-century England: the Oxford Philosophical Society. Central to its activities, museum objects gathered as curiosities became instead more like tools for experimental investigations. Consequently, as the records of both the Oxford Society's meetings and Plot's natural histories readily reveal, the process of establishing information often rested on much more than simply having an object and pointing to it, involving in addition an active inquiry into its properties, origins and causes. As the following passage makes clear, objects were not only observed by sight, but also often smelled and tasted and experimented upon (Knight, 1981: 54: Gunther, 1925: 24, 37, 49, 88–9, 101, 106–7, 113–14, 205). The findings that emerged from the meetings of the Oxford Philosophical Society and that formed the raw data for his natural histories had the quality of material artefacts and physical phenomena 'laid bare', with their hidden secrets exposed. Plot's work on a 'philosophical history' thus turned objects and observable phenomena into versatile clues in the unsolved mystery of how and why 'the universal furniture of the world', as Plot called it, was quite as it was.

NATURAL HISTORY OF OXFORDSHIRE

38.   Beside the *Brontie* of the *Forreign Naturalist*, we have others, which here in *England* we call likewise *Thunder-bolts*, in the form of *arrow heads*, and though by the vulgar to be indeed the darts of *Heaven*: which only in conformity to my own Country (though for as much reason as the foregoing *Brontie*) I have placed amongst the *stones* related to the *Heavens*.[1]

39.   From their form, by all *Naturalists* they are called *Belemnites*, from the *Greek* word Βελεμνον *telum*, which indeed there are some of them represent pretty well.[2] We have of them in *Oxford-shire* of divers sorts, yet all of them I find agreeing in this, that their *texture* is of small *striae*, or threds radiating from the *center*, or rather *axis* of the Stone, to the outermost *supersicies*; and that burn'd or rub'd against one another, or scraped with a knife, they yeild an odour like rasped Horn.[3]

40.   In magnitude and colour they differ much, the biggest I have met with yet, being that exprest in *Tab.3.Fig.3.* in *length* from what

above four inches, and in *thickness* much about an *inch* and a quarter. This was found in the Quarries in the Parish of *Heddington*, hollow at the top about an inch deep, and filled with a kind of gravelly earth; and has the *rima* or *chink*, which *Aldrovandus* and *Boetius* say all of them have; but I find it otherwise, as shall be shewn anon. Of colour it is *cinereous*, inclining to *yellow*, and if vehemently rubb'd, it is the only one amongst all that I have, that like *Amber* takes up *straws*, and some other light bodies.

41. There are of them also of a *bluish* colour, found at *Great Rolwright* in a *bluish* clay, of about a fingers length, hollow at the top, and have some of them, instead of one, three *clefts* or *rimae*, but neither so plain or long as the former, they ascending from the *cuspis* scarce half up the stone: two whereof are shewn *Fig.4.* and the third hidden behind the *Sculpture*; which may make some amends for that of *Fig.5.* which is of colour *cinereous* and hollow at the top, but has no *chink* at all; whereof there was a bed found in digging the *Sulphur* Well at Mr. *Lanes* of *Beddington*, as was mentioned before in the *Chapter of Waters*.

42. To which add a *fourth* sort, found in great plenty in the Gravel-pits without St. *Clements*, in the *suburbs* of *Oxford*, very few of them hollow at the top like the former, but radiated like a *star* from a closer center, as in *Fig.6*:[4] which made *Gesner* think it to be the *Astrapias* of *Pliny*, though expresly he says, 'tis of a *white* or *azure*, whereas this is always of an *amber* colour: yet draws not straws, it somewhat transparent, and may therefore pass for a sort of *Lapis Lyncurius*; not that it has original from the urine of that *Beast*, for we have plenty of the stones here and none of the *animals*, but from the unpleasant smell it has when burn'd or brayed; like the urine of *Cats*, or such like ramish creatures, whereof the *Lynx* perhaps may be one. These, most of them, are made tapering to a point like the former; yet sometimes having a blunter ending, and the *chink* on both sides, I thought fit rather to shew it in that form than the other, as in *Fig.6.* where the *cleft* runs not only the whole length of the *stone*, but quite under the end, and half way up the other side.

43. Many are the *Medicinal* uses of this *stone*, mentioned by *Boetius*, *Aldrovandus, and Gesner*: Whereof the chief are, 1. For the *stone*, for which (instead of the *Eurrhaeus*) 'tis used in *Spain* and *Saxony*. 2. For *exsiccation* of *wounds* in *Prussia* and *Pomerania*. And 3. for *ocular* distempers in *Horses*, in all parts of *England*.

44. Thus having run through the supposititious *stones* from *Heaven*, I next descend to the *Atmosphere*, or inferior Air, immediately encompassing the terraqueous Globe; which through incapable to itself to be represented in stone, yet having met with some related to its *Inhabitants*, I mean the *feathered Kingdom*, I thought fit to give them place before those of the *Waters*.[5]

45.   Whereof the first and only one, presented in *Sculpture Tab.3, Fig.7.* has perfectly the shape of an *Owls* head, which because not mention'd by any Author that I know of, I thought good to exhibit, and call *Lapis Bubonius*; it is a *black flint* within, and *cinereous* without, and was found near to *Hardwick* in the Parish of *Whitchurch*.[6]

46.   To which I might have annex'd the stone *Hieracites*, found frequently in the Quarries in the Parish of *Heddington*, but is not the *Hieracites* mention'd by *Pliny*, which he says alternately changes its colour; but of *Gesner*, to whose figure of it, ours is exactly like: but neither his nor ours resembling any thing of a *Hawks*, or other Birds *feathers*, so much as to deserve a *cut*, or the *Readers* view; I have saved *my self* the expense, and *him* the trouble.

Source

Plot, Robert, 1677, *The natural history of Oxfordshire, being an essay toward the natural history of England*, London: 93–5

Notes

1   Plot's point elucidates a concern with 'rational' as opposed to 'commonly accepted' taxonomy that was increasingly to exercise collectors and curators. It is interesting that Plot chose here, clearly against his own better judgement, to retain the 'vulgar' classification of these rocks within a section relating to the heavens.

2   Belemnites are a common fossil with a straight, smooth, cylindrical shape of some five to ten centimetres in length. They were commonly referred to as thunderbolts or thunderstones, owing to their supposed origin, and this is the reason Plot classifies them under stones relating to the heavens.

3   This treatment of museum specimens to vigorous experimental tests was entirely common amongst natural historical collectors such as Plot. It was really only in the eighteenth century that the eyes became almost the sole sense employed when visiting and examining a collection of specimens.

4   Plot here reduces to a footnote an anthropomorphic interpretation of the hollow and filled forms of belemnites – that they are female and male. This again suggests his keenness to distance what he saw as a more 'rigorous' and 'philosophical' approach to describing these specimens from the mystical and folkloric ideas that he would have encountered in rural Oxfordshire: 'These not being hollow at the top, nor containing any other stone, gravel, or earth, some call the male *Belemnites*: the three former being of the female kind.'

5   Despite his attempts to be 'modern' in his interpretation of a number of individual specimens, Plot's overall classification scheme was entirely

traditional, treating the world as a series of concentric spheres of earth, water, air and heavens in a fashion that would not have been disputed even by a medieval monk.

6   It was only during the eighteenth century that factors such as the shape of the stone Plot describes here became almost universally regarded as of incidental interest, without any intrinsic significance. By then, its classification as a stone tied by 'sympathies' to the 'feathered Kingdom' had come to seem at best a quaintly old-fashioned idea.

References

Gunther, 1925
Knight, 1981
MacGregor and Turner, 1986
Ovenell, 1986

17

James Petiver describes how to preserve natural specimens

James Petiver was a Warwickshire-born apothecary who set up shop in London and proceeded to accumulate on his premises a vast study collection of natural history specimens (Stearns, 1952). Far from an original thinker, Petiver's work summed up the standard methodology of a late seventeenth- or early eighteenth-century collector. His formula for publishing accounts of his findings was most frequently a simple transcription of what he himself termed 'Names, Descriptions and Vertues' (Petiver, 1698). Similarly, his prescriptions for the proper method of collecting specimens abroad summarised what could be found in a number of contemporary authors.

Inspired directly by Francis Bacon's philosophical directions on how to gather empirical knowledge, the Royal Society, for example, energetically pursued a programme of global investigations based on factual research. One effort in particular, inaugurated by the society's president in 1680, was to collect 'all the Journals of Voyages that had been made & had not been yet published' (Royal Society MS. 'Journal Book': 234). The society also initiated its own inquiries, sending out a series of specific queries to travellers in Bermuda, Greenland, Guinea, Iceland, India, Tenerife, Turkey and Virginia (Waller, 1689; Sprat, 1667: 156–7). In its first two years the society's journal, the *Philosophical Transactions*, included some twelve programmes of research for travellers. Typical was one sent to 'his Excellency the Lord Henry Howard' in Morocco, in which he was asked to inquire 'As to the Inhabitants men and women, what are their Inclinations, Diet, Oeconomy, Conveniences of Life, their Strength ... Arts, Practices, and Studies' (Royal Society MS. 'Register Book': 50–53).

Petiver's instructions, like similar works by Robert Boyle, Robert Plot, Edward Lhwyd and John Woodward before his, were more ambitious in setting out general questionnaires for voyagers to all foreign lands. No doubt gratifyingly for these authors, more than fifty pages of travellers' reports appeared in the 900 or so that made up the first three volumes of the *Philosophical Transactions* (Parks, 1951: 285–6).

Some of Petiver's prescriptions for dispatching specimens reveal a distinctly medical concern with the problem of preservation. A source for such knowledge could be found in a common medicinal encyclopaedia of the day such as Jean de Renou's *Dispensatory*. Samples derived from plants were, said Renou, 'either green or dry', and the green ones, in petrifying after a while, should only be kept 'for a half or a whole week'. Dry specimens, such as certain leaves, flowers, seeds, fruits and barks were to kept in dry places; others which might otherwise perish should be made up into 'spirits' and 'waters', and then kept damp and cool. Renou was also quite typical in describing various ways of preserving the remains of human bodies by the application of pitch, bitumen and other embalming agents – detailing, that is, the creation of a mummy. The same techniques were recorded by Nehemiah Grew in his catalogue of the Royal Society's repository (de Renou, 1657: 491; Grew, 1681: 2). Robert Boyle was another 'chemical' author who worked on the subject of preservation, describing in particular 'the use of Spirit of Wine for the preservation of Bodies from putrefaction', advocating in addition, the use of 'boiled down Venice Turpentine as a resin for preserving insects' (Boyle, 1663: 22–5; Cole 1975: 443–5). Methods that differ in technology but not intention have remained central to the treatment of zoological and vegetable collections ever since.

THE PRESERVATION OF SPECIMENS

Brief Directions *for the Easie Making and Preserving*
Collections *of all* NATURAL Curiosities
For JAMES PETIVER *Fellow of the Royall Society* LONDON

All small *Animals*, as *Beasts, Birds, Fishes, Serpents, Lizards*, and other *Fleshy Bodies* capable of *Corruption*, are certainly preserved in *Rack, Rum, Bandy* [sic], or other Spirits;[1] but where these are not easily to be had a strong *Pickle, or Brine* of Sea Water may serve, to every *Gallon* of which put 3 or 4 Handfulls of *Common* or *Bay Salt,* with a Spoonful or two of *Allom* powderd, if you have any, and so send them in any *Pot, Bottle, Jar* &c. close stopt, Cork'd and Rosin'd. N.B. You may often find in the *Stomachs* of *Sharks*, and other great Fish, which you catch at Sea, divers strange *Animals* not easily to be met with elsewhere, which pray look for, and preserve as above.

As to *Fowls* those that are large, if we cannot have their *Cases* whole, their *Head, Leggs* or *Wings* will be acceptable, but smaller *Birds* are easy sent entire, by putting them in Spirits as above, or if you bring them dry, you must take out their *Entrals*; which is best done by cutting them under their Wing, and then stuff them with *Ockam* or *Tow*, mixt with *Pitch* or *Tar*; and being thoroughly dried in the Sun, wrap them up close, to keep them from Moisture, but in long Voyages, you must Bake them gently, once in a Month or two, to kill the *Vermin* which often breed in them.

All large pulpy moist *Fruit*, that are apt to decay or rot, as *Apples*, *Cherries*, *Cowcumbers*, *Oranges*, and such like, must be sent in *Spirits* or *Pickle*, as *Mangoes*, &c. and to each Fruit, its desired you will pin or tye a sprig of its *Leaves*, and *Flowers*.

All *Seed* and dry Fruit as *Nutts*, *Pods*, *Heads*, *Husks* &c. these need no other Care, but to be sent whole, and if you add a Leaf or two with its Flower, it will be the more instructive, as also a piece of the *Wood*, *Bark*, *Root* or *Gum* of any Tree or Herb that is remarkable for its *Beauty*, *Smell*, *Use*, or *Vertue*.[2]

In Collecting PLANTS. Pray observe to get that part of either *Tree* or *Herb*, as hath its *Flower*, *Seed* or *Fruit* on it; but if neither, then gather it as it is, and if the Leaves which grow near the *Root* of any Herb, differ from those above, be pleased to get both to Compleat the Specimen; these must be put into a *Book*, or *Quire* of *Brown Paper* sitch'd (which you must take with you) as soon as gathered; You must now and then shift these into fresh Books, to prevent either rotting themselves or Paper. N.B. All *Gulph-Weeds*, *Sea-Mosses*, *Coralls*, *Corallines*, *Sea Feathers*, *Spunges*, &c. may be put altogether into any old *Box* or *Barrel*, with the *Shrimps*, *Prawns*, *Crabs*, *Crawfish*, &c. which you will often find amongst the *Seaweeds*, or on the Shoar with the *Shells*, which you may place in layers; as we do a *Barrel* of *Colchester* Oysters. All SHELLS may be thus sent as you find them, with or without their *Snails* in them, and wherever you meet with different sizes of the same sort, pray gather the fairest of all Magnitudes; the *Sea shells* will be very acceptable; yet the *Land* and *Freshwater* ones, are the most rare and desirable. In Relation to INSECTS, as *Beetles*, *Spiders*, *Grasshopper*, *Bees*, *Wasps*, *Flies*, &c. these may be Drowned altogether, as soon as Caught, in a little wide Mouth'd Glass or Vial, half full of *Spirits*, which you may carry in your Pocket. But all *Butterflies* and *Mouths*, as have mealy Wings, whose Colours may be rub'd off, with the Fingers, these must be put into any small Printed Book, as soon as caught, after the same manner you do ye Plants.

All *Metals*, *Minerals*, *Ores*, *Chrystals*, *Spars*, Coloured *Earths*, *Clays* &c. to be taken as you find them, as also such formed Stones, as have any resemblance to *Shells*, *Corals*, *Bones*, or other parts of *Animals*, these must be got as intire as you can, the like to be Observ'd in *Marbeld Flints*, *Slates*, or other Stones that have the Impression of *Plants*, *Fishes*, *Insects*, or other Bodies on them. These are to be Found in *Quarries*, *Mines*, *Stone* or *Gravel Pitts*, *Caves*, *Cliffs*, and *Rocks*, on the Sea Shour or wherever the *Earth* is laid open. NOTE If to any ANIMAL, PLANT, MINERAL &c. you can learn its *Name*, *Nature*, *Vertue* or *Use* it will be still more Acceptable.[3]

N.B. As amongst *Forreign Plants*, the most common *Grass, Rush, Moss, Fern, Thistle, Thorn* or vilest Weed you can find, will meet with Acceptance, as well as a scarcer Plant; So in all other things, gather whatever you meet with, but if very common or well known, the fewer of that *Sort*, will be acceptable to.

y[r] most Humble Servant

Aldersgate Street   JAMES PETIVER
LONDON

BOOKS &c. Printed for y[e] AUTHOR	
Musei PETIVERIANI Centuriae.X.Fig.	2s. 6d.
Labells for *Medicinall* Plants	1s. 6d.
Labells for *English* Wild Plants	1s. 6d.
FIGURES to *MR. RAY'S*, English *Plants*. with	
References to his *History & Synopsis, No.600*	
in 50 Folio Copper Plates.	2li. 3s. 0d.
An ENGLISH Catalogue *Engraved*	1. 6.
A Latine *Catalogue* Engraved	1. 6.

GAZOPHYLACIUM NATURAE & ARTIS.	
Containing above 1200 *Figures*, in 100 Folio	
Copper *Plates*' with their *Names* &c.	2li. 3s. 0d.
The *Catalogue & Descriptions* Separate	0. 5. 0.
Aquatilium, Animalium, AMBOINAE Jcones &	
Nomina, *Containing* near 400 *Figures* in 20	
Folio *Copper* Plates.	10s. 0.
The Printed *Catalogue* Seperate	6d.
Directions for *Collecting* Naturarall Rarities	6d.[4]

Such as *Buy* 5 of each, to have a 6th Gratis: PETIVER

Source

Petiver, James, 1767, 'Brief Directions for the Easie Making and Preserving collections of all natural Curiosities' in his *Opera, historiam naturalem spectantia; or gazophyl. Containing siveral 1000 figures of birds, beasts, reptiles, insects, fish, beelets, moths, flies, shells, corals, fossils, minerals, stones, fungusses, mosses, herbs, plants, &c. from all nations, on 156 copperplates*, London.

Notes

1   Nehemiah Grew, the cataloguer of the Royal Society's collections, credited Robert Boyle with the first experiments with different substances for preserving animals, though any number of other contemporary enquirers were interested in the same question. Boyle published his findings in 1682.

2   The idea of a substance's 'vertue' or virtue was principally a medicinal one, often with distinctly magical overtones. In short, the principle of a substance often closely reflected its outward appearance (such as walnuts, shaped like brains, being good for headaches). However, the reasoning for how the substances imparted their effects, and how virtues related to each other, was often a matter only to be uncovered by the most skilful alchemists and astrologers.

3   Though not made explicit in these instructions, this request for the name and local use of specimens encouraged interaction with the native inhabitants of the land being explored. Many travellers went prepared for such interactions, carrying cheap gifts which could be swapped, often for far more intrinsically valuable items. It also encouraged some explorers to learn at least some of the language and customs of the people whose lands they visited.

4   As this list of Petiver's other works indicates, much of his activities involved the listing and drawing of collections, mostly according to the taxonomic schemes of others such as the notable naturalist John Ray, who he much admired.

References

Boyle, 1663
Cole, 1975
de Renou, 1657
Grew, 1681
Petiver, 1698
Stearns, 1952
Royal Society MS. 'Journal Book' no. 6 (original)
Royal Society MS. 'Register Book' no. 4
Sprat, 1667
Waller, 1689

18

A show elephant becomes an anatomy exhibit

On Friday, 17 June 1681, an elephant was accidentally burnt in Dublin, with a sizeable crowd gathering to witness the extraordinary event. 'To prevent [the elephant] being taken away by the multitude, the Manager, Mr. Wilkins, produced a File of Musqueteers to guard him, till he should build a shed where he might securely disjoint him, in order to the making of a skeleton' (Mullen, 1682: 4). Our detailed knowledge of this event comes from an eyewitness account, from which an extract follows, which Allan Mullen included in the anatomical description of the elephant that he sent William Petty.

A medical man at Trinity College, Mullen was anxious to use the opportunity to study the elephant's anatomy, and so persuaded the elephant's manager to allow him to dissect it. To save the specimen from decay and the gathered 'rabble', the elephant was anatomised that night 'by Candle-light'. The rest of the story was provided by William Petty in a letter to his cousin, Sir Robert Southwell, written some three months later. 'It has become a public shew [he further explained] ... the Sceleton, the Trunk, Toung, Gutts, Penis ... with the Anatomicall description of some other parts not now to bee shewn. The Sceleton is suspended. That it turns round about upon a Swivle fixt in the Beam of the House' (Landsdown, 1928: 95, 97).

Mullen and then Petty thus jointly recorded, in finer detail than we are usually privy to, a process that was at the very core, or rather the very start, of any museum artefact – the process of transforming an object into an exhibit. In this particular case the process left some matters unchanged, in particular both were exhibited as objects of common public curiosity. However, the operation had also altered much. Most obviously, something animate had become inanimate: for museums did not contain living beings. An animal that had moved of its own volition, and that had required looking after, had been turned into a fixed and stabilised object able to be examined. Consequently, its significance changed too: for though both elephant and skeleton excited curiosity and attracted paying audiences, the former was offered up merely as an oddity or curiosity, which the latter had instead become a 'curious fact' and a piece of anatomical information.

Though at times seemingly an incidental and purely practical matter, this act of transforming an object as it was moved into a museum was absolutely crucial to the very conception of what museums stood for. Many other museum objects, of course, underwent much less elaborate transformations in order to become fit for museum exhibition, most simply being detached from their original location and moved to a new site. What the conceptually simple, though sometimes physically laborious, act of moving an object carried with it was the symbolically significant process of making objects discrete enough to be picked up and moved away from their original context (Parkes, 1925). Museums have ever since acted as islands of fixed location in a flux of artefactual information.

TRANSFORMING AN OBJECT INTO AN EXHIBIT

An Anatomical Account of the Elephant.
Accidentally Burnt in Dublin,
on Fryday, June 17 in the Year 1681

Sent in a letter to Sir. W. M. Petty,
Fellow of the Royal Society.

By A. M. [Allan Mullen]
Med. of Trinity Colledge near Dublin
(London, 1682)

Honoured Sir,

My Ambition to serve the R.S. in general, & my Obligations to your self in particular, are the only Motives that induce me to communicate my Observations on the Elephant burned here last Summer; for I understand that they are likely to be made publick, and am very unwilling to appear in Print, especially at the disadvantages which now I must: For People admiring the Elephant, as well for the docility, as bulk and rareness in these Countries, will expect so curious an account of him, as may funish them with the Reasons, why he comes to be more capable of doing things which seem to require Ratiocination, than any other Brute that we know. They may moreover think that from an exact description of the several parts of his Body, most, if not all Vessels and Organs being larger considerably in him than in other Creatures, a great light into the true uses of parts might be had.

Now Sir, I must desire you to inform that Honourable Society, for whom you design these following Notes, and of whom you are a Member with the Reasons why I cannot answer such great expecations. My want of Optick Glasses, and of other helps for curious Observations were considerable.[1]

Moreover the Circumstances of time and place were unfortunate; for the Booth wherein the Elephant was kept, took fire about Three a Clock in the morning, on *Friday* the 17th of *June*; upon this the City being alarm'd multitudes were gathered about the place: And when the fire was extinguished every one endeavoured to procure some part of the Elephant, few of them having seen him living, by reason of the great rates put upon the sight of him. To prevent his being taken away by the multitude, the Manager, Mr. *Wilkins*, procured a File of Musqueteers to guard him, till he should build a shed where he might securely disjoint him, on order to the making of a Skeleton.[2] This he got finished a Seven a Clock at Night, and about Eight I heard of his design. Being desirous to inform my self in the structure of the Elephant, I made search for him, and having found him I proffered my service to him: of which when he accepted, I endeavoured to persuade him to discharge some Butchers which he had in readiness to order the Elephant after their way, and to leave the whole management of the matter to me, and to such as I thought fit to employ, designing a general dissection, and that the *Icons* of each part should be taken in order by some Painter, with whom upon this occasions I could prevail. But my endeavours prov'd fruitless, because that about Ten a Clock that night, when we went to the shed, to find what condition the Elephant was in, he emitted very noisom steams. These made the Manager fear (the shed being very near the Council Chamber and the Custom House,) that the Ld. Lt. or Ld. Mayor would order it to be taken away as a nuysance, and that so in all probility it should be lost, and that perhaps he himself should be punished for suffering it to be there. When I considered, that in case he did not dispose of him that Night, the next Day being *Saturday*, I should be able to accomplish but a small part of what I designed, and that it would be both chargeable and difficult to preserve him from the rabble til *Monday*, and that then the stink would be altogether intolerable, if it should encrease in proportion to what it had done that day. I consented to have the business done that night, and for expedition sake, to make use of the Butchers as Assistants, but so as to be directed by my self in every thing: But their forwardness to cut and slash what came first in their way, and their unruliness withal did hinder me from making several Remarks which otherwise I would have made: Thus the Elephant was disjointed by Candle-light. Some parts were burnt, most of those that were not, were more or less defac'd by being parboiled. This may satisfie the R.S. how difficult it was to give a satisfactory Anatomical Account of the Elephant, and that the following slender one is given to shew my readiness to serve them, and my Obedience to your Commands.[3]

I shall not trouble you with a Repetition of what has been said of the Elephant by *Pliny, Gesner, Tavernier,* and others, being very little, if any way, instructive to any desirous to understand the Anatomy of that Creature, but shall faithfully, and as plainly as I can, acquaint you with what occured remarkable to me, upon a view of the several parts of his Body, and shall add only some conjectures of my own concerning the uses of some parts derived from their structure.

I shall begin with the *Cuticula* (of which I keep a piece which was raised by the Fire from a part of the *Cutis,* on which the Elephant was found lying, and which therefore was not defac'd) when I examined this, I found it covered all over with a strange sort of Scab, in many places resembling old Warts, deeply jagg'd, and the carnous Fibres of the Muscles of Beef, when much boiled, and transversly cut, but of a dirty tawny Colour. These Scabs (if I may so call them) both slit and cut, lookt like short peices of Whalebone. They did so firmly stick to the *Cuticula,* that I could not pull them from it, nor the parts of which they consisted (though they were much divided) from one another, without tearing it. And yet the *Cuticula* was much tougher and thicker than any that I have seen.[4]

The length of these Scabs was in some, ¼ or ½ but in other places not above ⅒ or ⅟₁₅ of an Inch. The cause of which difference I take to be the Elephants wearing, by rubbing or lying, some parts of them, whilst others were slightly or not at all worn.

Source

An anatomical account of the elephant accidentally burnt in Dublin, on Fryday, June 17, in the year 1681. Sent in a letter to Sir Will. Petty, Fellow of the Royal Society. By A. M. [Allen Mullen] Med. of Trinity Collage near Dublin, London, 1682.

Notes

1   The idea that the scientific examination of an object required the use of a set of widely used 'investigative instruments', such as the 'optick glasses' Mullen mentions, was itself a fairly recent innovation in natural philosophy. Along with museums and laboratories, such material was part of the growing material culture of the new sciences.

2   One of the many remarkable features of this quite bizarre tale is just how quickly the manager of the elephant thought of turning disaster into opportunity by creating a skeleton from his dead beast.

3   The servility of Mullen's tone in writing was typical of such correspondence

to the Royal Society, and is a clear indication of just how important the social as well as intellectual connotations were of dealing with the society.

4   The practice of 'testing' or experimenting with specimens which might be kept in a museum was very common, indicating how little reverence for objects in and of themselves there was, at least amongst seventeenth-century natural historians and philosophers.

References

Landsdown, Marquis of, 1928
Mullen, 1682
Parkes, 1925

19

Robert Hooke muses on language and memory, in which the idea of a museum or repository plays a significant part

Though never attracting the attention in England that it did in Italy, a substantial treatment of the 'art of memory' nevertheless did come from the Englishman John Willis in his *Mnemonica, or the Art of Memory*, published in Latin in 1618 and in English in 1661. (For Camillo's sixteenth-century memory theatre, see Chapter 1 in Part 1 of this volume.) Willis' scheme for improving memories was based on the use of a repository – that is, of 'an imaginary fabrick, fancied Artificially, built of hewn stone, in the form of a Theater' (Willis, 1661: 52–3). Willis' work suggested three fundamental keys to memory. One was the common notion that memory should be thought of as a space (Rossi, 1984: 121). The second was the role attributed to the elaborate 'method' by which 'lively and complete images' were to be created so as readily and fully to be remembered. The third rested on the issue of how to order those images (Yates, 1966: 372). In the search for an appropriate method to order things, it became widely accepted that nature's own was the most compelling; and by implication, the most powerful 'method' to adopt was quite simply that of a philosophical enquiry into nature – a method which, opined Robert Hooke, would 'afford ... a prospect into the most secret cabinets of Nature' (Oldroyd, 1987: 145–67).

As the following passages indicate, for Robert Hooke, the imaginary spaces that mnemonic artists had carefully divided up and filled with meticulously conceived images were, instead, carved out of the real world and filled with real objects, becoming, in short, repositories full of specimens. Hooke, as we shall see, offered some fairly detailed physiological and psychological speculations as to how philosophical investigations might actually feed the 'mental repository'. In Hooke's opinion, the human body was best understood through 'mechanical and sensible Figure[s] and Picture[s]'. The senses quite literally transported impressions about the body in the form of a series of different types of matter, with all this sensual material that was transported about the body eventually arriving at the mind: a 'Repository ... furnished with [a] variety of Matter adapted for the Uses to which the Soul applies them'.

Along with this very specific idea of how the mind worked, Hooke also formulated an equally graphic and particular notion of the philosophical enquiry that would most fittingly serve it – the best method by which 'to fill up the repository of the Memory withal'. In his attempt to match a mental process with a philosophical practice, the act of attention – whereby the soul fashioned and arranged ideas in the brain's repository – was also given a macrocosmic equivalent: namely the systematic accumulation and study of objects. Hooke's scheme was a 'method of describing, registering, and ranging ... particulars ... collected, as that they may become the most adapted materials for the raising of axioms and the perfecting of natural philosophy'. The cumulative implication of the elaborate correspondences that Hooke drew between macro- and microcosmic 'repositories' was then that the best method of philosophical enquiry was nothing other than the mental digestion of a well-ordered museum.

'THE PRESENT STATE OF NATURAL PHILOSOPHY'

I shall now pass on to consider of those other Faculties of the Soul, namely Memory and Ratiocination. The Business of the former being nothing else but a faithful Preservation of the things committed to it, and a ready recollecting them when necessary, will be rectified and perfected by this Method of the Philosophick Algebra, and the rectifying and perfecting of the Reason, we shall refer to another Opportunity.

The second thing therefore, is a Method of collecting a Philosophical History, which shall be as the Repository of Materials, out of which a new and sound Body of Philosophy may be raised.[1] This is to comprize a brief and plain Account of a great Store of choice and significant Natural and Artificial Operations, Actions and Effects, ranged in a convenient Order, and interwoven here and there with some short Hints of Accidental remarks or Theories, of corresponding or disagreeing received Opinions, of Doubts and Queries and the like, and indeed until this Repository be pretty well stored with choice and found Materials, the Work of raising new Axiomes or Theories is not to be attempted, left beginning without Materials, the whole Design be given over in the middle, for out of this are to be taken the Foundation Stones, on which the whole Structure should be raised, and those ought to be proportioned according to the rest of the Materials; for otherwise there may follow great Inconveniences, in prosecuting of it, here therefore ought to be laid up the more substantial Parts: But as for, the most curious and precious things which may serve for the finishing or compleating this grand Structure, they are to be fought for as occasion shall require and prompt. For as in any great building, none can be so perspicatious as to foresee every particular thing he shall need, for the compleating of it, but leaves the Care of providing them till occasions call for them, as being then best able to judge which of, that kind of Material which is wanting will be most fitting for his purpose, and so with that proceeds till other occasions call for other Requisites and Helps: And so from time to time furnishes himself with those more choice things, as the Occasions require; so there is none but before he sets upon such a Design, will be sure to provide himself of a sufficient Store of such Materials as he knows altogether necessary, nor will be neglect to lay hold on such things, as offering themselves by chance, put him in mind that he shall have occasion for them before he can finish his Design; and certainly much better it were, if the Architect were so skilful as to foresee to provide all kinds of Materials before he begins; for thereby his Work would be carried on the more compleately and uniformly, without Necessity of pulling down, or altering, or piecing, or transforming any part, or staying or interrupting.

The Case is much the same in providing a proper History for the perfecting of a new Body of Philosophy, the Intellect should first like a skilful Architect, understand what it designs to do, and then consider as near as can be, what things are requisite to be provided in order to this Design, then those Materials are to be carefully fought for and collected, and safely laid up in so convenient an Order, that they may not be far to seek when they are wanting, nor hard to be come by when they are found: In the choice of which, Care ought to be taken that they are found and good, and cleans'd and freed from all those things which are superfluous and insignificant to the great Design; for those do nothing else but help to fill the Repository, and to incumber and perplex the User, yet notwithstanding, Brevity is not so much to be studies, as to omit many little Circumstances which may be considerable in the use of it, for as in the laying up of Timber, the keeping on a branching part does make it serviceable for many Designs which it would be wholly unfit for, if it had been squared off, so it will be in the fitting and preparing the Particulars for a Philosophical History, there must be Judgment in the Historian to discern what will be material and useful in general, and what will be more especially adapted for the Inquiry whatever he designs.

This Similitude therefore hints unto us the whole Method of making a Philosophical History, according to which, I shall enumerate the several things necessary to this Design, and according to my Ability, endeavour to explain each Particular in such Order, and so far forth as to me seems most natural and consonant to my present Purpose. But first I shall permise some of the Accomplishments requisite for a Natural Historian.

There seem therefore these Requisites to accomplish one, that intends to prosecute or do any thing considerable in this Work, without which the

Collections may very much fail of the desirable Excellency in this or that Particular, though perhaps as to the kind they may contain many good things ...[2]

Memory then I conceive to be nothing else but a Repository of Ideas formed partly by the Senses, but chiefly by the Soul itself: I say, partly by the Senses, because they are as it were the Collectors or Carriers of the Impressions made by Objects from without, delivering them to the Repository or Storehouse where they are to be used.[3] Which Impressions being Actual Motions, as I have plainly proved in the Explication of the Organ of the Eye, and the Operation of Light, those Motions conveyed to this Repository become Powers sufficient to effect such Formations of Ideas as the Soul does guide and direct them in: For I conceive no Idea can be really formed or stored up in this Repository, without the Directive and Architectonical Power of the Soul; and the Actions or Impressions cease and fail without the concurrent Act of the Soul, which regulates and disposes of such Powers.

This Action of the Soul is that which is commonly called *Attention*, by which what is meant no one does further or more intelligibly explain, than only by giving the same Notion by some other ways of Expression, which, it may be are as little intelligible. My notion of it is this, that the Soul in the Action of Attention does really form some material Part of the Repository into such a Shape, and gives it some such a Motion as is from the senses conveyed thither; which being so formed and qualified, is inserted into and inclosed in the common Repository, and therefor a certain time preserved and retained, and so becomes an Organ, upon which the Soul working, finds the Ideas of past Actions, as if the Action were present.

This Repository I conceive to be seated in the Brain, and the Substances thereof I conceive to be the Material out of which these Ideas are formed and where they are also preserved when formed, being disposed in some regular Order; which Order I conceive to be principally that according to which they are formed, that being first in order that is first formed, and that next which is next, and so continually by Succession, from the time of our Birth to the time of our Death.[4] So that there is as it were a continued Chain of Ideas coyled up in the Repository of the Brain, the first end of which is farthest removed from the Centre or Seat of the Soul where the Ideas are formed; and the other End is always at the Center, being the last Idea formed, which is always the moment present when considered: And therefore according as there are a great number of these Ideas between the present Sensation or Thought in the Center, and any other, the more is the Soul apprehensive of the Time interposed ...

* * *

These *Nautili* are described by *Gesner, Aldrovand, Johnston*, and others, where you have their Names and a Picture or two of the Shells, and some Stones also tending to a Description of the Creature and two Species of them; but he that shall think to find any such Characteristicks by reading their Descriptions and seeing their Pictures of them, will be much mistaken. And indeed it is not only in the description of this Species of Shells and Fishes, that a very great Defect or Imperfection may be found among Natural Historians, but in the Description of most other things; so that without inspection of the things themselves, a Man is but a very little wiser or more instructed by the History, Pictures, and Relations concerning Natural Bodys; for the Observations for the most part are so superficial, and the Descriptions so ambiguous, that they create a very imperfect idea of the true Nature and Characteristick of the thing described and such as will be but of very little use without an ocular Inspection and a manual handling and other sensible examinations of the very things themselves; for there are so many considerable Instances that may be that means be taken notice of, which may be useful to this or that purpose for which they may be instructive, that 'tis almost impossible for any one Examiner or Describer to take notice of them, or so much as to have any imagination of them.[5] It were therefore much to be wisht for and indeavoured that there might be made and kept in some Repository as full and compleat a Collection of all varieties of Natural Bodies as could be obtain'd, where an Inquirer might be able to have recourse, where he might peruse, and turn over, and spell and read the Book of Nature, and observe the *Orthography, Etymologia, Syntaxis* and *Prosodia* of Natures Grammar, and by which, as with a *Dictionary*, he might readily turn to and find the true Figure, Composition, Derivation and Use of the Characters, Words, Phrases and Sentences of Nature written with indelible, and most exact, and most expressive Letters, without which Books it will be very difficult to be thoroughly a *Literatus* in the Language and Sense of Nature.[6] The use of such a Collection is not, for Divertisement, and Wonder, and Gazing, as 'tis for the most part thought and esteemed, and like Pictures for Children to admire and be pleased withy, but for the most serious and diligent study of the most able Proficient in Natural Philosophy. And upon this occasion tho' it be a digression, I could heartily wish that a Collection were made in this Repository of as many varieties as could be porcured of these kinds of Fossile-Shells and Petrifications, which would be no very difficult matter to be done if any one made it his care: For *England* alone would afford some hundreds of varieties, some Petrify'd, some not.

Source

Hooke, Robert, 1705 'A general scheme or idea of the present state of natural
  philosophy' (pp.18–19); 'Lectures of light' (p.140); 'Lectures and discourses
  of earthquakes and subterraneous eruptions' (p. 338) in *The posthumous
  works of Robert Hooke ... containing his Cutlerian lectures, and other discourses, read at the meetings of the illustrious Royal Society ...* ed. Richard
  Waller, London: 18–19, 140, 338.

Notes

1   Hooke's scheme for reforming the 'present state of natural philosophy'
    was in many respects a thoroughly Baconian inductive one, in which new
    general principles were to be raised from the accumulation of assured
    facts.
2   Amongst other attributes that he considers desirable in a natural historian fit
    to undertake his reform, he includes a knowledge of 'those several kinds of
    Philosophy already known', the understanding of 'mathematicks and
    mechanicks', and a need 'to get what Help he can from others'.
3   Hooke here is using the notion of a repository and collector as a metaphor
    for how the human mind gathers sensual input and stores up ideas in the
    form of a memory. However, since Hooke's philosophy of mind is such a
    strongly materialistic one, Hooke seems to imagine this repository of memo-
    ries (a sort of 'museum of the mind') to occupy some real physical space
    within the brain. Elsewhere, the metaphorical references to repositories are
    clearly also to be taken literally.
4   Hooke's emphasis on the significance of order in the arrangement of memo-
    ries had its direct parallels in contemporary museological concerns with the
    order and arrangement of specimens within a real-world repository.
5   In this lengthy sentence, Hooke both describes the methodology that he
    envisioned for 'museum science' – namely the 'ocular inspection ... manual
    handling, and other sensible examinations of the very things themselves' –
    and his philosophical argument for establishing natural history repositories –
    that the 'very things themselves' were infinitely more valuable than even the
    best descriptions and pictures.
6   Hooke's metaphorical discussion of the 'book of nature' both conjures up a
    favourite image of the work that seventeenth-century natural historians thought
    they were undertaking and, though not directly referred to, suggests the
    museum-based project undertaken by the likes of John Wilkins to create an
    entirely new and philosophically sound language (see Chapter 14 in this
    volume).

References

Oldroyd, 1987
Rossi, 1984
Willis, 1661
Yates, 1966

20

Nehemiah Grew writes the 1685 catalogue of the Royal Society's repository

Right from its earliest days, the premier scientific organisation in seventeenth-century England, the Royal Society, was given curiosities by members and well-wishers alike. This haphazard repository was considerably expanded by a collection of some thousands of natural rarities that a certain Robert Hubert (or Hubbard) had exhibited in London just after the Restoration. Hubert's collection had been acquired for the society with a £100 gift provided by the society's treasurer, Daniel Colwall. The collection's catalogue, from which the following extracts are taken, was duly dedicated to Colwall by Nehemiah Grew, the repository's first curator (Hunter, 1989).

The accumulation of a sizeable, well-ordered museum was held by many of its early members to be a high priority for the society. Following the Hubert acquisition, Christopher Merret and Walter Charleton were ordered to 'make a Catalogue of what is most desirable of all Sorts of Animals for the Repository', so that acting on their instructions, other members could then 'take care of sending into Forraigne parts, for such Animals' (*Royal Society Journal Book*, no. 2: 48–9). In addition to receiving 'whatsoever is presented as rare and curious', the naturalist Thomas Willisel was, in October 1669, paid £30 a year to travel up and down the country collecting rare specimens of birds, plants and animals for the society (*Philosophical Transactions*, 1666: 321; Birch, 1756: 358–433).

All those closely associated with the Royal Society's repository would have agreed with Robert Hooke who pronounced that the 'use of such a Collection is not for … Wonder, and Gazing, as 'tis for the most part thought and esteemed … but for the most serious and diligent study' (Hooke, 1705: 338). One way to pursue these studies was through the public examination of specimens. Thus, just as with the collections associated with Robert Plot and the Oxford Philosophical Society (see Chapter 16, this volume), the Royal Society's repository was partly kept, as the society's statutes explained, so that its members 'could view, and discourse upon the productions and rarities of Nature, and Art: and to consider what to deduce from them, or how they may be improv'd for use, or discovery' (Sprat, 1667: 145).

Largely inspired by John Wilkins' scheme for a new philosophical language, much effort was put into the rational organisation and accounting of the Royal Society's collections (see Chapter
14, this volume). Thomas Sprat, for example, reported that Robert
Hooke had set about reducing it 'under ... several heads, according to the exact Method ... which has been compos'd by Doctor
Wilkins and will shortly be publish'd in his Universal Language'
(Sprat, 1667: 251). And though Grew's 1681 published catalogue
derived its organising scheme more from an eclectic survey of
other authors – each suiting a different part of the collection – his
work nonetheless did bear the strong imprint of Wilkins' philosophy. Thus, for example, following Wilkins he declared that an
object's name should be 'a short Definition', 'taken from something more observedly declarative of their [the objects'] form, or
Nature', and elsewhere insisted like Wilkins that specimens should
be arranged 'according to their Nature', and their relationship
'one to another' (Grew, 1681: Preface).

THE ROYAL SOCIETY'S REPOSITORY

THE PREFACE
Nehemiah Grew

As to the following Catalogue, I have some things to say, of the Order,
Names, Descriptions, Figures, and Uses of Particulars, and the Quotations I have made therein.

As to the first, I like not the reason which *Aldrovandus* gives for his
beginning the History of *Quadrupeds* with the Horse; *Quod praecipuam
nobis utilitatem praebeat* [Which may be taken first from its noble use].
Being better placed according to the degrees of their Approximation, to
Humane Shape, and one to another: and so other Things, according to
their Nature. Much less should I choose, with *Gesner*, to go by the
Alphabet. The very Scale of the Creatures, is a matter of high speculation.[1]

As to the Names, where they were wanting, (which in our own Language were many) I have taken leave to give them. But have generally
reteind them, where I have found them all-ready given. Although, from
some distinguishing Note less convenient; as the Colour is, than the
Figure. And sometimes very Improper, as *Concha Persica*, and the like,
from the Place. For it often falls out, that the same Thing breeds in many
Places. But there is no Natural Reason, why it should be called by one,
rather than another. So that the Names of Things should be always taken
from something more observably declarative of their Form, or Nature.
The doing of which, would much facilitate and Improve the Knowledge

of them many ways. For so, every Name were a short Definition. Where as if Words are confus'd, little else can be distintly learn'd. Yet I took it not to be my part, actually to reform this matter; unless I have been writing an Universal History of Nature.[2]

In the Descriptions, I have taken care; First, to rectifie the mistakes of such as are given us by other Hands. Secondly, not to Transcribe any; as is too commonly done: but having noted something more special therein, to refer to the Author. Thirdly, where there is no Description at all, or that is too short, or the faults therein many, to give one at large. For the doing of all which, what the trouble of comparing Books together hath been, I say with *Sleydan* in another Case, *Post deum Immortalem Ipse novi* [After all this, I know how Immortal God felt].

In the Descriptions given, I have observed, with the Figures of Things, also their Colours; so far as I could, unless I have view'd them Living, and Fresh. And have added their just Measures. Much neglected by Writers of Natural History.[3]

If any object against their length: perhaps they have not so well considered the necessity hereof, for the cleer and evident distinction of the several Kinds and species, in so great a variety of Things known in the World. And wherein also regard is to be had, to all that after Ages may discover, or have occasion to enquire after. The Curiosity and Eiligence of *Pliny*, is highly to be commended. Yet he is so brief, that his Works are rather a *Nomenclature*, than a History; which perhaps might be more intelligible to the Age he lived in, than the succeeding ones. But had He, and Others, been more particular in the Matters they treat of: their Commentators had engaged their own and their Readers Time much better, than in so many fruitless and endless Desquisition and Contests. It were certainly a Thing both in itself Desirable, and of much Consequence; To have such an Inventory of Nature, wherein, as on the one hand, nothing should be Wanting; so nothing Repeated or Confounded, on the other. For which, there is no way without a clear and full Description of Things.

Besides, and in such Descriptions, many Particulars relating to the Nature and Use of Things, will occur to the Authors mind, which otherwise he would never have thought of. And many give occasion to his Readers, for the considerations of many more. And therefore it were also very proper, That not only Things strange and rare, but the most known and common amongst us, were thus describ'd.[4] Not meerly, for that what is common in one Country, is rare in another: but because, likewise, it would yield a great aboundance of matter for any Man's Reason to work upon. He that notes, That a *Grey* hound hath pricked Ears, but that those of a Hound hang down; may also the Reason of both: for that the former *hunts* with his *Ears*; the latter, only with his *Nose*: So that as a blind Man, minds nothing but what he Hears: so a

Hound, having his Ears half *Stop'd* with the Flaps, minds nothing but what he Smells. He that shall observe, That a Horse, which ought to have many and strong Teeth, and large and thick Hoofes, hath no Horns: and that an Ox, with Horns, hath fewer Teeth, and weaker Hoofs: cannot but at the same time see the Providence of Nature, In disposing of the same Excrementitious parts of the Blood, either way, as is most suitable to the Animal. One that considers the Teeth of a Horse, sees the reason, why he hath so long an upper *Lip*; which is his Hand, and in same sort answers to the *Proboscis* of an Elephant; whereby he nimbly winds the Grass in great quantities at once into his Mouth. So that for Nature to have made him a short Lip, had been to make a little *Hopper*, to a great *Mill*. The same Animal having need of great Lungs, how necessary it is also for him to have a broad Breast, well bowed Ribs, and wide Nostrils to give them play? That being much pester'd with Flys, he should have a long brush Tail to whisk them off. Whereas the Ass, which either for the hardness and dryness of his Skin, or other Cause, is less annoy'd with them, hath no need of such an one. That being heavy, he should not Treat or Leap stiff, as a Man; but have a Pastern made him, gradually and safely to break the force of his weight. By This, his Body hangs on the Hoof, as a Coach doth by the Leathers. Without this, the most thorow pas'd Horse, would treat so hard, that as it were impossible for any man to ensure long upon his Back: so his Joynts would be much chafed, and he must need presently tyre. Yet if it be too long, by yielding over much, it makes every step somewhat more laborious, and to loose some ground. He that would have one for Carriage, will choose him sshort, and high Back'd. For Running, long, and clean or slender Limb'd: another, were like a Man that should run a Race in his Boots. And a due length is as necessary: which is, when the Measure between the Main and the Tail answers to the hight, or thereabout. If much under, his hinder Feet will want their full scope: if much over, there will be more weight to be moved with the same force, as if the weight were less. But he that would have one for Draught, looks not that the Limbs be slender, if they are strong; especially those behind. for though the fore Legs pull sometimes, most when they make an acute angle with the Belly; yet the greatest stress usually lies upon the hinder; these being as the Centre of Gravity, and the Load, and Body of the Horse, the two Counter Weights. And when he Goes without Drawing, his fore Feet only support him; but his hinder, serve also as Leavers to carry him on. And therefore when he walks, he always moves his hinder Foot first.[5]

Together with such Notes as these, arising from the Description of the *outward Parts*; how largely and usefully might that of the *Inner*; his Generation, Breeding and the like, be also insisted on. And so the like of other Animals. Whereby a better History of them might be written in five years, than hath hetherto been done in two Thousand.

As for the Figures, I have given only those of such particulars, as are omitted by others. Saving one or two, found in some Authors less known, or common. Nor any, but what is also describ'd: which makes any further Explication of these needless, besides what the Reader will find next before them.

After the Descriptions; instead of medling with Mystick, Mythologick, or Hieroglyphick matters; or relating stories of Men who were great riders, or Women that were bold and feared not Horses; as some others have done: I thought it much more proper, To remarque some of the Uses and Reasons of Things.[6] Where also for the sake of the English Reader, I have undergone the transcribing some particulars. More I could have done, with less trouble. These I hope will compensate the room, they take up. Amongst Medicines, I have thought fit to mention the Virtues of divers Exoticks. Because the greatest Rarity, if once experienced to be of good use, will soon become common. The Jesuites Barque, of which, no Man get hath well describ'd the Tree, and very few known precisely where it grows; yet what great quantity, doth the much use of it bring over to us? Unicorns Horns, upon the like motive of Trade, would be as plentiful as Elephants Teeth.

I have made the Quotations, not to prove things well known, to be true; as one [*Aldrovandius*] (and he too deservedly esteemed for his great Diligence and Curiosity) who very formally quotes *Aristotle*, to prove a Sheep to be amongst the *Bisulca*: *Ovem, (inquit) ex genere esse Bisulcorum non solùm* αμτοιψιχ *ipsa loquitur, sed Aristoteles etiam scripto publicavit, inquiens*; as if *Aristotle*, must be brought to prove a Man hath ten Toes. But partly, To be my Warrant, in matters less credible. Partly to give the Authors, that which is their due: not at all liking the Malignant-way of some, who never mention any, but to confute him. Yet withall, To rectifie his Mistakes when I found them. And to mind the Reader, Not to peruse the most Honest, or Learned Author, without some caution.[7]

Source

Grew, Nehemiah, 1681, *Museum Regalis Societatis. Or a catalogue and description of the natural and artificial rarities belonging to the Royal Society and preserved at Gresham Colledge* ... , London: 'The preface'.

Notes

1 Here is a clear indication of how, by the 1680s when Grew was compiling his catalogue, the question of order had become within museums supremely important.

2 This notion of a name acting as a short definition for a specimen was one of the foundational ideas in John Wilkins' scheme for establishing a new 'philosophical' language. It had been envisaged by a number of language reformers that collections like those held by the Royal Society would play a significant role in the invention of such a language (see Chapter 14, this volume).

3 The plates included in Grew's work that illustrated some of the specimens in the society's repository were, indeed, accompanied by a scale, which as Grew pointed out was not by any means a standard practice of the time.

4 No matter how eager Grew and others associated with the Royal Society's repository were for the collection to include ordinary as well as extraordinary material, it was more often than not the latter that the society's members chose to send to it, which meant that a disproportionate amount of the collection was inevitably 'rare' and 'un-natural'.

5 This long digression on hounds, elephants and horses indicates Grew's conviction that the collection and description of natural history specimens was merely a necessary prelude to a fuller understanding of the natural world as a living entity.

6 Grew's unequivocally utilitarian approach to cataloguing a collection of curiosities such as the Royal Society's was clearly intended to be very distinct from earlier concerns with mystical powers and properties that played such a large part in the earlier formation of such collections.

7 It was commonly asserted by those involved with museums, that an acquaintance with the 'real' things themselves helped do away with the seemingly slavish need perpetually to find a classical source to legitimate a point made in a natural historical text.

References

Birch, 1756
Grew, 1681
Hunter, 1989
Philosophical Transactions, no. 1, 1, October 1666
Royal Society Journal Book, no. 2
Sprat, 1667

21

Elias Ashmole organises the Ashmolean Museum, Oxford

The accumulation in institutional settings (particularly universities) of apparatus, specimens and objects of interest took place considerably before the foundation of the first modern institutional museums in seventeenth-century Europe. The Bodleian Library in Oxford and the University Library in Cambridge, for example, had both long contained items that were frequently shown to visitors (Gunther, 1925: 149, 248, 252–4; Hunter, 1985: 160). Most of these collections were, in their origins at least, simply accidental accumulations of material that had to be stored somewhere. But they do represent the very beginnings of an important movement of knowledge and its material basis from private individuals to institutions. Thus, the London-based Royal Society's collection, for example, had at its core a collection amassed by Robert Hubert; Elias Ashmole used the Tradescant collection to found the university museum set up in his name in Oxford; and the British Museum, founded in the middle of the eighteenth century, was based on three major private collections, most notably Hans Sloane's.

The process of converting or transferring material from a private to an institutional collection had significant practical and intellectual consequences. In the first place, a fairly obvious difference was that institutional museums tended to be larger. More significantly, institutions came to provide, though truth be told far more often in promise than in practice, greater security and longevity for collections. The death of a collector, as John Evelyn observed in a letter to Samuel Pepys in 1689, could result in the 'sad dispersions', of what had 'with so much cost and industry [taken a lifetime to] collect' (Bray, 1889: 300).

The real significance of founding institutional museums, however, came in the attitude taken to them. It was on an intellectual plane, through the conscious designation of a space reserved for the accumulation of collections explicitly in order to further the goal of accumulating empirical information, that the launching of institutional museums came to exert such a profound influence on the whole concept of museums. The emergence of institutional museums was thus firmly located within the conception of investigative philosophy as a form of public knowledge that emerged in mid-seventeenth-century Europe, and particularly in England (Eamon, 1990: 334). It was this goal of harnessing a museum collection to the collaborative enterprise of producing publicly accessible and verifiable knowledge, that led Walter Charleton to pronounce the 'Museum Harverianum' (one of the earliest institutional museums, opened in 1654 at the College of Physicians) to be 'Solomon's House in Reality' – the fruition, that is, of Francis Bacon's elaborate plans for a full-scale research institute (Charleton, 1657: 34–42).

One of the most significant of England's seventeenth-century institutional museums was that set up in 1683, within Oxford University, by Elias Ashmole. The body of statues that Ashmole set out for his museum in 1686, which are reproduced below, at first glance seem predominantly concerned with practical and supervisory details, delivered in a somewhat pedantic tone. Under their surface, though, is enough evidence for exactly the sort of intellectual vision behind the institutional repositories of 'material facts' just outlined to make this document an essential text in understanding the early development of museums.

STATUTES, ORDERS AND RULES, FOR THE ASHMOLEAN MUSEUM IN THE UNIVERSITY OF OXFORD

Because the knowledge of Nature is very necessarie to humaine life, health & the conveniences thereof, & because that knowledge cannot be soe well & usefully attain'd, except the history of Nature be knowne & considered; and to this [end], is requisite the inspection of Particulars, especially those as are extraordinary in their Fabrick, or usefull in Medicine, or applyed to Manufacture or Trade.[1] I Elias Ashmole, out of my affection to this sort of Learning, wherein my selfe have taken, & still doe take the greatest delight; for wch cause alsoe, I have amass'd together great variety of naturall Concretes & Bodies, & bestowed them on the University of Oxford, wherein my selfe have been a Student, & of wch I have the honor to be a Member: lest there should be any misconstruction of my Intendment, or deteriorating of my donation; I have thought good, according to the Acts of Convocation, bearing date June 4: An:0 1683, and Sept: 19th. An:0 1684 to appoint, constitute & ordaine as follows.

1.   I Ordaine that the Vicechancellor for the tyme being, the Deane of Christchurch, the Principal of Brazenose, the Kings Prophessor in Phisick, & the two Proctors, or their Deputies, be Visitors of the said Musaeum.

2.   That there be a solemne Visitation of the said Musaeum yearely, upon the Munday next after Trinity Sunday, at eight of the Clock in the

Morning, to be continued by adjuournment, as it shall be found necessary; wherein shalbe examined the State of the said Musaeum, both in
reference to the diligence & fidelity of its Custody, & the accessions
made from tyme to tyme, by new Donations.[2]

3.   That the whole Donation already given or to be given, be distributed under certaine heads; and a number to be fixed to every particular;
& accordingly to be registred in the Catalogue of them.

4.   That the said Catalogue be divided into parts, according to the
number of the Visitors, see that the worke of Visitation may be expedited,
each Visitor comparing his part & seeing that all particulars are safe and
well conditioned, & answering to the Catalogue. As is done in the Visitation of the Bodley Library.[3]

5.   That beside the Catalogue, which is to remaine in the Musaeum,
another to be in the hands of the Vicechancellor, for the preventing of
fraude or embezelement; into wch, at the tyme of the Visitation, all the
additions made in the precident yeare shalbe entred: And that every
future Vicechancellor shalbe obliged, to deliver the same Catalogue over
to his Successor, when he delivers to him his Bookes & Keyes.

6.   That whatsoever naturall Body that is very rare, whether Birds,
Insects, Fishes or the like, apt to putrifie & decay with tyme, shalbe
painted in a faire Velome Folio Booke, either with water colours, or at
least design'd in black & white, by some good Master, with reference to
the description of the Body it selfe, & the mention of the Donor, in the
Catalogue; wch Booke shalbe in the Custody of the Keeper of the
Musaeum, under Lock & Key.

7.   That if there be in the Musaeum many particulars of one sort, it
may be lawfull for the Keeper of the Musaeum aforesaid, with the Con-
sent of three of the Visitors, whereof the Vicechancellor to be one, to
exchange it for somewhat wanting; or to make a Present of it, to some
Person of extraordinary quality.

8.   That as any particular growes old & perishing, the Keeper may
remove it into one of the Closets, or other repository; & some other to be
substituted.

9.   That all Manuscripts given to the Musaeum, shalbe kept by
themselves in one of the Closets, which shalbe called the Library of the
Musaeum, to the end the Curious, & such other as are desirous, may have
the View of them; but noe person to use or transcribe them, or any part of
them, but only such as the Keeper shall allow or appoint.

10.   That the Musaeum shalbe open, & attended by the Keeper or
the Under-Keeper in the same manner, & at the same tymes, as the
Bodley Library is; and at other tymes, if a particular or especiall occasion
shall require.

11.   That the Rarities shalbe shewed but to one Company at a tyme,

& that upon their being entred into the Musaeum, the dore shalbe shut; and if any more Company or Companies come before they be dispatcht, that they be desired to stay below, till that other come forth.[4]

12.   That no part of the Furniture of the Musaeum, nor Bookes out of the Library or Closets, be lent unto or carried abroad by any Person or Persons, upon any occasion, or pretence whatsoever, unless to be delineated or engraved, for the preservation of its memory in case it be perishable.

13.   That the Custody of the Musaeum during my Lyfe, to be at my appointment, who have at present names Doctor Robert Plott thereto; under the Title of Keeper, with an Allowqance or Pension to him & his Successors, in the same Employment, not exceeding the some of Fifty pounds per annum, the same to commence at Michaelmas One thousand six hundred eighty six, & to be deteyned by him, out of the Perquisits of the Musaeum. And in case of Vacancies after my decease, that then the Nomination & disposall of the Keepership, shall be in my Widdow during her lyfe & after her decease in the aforesaid Visitors or the Major part of them.[5]

14.   That the Nomination & Removall of the Under-Keeper shalbe in me during my lyfe, and after my decrease in my Widdow during her's, & after her decrease in the aforesaid Keeper & his Successors, and at all tymes he shalbe under his & their Survey & correction. And the said Keeper shall allow unto him a Sallary out of the Perquisits also, not exceeding the some of Fifteene pounds per annum, the same to commence at Michaelmas one thousand six hundred Eighty six. And further the said Keeper shall allow a person, to sweepe & clense the Musaeum & Closetts, with such other things therein preserved, as he shall appoit, a reward not less than Forty shillings a yeare, out of the Perquisits also.

15.   That a third Person shalbe chosen by the said Keeper, to be in readines to performe the Office of the Under-Keeper, when & at such tymes as Sicknes, or other allowable Occasions shall cause his absence; And that the said Keeper shall allow unto him for his particular service, out of the aforesaid Perquisits, so much money as he shall thinke convenient, not exceeding the some of Five pounds per annum.

16.   That at the tyme of each Visitation, the Keeper shall render to the Visitors, a true & perfect Account of all the Profitts & Emoluments, that have been made or received in the preceding yeare, by shewing the Rarities; the same annual Account to end at Michaelmas before.

17.   That a Honorary of Six halfe Guinies be yearely paid by the said Keeper upon the aforesaid Munday next after Trinity Sunday into the hands of the Vicechancellor for the use of the said Visitors; to be layd out either in an Entertainement, as is done in the Visitation of the Bodley Library, or in Gloves, as is done to the Visitors of the Savilian Lecture, at

the choise of the said Visitors, or the major part of them; & that this Honorary be paid by the sd. Keeper, out of the Profits by him received.

18.   That the Overplus of the sd. Profits after the aforesaid Honorary & Pensions, and the Allowance for sweeping & making cleane the Roomes to discharged, shalbe deposited in a Box or Chest, to remaine in the Library of the said Musaeum, with two different Locks & Keyes, the one Key to remaine with the Vicechancellor for the tyme being, & the other with the Keeper of the Musaeum for the tyme being; the said Money to be layd out in Painting or drawing such naturall Bodies, as are neere perishing, or in buying more Rarities, or Manuscripte Bookes, or other incident Charges, but not in anything that doth not relate to the said Musaeum.

Source

Bodleian Manuscript Rawl. D. 864, ff.187–9. Reproduced in Ovenell, R.F., 1986, *The Ashmolean Museum 1683–1894*, Oxford, Clarendon Press: 49–52.

Notes

1   Ashmole's opening statement almost stands as a manifesto for the intellectual role that he envisaged for his collection as converted into the institutional museum at the university.

2   The need to maintain such inspections was born out by many horror stories of what actually happened to material cared for by such early institutional museums. For many years such museums were far less safe than their formal façades might suggest. Significantly, once he had decided to leave his collections to a public institution, Hans Sloane ruled out their addition to any established repository.

3   A manuscript catalogue of some six volumes dating from this time, each relating to one of the areas assigned to the Visitors described by Ashmole, is still held by the History of Science Museum in Oxford (Ovenell, 1986: 39–46).

4   Viewed as amusing trinkets by many, a number of the items contained in the museum were nonetheless valued enough by others to make theft an ever-present threat, which a number of these statutes were aimed at reducing.

5   That the keeper of the museum, Robert Plot (see Chapter 16, this volume), was paid for his work, made him one of the earliest institutionally-funded museum professionals and, indeed, a very early example of an institutionally-funded scientist, if his work may be so characterised.

References

Bray, 1889
Charleton, 1657
Eamon, 1990
Gunther, 1925
Hunter, 1985
Ovenell, 1986
Simcock, 1984

22

Hans Sloane describes a 'China Cabinet'

Many early modern museums gave pride of place to collections of objects designated as 'artificial' (that is, man-made) and 'exotic' (that is, not from the West). Almost inevitably, the attention paid to these objects tended to draw its parameters from well-established categories. Examples of common and familiar indigenous objects clearly provided the most obvious points of comparison – the very necessary 'windows' through which to squint and try to make some sense of what was after all a flood of new, sometimes shockingly new, objects. It was this comparative process that allowed any understanding at all of the exotic foreign cultures from which these objects came.

The inclination to assume familiarity with an object's use and meaning was, however, in direct opposition with another equally powerful motivation. For at the same time, the attractiveness of a foreign object commonly seemed to be in direct proportion to its unusualness. Picked for their strangeness, however, they were then described and classified in terms of familiar attributes. Thus, the very process that allowed any understanding at all, simultaneously helped to iron out and absorb the puzzling contradictions and genuinely unsettling ideas that might have begun to lead to a fuller understanding of non-Western cultures (Arnold, 1996).

As a result of this tension, the objects that proved most satisfying, producing the most informed descriptions, were precisely those whose type was patently obvious, but that simultaneously manifested intriguing differences with familiar domestic examples. What these items essentially provided was the comfortable assurance that comes with any simple translation or conversion. The Leeds collector Ralph Thoresby, for example, had 'An Indian Comb', with five teeth, and 'Another that approaches nearer the form of the Europeans; having about forty Teeth' (Thoresby, 1715: 478). The extract that follows from Hans Sloane's article in the *Philosophical Transactions* for November 1698 similarly contains an account of a selection of instruments described as being 'new and of different shapes from the same used in Europe'. While in the Royal Society's Repository a 'China Statera' could be found, which, explained its cataloguer Nehemiah Grew, 'The Chinese carry ... about them, to weigh their Gems, and the like'. This last example could, in fact, serve as an emblem for this whole category of comfortably different objects; for on it was inscribed three 'rules, or measures ... The first, is our Europe-Measure; the other two, I take to be the Chinese-Measure, and that of some other Country trading with them' (Grew, 1685: 369). Here, then, was an object that could minutely translate practices and concepts across cultures, without in the least bit upsetting established conventions.

The inclination to allocate each object a categorical character, and the evident satisfaction provided by objects that were on this basis 'manageably' different, was nonetheless matched by an opposite tendency to accentuate what was not understood. This attitude was in part responsible for the habit of employing descriptive terms whose breadth verged on rendering them meaningless: the Tradescant museum, for example, had one section defined as a 'Variety of Rarities', part of the 'Ashmolean Museum Catalogue of Artificial Works' was simply labelled 'Various Objects', while most of the 'artificial curiosities' in Sloane's collection were to be found in his 'Miscelanies' [sic] catalogue. Played out through these contradictory inclinations to embrace the differently similar and indiscriminately to group all the foreign objects together, the curators of these early modern collections made some rather hesitant steps towards the analysis of non-Western material cultures.

A 'CHINA' CABINET

An Account of a China *Cabinet, filled with several instruments, Fruits, &c. used in* China: *sent to the Royal Society by Mr.* Buckly, *chief Surgeon at Fort St. George.*

By Hans Sloane, M.D.

Mr. *Buckly*, chief Surgeon at *Fort St. George* in the *East-Indies*, having lately presented the Royal Society with a *China* Cabinet, full of the Instruments and Simples used by their Surgeons, &c. amongst which, several are new and of different Shapes from the same used in *Europe*, they have commanded me some Account should be given of them.

The Rasors were of Two Sorts, either such as are represented to the natural Bigness, *Fig. 1.* and resemble some Sorts of Knives, and do not fold in; or *Fig. 2.* and *3.* which present another sort of Rasors, which are longer, and fold in after the manner expressed in the Figures. They were daubed over with a Substance, resembling, *Diachylum* Plaister, to keep them from Rust, which it had effectually done, through different Climates.

Fig 4. and *5.* represent an Incision Knife used in *China*, the whole being of Brass, excepting towards their Point *aa*, which is of Steel.

The most unusual instruments that came over in this Cabinet were, those contrived for the taking any Substance out of the Ears, or for the scratching or tickling them, which the *Chinese* do account one of the greatest pleasures.

Fig. 6. Does represent one of these Instruments which is a small Pearl, such as is used in Necklaces, through the Bore of which is put and fasten'd a Hog's Bristle, the other End of the Bristle being fast in a Tortoise-Shell-Handle.

Fig. 7. Represents an other Instrument for the Ears, made of small Silver Wire twisted, set into a Tortoise-Shell-Handle, the Wire being made into a round Loop at the End.

Fig. 8. Shows an Ear Instrument made of a piece of large Silver Wire, flatted at end, and set in a piece of Tortoise-Shell.

Fig 9. Is an Ear Instrument made likewise of Silver Wire in a Tortoise-Shell-Handle, the End of the Wire being made sharp, and shap'd like an Hook.

Fig. 10. Represents an Ear Instrument, very much resembling our common *European* Ear-pickers, being of Silver set in Tortoise-Shell.

Fig. 11. Shews the Figure of an Ear Instrument made of Several Hogs Bristles, set as in a common Pencil.

Fig. 12. Represents Instruments made of very fine Downy Feathers tyed together like a Pencil, or Brush on the end of a Tortoise-Shell-Handle.

Fig 13. Shows an Instrument exactly like that figured *Fig. 8*. only the flat end has a slit through it.

Fig 14. Is a *Chinese* Figure, wherein is represented one of that Nation, using one of these Instruments and expressing great Satisfaction therein. This I had of *William Charleton*, Esq; who favoured the Royal Society with a Sight of it at one of their Meetings.[1]

Whatever Pleasure the *Chinese* may take in thus picking their Ears, I am certain most People in these parts who have their hearing impaired and have advised with me for their Help, I have found have had such Misfortunes first come to them by picking their Ears too much, and thereby bringing Humours, or ulcerious Dispositions in them.[2]

Source

Hans Sloane, 'An account of a China cabinet, filled with several instruments, fruits, &c used in China: sent to the Royal Society by Mr. Buckly, chief Surgeon at Fort St. George', *Philosophical Transactions*, Vol. 20, 1699: 390–92.

Notes

1   This reference to the 'sight of' an object at a meeting indicates one of the chief uses of an institutional collection such as that of the Royal Society – namely, edifying entertainment. The likes of Robert Hooke and Nehemiah Grew (both closely involved with the society's repository) were thus periodically expected to find amongst the collections some item which could be shown, demonstrated and often experimented with at a meeting. The findings would then sometimes be written up in the Society's *Philosophical Transactions*.

2   Casual as it is, this sort of cross-cultural comparison is, from a modern perspective, surprisingly rare, given how much of these collections contained material from foreign lands. Apart from the occasional glimmer of economic interest in materials that might be exploited for commercial gain, any interest in how something was used within its native context was almost invariably accompanied by a dismissive note about the 'barbarity' of the foreign culture from which it came.

References

Arnold, 1996
Grew, 1685
Thoresby, 1715

23

Zacharias Conrad von Uffenbach describes Hans Sloane's collection

Born in Frankfurt in 1683, Zacharias Conrad von Uffenbach was a connoisseur, traveller and book-collector of considerable means, who by 1711 had amassed a library of some 12,000 books. He began his 'research trips' in 1702, and in 1710 stayed some five months in England. He took his last such trip in 1718 and died in 1734. His detailed descriptions afford readers a close inspection of the countries he visited. His trip to England did not leave him with an entirely positive view of the country and its culture. Many of the collectors that he spent a good proportion of his time accompanying, were clearly masters of their collections at the expense of any mastery they might have gained of social graces and niceties.

Uffenbach's travel accounts of the early eighteenth century complement nicely those made by John Evelyn some seventy years earlier when he had travelled in continental Europe (see Chapter 9, this volume). A comparison of the two gives a clear indication of how English museums and collections had, during the intervening period, grown to rival, and in some cases surpass, those of continental Europe. Spending as much time as he did amongst collectors, Uffenbach's accounts also give much insight into their world, indicating for example that a small-scale commercial market had developed to service collectors, a market buoyant enough to support a number of England's first auction houses (Herrman, 1972: 28–9).

The history of eighteenth-century English museums is partly set against the background of a rapidly expanding and increasingly established culture of collecting. By the middle of the century, it is tempting to think that almost every self-respecting nobleman or woman, doctor, merchant, or indeed anyone with a sufficient urge to better themselves and the wherewithal to do so, had equipped their home with some sort of gallery or cabinet of curiosities. At the centre of this competitive world of private collecting stood an undisputed champion – Hans Sloane, with whom, as Richard Richardson explained to his friend William Sherard in 1723, 'all things center' (Richardson, 1835: 194). It is Uffenbach's visit to Sir Hans Sloane, and his clearly gracious, and lengthy (four-and-a-half hour) tour of his collections, that is recounted in the following extract.

After moving to London at the age of nineteen, Hans Sloane pursued early studies in chemistry and botany. Professionally inspired by Thomas Sydenham and philosophically influenced by John Ray, Robert Boyle and Joseph de Tournefort, Sloane took up medical practice as an ideal calling that allowed him to combine work and virtuosic diversion. Like many early collectors, his habit began on youthful botanising trips; a voyage to Jamaica saw it flourish. Growing financial security in his middle years allowed him both to gather more and more objects, and also increasingly to buy up the fruits of the industry of other collectors. By 1753, his holdings included some 1,500 shells, over 12,000 vegetables, and no less than 23,000 medals. It was in amassing these gargantuan collections, and in the fashion that they were turned into a national institution (the British Museum) that Sloane was destined to change forever the shape of museums (MacGregor, 1994).

THE COLLECTION OF DR HANS SLOANE

In the afternoon Herr Campe took us to call on Dr Hans Sloane, who received us with vast politeness; in a very different manner from that coxcomb, Dr. Woodward.[1] He immediately addressed us in French, which was most amazing for an Englishman; for they would rather appear dumb than converse with a foreigner in any other language than their own, even if they should be quite capable of doing so. He took us into a room of moderate size, which was quite full. Above are three or four rows of books, while all the lower part is furnished with cabinets and natural curiosities. Not only is a large quantity here, but they are for the most part extraordinarily curious and valuable things. He has here the whole Charleton collection and many objects with Dr. Sloane brought from India himself, while he is daily increasing them in England for vast sums of money.[2] He assured us that the Venetian Ambassador had offered him fifteen thousand pounds sterling for this collection, but that he had refused. A great quantity of all manner of animals are to be seen here, some in spiritu vini and others preserved by drying. A prodigious variety of strange fishes, a large collection of ores, lapidibus figuratis, and an especially remarkable collection of lapidibus pretiosis, among them being several of uncommon size and value. He also had a handsome collection of all kinds of insects, which are kept in the same fashion as those we saw at Herr Dandrige's house, except that here, instead of glass, moonstone or Muscovy glass is used, which is much more delicate and light but more costly.[3] Dr. Sloane also showed us a cabinet of shells, which, through not at all numerous, consisted entirely of choice specimens. A Cochlea terristris

was especially remarkable; not so much for its elegance as for its curious
breeding from an egg, such as we had seen in no other collection. Dr.
Sloane showed us both a whole egg and various shells that were not yet
full grown and so were still partly surrounded by the crusta testacea. The
shell entirely resembles an egg shell, and, on holding the egg against the
light, one could see the concham lying concealed within it. The eggs are
not large, being rather smaller than doves' eggs. Another cabinet was full
of marinis, among which the collection of corals was especially charming, for they were not only of unusual size but also quality. Not only all
kinds of red, black and white corals are to be found here, but also those
half white, half red, red inside and white outside, etc. Next we saw a
cabinet full of all manner of butterflies; not so handsome as those of
Vincent in Amsterdam. Then we saw all kinds of Indian and other strange
costumes, weapons, etc. Also a sort of cloth that is said to grow on a tree.
Moreover some antlers well-nigh as large as those we saw at Windsor.
Dr. Sloane showed us further a small cabinet with about four hundred
varieities of most handsome agates, of which most were figured. He
considered them all to be natural, but this is extremely doubtful. Next a
cabinet of all manner of vessels and objets d'art of agate and other costly
stones and materials. We also saw a cabinet containing great quantities of
Numismatibus ex omni metallo and a tolerable number of cut antique
stones, but time was lacking to observe them all with care. Next a
remarkable cabinet of all kinds of stuffed animals, especially birds, and
also several nests of vastly curious structure. Among other things he
pointed out to us the nests that are eaten as a delicacy. It is said that the
material is formed in the sea like the succino and used by the birds to
build their nests. But, judging from its taste, appearance and feeling, I
took it for a gum or resin, though many persons, indeed, consider succinum
to be this.[4] After we had seen everything in all the rooms round about, as
far as time permitted, Dr. Sloane invited us into another rooms, where we
sat down at a table and drank coffee while he showed us all manner of
curious books. Namely, various large volumes containing nothing but
paintings from life of all sorts of exotic beasts, birds, plants, flowers,
shells, etc. A notable one with all kinds of national costumes. These
paintings were done by the best artists and collected sheet by sheet from
all parts of the world at a phenomenal cost, often by Dr. Sloane himself
on the long journeys he has taken. The book with excellent illuminations
by Mad. Merian of insects and plants was among them, but it was by no
means equal to the other. Finally he showed us some manuscrips, but
they were for the most part modern and on medical subjects. The best
was a description of the West Indian coasts in the Portuguese tongue,
accompanied by elegant paintings. It was a pity that we had so few hours
to look through this large collection and these handsome articles, since

the gentleman had no time on account of his extensive practice. They say that he could earn a guinea an hour. We thought, indeed, that he did us a very great honour by sparing us the time between half past two and seven o'clock. Being a much-travelled man he is vastly amiable, in especial to Germans and such persons as have some knowledge of this treasures. I presented him with a Lohenstein hystero lythibus, such as he had never seen before, and it was especially welcome; on this account he showed us more courtesy than to other persons. We then went to Thomas Smith's, who makes human eyes of coloured glass, with which he provides those who have lost them in war or by any other misfortune.

Source

Quarrell, W. H. and Mare, Margaret (trans. and ed.), *London in 1710 from The Travels of Zacharias Conrad von Uffenbach*, London, Faber & Faber, 1934: 185–8.

Notes

1   The geologist and collector John Woodward (see Chapter 24, this volume) was notoriously difficult and argumentative.
2   Sloane funded his collecting activities largely from a lucrative medical practice and from marrying well. His fortunes allowed him to acquire not just individual specimens, but whole collections, like that of William Charleton noted here.
3   It is clear from this detail, and from other similar passages, that the method of displaying material during the eighteenth century received increasing amounts of attention from collectors.
4   Visits to private collections clearly involved far more than just observing specimens in glass cabinets. However, the transference of Sloane's collections to an institutional museum (the British Museum) some forty years later put an end to such 'interactive' encounters with exhibits.

References

Herrman, 1972
MacGregor, 1994
Richardson, 1835

24

John Woodward sets out a classification for fossils

In the late seventeenth century the English geologist John Woodward ceaselessly collected 'fossils' (that is, geological specimens) by any means he could, so as, in his own words, to get 'as compleat and satisfactory information of the whole mineral Kingdom as I could'. To this end, he gathered what has been estimated at some 9,400 specimens, and to store them, four cabinets finished in a walnut veneer, each containing fourteen oak-lined drawers. At his death, Woodward left a large part of his collection to Cambridge University, thereby establishing an institutionally-based geological museum there which still survives (Woodward, 1695: 3; Price, 1989: 79–96, 82–3; Levine, 1977: 93–109).

As the following extract from Woodward's letter to Sir John Hoskyns makes clear, Woodward was intent on organising his specimens in a scientifically authoritative manner. His efforts to do this in practice, however, perfectly exemplify the problems of attempting to produce a systematic classification at the same time as enlarging the collection. Woodward ended up with twelve catalogues that covered some four basic fossil divisions. Always led on by the lure of an ever more complete collection, Woodward never quite managed to find the time to produce a single unified sequence for them. Even the lip service he paid to such aims, however, serves to highlight the nature of his primary objective: 'to methodise [his fossils] according to their several Species, and reduce them unto a Science' (Woodward, 1729: Vol. 2: IV, vol. 1: ix–x).

Within this taxonomic work, Woodward clearly saw his own contribution as that of filling a gap in a more comprehensive programme already begun by others of 'methodizing … natural Things, [distributing] each into their Classes, according to their natural Properties, and mutual Agreement amongst themselves'. But fossils, he claimed, 'of however great Worth and Importance, have been much neglected' (Woodward, 1728a: 2). What Woodward proposed was a balanced assessment of a wide range of 'rigorous Examinations, and exactest Experiments' upon his specimens that would yield a fossil classification based 'wholly upon their Nature and properties' (Woodward, 1729: x).

Despite a number of Woodward's own comments to the contrary, his classificatory enquiry was not, in fact, taken up as an isolated end in itself. Instead, he harnessed it to higher, more abstract goals; for Woodward treated his classificatory system as a mass of organised information that would indubitably prove a theory of the earth that he first related in his *An Essay toward a Natural History of the Earth* (1695) – a story in which God, angered at Adam's shameful fall, dissolved the earth by suspending gravity, only then to turn it back on and reconstitute the earth – rocks and fossils gradually being laid in strata according to the reapplied laws of gravity. This was the theory that provided the orchestration for much of his subsequent natural historical work.

Set in such a context, it becomes clear that Woodward was as intent on collecting arguments as specimens – arguments which together would amount to the articulation of a systematic support for his universal theory. For Woodward, then, taxonomy was both the natural extension of the collecting habit and a system by which to organise material that was destined to fit into a grand structure. 'Censure would be his Due', he declared in the Preface to his catalogues, 'who should perpetually be heaping up of Natural Collections, without Design of Building a Structure of Philosophy out of them ... This is in reality the only proper End of Collections, of Observations, and Natural History' (Woodward, 1729: xii–xiv).

THE STUDY OF FOSSILS

THOSE, which I have been hitherto displaying before you, Sir! are the chief Particulars, I would note to you relating to the extraneous Fossils.[1] And as to the *Native*, the Writers having been so little accurate as, you see, to confound Bodies of so very different Origin and Constitution with them, it cannot be thought strange, that their Accounts of the *native Fossils* themselves should be frequently erroneous and imperfect. In assigning their very Names, they give us commonly the same Body under different Names; as they do different ones under the same Name.[2] Then in their Methodozing and ranging of the native Fossils, 'tis no wonder that they fail, and that all Things are in disorder, and out of Course with them, when they so frequently make Choice of Characters, to rank them by, that are wholly accidental, and unphilosophical; as having no Foundation in Nature, or the Constitution of the Bodies themselves. Thus some rank them under the Heads of *common*, and *rare*, of *mean* and *pretious*: of less, and of greater *Uses*, in Medicine, Surgery, Painting, Smithery and the like; which would be proper in an History of *Arts* or *Mechanics*; but serves only to mislead them and their Readers in the History of *Nature*.[3] Besides, they rank, amongst the rest, Bodies that are

Mineral indeed, but *factitious*, and not in their native Condition. An Instance of this we have in the Pumex, which almost all the Writers of *Stones* place amongst *them*; whereas 'tis in Reality nothing but a *Slag* or *Cinder*, found either where *Forges* of Metalls have antiently been; or near *Aetna, Vesuvius*, or some other burning Mountain, forth of which it has been cast. Another Example of this we have in the *Lapis Spongiae*, which is a light, porose, friable Body, compos'd of a Matter chiefly *Corallin*, and generally made into the Form we find it, by a *marine Insect*.

BUT these are only a few of the many Instances that might be alledged to evince in how uncertain and perplex'd a Condition this Study has hitherto lain: And how little Light into the Nature of Fossils, and their Relation to one another, we are to expect from those that have theretofore wrote.[4] The classical Disposal of the native Fossils will indeed ever be a Work of Difficulty. It hath been prov'd from observations, made on the present Condition of them, that they have been one all in a State of Solution and Disorder: And such is the present Constitution of them that it is very hard, if not impracticable, to rank and reduce them into an exact Method.[5] For they want those fix'd Characters of Affinity or Disagreement that Animals, and that Vegetables carry along with them. It has been shewn, how little Certainty there is in their Colour and Figure, in their Situation in the Earth, and their Mixtures with each other. And few of them being pure, or unmix'd, 'tis plain there can be no determinate Rule as to their *Specific Gravity*, their *Consistence*, or Approach more or less to *Solidity*, or as to their Constitution. In fine, there being no single Character steady, or to be rely'd upon, I am oblig'd to make Use of one or other of them, as I see most fit, and conducing to my Purpose. My chief Regard is, to the Nature and *constituent Matter* of each; but since that Matter is frequently mix'd, and various in the same Sort of Body, I conduct my self by such other *natural Notes* as present themselves, and all such *Tests* and *Methods of Scrutiny*, as I find practicable. In particular, I have Regard to the *Bulk* each Sort of Fossil is naturally of: Also to its comparative *Gravity, Density, Solidity*, the *Grossness*, or *Fineness* of the Parts: The natural *Figure* of the form'd Stones, and other Bodies, their *Texture* and *Constitution*; as likewise the *Colours* observable in many Sorts of Fossils, the *Diaphaneity*, or *Opakeness*: Their Disposition to a *Solution* and Mixture with Water. Lastly, I consider in what Manner they affect the Organse of Sense, the *Smell* and the *Taste*; as also the *Touch*, as to their Roughness, Harshness, Smoothness, and their being unctuous, oyly, and the like.[6] With this Conduct, and assisted by these Lights, I range the native Fossils in the following Method. 1. *Earths*. 2. *Stones*. 3. *Salts*. 4. *Bitumens*. 5. *Minerals*, or Bodies nearly approaching the Nature of Metalls. And, 6. Metalls themselves. The particular Reasons for my adjusting them thus, you will be better Judge of, when you come to see the Details of the whole Method.

I am, Sir, &c.

Source

Woodward, John, 1728, 'The study of fossils never hither to reduced to rule, nor any form of art.' Written in the form of a Letter to Sir John Hoskyns in *Fossils of all kinds, digested into a Method*, London: 19–23

Notes

1 Woodward's classification scheme for fossils was fourfold: English native, foreign native, English extraneous and foreign extraneous. The term 'extraneous' more or less corresponds to what are today called fossils, while 'native' fossils refers mostly to geological specimens that are today not thought to have fossil origins.
2 Woodward here clearly indicates that the relationship between specimens and their names should not be an accidental one. The full philosophical implications of this position had been proposed by John Wilkins in his *An essay towards a real character and philosophical language* (1668) (Chapter 14, this volume).
3 The seventeenth century saw collectors not only distinguish the 'artificial' from the 'natural' with more and more rigour; but also both physically to separate them within their repositories and to treat them (present, analyse, catalogue them, and so on) in entirely different ways.
4 Woodward's reference to the relationship of specimens to each other provides clear evidence of a shift away from searching for intrinsic characteristics, or 'virtues' as he would have called them, towards a concern to compare relative properties.
5 Woodward here is referring to his diluvial theory in which the creation of fossils is related to the biblical tale of Noah's Flood.
6 From this description we get a clear picture of how Woodward worked in his museum – arranging his specimens only after having tested their consistency, texture and specific gravity, their reaction with water, as well as their smell and taste.

References

Levine, 1977
Price, 1989

Woodward, 1695
Woodward, 1728a
Woodward, 1729

Part III
Enlightened Voices

25

Michael Valentini lists contemporary collections

As the seventeenth century passed into the eighteenth, the development of ideas about museums and collections played a significant role in the generation of ideas about the world, and man's place in it, building upon the developments written about by Quiccheberg (Part I, Chapter 2, this volume.) Particular interest concentrates upon three authors: Johann Major, Michael Bernhard Valentini and Kaspar Friedrich Einchel (or Jencquel) otherwise known by his pseudonym of 'C. F. Neikelius'.

Johann Daniel Major was born in Kiel, in north Germany, in 1636. His chief work, issued under the pseudonym 'D.B.M.D.', was entitled *Unvorgreiffliches Bedenken von Kunst – und Naturalien – Kammern Insgemein* (that is, broadly speaking, *Thoughts on Collections of Natural History and Art*) and appeared in Kiel in 1674. The work was quite short – only twenty-eight folio sheets – but it encapsulates his experience as a doctor and as Inspector of the Kiel Botanic Gardens. In his book he begins with the question of why people collect, which he believes is an inborn human urge linked with the desire for fame and also the desire to give expression to the wonderful works of God. The notion that categorisation of the material world, natural and man-made, draws us closer to the mind of God, was a fundamental thought in the earlier decades of the philosophical Enlightenment, whose thinkers saw no conflict between science and religion.

Major then gathers some forty different names used in his day for collections, the differences between which he defines, and follows this with practical instructions about the ordering and care of the contents of a collection. For him, the complete collection should have a cabinet of naturalia, that is, natural history specimens, and a library wherein also will be sculptures, coins, urns and so on: the kind of material we would call historical or archaeological. Three other important elements are identified: collections of mathematical instruments, of armour and of art. All this is to be supported by a written catalogue, known as the Rarity Book, which includes both material held in the collection, and other objects, so making the collection even more comprehensive.

Michael Bernhard Valentini belonged firmly to the next generation. He was employed as doctor to the ruling family of Hesse, a north German principality, and was also Professor of Medicine at Giessen University. His work appeared in two volumes in 1704–14, entitled *Schaubuhne oder Natur – und Materialienkammer* (or *Consideration of Collections of Natural History and Man-Made Material*) and part of its (very lengthy) title describes it as '*Museum Museorum*', a 'museum of museums'. Valentini reprinted the whole of Major's short work in his first volume. Valentini's first volume is a general discussion of the nature of collections, which he, too, sees as a natural way for man to appreciate almighty God's creation. He embraces the notion of the three realms of nature, which runs back to the Roman Pliny (see Volume 1, this series), and describes insects, birds, fish, mammals and finally trees. He discusses the material required for painting, and makes a separate list of exotic things, called 'East Indian'. The second volume, published in 1714, gives a detailed list of the individual collections known to Valentini, including his own. The publication concluded with an index and a bibliography, both crucial advances in the recognition that scholarship could only progress through a conscious development of its own techniques by which knowledge could be delivered to a steadily widening public.

Museographia, by 'C. F. Neikelius' was published in 1727. Its author had left it unpublished and it was edited by Dr Johann Kanold of Vienna. Neikelius emphasises in his Foreword that his book is to be seen as a work of reference, and it built upon previous publications. It, too, includes an index and bibliography, which includes the *Catalogue* of the Tradescant collection (Part I, Chapter 12, this volume). Neikelius divides nature into the three realms of animal, vegetable and mineral, a triple classification which has acquired a proverbial status among English speakers. Works of art should also be collected, as originals not copies, and there should be a separate cabinet of artificialia, that is, man-made materials.

Neikelius also gives detailed instructions on what we would call collection management. Shelves must be orderly and rooms well arranged for easy access; visitors must have clean hands and work in silence. The room should be airy, preferably with a south-easterly orientation, and painted in a light colour. A register of new acquisitions and a catalogue-general are indispensable. In addition, the book contains a detailed list of all the collections known to the author, which includes much useful information about some of the major Italian art collections.

The interrelationships of this group of writings, complicated by the authors' habits of using *noms de plume*, of passing material around in manuscript, and of relying on other editors in the publication of their works, are very complex. Only small parts of the body of material is easily available, and this is a great pity. The piece given here is the list of major collections, together with some notes of where he found the information, published by Valentini in 1714, as reprinted by Murray. This list concentrates upon German collectors, who were best known to Valentini, and is far from exhaustive: there were many important collections in Italy, some in France and some others in Britain (for example Sloane) which are omitted. Nevertheless, the list is important, partly because of what it does include, and partly because its compilation was reckoned to be of interest to the learned public.

RELATING TO PARTICULAR MUSEUMS

I.   Royal Museum at Vienna.[1]
        From Edward Brown's *Travels* (German translation), cap. xi., p 247.

II.   Treasury of the Abbey of St. Denis: an Extract.[2]
        The Anatomy Cabinet in the Royal Gardens at S. Victoire.[3]
        Notes on the Louvre.

III.   The Royal Museum at Copenhagen: an Extract.[4]

IV.   The Royal and Electoral Museum at Dresden.[5]
        From Martin Zeiler's *Handbuch*, f. 475.

V.   The Museum at Hesse Cassel: an Extract.[6]

VI.   The Treasury of Loretto.[7]
        From Sprenger's *Roma Nova*.

VII.   Relics in the Liebfrauen Kirche at Aachen.[8]
        From Edward Brown's *Travels*, p. 312.

VIII.   The Museum of the Royal Society of London.[9]

IX.   The Curiosities in the Gallery of the Garden of the University of Leyden.[10]

X.   Museum of Tobias Reyner of Lüneburg.[11]

XI.   Museum of Christian Maximilian Spener of Berlin: an Extract.[12]

XII.   Museum of Burgomaster Lorentz von Aldershelm of Leipzig.

XIII.   Catalogue of the Fossils in the Museum of Johann Georg Kisner of Frankfort, August, 1711.[13]

XIV.   Apothecary Petivers Catalogue.[14]

XV.   Rarities in the Anatomy Theatre at Amsterdam: And in the Anatomy Theatre at Leyden.[15]

XVI.   Collection of Mathematical Instruments at Giessen.[16]

XVII.   Museum of Astronomical Instruments belonging to Professor Erhard Weigel of Jena: an Extract.[17]

XVIII. The Cabinet of Johann Conrad Rätzel of Halberstadt.[18]

XX.   Museum Brackenhofferianum, delineatum a Joh. Joachimo
           Bockenhoffero, Argentinensi.[19]
XXI.   Museum Curiosum of Gottfried Nicolai of Wittenberg.[20]
XXII.   Cabinet of an unnamed Collector: coins, medals, gems, natural
           and artificial curiosities, and mathematical and other instru-
           ments. The Author notes that it is for sale.[21]
XXIII.   Repositorium Valentinianum.[22]
XXIV.   Joh. Dan. Major's Himmelische Beschauung der Göttlichen
           allergröst-und herrlichen Kunst-Kammer der gantzen Welt.[23]

Source

Murray, D., 1904, *Museums, their History and their Use*, Vols 1–3, Glasgow,
James Maclehore & Sons: 229–30.

Notes

1   The Hapsburg collections at Vienna were large and very important. They
    included the Imperial Treasury, the Cabinet of Coins and Antiquities, the
    Imperial Museum, the Natural History Cabinet and collections of arms and
    armour. See Impey and MacGregor, 1983.
2   The Abbey Church of St Denis has already appeared twice in this series
    (Volume 1, *Ancient Voices*, Chapters 59 and 60). Its collections embraced
    the material gathered by Suger, and a considerable accumulation acquired
    since his time. The collection was broken up and most of it disappeared
    during the upheavals of the French Revolution.
3   For the Louvre, and the French royal collections generally, see Impey and
    MacGregor, 1985.
4   The Royal Collections at Copenhagen embraced particularly important
    northern antiquities collected from the seventeenth century onwards. See
    Impey and MacGregor, 1985.
5   The collections accumulated by successive Electors of Saxony in their
    capital, Dresden, were among the most famous in Europe. They included
    the renowned Green Vaults, the Saxon Treasury, and much classical archae-
    ology, natural history, and eventually porcelain. See Impey and MacGregor,
    1985.
6   The Hesse Cassel museum contained the collection of the ruling princely
    family, and included art, antiquities and natural history.
7   One of the important Italian collections.
8   The Liebfrauen Church at Aachen had a renowned collection of relics,
    contained in precious caskets of various kinds.
9   For the Museum of the Royal Society, see this volume, Chapter 20.
10 Leyden University, Holland, had one of the most famous European collec-

tions. The specimen collection of the Anatomy School was especially re-nowned, and the material displayed off the garden included plant and animal specimens preserved in spirits and many curiosities.

11   This is another famous German collection, eventually embraced within that of the ruling ducal family.

12   Johann Jacob Spener was Professor of Physics and Mathematics at the University of Halle, Germany. His museum embraced ancient and recent man-made material and natural history material, from outside and inside Germany. However, the relationship of Johann to Christian is unclear.

13   Johann Georg Kisner of Frankfurt-am-Main had a significant collection of fossils.

14   James Petiver (c. 1663–1718) was apothecary to the Charterhouse, London, and had a large collection of natural history material. His collection was bought by Sir Hans Sloane in 1718, and went with the Sloane Collection to the British Museum when it was formally created by Act of Parliament in 1753 (see this volume, Chapter 17).

15   The anatomy courses offered by these two Dutch universities were particularly famous, and the 'theatres' were lecture rooms with specially raked seating in which dissections could be performed so as to be visible to students. Specimen collections were maintained as part of them.

16   The collection of the University of Giessen, Hesse Dormstadt, Germany.

17   The University of Jena was one of the premier German seats of higher education and learning.

18   Rätzel had a significant collection of natural and man-made material; it was one of the major German collections.

19   Elias Brackenhoffer had a major broad collection of art and natural history material. An account of the collection was published by Johann Joachim Bockenhoffer in 1683.

20   Gottfried Nicolai's collection of rarities was published at Wittenberg by Christian Warlitz (1648–1717), Professor of Medicine at Wittenberg University in 1710.

21   The identification of this collection remains unclear.

23   This is, of course, an account of Valentini's own collection.

24   Valentini's book included a reprint of Johann Daniel Major's view of the moral significance of the art collection, his *Heavenly Vision of the Divine all encompassing and noble Art Gallery of the Whole World*.

References

Findlen, 1996

26

The collections of Carl Linnaeus and their arrival in Britain

It has been said that God created nature and Carl Linnaeus gave it order. Linnaeus, a Swede born in 1707, made his first collection of flora in Lapland in 1733, and published the first edition of his *Systema Natura* in 1736. It was not until the tenth edition, published in 1758, that Linnaeus gave to all the animals known to him their binomial names (generic and specific), and this system remains the starting point for modern classification of the natural world, although since subject to considerable modification and rethinking. Linnaeus named nearly 4,400 animal species, and he divided them into six classes as *mammalia* (mammals), *aves* (birds), *amphibia* (amphibians), *pisces* (fish), *insecta* (insects) and *vermes* (worms).

Carl himself, and his father, were both substantial collectors. When Linnaeus became Professor at Uppsala University he set about acquiring animal specimens for the university, and as his reputation grew, more material was sent to him. Some of this material still exists at Uppsala.

The private collection, however, was disposed of differently. Following Linnaeus's death in 1778, Sir Joseph Banks offered £1,500 for the plant specimens in the Herbarium, but the collection went to Linnaeus' son and, after the son's early death, to Carl's widow and daughter. The family then offered the whole cabinet to Banks for 1,000 guineas (a guinea was £1 1s) and Banks passed the letter to a young medical student friend of his, James E. Smith.

Smith agreed to buy it, and (after efforts to keep it in Sweden which included an attempted interception in the Channel by a Swedish warship sent by King Gustavus III) it arrived safely in England on 29 October 1784. In 1788 Smith moved to 12 Great Marlborough Street, London, and there, with two colleagues, he set up the Linnaean Society for the study and publication of natural history. On Smith's death, however, in 1826, the Society learnt that if it wanted the collections it would have to buy them: in the end, a sum of £3,000 was agreed, largely paid by the Treasury, but leaving the Society with a considerable debt.

The Linnaean Collections remain at the heart of the Society, and represent primary material for understanding how one of the most influential modern scientists thought and worked.

THE PURCHASE

HISTORICAL CHRONICLE

A gentleman[1] in the country of Suffolk has lately made a purchase of the entire library and collection of the two Linnaeus's. The books are not numerous, being about 2000 vols. but many are extremely rare and valuable; but there are, besides a great number of manuscripts, drawings, &c. 19,000 specimens of dried plants, a good collection of insects, a very fine one of shells, and many fishes and other subjects; in short, everything relating to natural history and medicine, which was in the possesion of the two Linnaeus's, except the fossils of the elder, which his son gave to the university of Upsal.[2] The specimens of plants are more peculiarly valuable, as they are the basis of the Species Plantarum,[3] and certainly refer to that work. This collection is at present in Sweden, but will be shipped off as soon as possible for England.

THE ARRIVAL

October 29

This day was landed at the custom-house, the valuable collection and library of the late celebrated Linnaeus, purchased by a private gentleman in Suffolk, as mentioned in a former Magazine.

Source

Gentleman's Magazine 1784, 54: 393, 869.

Notes

1 The 'gentleman' was Smith.
2 *Species Plantarium* was one of Linnaeus's principal books on plants. It first appeared in 1753.
3. Upsal = Uppsala.

References

Allen, 1978

Larson, 1971
Stafleu, 1871
Schiebinger, 1993

27

Sir Joseph Banks and Dr Daniel Solander collect in the South Seas

The three voyages of exploration commanded by Captain James Cook (1728–79), all of which involved extensive travel in the Pacific Ocean, generated an extensive range of collecting activity, in both ethnography and natural history, which was to have an immense effect upon scientific progress and the nature of collecting. Of the three, the first, in the *Endeavor*, was perhaps the most important. In 1768 the Royal Society was granted £4,000, a ship, and the full backing of the Admiralty for an expedition to observe the transit of Venus across the sun and make astronomical calculations of great importance. The best place from which to make the observations was Tahiti ('Otaheite') in the Pacific, and so James Cook was chosen as captain of the *Endeavor*, which sailed in 1768, and returned in 1771. He probably also had more secret instructions to search for the great southern continent believed to exist in the South Seas.

With Cook sailed Daniel Carl Solander and Joseph Banks. Solander (1733–82) was a former pupil of Linnaeus. On his return to England in 1771 he was employed by the Duchess of Portland to work on her shell collection (see Chapter 28, this volume). Banks was born in 1743, and in 1764 he succeeded to his father's considerable fortune. In 1766 he had taken part in an expedition to Newfoundland and Labrador to collect plants and insects, and saw the *Endeavor* voyage as a major opportunity, for which he was prepared to pay his own expenses. The collections which he and Solander made in the South Seas and elsewhere on the voyage were of prime importance in filling out the classification of the planet's flora and fauna.

In 1778 Banks was made President of the Royal Society, an office which he held until his death. In 1781 he was made a baronet, and he became a trustee of the British Museum. In effect, he was the point of reference for all decisions made in London affecting the museum and scientific establishment during the later part of his long life until his death in 1820. He bequeathed his collection and his books to the British Museum.

DANIEL SOLANDER TO MR ELLIS, DATED FROM RIO DE JANEIRO, 1 DECEMBER 1768

My Dear Sir,[1]

In my last from Madeira of the 18th of Sept. I only had time to let you know we were all well, and that we there met with a very good reception, which is more than I can say of this place, where the Vice Roy has been so infernally cross and ill-natured, as to forbid us to set out feet upon dry land. How mortifying that must be to me and Mr. Banks you best can feel, especially if you suppose yourself within a quarter of a mile of a shore, covered with palms of several sorts, fine large trees and shrubs, whose very blossoms have had such an influence upon us, that we have ventured to bribe people to collect them, and send them on board as greens and sallading for our table.

Now and then we likewise botanized in company with our sheep and goats, when grass has been sent on board for them. Once I have ventured, as belonging to the watering boat, to land at the watering place, which is in the middle of the town, where happening to meet with a civil captain of the guard, and telling him I was the surgeon's mate, and should be glad to go up to some apothecaries shops to buy drugs, he granted me a guard; which happened to be a very good-natured serjeant, that followed me not only all round the town, but likewise a little way into the country, where I collected a few plants and insects; but I could not get so far as the uncultivated places where the palms grow. This place is very large and well built, very regular and well paved. They reckon 37,000 white inhabitants, and above 400,000 blacks; some say half a million. Their churches are very rich, as are their numberless convents. The Opera-house is large, but they say the performers are indifferent. Every body that lives here cannot be called any thing else but a slave; none dare do any thing without the Viceroy's leave.

We have, nevertheless, by fair means and foul, got about 300 species of plants, among them several new, and an infinite number of new fish. We can hardly buy a plate of shrimps, without finding a dozen of your *Pennatula reniformis*, or kidney shaped sea-pen, among them.[2] This harbour swarms with rays and sharks; among the last, the *zygaena* [*malleus*][3] and *tiburo* of Linnaeus, or hammer-headed and shovel nose sharks, have given us a great deal of pleasure. It is never heard that sharks do any harm, but in the sea and open roads. In our voyage between England and Madeira, as well as afterwards, we have been lucky enough to meet with a great variety of mollusca, especially of the tribe which Dr. Peter Browne calls Thalia, but very ill described by him. We have made above eight or ten new genera, and, I believe, rather too few: I think we have seen above an hundred species of mollusca, especially when we were becalmed near the line; we then every day hoisted out Mr. Banks's board, and sometimes might have caught boat-loads of what the sailors called sea-blubbers, and thought they were all of one kind; but they soon became such good philosophers, that they even recollected the different names, and could remember what we had shewn them, and, consequently, could look out for new ones; some of the sailors have proved very useful hands.

Many of our ship's company have, for a few days, been low spirited from a bilious complaint, which our surgeon generally cured in a week's time.

We have lost no men yet by sickness. Our first mate was drowned at Madeira.

If any of your friends go to Madeira, advise them to get recommendations to Dr. Heberden,[4] he has more influence there than the governor. He is just such a philosopher as my friend, and very communicative. His many instruments, mathematical and optical, have procured him the name of *il Doctore Docto*. His being a member of the Royal Society of London, has not added a little to his reputation. He procured us access into a nunnery, and when they heard that Mr Banks and myself belonged to the Royal Society, they immediately took us for men of supernatural knowledge, and desired us to walk into their gardens, and shew where they might dig for water; they wanted to know by what signs they should be able to foretel tempests, rain, and thunder and lightning. The answers and explanations of all this would have taken us several days; but our captain would not stay for the gratification of the nuns.

The governor was highly pleased with the performance of the new electrical machine; it worked prodigiously well at Maderia, but not half so well near the line; perhaps the air is too damp at sea.

These letters are sent to Europe in a Spanish king's packet, that came here in her way to Buenos Ayres; there is on board of her an officer that has lived seven years in the missions of Paraguay, which he describes as the finest country under the sun. It was not a little mortifying to us, to see all the Spaniards get leave to hire a house on shore, when we were denied to land on any island, or other place that we desired the Vice Roy might appoint, and that under a guard, the very day when our ship was keel'd for to clean her sides, so that we could hardly make a shift to walk. I hope I shall live to see the day when Conte de Azambuja, the new Vice Roy of Brazil shall be shamed of his impolite behaviour towards us. This letter goes in a Spanish man of war; my last, from Maderia, was sent in an Irish ship. The Spanish officers are the only people that we are allowed to converse with; they are very civil and agreeable, and seem to be unreserved. The captain has been in the South Seas, and went round Cape Horn, which, I believe, will be our route. The fruits of this country are nothing near so good as ours are in Europe. Their pineapples are extremely sweet, but no flavour; their grapes bad, so are their few apples, likewise their melons; oranges are good, but rather want acid to give them flavour. Bananas, plantains, very little better than those you might have tasted at Kew. Water melons very good, Mangoes are not so good as they are described in 20.18. taste of a disagreeable turpentine.

Their other fruits, as Iamboeira (*Eugenia Iambos* of Linnæus,) Papayas, Mammeas, &c. can no ways be equivalent to our fruits; but they have one advantage, that they have here a succession of fruit the whole year round. Their few peaches are abominable; their greens tough and leafy. The country people eat almost every fruit that grows, but very few of them would be acceptable, even to boys in Europe.

DAN. CH. SOLANDER

Source

Gentleman's Magazine, 1769: 530–1.

JOSEPH BANKS TO THE COMTE DE LAURAGAIS, DATED DECEMBER 1771, LONDON

My Dear Count[5]

The abstract of my Voyage which I have so long Promis'd you, I at last begin to write: the multiplicity of employments in which I am engaged will I know, with you plead my excuse for having so long delay'd it.

On the 25th of August 1768 we set sail from Plymouth and on ye 12 of Sepr arriv'd at Madeira after a moderate Passage. Here we were receiv'd with great Civility by our Consul, and not uncivily by the Portuguese Governor: and during our stay we collected some specimens of Natural Curiosities not unworthy our Notice.

On ye 18th of ye same Month we set Sail from yt Place, and on the 13th of November arriv'd at *Rio de janerio*: where instead of being received as friends and allies, of his most faithful Majesty; orders were immediately issued out, yt every insult possible should be offered to the officers of our ship, whose duty obliged them to land: and as for us (*Foutres Philosophers*) we were refus'd to land, on any pretence whatsoever on the peril of being sent to Portugal in Irons. A thing I verily believe their absurd Viceroy would have done, had he caught either Dr Solander or myself upon any of our little Excursions.

Notwithstanding the Vigilance of his Excellence le *Comte D'Azambusio*, however we ventur'd a shore each of us once: and had several parcels of Plants brought off to us under the title of grass for our

Cattle: as we were absolutely forbid to have them under any other De-nomination.

The abject slavery of the Portuguese in this Colony, is beyond imagination: suffice it to say, that to prevent any attempt against Government, every officer and other person of any Distinction, is oblig'd to attend ye Levée of ye Viceroy twice every day; under penalty of his displeasure: which is follow'd by an Instant excommunication from all Society. For whoever speaks to a man under these circumstances, is instantly himself under ye same.

From these unfriendly and illiberal people, we departed on ye 7th of Decr not forgetting in our way out of ye Harbour to land upon a small Island Call'd *Raza* off ye mouth of it; where in a few hours we much increas'd our natural Collections.

On ye 15th of january we arriv'd at *Terra del Fuego*, and soon anchor'd in a small bay near ye middle of ye *Streight le Maire*, which had been formerly call'd by the Nassau fleet the Bay of good Success: here we lay some Days in a tolerable Harbour, which offered plenty of Woods and water; and an innumerable quantity of Plants incomparably different from any which had before been describ'd by any writers on Botany. The inhabitants who were of a moderate size, were friendly to us: but seem to have no provisions to spare, nor if they had would it have suited our Palates: being generally the Flesh of Seals. We found however a kind of watercress (cerdamine) and a kind of Parcely (apium) which we made into Soupe; and no doubt, re'p'd benefit from their antiscorbutik virtues; tho' in reality none of our people were absolutely ill of the scurvy.

From hence we Sail'd on ye 21st january, and having passed *Cap Horn*, and ass'd sufficiently to the westward of ye Coast of America; we sail'd in almost a N.W. direction for ye Island of Otaheite; ye Taiti of Mr Bourgainville, which was ye Place of our Destination: On ye 4th of April we saw land, may be the 4 Facardin of that gentleman, and from thence passing by several low Islands, arriv'd at ye place of our Destination. On ye 13th of the same month the inhabitants receiv'd us wth great politeness: but it was visibly the Effect of Fear we immediately erected a small stockade defence, and in yt observ'd the transit of the Planet Venus over ye Sun on the 3rd of June 1769: for which observation we had ye most favourable weather imaginable.

The inhabitants of this Island during our whole Stay of 3 months behav'd to us wth great affibility: Mr Bourgainville's account of them is as good as cou'd be expected from a man who staid among them only 9 Days; and never (tho' a native went away with him) made himself master of their Language, (This, not only myself, but several of our Company did;) and of it I shall only say, that Mr Bourgainville has omitted in his vocabulary every aspirate in it: (tho' the use of them is very Frequent,) I suppose in Confirmity to his Mother Tongue. After a stay of 3 Months we left our belov'd Islanders; wth Much regret on ye 13th of July, and sail'd to ye Westward in search of other Islands; wch a native of Otaheite who chose to emark wth us offered to direct us to; we found them with great facility, they were in number 6 Huaheine, Vehieta, Otaha, Bolabola, Maurua, and Tupi; the Natives of which we found to be of exactly the same manners, Customs, and language, as those of Otaheite. After a month's stay among them, we left them on ye 9th of August; in order to steer to ye southward, in hopes of finding a land more worthy our Notice tho' we were absurdly forbid to proceed [to a] higher Latitude than 40d into which Latie we arriv'd by a due South course, and turning then to the westward on ye 3d of october, fell in wth the Easter[n] side of New Zeland. The extent of this Country which extends from ye Late of 34d to that of 47dS: took us up to six Months before we could compleat our Circumnavigation of it: in ye Time however we discover'd that Instead of being as generally suppos'd part of a Southern Continent, it was in reality only 2 Islands, without any firm lands[6] in their Neighbourhood.

The coast of these Islands abounds in Harbours, the country is fertile, and ye Climate Temperate, the inhabitants are a Robust, lively and very ingenious People: they always strenuously oppos'd us, so that we sometimes were laid under the desagreeable necessity of effecting our Landing by Force; they were however when subdued, unalterably our friends and carried ye sentiment to lengths which in Europe we are unacquainted with. Notwthstanding that their barbarous customs taught them to eat ye Bodies of such of their Enemies as were kill'd in Battle. But what surpriz'd us ye most, was that notwithstanding ye distance, these people all along that large extent of Coasts, spoke different dialects of ye language of Otaheite, every one of which were tolerably well understood by ye Indian who accompanied us.

From these brave people we departed on the 1st of april 1770, and steering a Course nearly West in the 19th of ye same Month fell in wth the Coast of New Holland in Latie 38 S. a coast which had never before been investigated by any navigator. Along this Coast we sail'd often carrying [sic] to an anchor, generally in very fine Harbours. 'till on ye 10th of June we struck upon a Rock in Latie 15 S. nearly about ye same place where Mr Bourgainville heard ye voice of God:[7] on this Rock we lay 23 hours in ye utmost danger; and when ye ship got off, which was effected by throwing over board almost every thing heavy, we found her so leaky, that she would hardly swim: we got her however into a small harbour, where with great difficulty in two Months we refitted her.

During our stay in this harbour, we made friendship wth several of ye inhabitants, whom from their shy dispositions we had not before well seen; they were of a moderate size but slender Limbed, dark brown, and stark naked both sexes; their Language is not unmusical, but different from any we have either before, or sence met wth, their arms are *Assagayes*, headed wth ye Boardeda[8] Bones of Rays they were however not uncivil, tho' very timorous and Jealous of their Sooty Wives.

After having repaird our ship as well as we could, we on ye 4th of august sallied first into a sea of Dangers, more difficult to imagine than to describe:[9] without a wall of rocks, ran paralel to ye shore at ye distance of 8 or 10 Leagues within were Shoals innumerable, which ye smoothness of ye water, caus'd by a barrier that prevented our retreat, prevented us from discovering. In this Sea of Dangers we remained, after haivng once escaped and having been driven back again into it with ye utmost hazard of our Lives 'till we carried in Latie 10 S. where to our great Joy we discovered an opening to ye west of us, which seem'd to promise a passage into ye Indian Sea: we accordingly followed it and found it indeed a Streigth between New Guinea and New Holland through which we passed and became at once easy and happy.

We now resolved to see the Coast of new Guinea, in order to ascertain whether or no ye Chart had laid down that Country in a right Position: and accordingly on ye 3d of sepr fell in wth it about the Island of *Vleer Moyen*, as it is laid in the Charts of the ingenious President de Brosses.[10] From hence we coasted along round the cape St Augustin: finding the land very low every where, and shoaling off so far, that in 6 fathom of water we sometimes could not see it from ye deck, nor could we ever get nearer it than a league, tho' our ship did not draw above 13 feet of Water.

Nearly about the place call'd *Kerr Veer* in ye Dutch Charts, we landed with our Boat, and Saw Cocoa nut trees, and a fertile or at least a Rich Soil: the natives soon attack'd us wth their arrows, and we being but 8 in number not able to bring our ship nearer, than a League, or our Boat than a quart[er] of a Mile of the Shore, we were oblig'd to retire: wch we did in Safety, tho' followed by near 300 of ye inhabitants; who to our great surprise threatened us with fire thronk[11] out of reeds, I know not how, but exactly ressembling the flash of an Musquet so much so, that those who remain'd in the ship were much alarm'd.

From this place than we saild immediately, and passing by Islands which by their situation we judged to be *Arrow* and Timorlaut we arriv'd in sight of Timor, from whence passing between *Rote*, and *Simau* we fell in wth a small Island call'd *Savu*; here we Came to an anchor; and bought from ye Natives Sheep, Goats, Buffaloes &c the first we had met since we left Rio de janerio: Then Passing along ye south side of Java, and into the Streights of Sunda, we arriv'd at Batavia on ye 9th of october, where we resolv'd to repair well our ship which had suffer'd when lying on ye Rocks on the Coast of *new South Wales*, as we Call'd it very materially.

Tho' we had been remarkably Healthy, through the great Variety of climates which we had pass'd before, yet the uncommon Malignity of ye air of Batavia so fatal to Europeans, was not the less terrible during our stay here about two Months, and afterwards at sea of Distempers contracted here:[12] we lost above ⅓ of our people among whom were all my Artists, and the two poor Indians, whose loss especially I much regretted, I hope[d] to have pleas'd my country men much with the answeres they would have made to their questions; wch I was capable of doing having learnt tolerably well their Language.

From hence touching at the *Cape of good hope* and *St Helena*, as is ye Customs of India ships, we arriv'd in the Downs on ye 13th of July 1771 so well satisfy'd with the discoveries which we had made in ye three Kingdoms of nature, that we resolv'd to solicit the Government to furnish Ships for an other undertaking of ye same Nature which they have accordingly done: and in the Month of March 1772 we hope to enter upon our new undertaking.

The Number of Natural productions discover'd in this Voyage is incredible: about 1000 Species of Plants that have not been at all describ'd by any Botanical author; 500 fish, as many Birds, and insects Sea and Land innumerable: out of these some considerable oeconomical purposes may be answer'd particularly with the fine Dyes[13] of the Otaheitians and the Plant of which the new Zealanders make their Cloth of which we have brought over ye seeds. The fine red Colour us'd by the inhabitants of the Islands situated between the tropicks in the South Sea the tinge of which seems to be between that of Scarlet and a pink is made by mixing the juice of the Fruit of a Fig Tree suppos'd to be peculiar to those Islands with the juice of the Leaves of the *Cordia Sebestena orientalis* Lenius.[14]

NB: The fig tree is now describ'd under the name of *Ficus Tictoria* and probably did not escape the researches of so accurate a Botaniste as Mr de Commerson who sail'd with Mr Bourgainville, is disputed[15] to be. – Quadrupedes we found few and none remarkable but one Species totally different from any known kind the full grown of it was as large as Sheep, Yet went totally on its hind legs as the *Jerbua* and the *Tarsier* of De Buffon, yet in every other part of its external Structure was totally different from either of these Animals.

Thus (my dear Count) I have Given you an abstract account of my last Voyage the narrative of which will appear (I hope) some time next Winter: as I have put all the Papers relative to ye adventure of it into ye hands of Dr Hawkersworth [*sic*] who I Doubt will not do justice to ye work which ye shortness of my Stay in England would not permit myself to attempt. in march Next we shall sail upon a new undertaking of ye same kind in which we shall attempt the Souther[n] Polar Regions, O how Glorious would it be to set my heel upon ye Pole! and turn myself

round 360 degrees in a second. But that as the unexplained Secret of the creation shall Please – whatever may Happen to me, I hope for the Pleasure of relating to you at my return: and truly sign myself
Your oblig'd and affectionate
sign'd Jos.BANKS
London xxx December 1771

Source

Beaglehole, J. C. (ed.), 1962, *The 'Endeavour' Journal of Joseph Banks 1768–1771*, Sydney, Public Library of New South Wales and Angus & Roberston, Vol. 11: 324–9.

Notes

1 It should be noted that for this voyage Solander had designed a particular form of opening box for storing collected specimens. These are still called 'Solander boxes' and are still used in museums.

2 'The kidney-shaped sea pen had been discovered before on the coast of South Carolina, and sent to Ellis by John Gregg of Charleston (*Gents Mag* 1794, xxxiv: 370). It is now called *Renilla reniformis* (Pallas).' (Note from *Gentleman's Magazine*.)

3 'The sense requires the addition of this word, omitted either by Solander or by the printer.' (Note from *Gentleman's Magazine*.)

4 The Heberdens were a family possessing several men of medicine and natural history. William (1710–1801) became an FRS in 1749, and his son William (1765–1845) was Physician-in-Ordinary to the King (1809). It is not clear which Heberden this was.

5 This letter had a very complex history, and existed in several forms.

6 'firm land' (*terra firma*), that is, a mainland, or continent.

7 This is a reference to Bougainville's description of his approach to the Great Barrier Reef on 6 June 1768. He had described the rocky coast as 'the voice of God' and had abandoned his exploration of it at that point. New Holland was the contemporary name for Australia, but as the letter shows a few lines further on, New South Wales was used in England. Louis Antoine Bougainville (1729–1811) was a soldier, mathematician and explorer. Between December 1766 and March 1769 he sailed round the world, stopping at Tuamoto, Tahiti, Samoa and the New Hebrides in the Pacific. He published his *Voyage autour du monde* in 1771.

8 '*sic*, i.e. bearded.' (Beaglehole's note.)

9 'Does he mean the reverse – 'more difficult to describe than to imagine'?' (Beagleholt's note.)

10 'The MS has here a marginal note: "author of L'Histoire de Navigations aux Terres Australes".' (Beaglehole's note.)
11 '*sic*; obviously a slip for "thrown".' (Beaglehole's note.)
12 'MS "contracted: here" etc, which leads to a quite erroneous statement, as only a few men died actually at Batavia.' (Beaglehole's note.)
13 'MS "Clayes" with the "a" deleted; obviusly "Dyes" is meant; Cameron prints "dye".' (Beaglehole's note.)
14 'That is, Linneaus.' (Beaglehole's note.)
15 '*Sic*, i.e. "reputed".' (Beaglehole's note.)

References

Beaglehole, 1962
Lyte, 1980

28

The Duchess of Portland collects shells and antiquities

After the Cook voyages, many shells collected during those voyages were circulating among collectors, but one of the best collections was recognised as that of Margaret Cavendish Bentinck, Duchess of Portland (1714–85). At her town house in Whitehall and her country estate at Bulstrode in Buckinghamshire, Margaret established a salon which welcomed serious men of science, political writers like Jean Jacques Rousseau (1712–88), King George III, and the fashionable world. On the return of the *Endeavor* in 1771, in particular, she was able to add considerably to her shell collection, and to make the acquaintance of Daniel Carl Solander.

Solander had a profound knowledge of conchology, and was glad to be employed by the duchess to work on her shell collection. He was considering producing an updated edition of Linnaeus's *Systema Natura*, and the duchess had examples of a number of shells not yet described and published. Solander began working in January 1778, spending each Tuesday working on the material. He worked solidly, but died in 1782 leaving the work unfinished. Nothing had been published, although the descriptions of the shells, written on slips of paper, were acquired by Banks, and passed with his own collection to the British Museum. Three years later, Margaret herself died, by now heavily in debt, partly (or largely) as a result of her collecting habit.

To meet her debts, it was necessary to sell her collection at auction. The sale catalogue was published in 1786, and listed 4,156 lots, the majority of which were shells and other marine specimens. The sale took place in April and realised £11,546 14s. The Portland Collection became widely dispersed, but the catalogue is still of importance to systematic conchologists because it contains many validly proposed names for new species in the collection which were described in the catalogue for the first time; many of these were, of course, the names which had been proposed by Solander.

Margaret collected antiquities as well as shells, and by far the most renowned of her antique pieces was the Portland Vase, a cobalt blue blown-glass vase with cameo-style decoration created by cutting away white opaque glass; the decoration is of a mythological subject, possibly the story of Peleus and Thetis. The vase was made in the first century BC and may have had imperial connections. It is now in the British Museum. The vase resurfaced in 1600, and passed into the hands of the Barberini, in whose famous collections it, too, became very famous. In 1782 the vase came into the possession of Sir William Hamilton, who sold it to the duchess in 1784. In the sale following her death, it was almost the last lot and fetched £1,029, a very large sum.

EXTRACT FROM THE SALE CATALOGUE OF THE PORTLAND SALE (1786), GIVING A SELECTION OF THE MOST SIGNIFICANT LOTS

Lot 1455:– Buccinum Iris, *S. Martyn,*[1] *very* fine and extremely scarce [*Latirus iris* Lightfoot]   [Humphrey £2 2s.][2]
Lot 2559:– A very fine and large specimen of Conus Ammiralis, L. or High Admiral, from *Amboyna-rare [Conus ammiralis L.]*
                    [Cash £1 11s. 6d.]
Lot 3823:– A very large and fine specimen of Serpula Penis, L. or the Watering Pot, from *China – extremely scarce [Penicillus penis* L.]
                    [Cash £8 8s]
Lot 3831:– An exceeding fine and large Cypraea Aurora, S. or the Orange Cowry, from the *Friendly Isles*, in the *South-Seas, extremely scarce. Martyn, [Cypraea aurantium* Gmelin]   [Humphrey £3 5s.]
Lot 3832:– A very large and fine specimen of the white variety of Ostrea Malleus, *L.* brought by *Capt. Cooke* from the *Coral Reef*, off *Endeavour River*, on the Coast of *New Holland – very rare [Malleus albus* Lamarck]   [Cash £4 4s.]
Lot 3900:– A pair of large and beautiful specimens of Helix picta, or the painted Helix, a terrestrial shell, from the *W. Indies, very fine, – Rum.* 22. 1. [*Polymita picta* Born]   [Dillon £5 5s.][3]
Lot 3906:– Nautilus scrobiculatus, S. or Great umbilicated Nautilus, from *New Guinea, very rare. – Lister, 552. 4.-Knorr* IV. 22. 1. [*Nautilus scrobiculatus* Lightfoot]   [Dillon £4 6s.]
Lot 3926:– A large and fine specimen of *Voluta Nobilis, S.* an extremely rare, and very beautiful shell of the Wild Music kind, from *China. – Lister, 799. 6.-Martin III. 774. (Voluta corona nobilis* Lightfoot[4]
                    [Dillon £6 8s. 6d.]
Lot 3965:– A fine specimen of Voluta Arausiaca, S. or Prince of Orange's Flat Musick, from *Amboyna, very rare – Rum. 37. 2. [Harpulina arausiaca* Lightfoot]   [Dillon £5 5s.]
Lot 4021:– A very fine specimen of Voluta Aulica, S. a beautiful red clouded species of the wild Music kind, its country unknown, *unique* [*Aulica aulica* Sowerby]   [Dillon £12 12s.]

Lot 4024:– A most beautiful and perfect specimen of Voluta Gambaroonica, an undescribed species, from *Gambaroon*, in *Persia*, of which there is only one other known [*Aulicina nivosa* Lamarck]   [Dillon £23 2s.]

Lot 4025:– TURBO PULCHER, *or the* BEAUTY, *a marine turret-shaped Shell, smooth, of a white ground, with six broad undulated pink stripes,* extremely beautiful, *unique* [*Phasianella australis* Gmelin]
[Dillon £12 1s. 6d.]

Lot 4027:– A large and complete specimen of Conus Aurisiacus, L. or Orange Admiral, rich in colour, from *Amboyna* – *extremely scarce* [*Conus aurisiacus* L.]   [Dillon £18 7s. 6d.]

Lot 4041:– A magnificent specimen of Voluta Imperialis, the most perfect one known, from the *Straits of Malacca* – extremely scarce [*Voluocorona imperialis* Lightfoot]   [Dillon £24 3s.]

Source

Sale Catalogue of the Portland Sale, 1786, drawn up by Revd. John Lightwood, Chaplain and Librarian to the Duchess of Portland.

THE PORTLAND VASE AND THE SARCOPHAGUS IN WHICH IT WAS FOUND

THE interest, which has always been taken by men of taste and learning in that singular example of ancient art, now known as the Portland Vase, and which has been long fostered by its exhibition, through the favour of its noble owner, in a prominent position amidst the national collections, has been recently more deeply excited by the wanton attack which threatened its total annihilation.[5] From that lamentable condition we are happy to state it is now restored. Perhaps no broken vessel was ever before put together that had been shattered into so many pieces. This of course could never have been affected with certainty, had not the many models and drawings which have been made of it formed a decisive record of all its features in their proper position. Its reconstruction thus became merely a long and laborious puzzle; but the skilful ingenuity with which the task has been accomplished by Mr. Doubleday of the British Museum, and the cleverness with which he has in a great degree contrived to render imperceptible the innumerable lines of conjunction, would be sufficient to establish his immortality as the prince of restorers, and could not have been surpassed by the most experienced of the antiquaries of Italy. Most ordinary spectators, indeed, whose curiosity may have been raised on the matter, will perhaps be disappointed that they can detect so few traces of the havoc they look for; but a monument of Mr. Doubleday's skill will be preserved in a large water-colour drawing, which shows upon one surface, the multitudinous fragments into which the vase was separated, including a small box of minute portions, which have also now been worked up, (together with the cement,) in order to fill the smallest vacuities that would otherwise have been really deficient. The circular bottom, which the best judges now pronounce not to have been a part of the original vase, is alone omitted. It was formally invisible, from the vase always standing in a fixed position; but will now be set into the front of the pedestal below the vase.

Mr. Windus whose publication it is now our intention to notice, and the title of which we have subjoined below, was not attracted to the investigation of the Portland Vase by the late calamity. His work was at that time ready for the press, having been the subject of his studies from an early period of his life, and the principal object of his literary pursuits during the last five years. It must be a source of much gratification to Mr. Windus to have at length accomplished his favourite undertaking, and to have been enabled, by personal superintendence of the artists employed, to accompany his *New Elucidation* with plates which so faithfully represent the beauties of the original, and so highly embellish his volume.

The Portland Vase was first restored to mortal view during the papacy of Urban VIII, a member of the Barberini family, between the years 1623 and 1644. The accidental opening of an artificial hill called the Monte del Grano, three miles from Rome on the road to Frascati, disclosed the existence of a subterranean sepulchre of four several chambers, delineated in a plate of Bartoli's *Antiqui Sepolchri*, 1704, and of which Mr. Windus has given a copy. In one of the chambers was found a sarcophagus, carved with basreliefs on its sides, and surmounted by reclining effigies in the usual Roman style, resembling those which were brought from Etruria a few years ago, and placed in the British Museum, from the collection of Campanari.

Within this sarcophagus was found what is now called the Portland Vase. It contained the ashes of the decreased, which apparently had been inserted by its bottom being cut off or broken.

The sarcophagus on being removed was deposited in the museum of the Capitol, where it still remains; and the vase was placed in the library of the palace of the Barberini. The private circumstances of that family, about seventy years ago, induced their parting with some of their treasures, and this vase was purchased by James Byers esquire, an Englishman then resident at Rome. From his hands it passed into those of Sir William Hamilton, who sold it to the Duchess of Portland. At the sale of her Grace's valuable collection in 1786 it was purchased by her son the late Duke, and, by the permission of the present Duke, it has, since the year 1810 been exhibited in the British Museum.

The greatest curiosity of the Portland Vase perhaps, consists in its material, which for some time divided the opinions of connoisseurs as much as its designs. Many of the best of them believed that it was a natural stone, wrought within, as well as without, by the tool of the workman. Breval, in 1738, called it 'the famous vase of Chalcedony'; Bartoli termed it a sardonyx, De la Chausse an agate, and Montfaucon a precious stone. Count Caylus, better informed, referred to it as being of glass; and Wickelman speaks of it more particularly at the highest of the ancient works in that material.

We shall not attempt on the present occasion to go through the various interpretations which have been assigned to the bas-reliefs and other devices which are seen on this beautiful specimen of ancient glass. For them we shall refer to Mr. Windus's volume, and to that of Mr. Wedgwood which he has reprinted. We may content ourselves with repeating (what we before stated when describing the injuries of the Vase, in our Magazine for March last, p. 300) that the explanations which have been most accepted, since Mr. Wedgwood wrote, are those of Millingen and Thiersch.

Mr. Windus's theory is that both the Vase and Sarcophagus are commemorative of the great physician Galen. On one side the Vase exhibits three figures, a male and two females, naked to the waist, each seated on a rock. The central figure is a young female holding an inverted torch. This subject is considered by Milligen to represent the marriage of Peleus and Thetis, and by Thiersch that of Jason and Medea.

Mr. Windus explains it as follows:

A noble lady was said to lie in a very dangerous state, whose disorder Galen the physician discovered to be love, the object of which was a rope-dancer, Pylades. Galen valued himself most on this cure, as having rivalled the discovery of the love of Antiochus for his mother-in-law Stratonice, which gave so much celebrity to Erasistratus. The desponding female to the centre, with an inverted torch, is presumed to represent either Lucilla or Fadilla, daughters of Marcus Aurelius and the Empress Faustina * * * The male and female figures on the right and left of this figure are sympathising relatives. * * * These may represent Marcus Aurelius and Faustina.

On the other side,–

The noble lady appears rapidly restored by the approach of the object of her affection, allegorised by the springing up of the gyrating Hygeian serpent, the emblem of healing. Pylades, the rope-dancer, is advancing timidly from the Grecian portico or scena; although encouraged by the lady, who takes him by the arm, he appears to hesitate, and looks to Galen for advice with a very anxious countenance. The beautiful contemplative attitude of the great physician, as well as his dignified appearance, is worthy of notice. * * * Cupid soars above with blazing torch (in contrast to the one in the first compartment, nearly extinct,) expressive of the complete restoration of health as well as the torch of Hymen.

However, Mr. Windus finds even the accessory ornaments conducive to the support of his elucidation. The masks under the handles are

face-skins, allegorical of Esculapius, Hippocrates, or Galen, and are gracefully filleted on the handles of the vase, which scaled as serpents, constitute physical emblems. These visages are hypothetically characteristic of the profession of surgery; ... and the two leeches almost dropping from the extremity of the beard of one, complete the allegory without futher comment.

Such is Mr. Windus's *New Elucidation*, on the reality of which we cannot pretend definitively to decide, but must leave it to the judgment of the learned. If we have detailed it more concisely than is due to its merits, we must plead in excuse our limited space, and refer the reader for further satisfaction to Mr. Windus's work, in which many accessory arguments and illustrations will be found. Nor is he, after all, a bigot to his theory. Even the leeches do not adhere desperately to him; for he admits that many have supposed them to be leaves of the adjoining tree, but, he adds, 'on this point I crave a little indulgence to the phantasmagoria of my mind, in making out the novel thesis'.

With regard to the bottom of the vase, we have been informed that its material and execution are not equal to the vase itself, although of the same description. It appears to have been a portion of another vase of the same kind, fitted on after the original bottom had been destroyed, either at the time when the ashes were inserted and the vase deposited in the sarcophagus, or possibly in the 17th century, when it was restored to the upperworld. Restorations and matchings, equally difficult, are common with the ingenious Italians.

Its ornament is a hooded bust, which was described in our former article as 'Atys or Adonis, raising his hand to his mouth in the attitude of Horus'. Mr. Windus considers it to represent Angerona, the secret divinity who presided over the fate of Rome.

The first cast of the Sarcophagus that has ever been brought to this country has been imported at the expense of Mr. Windus, and has been recently exhibited at the Polytechnic Institution in Regent Street. Mr. Windus totally dissents from the idea of Bartoli, that the sepulchre was that of the Emperor Severus and Julia Mammaea, because that emperor died when under thirty years of age, and the effigy represents a man upwards of fifty; but he considers the reclining effigies to be those of Marcus Aurelius and his wife Faustina: the later 'represented as the goddess Ceres, with wheat-ears in her right hand'. The bas-relief in front he describes as follows:

> The principal, or front group, represents many patients, many well authenticated, as having been restored from illness by Galen at different periods. In the centre, of the greatest altitude of the whole, is the princess Faustina, wife of Marcus Aurelius, with her hand on the shoulder of a gladiator, whose fine attitude and characteristic appearance reminds us of Achilles. The next figure in front, a small female, is presumed to be Lucilla, or Fadilla, his daughter. The different braiding of the hair fully warrants, as is well known to antiquaries, the distinctions of mother and daughter. She is looking very earnestly, which is reciprocal, on an athletic character, with a horn in one hand and a pole in the other; this is supposed to be Pylades, the actor, or rope-dancer.

Mr. Windus thus pursues through-out the story of Galen, which has won his favourable attention,[7] less partial observers may be able to detect in the bas-reliefs nothing more than some of the best-known scenes of the Homeric poems. That in the front of the Sarcophagus appears to be the claim of Achilles for possession of the captive Briseis, in the presence of Agamemnon and Menalaus, who, as kings, are represented seated, but the former with emblems of greater dignity than the other. The bas-relief on the back of the Sarcophagus, Mr. Windus describes as *Galen, personified* as Priam, begging the body of Hector; such is evidently the subject, but Priam is surely *in propriâ personâ*.

We cannot conclude without the expression of a wish that the cast of the Sarcophagus may be admitted into the British Museum, as we think that, though even its original may be of very far inferior curiosity to the Vase itself, still it would be a very interesting addition to the repository in which the vase of which it was formerly the shrine, is now preserved.

Source

Gentleman's Magazine, 1846, 25: 41–4.

Notes

1   Martyn is Thomas Martyn (1760–1816) who is not to be confused with the Thomas Martyn, son of John Martyn (Chapter 31, this volume). This Thomas Martyn (1760–1816) was born in Coventry, moved to London by 1784 and ran a drawing academy in Great Marlborough Street. He was a natural historian and draughtsman, and published the *Universal Conchologist* (1784) which gave a drawing of every known shell.
2   The details in square brackets record the name of the buyer where this is known, and the price.
3   Dillon was a sales agent acting for the Duke of Calonne, who was a major continental shell collector. The catalogue of his collection is the *Museum Calonnianum*.
4   Most of these shells were valued partly for their rarity, and partly for their colours and exotic shapes, which attracted a corresponding romantic superstructure.
5   The vase had been loaned by the Portland family for display in the British Museum. On 7 February 1845 it was smashed in an act of vandalism by a young man apparently suffering from a hangover.
6   *A new Elucidation of the Subjects on the celebrated Portland Vase, formerly called the Barberini: and the Sarcophagus in which it was discovered.* By Thomas Windus, F.S.A. It is accompanied by a corresponding *Reprint of a Description of the Portland Vase, formerly the Barberini; the manner of its formation, and the various opinions hitherto advanced on the subjects of the Bas-reliefs.* By Josiah Wedgwood, F.R.S. F.S.A., with the addition of Notes by Thomas Windus, F.S.A. in juxtaposition to the most favoured theories, with his contrary opinions thereon.
7   Opinion has not supported Windus's view of the character of the scenes on the vase. It is now generally considered to depict events leading up to the birth of Achilles.

References

Dance, 1966
Williams, 1989

29

Captain Chapman sends Whitby fossils to the Royal Society Collection

The Royal Society (see Chapter 20, this volume) continued to meet throughout the eighteenth century, and to publish its *Philosophical Transactions*. In 1710 it had moved from Gresham College to new premises in Crane Street, and here it met and its collection was kept. However, in 1780, under the presidency of Sir Joseph Banks (this volume, Chapter 27), the society moved again to rooms in Somerset House in the Strand. The collection seems to have been something of a problem for some time, and in 1781 it was presented to the British Museum as a single donation, where it remains.

During the eighteenth century, the society continued to record finds of important material in its *Transactions* and, until 1781, to receive material into its collection. This letter from Captain William Chapman to John Fothergill, dated from Whitby, 20 January 1758 and read out at a Society meeting on 4 May 1758, records the discovery and subsequent presentation of the fossil bones belonging to a marine reptile over 2 metres long. The letter gives a good description of the circumstances of the find and the character of the bones.

Whitby is a small coastal town in Yorkshire on the mouth of the River Esk. It was the site of the famous Northumbrian religious house associated with Abbess Hilda and founded, Bede tells us, in 653. In the eighteenth century its yards built the ships for Captain Cook's voyages, and in the nineteenth it was to be made famous as the setting for Bram Stoker's novel *Dracula* (published 1897). The coast at Whitby has fragile cliffs composed of Jurassic Lias limestone, which represent the north-eastern end of the band of Jurassic limestone which runs across Britain, the cliffs at Lyme Regis (see this volume, Chapter 37) representing the south-western end. Both places were, and are, famous for the fossils which are preserved in the rocks of the seashore. The Whitby cliffs also produce jet and alum, needed for a large range of industrial processes.

Captain Chapman's account demonstrates how geological interests were progressing among the educated classes around the middle of the century, and how the collections of the Royal Society were growing. It also shows how the communication of intel-

lectual matters, through networks of contacts, letters and publications, was making enlightened study possible.

WHITBY FOSSILS

*An Account of the fossile Bones of an Allegator, found on the Sea-shore,
near* Whitby *in* Yorkshire. *In a Letter to* John Fothergill, M.D.[1] *from
Capt.* William Chapman.

Whitby, 20th of 1st mo. 1758.

Read May. 4, 1758.

A Few days since we discovered on the sea-shore, about half a mile from
this place, part of the bones of an animal, appearing as in the annexed
figure. The ground they laid in is what we call allum-rock; a kind of black
slate, that may be taken up in slates, and is continually wearing away by the
surf of the sea, and the washing of stones, sand, &c. over it every tide.

The bones were covered five or six feet with the water every full sea,
and were about nine or ten yards from the cliff, which is nearly perpen-
dicular, and about sixty yards high, and is continually wearing away, by
the washing of the sea against it; and, if I may judge by what has
happened in my own memory, it must have extended beyond these bones
less than a century ago. There are several regular strata or layers of stone,
of some yards thickness, that run along the cliff, nearly parallel to the
horizon and to one another. I mention this to obviate an objection, that
this animal may have been upon the surface, and in a series of years may
have sunk down to where it lay; which will now appear impossible, at
least when the stones, &c. have had their present consistence.

References to the Draught.[2]

A, B, C, the head and bill, not in the same line or range with the rest of the
    bones.

a, b, A bone, with its processes, which I take to be similar to that, which
    includes the brain in fishes. The part between the bone and outlines
    appeared to be a smooth membraine; but was so thin, that in taking up
    it broke. It is evident this is the upper part of the head inverted.

B, C, the superior *maxilla* intire, and in some places covered with the
    inferior one for four or five inches together. Where this happens, the
    vacuity is filled with matter like the rock in which it lays; and there
    are large teeth in each jaw, at such distances, and so posited, that those
    in one jaw fill up the vacuities in the other, and appear like one
    continued row, the mouth being shut.

Where there is only the superior *maxilla* remaining, there are no teeth; but the sockets are visible and deep, and at the same distances from each other as the teeth in the other part of the jaw. The tip or extremity of the bill was intire for four or five inches, having both *maxillae*, with their teeth, and towards the point large fangs. Part of the bill and head were covered with the rock; which was removed before they appeared as in the figure.

A, D, F, G, cavities in the rock, about two inches deep, where, I suppose, the wanting *vertebrae* have laid, as they are exactly suited to have received them.

D, F, Ten *vertebrae*, from three to four half inches in diameter, and about three inches long, some of them separated in taking up. They were about two inches in the rock.

E. Here is observed something like bone to stretch from the *vertebrae*, and intending to take it up whole, begun to cut at what we thought a proper distance; but found we cut thro' a bone; and with the *vertebrae* brought up three or four inches of the *os femoris*, with the ball, covered with the *periosteum*: but the animal has been so crushed hereabouts, that we could make little of the socket or *os innominata*. Several of the ribs came up with the *vertebrae*: they were broke, and laid parallel to the *vertebrae*; but not quite close, there being some of the rock between them. The *periosteum* is visible on many of the bones.

G, H, Twelve *vertebrae* remaining in the rock, with which they are almost covered, especially towards the extremity.

The place, where these bones lay, was frequently covered with sea-sand, to the depth of two feet, and seldom quite bare; which was the occasion of their being rarely seen: but being informed that they had been discovered by some people two or three years ago, we had one of them with us upon the spot, who told us, that when he first saw it, it was intire, and had two short legs on that part of the *vertebrae* wanting towards the head. Altho' we could not suspect the veracity of this person, we thought he was mistaken; for we had hitherto taken it for a fish. But when we took it up, and found the *os femoris* above-mentioned, we had cause to believe his relation true, and to rank this animal amongst those of the lizard kind: by the length (something more than ten feet) it seems to have been an allegator; but I shall be glad to have thy opinion about it.[3]

I am thy friend,

William Chapman, *Sen*
The bones were sent up, and are herewith presented to the Royal Society
by J. Fothergill.

Source

Philosophical Transactions of the Royal Society, 1758, 50, Part 2 (entry XCII): 688–91

Notes

1   John Fothergill was a medical doctor, and a member of the Royal Society.
2   This, and the letters, refer to an engraved plate which accompanied the letter.
3   The fossil bones, duly received into the Royal Society collection, passed with the rest of its material to the British Museum.

References

Birch, 1756
Hunter, 1989
Sprat, 1667

30

The Resta Collection of drawings is sold

One of the most celebrated collections of drawings ever to have come on to the English market was that assembled by Padre Sebastiano Resta, a Milanese collector, during the seventeenth century. Resta was born in Milan in 1635 and studied at the city's university. He went to Rome in 1665 and entered the Order of St Philip Neri. Apart from collecting drawings, he was the author of various Latin works, and he died at Rome in 1714. He had compiled a number of volumes of original drawings, one of which he presented to Philip V of Spain. The other volumes of drawings passed into the hands of Giovanni Matteo Marchetti and, after his death in 1704 to his nephew Marchetti of Pistoia, by whom they were offered for sale in 1709. The drawings numbered over 2,000, and were offered for £750 which could perhaps be beaten down to £600.

Letters from Resta to Guiseppe Magnavacca survive in Correggio, and one of these, dated from Rome on 19 April 1699, describes a collection of drawings, apparently bound in three books. The first volume is said to be full of old drawings from Giotto (represented by a crucifixion), Fra Angelico, Donatello, the young Raphael, Dürer and others. Its second part is described as containing works by Michelangelo, Leonardo and the mature Raphael and Titian. The second volume was said to have later material by artists like Valerio Campi, Passarotti and Carracci. (This letter seems to refer to the volumes marked I, II and III in Talman's letter: see extract below.) However, the real provenance of many of the drawings seems to have been very different. Popham (1936: 13) concluded that the collection as it survives contains no genuine material by Leonardo, Correggio, Raphael or Titian, but only copies of their work; what the collection may have had are drawings by the mannerists of the second half of the sixteenth century and the seventeenth century, not of the earlier masters.

The agent for the sale was John Talman (d. 1726) the son of William Talman, the architect of Chatsworth House, built by the second Duke of Devonshire (1665–1729), who himself was a significant collector of drawings. Talman spent much of his time in Italy, but in England became the first Director of the Society of Antiquaries in 1718. He, too, was a considerable collector, and his own collection is now in the Ashmolean Museum.

The letter from Talman printed here was addressed to Dean Aldrich of Christ Church, Oxford, and is the most thorough account of Resta's collection which has appeared in print. Talman sold part of the Resta Collection to Christ Church College, Oxford, and most of the rest to John Lord Somers (1651–1716), although his holdings were dispersed by auction after his death. The collection was sold at Mr Motteux's Auction Room in the Little-Piazza, Covent Garden on 16 May 1717. Many of these drawings are now in the Devonshire Collection at Chatsworth House.

JOHN TALMAN ON THE RESTA COLLECTION

Florence, March 2, N.S.[1]
17 09/10

Sir,
I have lately seen a collection of Drawings, without doubt, the finest in Europe, for the method and number of rare designs; nor is the price, considering the true value, at all too much. Mr. Envoy is of the same opinion, and has desired me to let an abstract of my catalogue, which I am making with all exactness, be copied out, to send to my Lord President – I send an abstract with this post, as I have done to Mr. Topham – to shew to several lords.

This collection belonged to Monsignor Marchetti, bishop of Arezzo, now in possession of Chevalier Marchetti of Pistoia, nephew to the said bishop; which collection is to be sold. It consisteth of 16 volumes, folio (14 inches broad, and 20 high) gilt, and bound in red Turkey leather: They were at first collected by the famous Father Resta, a Milanese, of the oratory of Philippo Neri at Rome; a person so well known in Rome, and all over Italy, for his skill in drawings, that it would be needless to say any more of him, than that these collections were made by him, and that through the whole work, he has abundance of observations (gathered by the application and experience of fifty years), no where else to be seen; every book being filled with Notes on each drawing, with several recollections of those who have wrote the lives of Painters. The design of this work is to shew the rise and fall of painting in divers periods of time.

In the 1st Vol. (which is bound as above mentioned, and is fourteen inches broad and twenty high) painting is divided[2] into 'Pictura, nascente, crescente, et adulta.' In the first page are the heads of those Popes, who reigned during the said periods in the time of Gregory IX, 1227, containing twenty-one Popes. The IId, in the time of Innocent VI, 1352, containing fourteen Popes. The third period in the time of Paul II, 1464, containing five Popes. In the Index are all the names of the painters whose works are contained in this volume. It contains pages 69, and drawings 137, of the most considerable masters. In this book are Albert Durer, 2. Leonard de Vinci, 3. M. Angelo, 4. Andreas Mantegna, 27. P. Perugino, 4. Raph. Urbin, 7. Under every drawing in this and all other books is set down the master's name, from whence it came, by whom given, and when.

The IId Vol., red as the former, containeth the golden age, or painting compleat, with a copious Index; there are nine pages relating to the work of Buonaroti, Raphael, Titian, and Correggio, the heads of the golden age. Leonardo da Vinci, as being the most antient, and first who gave light to this age, is placed by himself, and forms a class alone; but by way of introduction, to shew the drawing of this bright period, here are exhibited some specimens of the masters of the aforesaid four heads of grand families, viz. of Girlandaio, master to M. Angelo; of John Bellini, master to Giorgione and Titian; of P. Perugino, master to Raphael; of Andr. Mantegna, master to Correggio. The first drawing in this book, is the Ritratto of Bramantino, a Milanese painter, who, though properly belonging to the former period, yet to do honour to the country of Father Resta, a Milanese, where he did so much in the art of painting as to be esteemed the introducer of the golden age into that city, is therefore placed in the front. Before the annotations is set the Ritratto of Father Resta, looking on this Vol. and as it were shewing it with great joy to Carlo Maratta: This drawing was made by the said Carlo, 1689, as his own handwriting undernearth shews.

This book contains 169 pages and 300 drawings. This age began in the pontificate of Julius II, and comprises that of Paul III, &c. This tome ends in the reign of Julius III. And the last design but one is a beautiful Cartel, containing the arms of that Pope, supported by the figures of Justice and Victory, to intimate that this age terminated triumphantly. The number of Drawings of the principal masters are, Andr. del Sarto, 6. B. Baninelli, 6. Correggio, 5. Dan. di Volterra, 9. Giorgione, 7. Giulio Romano, 15. Leonardo da Vinci, M. Angelo, 14. Portenone, 9. Polidoro, 28. Parmeggiano, 16. Penno, 19. Raphael, 7. Titian, 6. Vasario, 4.

The IIId Vol. contains the practical or age of experience, beginning in the time of Pius IV. 1560, comprehending ten Popes, to 1591. The division is into three grand schools, Zuccari, Mutiano, and the Carracci; under which three heads, all the other masters are ranged. This book has 222 pages, 330 drawings.

Vol. IV. This is called the age of painting restored by Carracci, is bound as the former, and is as it were a second part of the last school in Vol. III.–Pages 144. With an appendix, 7 pages, and drawings 221.

Vol. V. This Volume, bound more richly than the other four, is against Visari, or Florentin Vasari against Bolonese Vasari. The title of the book is 'Felsina vindicata,' or, 'Felsina in aureo seculo argentea, in argenteo aurea.' The last drawing in this book, is a victory of Correggio, to shew that Lombardy justly triumphs over Tuscany, pages 87, drawings all bordered with gold, 109.

Vol. VI. This contains the ancient Greek paintings in the Mosaicks at Rome, and elsewhere, all by one hand, number 24, bound in parchment, gilt back and sides.

Vol. VII. Curious landskips and views of towns, with borders of gold. Pages 60, drawings 96. Bound in plain parchment, no index. These drawings are all of the great masters.

Vol. VIII. Saggio Dei Secoli (curiously bound in blue Turkey leather, all gilt sides and back gilt) or specimens of painting for five centuries, viz. 1300 to 1700 inclusive, beginning with the story of Coriolanus, done by Carracci, from the baths of Titus at Rome, and a most curious miniature of Cimabue: No index. The drawings are bordered with gold. Pages 79, drawings 110. The two last drawings are of Caracci, as well as that in the beginning after Corial; for which reason there is wrote underneath: 'Let us end with the best, since that, Finis habet rationem optimi, et sic respondent ultima primis.'

Vol. IX. This is called, senators in the Cabinet, or, The cabinet council of the grand Judges of art, to whose works, exhibited in this book, all causes of appeal are to be carried. These senators are Leonardi da Vinci, M. Angelo, Andr. del Sarto, Georgione, Titian, Raphael and Correggio, for the grand tribunal, or high court of Parliament, for the golden age. For the prerogative court, in the beginning of the silver age, or Hilary term, the judges are Zuccari, Barocci and Procaccino; none are permitted to plead in these courts, but such as are truly worthy and experienced persons: Lafranco, with his great Correggiescan Carracescan genius, is the last of those in this book, and of the cabinet council. His school opens the grand senate of both houses of parliament, and courts of common law: But Hannibal Caracci, by a special privilege, can vote in all courts, and in all causes. The drawings 43, all bordered with gold, and of the prime masters only. Pages 24. No Index.

Vol. X. Saggio Dei Secoli, shewing specimens of paintings in the early ages, beginning with the drawing of a Greek, in the time of Cimabue and Giotto. Drawings 150, bordered with Gold; the Index not finished.

Vol. XI. and XII. Two books (red Turkey leather), eleven inches broad, sixteen inches high, full of curious drawings of all sorts of masters, for 200 years; designed for entertainment, without any regard to the history of painting; through every drawing hath notes to it. In the first book, pages 111, drawings 144. In the second, pages 70, drawings 172; among which are a great many of Raphael's, and the other great masters.

Vol. XIII. A small, but very excellent series of drawings (bound in parchment gilt), placed in order of time and beginning with P. Perugino, 1446, are brought down to the present time. Here among the drawings of

Raphael, is one, which the father calls the Oriental Pearl. Pages 40, drawings 72; adorned with gold.

Vol. XIV. This book contains 'Schemata prima Tholi, magni monuments laboris,' or several designs for the Cupola of Parma, viz.. three different designs for the assumption, and two for the apostles, all in red chalk, by Correggio. Pages 7, drawings 5; with large notes.

Vol. XV. This Volume has more designs for the said Cupola, of the hand of Correggio: and with abundance of notes. This volume, with the last, are of a size bigger than all the rest, broad eighteen inches, high twenty-eight inches.

Vol. XVI. This Volume contains a variety of designs of all the great masters, as of Correggio, his disciples and imitators, &c. In the title page is an emblem, with this motto. 'Nostri quondam libamen amoris.' Pages 65, drawings 219. Of the principal masters, del Sarto, 4. Procacino, 3. Baroci, 4. Bernin, 2. Correggio, 35. Lod. Caracci, 12. Anab. Caracci, 12. Polidoro, 4. Parmeggiano, 19. Cortona, 3. Raphael Urbin, 10. A Sacchi, 2. Titian, 4. Zuccari, 5. The last drawing but one is a lofty and noble portico, called the Academical; in which are represented Father Resta, and several other figures, bringing this collection to the bishop, who is sitting in a chair with the Cavalier Marchetti, his nephew, standing by him; to whom the bishop, by laying his hand on his heart, shews the great satisfaction he has in being the possessor of so noble a collection, which consists of 2111 drawings.

This great drawing is of Passeri, and finely coloured. Total number of drawings in this whole collection, excepting those books where there are no Indexes: Leon. da Vinci, 12. M. Angelo, 27. Andr. Mantegna, 23. Perugino, 6. R. Urbini, 25. Andr. del Sarto, 10. B. Bandinelli, 6. Corregio, 63. Dan di Volterra, 6. Georgione 7. Jul. Romano, 15. Pordinone, 9. Polidoro, 32. Parmens, 35. Perino, 21. Titian, 12. Bernin, 14. Sacchi, 8. The 5 Caracci, 74. Domenichino, 45. Guido, 6. Della Bella, 12. Callot, many. In all, with the rest mentioned in this catalogue, 527. For which 2111 drawings, they demand three thousand crowns, or 750 L sterling. I hope they will fall one thousand, which will bring it to Five hundred pounds. If they are worth any money, they are worth six hundred pounds sterling.

Sir,
Your most humble servant,
JOHN TALMAN.

Source

Herrmann, F., 1972, *The English as Collectors*, London, Chatto & Windus: 107.

Notes

1 This date reflects the use by Talman of the improved calendar: NS = New Style
2 The collection was arranged in a complicated historical and metaphorical system

References

Herrmann, 1972
Popham, 1936

31

Thomas Martyn collects collectors

In 1766 a work called *The English Connoisseur: containing an account of whatever is curious in painting, sculpture etc. in the palaces and seats of the nobility and principal gentry of England both in town and country* was published in London. This cumbersome title, in the style of the day, hid a compendium of information about fine art collections then existing in England. The style is sometimes rather monotonous, but the quantity of detail of great interest.

The editor of the work was subsequently identified as Thomas Martyn (1735–1825) who is chiefly known as a botanist (and not to be confused with the Thomas Martyn (1760–1816), who published the *Universal Conchologist* in 1784). Thomas was born in London, the son of John Martyn. He was an undergraduate at Cambridge and in 1762 was elected Professor of Botany at Cambridge. He was ordained a minister of the Church of England as a young man, and held a series of livings, taking two years away between 1778–80 to undertake a protracted Continental tour. In 1773 he began publication of *The Antiquities of Herculaneum*, translated from the Italian, although this caused some difficulties with the court of Naples, and the project had to stop. He published many botanical works, as well as *The English Connoisseur*. His father John, who was also a botanist, was a friend of Sloane and a correspondent of Linnaeus, and also held the Chair of Botany at Cambridge. When he died, there were 2,600 specimens in his herbarium.

The two volumes of *The English Connoisseur* describe the contents of the collections at Blenheim (owned by the Duke of Marlborough), Chatsworth (Duke of Devonshire), Ditchley (Earl of Litchfield), Hampton Court (part of the royal collection) and Houghton Hall (Sir Robert Walpole) among other country houses. In London, they give details of the material held by the Society of Antiquaries, the Foundling Hospital in Lamb's Conduit Fields, the College of Physicians, St Paul's Cathedral, Shaftesbury House and Somerset House, among others. In Oxford the books cover collections in the Ashmolean Museum and a number of colleges.

Among the 'country' collections, Martyn described the collection of Mr Paul Methuen, based on a catalogue of his material compiled by Horace Walpole. The collection descended to Lord Methuen of Corsham House, near Bath, where many of the paintings are still; others were sold at Christie's in 1840, 1899 and 1920. The Preface to the volumes, and the account of Methuen's collection, are given here.

ENGLISH COLLECTIONS IN 1766

PREFACE

The great progress which the polite arts have lately made in England, and the attention which is now paid them by almost all ranks of men; seem to render an apology for a work of this nature wholly unnecessary. The only way, by which we can ever hope to arrive at any skill in distinguishing the stile of the different masters in Painting, is the study of their works: any assistance therefore in this point cannot but be grateful to the rising Connoisseur. It is well known at how few of those houses into which, by the indulgence of their illustrious owners, the curious are admitted, any catalogues of the paintings and other curiosities, which adorn them can be obtained; and without such catalogues it must be confessed little use can be made, by the yet uninformed observer of these valuable collections, besides that general one of pleasing the eye and the imagination, by viewing a variety of delightful objects. The editor of the following trifle, aware of the necessity of such assistance, when he first designed to travel about his native country, in order among other views to become acquainted with the manner of such principal masters in painting, looked out for books giving an account of the curiosities which the seats of the nobility and gentry, in various parts of the kingdom, contain. From the few that fell into his hands, he abstracted what he thought was to his purpose; and in his progresses, corrected in them whatever he thought amiss, and made addition when he found them deficient. Where no catalogue had been before printed he endeavoured to obtain one, or to make out such a one as he was able to do, from a survey of the house and information. If this work, which the editor here offers the young student in the polite arts, should at all contribute to promote of facilitate the study of them among his countrymen, he will have gained all the end which he aims at.

The curious observer will find ample and instructive lessons on the Italian schools in the houses of our nobility and gentry. Mr. Walpole[1] scruples not to assert that 'there are not a great many collections left in Italy more worth seeing than that at Houghton. In the preservation of the pictures it certainly excells most of them.'

It should be observed in commendation of the taste which our illustrious countrymen in general have showed, that they have preferred the greatness of design and composition in which the Italian masters are so well known to excell, before the gaudy Flemish colouring, 'or the drudging mimickry of nature's most uncomely coarseness, upon which the Dutch so much value themselves. To deny these their proper share of merit, or to refuse them a place in a colleciton, would be ridiculous; but surely to set them in competition with Italian sublimity is much more so.

When the editor was in Holland, the great predilection of the Dutch for their own painters could not escape his observation; scarce anything being seen in their cabinets but the laboured productions of their own masters. In France, where he had the pleasure of surveying abundance of Italian pictures, and where the Orleans Collection alone would compensate the pains of any traveller; he could not but often smile to see the tawdry productions of their own artists set upon a level, nay sometimes, with true French vanity even jostling or thrusting aside the divine productions of the Italian Pencils. At this time he could scarcely help felicitating his own countrymen, upon their not having produced artists of sufficient eminence, to give them a pretence of buying a taste for real merit and greatness under national projudice.

When this, however, is said in commendation of the predominant taste of the English, it is not to be understood, as if there were wanting among us sufficient specimens of their Dutch or Flemish schools; we only have them not in so great number of perfection as in Holland and Flanders ...

The editor cannot help concluding with a wish that the nobility and gentry would condescend to make their cabinets and collections accessible to the curious as is consistent with their safety. The polite arts are rising in Britain, and call for the fostering hand of the rich and powerful: one certain way of advancing them, is to give all possible opportunities to those who make them their study, to contemplate the works of the best masters that they may not form a bad taste and a poor manner upon such productions as chance throws in their way. It ought to be acknowledged with gratitude, that many of the collections of the great, are ever open to the inspection of the curious; who have been permitted by some in the most liberal manner to take copies of their paintings, and to make drawings from them; but at the same time it must be lamented that some cabinets are not accessible without difficulty and interest. It should be mentioned to the honour of the French nation, that their collections are come at, even by foreigners, with great facility: in particular the royal pictures are not locked up in private apartments from the eye of the people, but are the pictures of the public.

To anyone who is desirous of becoming acquainted with the principles of Painting without much labour, the editor would recommend *Count Algarotti's* elegant little treaties or *Essay on Painting*, written in the Italian language and lately translated into English.

THE COLLECTION OF MR PAUL METHUEN

PAUL METHEUN ESQ.
In Grosvenor-Street

ON THE FIRST FLOOR [The second floor has been omitted.]

IN THE HALL AND STAIR-CASE

Over the Chimney
A Naked Boy blowing bubbles, and treading on a Death's Head, representing Vanity by *Elizabeth Sirani.*

Near the Street Door
A large picture of Dogs and Foxes, by *Peter Snyders.*

Over the Door that goes into the first Parlour
A Man's Head, by *Gioseppe de Ribera*, commonly called *Il Spagnoletto.*

On the Landing Place
A large picture of David and Abigail, by *Sir Peter Paul Rubens.*

Over the Door
The Adventure of Don Quixote and the Barber, by a Spanish Painter.

Fronting the Landing-Place at the Top
The Portrait of the Duchess of Mantua, Grand-daughter to the Emperor Charles the Fifth, with her Son in her lap, who was the last Duke of Mantua, with some allegorical figures, armour, &c. by *Giovanni Benedetto Castiglione.*

Under it
A Landscape, and a musical conversation, painted by *Sir Peter Lely*; being the portraits of himself and his whole Family, drawn by the life.

Fronting the Windows
The Judgement of Paris, by *Gerard Lairess.*

Under it
The Judgement of Midas, by the same hand.

Over the Looking-Glass
A young Lad blowing bubbles, said to be painted by *Annibal Caracci.*

IN THE FIRST *PARLOUR*

Over the Chimney
A Dutch Kermis, or Country Friar, painted by old *Peter Brughel.*

On each side of the Chimney – Next the Window
The Portrait of a Turk, by *Rembrandt Van Ryhn.*
David with the Head of Goliath and his sling, by *Leonello Spada.*

Between the Windows
A Man's Head, said to be that of Massaniello the Fisherman, who caused the great revolution of Naples, by *Salvator Rosa.*
The Portrait of Francisco de Taxis, the first inventor of the Posts in Europe, for which reason the direction of them had always reminded in one of his Family in all the dominions that belong to the House of Austria, by a hand not certainly known.

Over the Doors out of the Hall
The Folly of spending our Lives in the Pursuit of Love, Wine, Music and play, an emblematical picture by *Johannes Schorel.*
The Virgin, Our Saviour, Mary Magdalen, St Peter, John the Baptist and St Jerome, by *Jacobo Palma.*

Over the Marble Table
The Birth of Our Saviour, and the Adoration of the Shepherds, by *Giac. Bassan.*

Under it in the Middle
St John the Baptist asleep in the desart, by *Andrea del Sarto.*

On both Sides of it
Two small Sea Pieces, a port in the Mediterranean, and a fight with the Turks, by *William Vandervelde*, Junior.

Under them, in the Middle
An emblematic picture, representing a guardian Angel pointing out the way to Heaven to a soul, under the figure of a young girl, by *Carlo Dolce.*

On both Sides of it
Two very highly finished Landscapes on Copper, by *Salvator Rosa.*

Between the two Doors
The Portrait of the Duke of Richmond and Lenox, of the Stuart Family, at whole length, with a Dog, by *Vandyke.*

Over the Door to the Back Parlour
Vulcan at his forge, with the Cyclops, by *Jacob Jordans*, of Antwerp.

Over against the Windows – in the Middle
The Head of our Saviour crowned with Thorns, by *Ludovico Caracci.*

On both Sides of that
Two Fruit Pieces, by *Michael Angelo Pase*, called *Michael Angelo del Campidoglio.*

Under them, in the Middle
A Bacchanal in two colours, by *Rubens.*

On both Sides of it
Landscape, with a Robbery, and a Beatle, both painted by *Giacomo Cortese*, commonly called *Il Bourgognone.*

Under them, in the Middle
A pretty large landscape, and figures of Dutch Boors, by *Adrian Van Ostade.*

On both Sides of it
A Stag-hunting, and another of Hern Hawking, by *Philip Woverman.*

Under them
Two Conversations of Boors within doors, by *Ostade.*

IN THE SECOND PARLOUR

Over the Chimney
Lot and his two Daughters, with the city of Sodom on Fire, by *Lorenzo Lotti*, a great imitator of *Giorgione* and *Titian.*

Over the Closet Doors – Next the Window
The great amphitheatre at Rome, and other buildings, by *Viviano Cadaborra.*
A Sea Port, with Buildings and Ruins, by *Salvoiuch*, and the Figures by *John Miele.*

Over the Door to the First Parlour
Amphale the Mistress of Hercules, with the Lion's Skin and his Club by her, by *Augustin Caracci*.

Over the two Doors
Two Battles in the style of *Bourgognone*, but the hands not certainly known.

IN THE PASSAGE ROOM

Over the Doors
A Philosopher with a Book in his hand, by *Pier Francesco Mola*.
Mary Magdalen, by *Giacinto Brandi*.
Our Saviour meditating on the Sins of the world, by *Giovanni Antonia Regillio*, a competitor of Titian, and commonly called *Il Portanone*.

IN THE GREAT ROOM

Over the Door at which you go in
The Portrait of a young Man on wood, by *Andrea del Sarto*.

Between that Door and the Windows
The Head of St James the Apostle.
The Head of St John the Evangelist.
N.B. These two last pictures are by a hand not certainly known.

Under them
A Bacchanal painting on copper, by *Cornelius Polemburgh*.

Between the Door and the Wall – in the Middle
A pretty large picture of Our Saviour and the Samaritan Woman, by *Giovanni Francesco Barbiori da Cento*, commonly called *Il Guercino*.

On the Side towards the Door
The Virgin and Child, by *Il Cavalier Giovanni Langranchi*.

On the Side towards the Wall
Venus dressing, and Cupid holding her Looking Glass, by *Paolo Veronese*.

Under them, in the Middle
The Virgin and Child, by *Raphael de Urbino*.

On the Side towards the Door
The Virgin and Child in the Clouds, and several Angels, by *Bartholomeo Murillo.*

On the Side towards the Wall
The Virgin and our Saviour, by *Carlo Cignani.*

Next to the Door
The Annunciation of the Virgin Mary, by *Paolo Veronese.*

Next to the Wall
The Birth of our Saviour, &c. by *Jacopo Robusti*, commonly called, *Tintoretto.*

Over the Chimney
Tobit and the Angel, by *Michael Angelo Caravaggio.*

Between the Wall and the Chimney – in the Middle
The Portrait of a Man, by *Antonio Allegri*, commonly called *Il Corregio.*

Towards the Wall
The Head of some Spanish General, by *Giovanni Giachinette*, commonly called *Il Bourgagnone delle Teste.*

Towards the Chimney
The Portrait of the Famour Fernando Cortes, conqueror of Mexico, by Titiano Vecelli, called *Il Titiano.*

Under them
A large Battle in an oval, painted by *Luca Jordano.*

Between the Chimney and the farthest Wall – in the middle
St Sebastian, by *Guido Reni.*

Next to the Chimney
The Portrait of St [sic] Anthony Vandyke, painted by *Himself.*

Next to the Wall
The Portrait of a young Girl, with a little dog asleep in her hands, by *Rembrandt.*

Under them
A large oval Battle, painted by *Luca Jordano.*

Over the Closet Door
The Portrait of a Man with a book in his hand, said to be the famous satyrist Berni, by *Giorgio Barbarelli*, called *Il Giorgione*.

Between the Door and the Wall
A She Saint, with Angels, by *Pietro Beretini*, called *Pietro Cortona*.

Under it in the Middle
A small Battle, by *Bourgognone*.

On both sides of it
Two small pictures, done from the Gallery of Arch-Duke Leopold, the one from Paris Bourdon, and the other from young Palma, by *David Teniers*.

Between the Door and the Window
A large picture, representing our Saviour at the Pharisee's house, and Mary Magdalen annointing his feet, with the portrait of the person for whom it was painted, as a servant waiting at table, by *Carlo Dolce*.
N.B. This Picture is out of the stile of *Carlo Dolce's* painting, who never before attempted so great a subject and composition; and was done by him after the drawing of *Ludovico Cigoli*.

Under it in the Middle
The Portraits of three of Henry the 7th's Children, viz. Prince Arthur, Henry the 8th, and Princess Mary, who was afterwards Queen of France, and Dutchess of Brandon, by a hand not certainly known.

On both sides of it
Two pieces of the history of Judith, the one where she is presented to Holofernes, and the other where she is entertained by him at a feast, by *Paolo Veronese*.

Source

Martyn, T., 1766, *The English Conoisseur ...*, London

Notes

1   Walpole expresses this view in his *Aedes Walpolianae*, Introduction. Martyn quotes the same source a few lines on.

2 The reader will notice that the Methuen collection includes a considerable
   range of paintings.

References

Herrmann, 1972
Simpson, 1950

32

Alexander Pope mocks collectors and their habits

During the first half of the eighteen century, the connections between literary and political London were particularly close. One important group centred on the Whig leader, Sir Robert Walpole, and the other considered itself to be Tory and gathered around the Prince of Wales, Frederick (the son of George II and father of George III; he never reigned himself, dying before his father). The Tory group included writers like Swift, Congreve and Gay, and with these was Alexander Pope.

Pope was born a Londoner and a Catholic, his father was a linendraper, and he had both poor health and a poor education. However, his talent for poetry was recognised early by powerful Catholic connections and his first major work, *Essay on Criticism*, was produced in 1711, to be followed by the two versions of his *Rape of the Lock* (1712 and 1714), a mock-heroic epic. His translation into verse of Homer's *Iliad* was completed in 1725, and made him enough money to settle comfortably in his villa at Twickenham, on the Thames, near London. Here he built his famous 'grotto', actually a tunnel connecting his garden with a lawn running beside the river.

Pope planned a work entitled *Moral Essays* which was to have been ten epistles, but of which only the first four were written, between 1731 and 1735. Epistle IV was addressed to Richard Boyle, Earl of Burlington, a friend of Pope's and the man who rebuilt Burlington House in Piccadilly, London, along classical lines and did much to set the classical tone of Georgian architecture. The plan of the poetic epistle was to discuss the use of riches, with the need to temper expense with proportion and harmony.

Like much of Pope's work, the epistle is full of references to contemporary people and events, often sarcastic and critical in tone. Some of this was part of the political in-fighting of the day, but some seems simply to be a part of Pope's own temperament and vision of the world.

EPISTLE

'Tis strange, the Miser should his Cares employ,
To gain those Riches he can ne'er enjoy:
Is it less strange, the Prodigal should waste
His wealth, to purchase what he ne'er can taste?
Not for himself he sees, or hears, or eats;
Artists[1] must chuse his Pictures, Music, Meats:
He buys for Topham,[2] Drawings and Designs,
For Pembroke,[3] Statues, dirty Gods, and Coins;
Rare monkish Manuscrips for Hearne[4] alone,
And Books for Mead,[5] and Butterflies for Sloane:[6]
Think we all these are for himself? no more
Than his fine Wife, alas! or finer Whore.
    For what has Virro painted, built, and planted?
Only to show, how many Tastes he wanted.
What brought Sir Visto's ill got wealth to waste?
Some Daemon whisper'd, 'Visto! have a Taste.'
Heav'n visits with a Taste the wealthy fool,
And needs no Rod but Ripley with a Rule.[7]
See! sportive fate, to punish aukward pride,
Bids Bubo[8] build, and sends him such a Guide:
A standing sermon, at each year's expense,
That never Coxcomb reach'd Magnificence!
. . .

    At Timon's Villa[9] let us pass a day,
Where all cry out, 'What sums are thrown away!'
So proud, so grand, of that stupendous air,
Soft and Agreeable come never there.
Greatness, with Timon, dwells in such a draught
As brings all Brobdignag before your thought.
To compass this, his building is a Town,
His pond an Ocean, his parterre a Down:
Who but must laugh, the Master when he sees,
A puny insect, shiv'ring at a breeze!
Lo, what hugh heaps of littleness around!
The whole, a labour'd Quarry above ground.
Two Cupids squirt before: a Lake behind
Improves the keenness of the Northern wind.
His Gardens next your admiration call,
On ev'ry side you look, behold the Wall!
No pleasing Intricacies intervene,

No artful wildness to perplex the scene;
Grove nods at grove, each Alley has a brother,
And half the platform just reflects the other.
The suff'ring eye inverted Nature sees,
Trees cut to Statues, Statues thick as trees,
With here a Fountain, never to be play'd,
And there a Summer-house, that knows no shade'
Here Amphitrite sails thro' myrtle bow'rs;
There Gladiators fight, or die, in flow'rs;
Un-water'd see the drooping sea-horse mourn,
And swallows roost in Nilus' dusty Urn.
 My Lord advances with majestic mien,
Smit with the mighty pleasure, to be seen:
But soft – by regular approach – not yet –
First thro' the length of yon hot Terrace swet,
And when up ten steep slopes you've dragg'd your thighs,
Just at his Study-door he'll bless your eyes.
 His Study! with what Authors is it stor'd?
In Books, not Authors, curious is my Lord;
To all their dated Backs he turns you round,
These Aldus[10] printed, those Du Suëil has bound.[11]
Lo some are Vellom, and the rest as good
For all his Lordship knows, but they are Wood.
For Locke or Milton 'tis in vain to look,
These shelves admit not any modern book.

Source

Epistle IV to Richard Boyle, Earl of Burlington, Alexander Pope.

Notes

1 'Artists' here means 'experts'.
2 Richard Topham (d. 1735), Keeper of Records at the Tower. His important collection of artworks was bequeathed to Eton College.
3 Thomas Herbert, Earl of Pembroke (1656–1733), a Whig politician who collected art and antiquities.
4 Thomas Hearne (1678–1735), an Oxford man who edited medieval manuscripts and left his collection to the Bodleian Library in Oxford.
5 Richard Mead (1673–1754), Physician-in-Ordinary to George II and Queen Caroline. He had a major library of some 30,000 volumes.
6 Sir Hans Sloane (1660–1735) see this volume, Chapter 23.

7 Ripley was said to be a carpenter, employed by Sir Robert Walpole and commissioned by him to act as architect for various public buildings; Walpole finally made him Comptroller of the Board of Works.

8 'Bubo' was George Bubb, who later called himself Doddington and finally became Baron Melcombe (1671–1762). 'Bubo' is Latin for 'fowl'. Bubb completed the building of the mansion at Eastbury, Dorset.

9 'Timon' has sometimes been identified as John Brydges, Duke of Chandos, who had a magnificent house at Canons. He was one of Pope's patrons, and the identification may not be correct.

10 Aldo Manutio was a famous Renaissance Venetian printer.

11 Abbé du Sueil was a famous early eighteenth-century Parisian bookbinder.

References

Butt, 1963: 58–93

33

Gowin Knight's proposal for the establishment of the British Museum and for Sloane's collection within it

At the age of eighty-one, Sir Hans Sloane retired from his house at Bloomsbury to his country home at Chelsea. He planned to make his great collection the nucleus of a national collection, and accordingly left a will, the final form of which, prepared in 1751, made his intentions clear. The purchase price to be asked of the King, George II, was £20,000, and Sloane named a number of trustees, one of whom was Horace Walpole. George did not wish to make the purchase, and eventually a state lottery was instituted to raise the purchase price and funds for the purchase of a suitable building. This would house not only Sloane's collection, but also the books and manuscripts collected by Cotton and Harley. On 7 June 1753, George II assented to the Act of Parliament which created the British Museum.

An existing, rather than a new, building was needed because it would be less expensive, and Montague House in Bloomsbury was chosen. It was built around 1680 by the Duke of Montague in the French style, and had had its interior refitted soon after 1686 following a serious fire. The museum conversion work took some time, and the building did not open until 1759. In theory, access was free to all, but this was impossible in practice, and both opening hours and the issue of tickets were deliberately used as limiting devices. Until 1863, armed sentries stood at the entrance, who must have made their own point.

Sir Gowin Knight was the British Museum's first Principal Librarian, whose plans for the institution (extracted below) were drawn up some three years before its official opening in 1759. The extract here makes very clear a number of basic parameters for what might be termed a new 'museum science' – a museological rationale that stood in marked contrast to the thinking that had informed museum practice throughout the seventeenth century. Firstly, it reveals just how much careful thought was given to the manner in which the visiting public, or 'spectators' as Knight calls them, would perceive the collection. Secondly, it shows the extent to which he clearly expected the display to exemplify a very particular vision of the natural order. And finally, it indicates the way in which this preoccupation with taxonomic order descended to quite specific matters of display – of room layout and even exhibition furniture. In line with Knight's proposals the initial layout of the British Museum in Montague house in 1759 duly had four successive rooms designated K, L, M and N devoted to fossils, shells, plants and insects, and zoology; though some of the finer details of Knight's scheme had inevitably to be sacrificed for the sake of practical utility.

By the 1760s, the ideas expressed by Knight were being echoed in the attempts of other 'curators' charged to rejuvenate established museums like the Ashmolean and the Royal Society's Repository. William Huddesford, describing his task at the former, talked in terms of 'bringing them [the "Good and Valuable Specimens"], to Light in proper and decent ornaments'; while Henry Baker, working with the latter, set about cleaning and arranging the collections, so 'as to make an handsome Appearance, ... to be seen with Ease' (MacGregor and Turner 1986: 653; Additional MS. 5166: 240).

Particularly potent evidence for the character of this late eighteenth-century regime is to be found in the museum furniture associated with it, some of which still survives in museums and historic houses today. Indeed, the English cabinets of the late eighteenth century – 'those curious and neat pieces of furniture, used by ladies, in which to preserve their trinkets, and other curious matters', as Thomas Sheraton described them – embody something of a caricature of this mentality (Sheraton 1803: 115). It is their careful, almost fussy, distribution of doors, wings, shelves, drawers and niches that speaks loudest of the consuming passion for order; and their wide glass fronts, delicate inlays, well-turned legs, and showy panels that so dramatically portray the equally dominant concern for presentation and display.

THE PLAN FOR THE COLLECTIONS BY DR GOWIN KNIGHT, 1756

Agreeable to the desire of the Committee, Dr. Knight delivered in *a plan for the General Distribution of Sir Hans Sloane's Collection* of natural and other products.

The Greatest and most valuable part of this Collection consists of things relating to Natural History: wherefore that part will first claim our attention, and will merit a particular regard in the general distribution.[1]

All the articles that come under the head may be properly classed in the three general divisions of Fossils, Vegetables and Animals. Of these the Fossils are the most simple; and therefore may be properly disposed in the first Rank: next to them the Vegetables; and lastly the animal substances. By this arrangement the Spectator will be gradually conducted from the simplest to the most compound, and most perfect of nature's productions. I would therefore humbly propose that the Fossils may be placed in the first room next to the Saloon; and when they are properly disposed, to begin with the Vegetables where the Fossils end, either in the same room or in the next according as the space will permit. In like manner the Vegetables may be succeeded by the Animals and animal substances: and since there is found in Nature a gradual and almost insensible transition from one kind of natural production to another, I would endeavour both in the general and particular arrangement, to exemplifie those gradual transitions as much as possible.[2]

As the class of vegetable productions will be imperfect unless a good collection of dried plants make a part thereof, such a collection seems to be much wanted to render this branch of Natural History complete. I would therefore beg leave to propose, as the *Hortus Siccuses* would take up too much room, and are already otherwise disposed of, to make a collection quite new; and to digest them according to Linnaeus's System, and deposit them in a cabinet to be constructed for that purpose according to the proportions laid down by Linnaeus himself in his *Philosophia Botanica*. His proportions are, in Paris measure 7 feet & 1/2 in height, 16 inches in bredth, and 12 inches in depth. Such a cabinet may very well stand against one of the jambes of the windows, which are at present vacant.[3]

If the Fossils and Vegetables can be contained in the first rooms, the room at the west end, with the lip adjoining, will remain for the Animals and animal substances.

Some of the Vegetables, and a considerable and valuable part of the Animals are preserved in spirits, and would be a great ornament to the Collection if placed in the cabinets; and I presume it would give more satisfaction to the publick to see them each arranged there with the things of the same kind, than to have them put together in the Base Story.

At the same time the Monsters and anatomical preparations, will be best joined with the skeletons, and other parts of anatomy in the Base Story: more especially as all these are not proper objects for all persons, particularly women with child.[4] The large room in the Base Story at the west end will be very fit for this purpose; and being under the rooms to which its contents belong, will have a communication with it (them) by the back stairs.

If on account of this disposition the two rooms allotted to the animalia should be found too small to contain the whole, a continuation of this class may be made in the two rooms adjoining the Committee room.

As to the antiquities they may be put in the largest room in the Base Story at the east end, to which the next room may be added if necessary.

This situation will be the more proper on account of the medals, if they should be placed above, as there will be a communication by the back stairs.

The little room at the west end opening upon the back stairs may contain the miniature pictures, and a cabinet of some of the most valuable and curious productions of art. The rest may be put in the Base Story, as also the instruments, habits, indian curiosities, etc.

Source

'The Plan for the Collections by Dr. Gowin Knight, 1756'. Appendix 1 in Gunther, A.E., 1980, *The founders of science at the British Museum, 1753– 1900*, Halesworth, Suffolk, Halesworth Press: 158–9.

Notes

1 The natural history specimens were destined not to remain at the British Museum at all. Those that remained of Sloane's original collections (most notably his herbaria) were eventually transferred to the Natural History Museum.
2 Knight's scheme, like a number of others then being worked on for the purposes of rearranging existing institutional collections, bore the strong imprint of a taxonomy derived from contemporary natural theological thought.
3 Along with employing differnt systems of taxonomy and nomenclature, Sloane and Linnaeus also differed in how they set out their books of dried plants (*Hortus Siccuses*), for, unlike Linnaeus, Sloane arranged his with more than one specimen per page. Consequently, Sloane was far less able to rearrange the pages of his Herbarium when particular specimens needed to be reclassified. Sloane's original books of botanical specimens may still be consulted at the Natural History Museum in London.
4 This sensitivity to the potential likes and dislikes of visitors betrays a con- siderably stronger notion of using a museum collection to make a public spectacle than can be found in most similar schemes of the previous century. Knight's fears over the effects of 'monsters' on pregnant women indicates the persistence of a belief in birth defects and miscarriages resulting from the 'antipathetic' effects of disfigured specimens, particularly human ones. There is also a strong suggestion here that Knight had in mind visitors to the museum from the 'politer' middling sort rather than the working classes.

References

Additional MS. 5166, f. 240 (British Museum)

Edwards, 1870
Eri, 1985
The General Contents of the British Museum, London, 1761
Gloag, 1952
MacGregor and Turner, 1986
Sheraton, 1803
Wills, 1971

34

Overseas and native visitors view the British Museum

The British Museum had opened in Montague House in 1759, and its collections were installed in the series of rooms existing in the house. The arrangement of the collections within the museum seemed chaotic to most visitors. The entrance hall contained a mixture of Oriental statues, marble busts, stuffed elephants and polar bears, fossils, Roubiliac's statue of Shakespeare, Chantrey's statue of Banks, and several stuffed giraffes. The visitor proceeded through these pieces to the great staircase, and so to the saloon, where there was more of the same. The rest of the museum was divided, rather more sensibly, between the three original departments: Manuscripts, Medals and Coins in six rooms on the eastern side of the first floor; Natural and Artificial Productions on the western side of the first floor; and Printed Books, Maps, Globes and Drawings in the twelve rooms on the ground floor. The whole assemblage struck some people as lacking in order and classification, and unworthy of its national position, although others were impressed by the collections and their lofty surroundings.

The very presence of the National Museum acted as a magnet for other collections, some presented, others purchased by special Parliamentary grants. The Parliamentary Papers arrived in 1772; Hamilton's antique vases in the same year; Cracherode's fine library in 1799; the Egyptian antiquities captured at Alexandria (including the Rosetta Stone) in 1802; the Townley Marbles by 1814, and Charles Greville's mineral collection in 1810. These and others, forced the rebuilding and reorganisation which characterised the nineteenth century.

DESCRIPTION OF THE BRITISH MUSEUM BY KARL PHILIP MORITZ OF BERLIN, 1782

In general, you must give in your name a fortnight before you can be admitted. But by the kindness of Mr. Woide,[1] I got admission earlier ... Yet after all, I am sorry to say that it was the room, the glass-cases, the shelves ... which I saw; not the museum itself, so rapidly were we hurried on through the departments. The company who saw it when I did, and in like manner, was variously composed. They were of all sorts, and some, as I believe, of the very lowest classes of people of both sexes, for, as it is the property of the Nation, every one has the same 'right' – I used the term of the country – to see it that another has. I had Mr. Wendeborn's book[2] in my pocket, and it, at least, enabled me to take more particular notice of some of the principal things ... The Gentleman who conducted us took little pains to conceal the contempt which he felt for my communications when he found it was only a German description ... which I had ... So rapid a passage through a vast suite of rooms in little more than one hour of time, with opportunity to cast but one poor longing look of astonishment on all the vast treasures of nature, antiquity and literature, in the examination of which one might profitably spend years, confused, stuns and overpowers the visitors.

Source

Quoted in Crook, J. M., 1972, *The British Museum: A case-study in architectural politics*, London, Allen Lane: 64

DESCRIPTION OF BRITISH MUSEUM BY WILLIAM HUTTON OF BIRMINGHAM, 1785

I was not likely to forget Tuesday, December 7th, at eleven ... We began to move pretty fast, when I asked with some surprise whether there were none to inform us what the curiosities were as we went on? A tall genteel young *man in person*, who seemed to be our conductor, replied with some warmth: 'What! would you have me tell you everything in the Museum? How is it possible? Besides, are not the names written upon many of them?' I was much too humbled by this reply to utter another word. The company seems influenced; they made haste and were silent. No voice was heard but in whispers. If a man spends two minutes in a room, in which a thousand things demand his attention, he cannot bestow on them a glance apiece. When our leader opens the door of another apartment, the silent language of that action is, *come along* ... I consider myself in the midst of a rich entertainment, consisting of ten thousand rarities, but, like Tantalus, I could not taste one. It grieves me to think how much I lost for want of a little information. In about thirty minutes we finished our silent journey through the princely mansion, which could well have taken thirty days. I went out much about as wise as I went in, but with this severe reflection that, for fear of losing my chance, I had that morning abruptly torn myself from three gentlemen with whom I was engaged in an interesting conversation, had lost my breakfast, got wet to the skin, spent half-a-crown in coach-hire, paid two shillings for a ticket, [and] been hackneyed through the rooms with violence ... I had laid more stress on the British Museum, than on anything else which I should see in London. It was the only sight which disgusted me ... Government purchased this rare collection ... at a vast expense, and exhibits it as a national honour ... How far it answers the end proposed this chapter of cross incidents will testify.

Sources

Hutton, W. *Journey to London*, 1785, quoted by Crook, J. M., 1972, *The British Museum: A case-study in architectural politics*, London, Allen Lane: 65

Notes

1   Mr Woide was a German Assistant Librarian at the Museum.
2   F.A. Wendeborn had published a *View of England*, translated into English in 1791.

References

Crook, 1972
Edwards, 1970

35

Collecting as revolution

During the eighteenth century, the French royal collection grew considerably. The sale of the English royal collection after the beheading of Charles I in 1649 provided a major opportunity, and so did the financial difficulties of the French banker Jabach in 1671, for Jabach possessed pictures that had belonged to the Duke of Mantua. By the end of his reign Louis XIV owned nearly 1,500 pictures by Old Masters, a fine collection of classical antiquities, and thousands of drawings. As early as 1692, it had been recognised that these works of art should be more publicly available, but in practice policy fluctuated. By about 1785 most of the paintings were in the Louvre, then still a royal palace.

Quite apart from the royal collections, there were, of course, in France very considerable collections of artworks held by aristocrats and other wealthy men, like the huge collection possessed by Cardinal Mazerin, who had presented his pieces to the King. Similarly, the churches of France had a great deal of material, much of it medieval: the riches of the abbey church of St Denis, for example, have already been described (see Volume 1 in this series).

When revolution broke out in France in 1798, all this collected art constituted a serious problem, theoretical and practical. At the theoretical level, it was not clear how works which were valuable but indelibly associated with the *ancien régime* should be treated, and at the practical level, the quantity of material created a real problem. Much material was destroyed in the revolutionary fervour which came to be called 'vandalism', a name coined at this time. Steps, however, were taken to deal with the rest.

A commission known as the Conservatoire du Muséum National was put in charge of the Louvre in 1792, and the old palace was opened as a public museum. A decree of 1789 had transferred ecclesiastical property to the state and a number of arrangements to deal with the mass of material were made, including the creation of the Commission Temporaire des Arts. This created depots, like the Dépôt de Nesle (1793) on the corner of the present Quai Voltaire in Paris, run by Jean Naigeon. Here works of art were collected, inventoried and stored, to await auction, return, or transfer to the Louvre, or other public buildings. The Dépôt was closed in 1796, although Naigeon continued to curate the collection until 1799.

Meanwhile the revolutionary wars with the European royal powers, which broke out in 1792, followed by those of Napoleon, were deliberately made the means of transferring European artworks to France. These came in quantity, first from northern Europe and then from Italy. In 1798 there was a triumphal entry into Paris of captured works of art, when masterpieces like the four bronze horses from St Mark's church, Venice, and the Venus di Medici were paraded on elegant carts in the Champs de Mars before delivery to the Louvre. Some of these, but not all, were returned following Napoleon's defeat in 1815.

In revolutionary and Napoleonic France, art and collections in museums were given new overt meanings: educational, republican, patriotic and moral.

STATEMENTS MADE BY JEAN NAIGEON

I have made innumerable sacrifices for the cause of the Revolution, employing all my free time at my task, giving all my care to collect and conserve art work, first as a member of the Commission des Arts with no material compensation, and then as a member of the Commission Temporaire des Arts. It was the Comité d'Instruction Publique which assigned me to my position at the Dépôt de Nesle; I did not seek it. ...

I assumed my work with the most ardent zeal, at first without pay. The Comité d'Instruction Publique and the Commission Temporaire des Arts chose me to be Keeper of the Dépôt de Nesle. To merit this display of confidence I abandoned my studio and spent all my moments watching over a precious collecton which grew daily. Despite the multiplicity of the objects under my care, despite the speed (necessary in this stormy time) with which inventories were drawn up and transports were arranged in the Dépôt, everything was maintained in fitting order, nothing was lost, and it can be said that my collection had an air of a museum rather than a temporary warehouse. A multitude of objects have been withdrawn for museums, libraries, and public buildings, and the Musée Central in particular chose the rarest and most important paintings, statues, bronzes, prized marbles, etc. Moreover furniture and personal property was returned, while lesser works were sold to help liquidate the national debt ... I can produce perfect records of all of the transactions that took place in this immense operation.

Source

Wisner, D., 1996, 'Jean Naigeon at the Dépôt de Nesle: a collector and culture-broker in the First French Republic', *Journal of the History of Collections*, 8, 2: 159–60.

POLICY OF COMITÉ D'INSTRUCTION IN RELATION TO CAPTURED WORKS OF ART (1794)

The Committee proposed to:

despatch secretly in the wake of our brothers in arms artists and men of letters with a solid educational background. These honest citizens of proven patriotism will remove with all due care such masterpieces that exist in the territories into which republican arms have penetrated. The riches of our enemies are, as it were, buried in their midst. Arts and letters are friends of liberty. The monuments erected by slaves will acquire, when set up among us, a splendour which a despotic government could never confer on them.

Source

Hemmings, F.W.J., 1987, *Culture and Society in France 1789–1848*, Leicester University Press: 78.

LETTER OF COMMISSAR THOUIN, ANNOUNCING THE ARRIVAL OF ART TRANSPORTS FROM ITALY, TO THE DIRECTORY IN 1797

... Are the precious relics of Rome to arrive like loads of coal and to be put on the quai of the Louvre as if the cases contained nothing but soap? ... I admit that the idea of such an arrival pains me ... Citizens of all classes of the population ought to be aware that the Government has given them consideration and that all will have their share of the great booty. People will be able to judge what a Republican Government means if compared with the rule of a monarch who makes conquests merely for the pleasure of his courtiers and the satisfaction of his peronal vanity ...[1]

Source

Witlin, A., 1949, *The Museum: its History and its Tasks in Education*, London, Routledge & Kegan Paul: 250.

REMARKS MADE BY VIVANT DENON, DIRECTOR-GENERAL OF THE LOUVRE, IN 1815

Let them carry them away! They have no eyes to see them! Masterpieces of art could be kept nowhere more appropriately than in France, the country which always will be leading in matters of art.[2]

Source

Witlin, A., 1949, *The Museum: its History and its Tasks in Education*, London, Routledge & Kegan Paul: 251

LETTER BY VIVANT DENON'S SON, DESCRIBING EVENTS AT THE LOUVRE IN 1815

I have seen my father persistently removing ... pictures from the carts on which they had been loaded by the foreign commissars ... [I have seen him] carrying the pictures back to the gallery and trying to secure them by dint of will ...

Source

Witlin, A., 1949, *The Museum: its History and its Tasks in Education*, London, Routledge & Kegan Paul: 251.

Notes

1   This letter preceded the triumphal parade mentioned in the introduction.
2   This, and the next extract, refer to the return of stolen art to its country of origin, following the defeat of Napoleon in 1815.

References

Hemmings, 1987
Wisner, 1996
Wittlin, 1949
Wittlin, 1970

36

Miss Benett collects fossils in Wiltshire

Miss Ethelred Benett created a remarkable collection of fossils through her activities in Wiltshire, southern England, during the 1810s, 1820s and 1830s. Part of this collection is now housed in the Academy of Natural Sciences, Philadelphia, having been purchased and donated by T. B. Wilson in the late 1840s. The whereabouts of the rest remains as yet unclear. The collection originally contained thousands of specimens, mostly from the Jurassic-Cretaceous strata local to Wiltshire.

Ethelred Benett was born in 1776 of a well-off family, and, remaining unmarried, devoted her life to her collecting. She became well known in geological circles, and her work and her fossils with their carefully stratigraphical contexting, were used by men like James, Sowerby and William Smith, and institutions like the British Museum and the Geological Society of London. She was very generous with both her findings and her collection, passing specimens to other geologists very freely. When she died on 11 January 1845, her sister, Anna Maria Benett, disposed of what was by then a very considerable and important cabinet.

Benett's catalogue of her Wiltshire fossils was her only published work. The list appeared in two forms, first (1831) as part of a history of Wiltshire by Sir Richard Colt Hoare, and then as a privately printed pamphlet. In both, the lists of material occupied about nine pages of text and the second version, printed later the same year, included eighteen plates of figures. The two versions differed in various arrangements of the lists, chiefly in order to improve the presentation of some of the newly discovered material which she was here making known to the scientific world for the first time. The publication included seventy-seven new species and one declared new genus and these, as a part of the total of 443 identified fossils, were, like the rest, given Linnaean binomial descriptions in order to establish their scientific status. One of the most important genuses in the collection was *Polypothecia* and to it Benett referred nineteen species of fossil sponges, found in the Greensand beds: Spamer, Brogan and Torrens suggest that she should be credited with the erection of this genus (1989: 135–42). The new genus claimed by Benett herself was *Drepanites*, which involved shell forms (although subsequently her name did not become part of the general scientific usage).

The degree of acceptance Benett achieved in the scientific world of her day was quite remarkable for a woman, debarred by her sex from the universities and the learned societies. Her name, which is a masculine form of an Anglo-Saxon personal name (an acceptable feminine form would be Ethelreda), is a curious side-note to her career. A mistake over her gender, caused by her name, led to her award by the Emperor of Russia of an honorary degree of Doctor of Civil Law from the University of St Petersburg in recognition of the fine collection of fossils she had sent there.

BENETT'S COMMENTS ON THE GENUS *POLYPOTHECIA*[1]

If it should be objected to my new names in the genus Polypothecia, that they are all derived from external form; I beg to state, that three scientific gentlemen undertook, at different times, to describe and name this class of fossils, and to each I offered all the assistance which my very large collection of them afforded; that all have disappointed me; and having waited fifteen years, and the fossils now, by the death of the late Mr. J.S. Miller, again on my hands unnamed, I have done the best I could. Mr. Miller did, however, publish a Prospectus of a work on them; to that I am indebted for the generic name 'Polypothecia' …

Source

Benett, E., 1831, *A Catalogue of the Organic Remains of the County of Wilts*, Warminster, J.L. Vardy, quoted in Spamer et al., 1989, 'Recovery of the Ethelred Benett Collection of Fossils mostly from the Jurassic-Cretaceious Strata of Wiltshire, England', *Proceedings of the Academy of Natural Sciences of Philadelphia*, 141: 136.

BENETT'S LETTER TO SAMUEL WOODWARD ON THE GENUS *DREPANITES*[2]

As to my genus Drepanites I am rather at a loss what to say about it, the late Mr. Parkinson examined the specimen figured very minutely and said it was certainly quite a new thing and gave me the name of Pedum for it but that being preoccupied by a bivalve could not stand of course and I of course changed it but I brought the specimen to London to be figured and afterwards shewed it to Mr. Sowerby and I see he is decided it shall be his Ammonites falcatus [i.e. *Hyphoplites falcatus*, the type species of *Hyphoplite*] which I do not believe, Mr. Parkinson could not make an amonite out of it and he tried to do so thinking at first it was one, there appears to be some appearance of septa at the larger end but the smaller cannot be brought within the other any way I think and beside it appears to be a perfect termination; I should place it with the chambered shells and I think I have done so in Sir R. Hoares work I will see before I close this letter. I have placed my Drepanites between the Hamites and Scaphites and I think it had better remain unless Mr. Sowerby can prove it to be an *ammonites* but I have just compared his A. falcatus the figure I mean of course and my own positive specimen and though they are as near as possible the same size they are not the same thing the inside of the curve of mine is decidedly much wider and will not come into that figure.

Source

S. Woodward Archive, Vol. 5, folio 63, 1831, Norwich Castle Museum, quoted in Spamer et al. 1989: 149.

BENETT'S DESCRIPTION OF THE CHIEF FOSSIL-BEARING LOCALITY[3]

The town of Warminster stands on the Green Sand; and the remains of Alcyonia with which it abounds, more particularly on the west of the town, seem almost inexhaustible: a few remains of Testacea are sparingly scattered among them, but at Chute Farm, near Longleat, in a field called Brimsgrove, it would seem, said the late Mr. Wm. Cunnington, as if a cabinet had been emptied of its contents, so numerous, and so various, *were* the Organic Remains found there; now become scarce; but chiefly small species.

Source

Benett, 1831, quoted in Spamer et al., 1989: 152.

Notes

1   J. S. Miller had previously mentioned the name in a privately printed pro-spectus (1822).
2   James Sowerby published Benett's detailed description of Chickgrove Quarry,

Tisbury, Wiltshire, in his *Mineral Conchology of Great Britain* (1816, 2: 57–9). Gideon Mantell was a noted contemporary scientist.

3   Warminster is in Wiltshire: Chute (or Shute) Farm was a famous fossil location. The fossils mentioned are varieties of shells.

References

Torrens, 1985

37

Mary Anning: collectrice extraordinaire

The Annings were a working-class family living in Lyme Regis, Dorset, in the early decades of the nineteenth century, who made part of their living by selling local shells and fossils to those who visited the small watering place. Lyme Regis is on the coast, and possesses particularly spectacular cliffs of the Blue Lias limestone beds, which carry very significant remains of the Jurassic fauna. Moreover, the cliffs are unstable, and subject to frequent collapses, which reveal hitherto inaccessible deposits, so important fossils are continually being brought to light. The Annings, particularly the mother and daughter, both called Mary, proved to be particularly adept at locating fossil material, and their efforts coincided with an important upsurge in geological interest among the educated classes in England.

In 1812, the local paper published a short account of the find of a 'crocodile' – actually a 5-metre-long ichthyosaur, a sea reptile, 180 million years old – in the Dorset cliffs. Mary the younger recognised an opportunity and began to build up an expertise in the cliffs, and contacts in the scientific world who would be prepared to pay quite highly for her finds. In 1825 she met Charlotte Murchison, wife of Roderick Murchison, an important London-based geologist, and through this network men like William Buckland, Professor of Geology at Oxford, became her customers.

In 1823 Mary discovered her first major complete fossil, of the marine reptile plesiosaurus, and five years later she found a nearly complete skeleton of a winged reptile, a pterosaur. The plesiosaurus passed, via the Duke of Buckingham, to the British Museum (Natural History). The pterosaur was published by Buckland in the *Transactions of the Geological Society* (1829), and the further discovery of a new plesiosaurus followed, which was formally named by Buckland. These major fossils were accompanied by large numbers of fragments and lesser material, which were sold to collectors. Further ichthyosaurs were found in the 1830s, the largest of which was bought by the British Museum. The principle fossil hunter here was Thomas Hawkins, an eccentric who lived at Sharpham Park near Glastonbury in Somerset. He seems to have operated in friendly rivalry with Mary, and he published long-winded accounts of his activities.

Meanwhile, Mary continued to have distinguished patrons, like the King of Saxony who visited Lyme in 1844, and to find and sell fossils. She died in 1847, aged forty-seven. Her life and work bring together a number of threads. As a south Dorset working woman, she knew her locality extremely well; this locality happened to be exceptionally fossiliferous; and she lived in a generation eager to gather the specimens which she knew how to acquire. As a result, although an uneducated woman, she was able to create for herself an important reputation in the scientific world of her day, and in the historiography of science.

THOMAS HAWKINS DESCRIBES HIS FIRST FOSSIL-HUNTING VISIT TO LYME

In the month of July, 1832, Miss Anning obtained from the indurated marl of the lias limestones near the Church at Lyme, part of the head of the Chiroligostinus[1] figured in the third plate. Happening to arrive at Lyme the same day, I was fortunate in availing myself of the specimen. Accompanying Miss Anning the next morning on the beach, she pointed out to me the place whence it was brought. Persuaded that the other portion of the skeleton must be there, I advised its extraction, if it were possible, but Miss Anning had so little faith in my opinion, that she assured me I was at liberty to examine its propriety or otherwise myself. Hereupon I waited upon Mr. Edwards, the owner of the land, and request permission to throw down as much of the cliff as was necessary for such intention, which he very handsomely allowed me to do.

If our reader knows Lyme he will remember that four or five hundred yards of the coast from the borough Eastward has an elevation of from sixty to a hundred feet above high-water mark, and that a bed of diluvial gravel conceals the blue-marl of the lias from observation, except in those places where the rain has ploughed itself a channel towards the sea. At this spot was seen two or three years ago a kind of peninsular rock, which had long defied the fury of the destructive current that a South-Wester invariably propelled against it from the cob. There it is abutted upon the angry waves, reft of its gravelly covering by the storm, with its grey sides slowly crumbling beneath the frost and saline atmosphere; but its foundations sound and unmoved. Nature seems to have made this depository of *the chef d'oevre* of her *ancient regime*, for here was the Chiroligostinus, her especial care. But that venerable though tiny promontory is no more. What the warring elements failed in, curiosity achieves; the hand of man came upon it, and it departed like a shadow.

The sun rose bright on the 26th day of July, 32, and the morning mists were hardly rolled from the hill's side ere many men busily engaged with spade and pick-axe to humble the doomed summit of this cliff. Progress was also made on the following day, when people from the adjacent country flock to witness the execution of a purpose which seemed to stagger their faith in our rationality. By next day's noon twenty thousand loads of earth, cast from the crown of the rock, constitute a good roadway to the beach from that part of it to which we had dug, and a few minutes more suffice to demonstrate the wonderful remain I tell of. Who can describe my transport at the sight of the colossus! My eyes the first which beheld it! who shall ever see them lit up with the same unmitigated enthusiasm again! and I verily believe that the uncultivated bosoms of the working-men were seized with the same contagious feeling, for they and the surrounding spectators waved their hats to a hurra, that made hill and mossy dale echoing ring. Ah but the tug of war! – the bones with the marl in which they lay, broke into small fragments, so that I almost despaired of their re-union; albeit, with the kind assitance of Miss Anning, the whole of them were packed, and by night-fall the last heavy box-full was deposited in a place of safety. So secured, the skeleton and its matrix weighed a ton.[2]

THOMAS HAWKINS DESCRIBES HIS SECOND VISIT IN 1833

'Have ye sid my animal sir,' said the fossilist Jonas Wishcombe of Charmouth as I called at his house to enquire if he had anything worth buying; – 'I should like vor yer honour to see 'im.' My heart leaped to my lips – 'animal! animal! where?' Can't be sid to day sir – the tide is in … Can't see 'un now yer honour – the tide's rolled atop'o'im fifty feet high' 'In marl or stone?' 'Why in beautiful ma-al'.Wishcombe could not persuade me that it was at all possible for a fragile delicate saurian remain to continue unharmed beneath the tremendous breakers which I but too well knew were at that moment wildly careering over the spot where he said it was situated … We determined … to be on the beach next day at the hour of low-water, if by hap we might then snatch a glance at the buried saurus … The weather-cock looked the right way as we descended the execrable path by which the good people of Lyme are content to wade to the seashore between their delightful town and the pleasant village of Charmouth … Let every naturalist make pilgrimage to the beetling crags mid-way of the rivers Char and Lim. A waterfall issuing from a placid lake in their lone bosom bound from ledge to stony ledge and is swallowed up of the thirsty shingle at their base:– … there lay the Chiropolyostinus the mark of the vertebral column of which was scarcely perceptible through the selenitic layer that had preserved it from the roaring waters … Jonas gladly sells me the right to the skeleton, of which I have heard he had known many months, while no opportunity presented him for its extraction.

He chuckled when I gave him a guinea earnest-money, convinced that he had made brave use of a discovery that no one could render, useful ... 'You will never get that animal,' said Miss Anning, as we made our devious way towards Lyme through the mist and flashing spray. 'Or if you do, *perchance*, it cannot be saved ... because the marl, full of pyrites, falls to pieces as soon as dry.' 'That I can prevent,' 'Can you?'

[For some weeks the wind remained in the south-west, and Hawkins had to wait until it blew off shore. At last it veered, and it was possible to make the attempt upon the Ichthyosaur.] 'Make haste; the tide's going out fast,' said Miss Anning as I passed her on the way ... I seized this opportunity of thanking her for the brief exhortation; it secured me the saurus that same day. Really the tide seemed to gallop away. Half a dozen of us – all lusty and eager for the occasion – meet; we arranged the mode of exhumation, disposed our instruments and wait for the crisis when the retreating waves shall desert the remain ... 'What d'ye think zir to dig'un out a whool' exlaimed the best tempered but unhappily Bacchinal fellow that every lived. 'Yes.' The tide goes back-back ... the crowbars and pickaxes loosen it from its bed ... The spectators say the tide flows – it does: we attempt to raise the heavy mass upon its side but our strength fails us ... To Sir Henry Baker, the reverent Benjamin Jeanes, Mr. Edwards, Waugh and other gentlemen, who came to our help, and by whose additional exertions we at length effected it, my thanks have been already made. I thank them again; their condescension can never be sufficiently estimated ... As Miss Anning anticipated, the marl – as soon as it dried – cracked, but by the assistance of some clever carpenters we secured it in a tight case with plaster of Paris so that no power can now disturb it!

Source

Hawkins, T., 1832, *Geological Sketches and Glimpses of the Earth*, London: 12–13, 25–7.

MRS GORDAN, BIOGRAPHER OF WILLIAM BUCKLAND, DESCRIBES THE VISIT OF THE KING OF SAXONY TO THE ANNING'S FOSSIL SHOP IN 1844

We had alighted from the carriage, and were proceeding along on foot, when we fell in with a shop in which the most remarkable petrefactions and fossil remains – the head of an Ichthyosaurus, beautiful ammonites, etc., were exhibited in the window. We entered, and found a little shop and adjoining chamber completely filled with fossil productions of the coast. It is a piece of great fortune for the collector when the heavy winter rains loosen and bring down large masses of the projected coast. When such a fall takes place, the most splendid and rarest fossils are brought to light, and made accessible almost without labour on their part. In the course of the past winter there had been no very favourable slips; the stock of fossils on hand was therefore smaller than usual; still I found in the shop a large slab of blackish clay, in which a perfect Ichthyosaurus of at least six feet was embedded. This specimen would have been a great acquisition for many of the cabinets of Natural History on the Continent, and I consider the price demanded – £15 sterling – as very moderate. I was anxious at all events to write down the address, and the woman who kept the shop, for it was a woman who had devoted herself to this scientific pursuit, with a firm hand wrote her name 'Mary Anning' in my pocket-book, and added, as she returned the book into my hands, 'I am well known throughout the whole of Europe'.

Source

Gordon, Mrs, 1894, *Mary Anning, the Heroine of Lyme Regis*, London: 115.

Notes

1   'Chiroligostinus' was the name by which Hawkins calls this fossil. It was an ichthyosaurus.
2   This specimen was subsequently bought for the British Museum.

References

Lang, 1939
Lang, 1959
Vines, 1992

Part IV
Antique Voices

38

Johann Winckelmann describes the antiquities discovered at Herculaneum and Pompeii

Johann Winckelmann was the most significant thinker to emerge in the context of the eighteenth-century classical Greek revival, and the man who contributed most to its overwhelming influence on taste and education during the later eighteenth and nineteenth centuries. His own character and tastes were an important aspect of how he approached the classical world: if he had been a different man, our inherited view of 'Greekness' and its immense cultural significance might have been quite different. Winckelmann's career exemplifies the undoubted fact that cultural values are constructed, not preordained, and that the views of influential individuals play a large part in their creation.

Winckelmann was born in 1717 at Stendal in Brandenburg, in north-east Germany. He was the son of a poor shoemaker, but he succeeded in attending school in Berlin, and then classes at the universities of Halle and Jena. In 1748 he went to Nüthenitz near Dresden and here he was able to become acquainted with the extensive Dresden collections of art and antiquities gathered by successive Electors of Saxony, whose capital was Dresden. This, and his growing passion for Greek literature, took him in 1755 to Rome, where he became librarian to Cardinal Archinto, and also a Roman Catholic.

Once in Rome, he moved easily into a circle of socially well-placed connoisseurs, including the household of Cardinal Albani, who was forming a magnificent collection of classical art at Porta Salara. In 1763, Winckelmann was made Librarian and President of Antiquities at the Vatican. From then on, he immersed himself in the study of ancient art and architecture. His most important book, *History of Ancient Art*, was published in 1764. In 1768 he went to Vienna, where he was received with honours by Maria Theresa, Empress of Austria, but on his way back, at Trieste, he was murdered for the sake of some coins he was carrying.

Winckelmann's views on ancient art were deeply influential. He set forth both the history of Greek art and the principles upon which he believed it to be founded. This involved a discussion of the political, social and intellectual condition which, he believed, fostered creative activity in the Greek city-states, especially

Athens. His fundamental idea is that the end of art is beauty, and that this involves the true artist selecting from nature those features best shaped for this purpose, and then combining them through imagination into the creation of ideal types, particularly of the human form. For Winckelmann this could only be understood through reference to the actual remains of antiquity, closely observed by himself during his travels, and it is this which gives his book a particular archaeologically-rooted strength.

Historically, Winckelmann divided Greek art into four periods. The first, 'straight and hard', comprised the relatively primitive Archaic style. The second, 'grand and square', was that of the young but mature fifth century BC, best displayed by the Athenian sculptor Pheidias. The third, 'beautiful and flowing', was that the 'older' fourth century BC, exemplified by the soft, naturalistic style of the Athenian sculptor Praxiteles; and the fourth, decadent and imitative, which characterised the decline of art in late Greek and Roman times. His work helped to encourage this 'rise and fall' approach to art history, based ultimately upon the model of the human cycle.

A number of criticisms can be levelled against Winckelmann. His work was built upon the material he had seen in Italy (he never visited Greece) and he did not realise that many of what he took to be original Greek works were in fact later copies from the supposed inferior late Roman period. Essentially, therefore, his view of the glory that was Greece depended not upon direct physical study of surviving Greek materials, but upon a nostalgia for a perceived Greek golden age which transcended mere material. Nevertheless, the existing collections of classical sculpture, like those of Thomas Howard, linked with the inspiration provided by Winckelmann's works on Greek art, stimulated much collecting in Greece in the late eighteenth and nineteenth centuries, and it is intimately bound up with the whole 'classical revival' in taste, particularly of interior decoration and applied art, which dominated the decades either side of 1800.

In 1758 and 1762 he visited Naples, and his work on Herculaneum and Pompeii, Roman towns preserved intact by the lava flow from the eruption of Vesuvius in AD 79, was the first serious information to reach scholars about the new finds.

POMPEII AND HERCULANEUM

As to the monuments found in Pompeii, I shall confine myself to a little temple, or square chapel, which was discovered in the year 1761. This temple belonged to a large *Villa*; or country seat.[1] The front, richly ornamented with different kinds of foliage, was supported by four stone columns, covered with stucco; a palm[2] and a half in diameter, and seven palms seven inches high; the shafts fluted. One of them is to be seen in the cabinet of Portici.[3] The body of this temple stood five steps above the ground. Two of these steps lay on the outside of the colonnade; and the other three, which were of a circular form, within the middle inter-columniation, which was much longer than the other two; and led to the body of the temple; so that the middle intercolumniation stood the height of the steps above the other two. These steps were paved with squares of a common kind of marble, called *Cipolino*. Within this little temple there was found a marble Diana, of Etruscan[4] workmanship, on a pedestal, which was likewise of marble. Before it, towards the right hand corner, there stood another round temple; on the other side a wall; and, opposite to the temple, a cistern with four wells, or rather openings, in the angles of it, to facilitate the drawing of the water. The only building of two stories, found since they began to dig for antiquities, is in this place; and it is now laid quite bare...

One of [these] was found at Herculaneum. Three Priaputes,[5] each terminating at bottom in a goat's leg, form the feet of it. Their tails, issuing from above the *Os sacrum*,[6] extend horizontally to a ring in the middle of the trevet, and by twining above it, unite and secure the whole, just as the crosspiece in our common tables. The other trevet[7] was found at Pompeii, some time after that I have been describing. It is of admirable workmanship. On that part of each leg where it takes a bend to appear with the greater grace, there fits a sphinx, whose hair, instead of falling directly over the cheeks, passes under a diadem. This headress may be considered as allegorical especially in a tripod of Apollo, and allude to the obscure and enigmatical answers of the oracle. The large brims of the chafingdish are ornamented with ram's heads and bound together by garlands of flowers, and other excellent carvings. In the sacred tripods, the chafingdish on which they placed the coal-pan, was made of baked earth. That found at Pompeii had still the ashes in it. In the year 1761, they found in a temple of Herculaneum, the discovery of which has not as yet been finished, though for what reasons I cannot say, a large square chafingdish, in bronze, such as they commonly use in Italy to warm their large apartments, about the size of a middling table. It stood upon lion's paws. The brims were curiously incrusted with a foliage composed of copper, brass, and silver. The bottom consisted of a very substantial iron grate, lined with brick-work, as well above as below, so that the coals could neither touch the upper part of the grate, nor fall down through the lower. But this curious piece was found all in pieces.

I must likewise reckon, amongst the necessary houshold furniture, the lamps, in which the ancients were so industrious to display their elegance, and even magnificence; mould or dipt candles not having in general use among them. There are lamps of every kind in the cabinet of Herculaneum, both in baked earth and in bronze, especially the later; and, as the ornaments employed by the ancients have generally a relation to some particular object, we often find some singular subjects on them. Most of those in baked earth represent a bark, with seven prows or rostrums at each side, to hold as many wicks. The vessel, used to pour oil into these lamps resembles a little round close decked bark, with a sharp rostrum at one end, and at the other end a little convex plate, having a hole in the middle of it, to pour in the oil, which was afterwards to supply the lamp. One of the largest in bronze terminates, behind, in a bat with expended wings, which may be considered as an emblem of night. The delicate tissue, for which the wings of this bird are remarkable, the tendons, the veins, and the skin which covers them, are all of admirable workmanship. On another of these lamps there is a mouse, which seems to be watching an opportunity to get at the oil; and, in a third, a rabbit browsing the grass. But nothing displays better the magnificence aimed at by the ancients, than a square pedestal or base, in bronze in which there stands a naked boy, two palms in height, with a lamp hanging by three chains, four times interwoven, in one hand, and in the other the hook used to trim the wick, suspended by a chain like the first. Near him there is a column adorned with a spiral fluting, and, instead of a capital, terminating in a mask, which likewise answered the purpose of a lamp, the wick issuing at the mouth; and there being a hole in the crown of the head, with a little hinged door or valve, to fill it by.

The ancients used their candelabres to carry lamps. These candelabres resembled our stands and were as curiously wrought as the lamps themselves. The stem of the candelabre, curiously moulded, rested on a foot usually supported by three lion paws. This foot, as likewise the upper part, or plate of the candelabre, were turned, and adorned with pretty eggs on the edges, and foliages on the surfaces. The foot of the largest candelabre is a palm and an inch, Roman measure, in diameter. I believe there are near an hundred of them in the cabinet, the highest seven palms and a half high, whereas all Rome cannot produce a single one in bronze.

Source

Winckelmann, J., 1770, *Critical Account of the Situation and Destruction by the first eruptions of Mount Vesuvius of Herculaneum, Pompeii and Stabia*; this was in the form of a published letter written to Count Bruhl of Saxony. The English version was published by Carham, T. and Newberry, F., St Paul's Churchyard, London. The text is pages 35–6, 62–4.

Notes

1   Pompeii was the Roman seaside retirement town, ideally situated on the Bay of Naples; and as such it had a number of luxurious private houses as well as high-quality public amenities.
2   This is the eighteenth-century Neapolitan measurement. There was also a Roman palm.
3   The royal (Neapolitan) collection of material found at the site.
4   Great confusion existed between 'Etruscan', Greek and Roman copies of Greek material as labels of origin. See this volume, Chapter 43 on Sir William Hamilton.
5   Phallic figures.
6   The bone at the bottom of the spine.
7   'Trevet' or 'trivet': these are metal frames intended to hold the 'chafingdish' described in the following lines. These acted like braziers to heat rooms, carry out simple cooking and offer sacrifices.

References

Bernal, 1987
Haskell and Penny, 1981
Morris, 1994
Potts, 1994
Shanks, 1996

39

Charles Townley and his marbles

Charles Townley (sometimes spelt Towneley) came from an important Lancashire landed family who had been settled at Townley since the twelfth century. They had remained Catholic, which meant that up to 1829 all public careers in Britain were closed to them, and this possibly helped to direct Charles's thoughts (like those of the Earl of Arundel before him) towards collecting, as a prestigious activity which he was allowed to undertake.

Charles Townley was born at Towneley Hall in 1737, and through his mother he was connected with the Howard family of the dukes of Norfolk, also Catholics. Like many wealthy Catholic boys, Charles was educated at Douay; he succeeded his father in 1742, and travelled extensively in Italy, staying in the country for nearly eight years. He knew Sir William Hamilton at Naples, and Thomas Jenkins and Gavin Hamilton, artists and dealers in Rome. In 1768 he made his first important purchase, of the well-known statue of a boy playing at the game of tali which had been in the Barberini Palace at Rome, and thereafter his collecting continued until his death in 1805. The pieces were displayed in his house until his death, and were then acquired for the British Museum at a cost of £20,000 paid to the Townley estate, and from 1808 exhibited to the public.

It will be seen from the accompanying text that Charles built his collection up by purchase, either from agents like Hamilton who were excavating in Italy, or on the open market. The great bulk of his classical material came from Roman sites in Italy, not from mainland Greece, or the ancient Greek colonies in Sicily, southern Italy or Asia Minor. Consequently, most of his pieces are of relatively late Roman date. For a brief period around 1808 they were regarded as the most important collection of ancient sculptures in Britain, but after the Elgin Collection of fifth-century Greek material came to London, their reputation went into an eclipse which lasted until the last few decades, during which Roman art has been reappraised.

TOWNLEY'S MARBLES

[Townley] visited Naples, Florence and Rome, and from time to time made many excursions into various parts of Magna Graecia and of Sicily.

At Naples he formed the acquaintance of Sir William HAMILTON and of D'HANCARVILLE. At Rome he became acquainted with three Englishmen, James BYRES, Gavin HAMILTON, and Thomas JENKINS, all of whom had first gone thither as artists, and step by step had come to be almost exclusively engrossed in the search after works of ancient art. The success and fame of Sir William HAMILTON's researches in the Kingdom of the Two Sicilies and of those, still earlier, of Thomas COKE of Holkham (afterwards Earl of Leicester), had given a strong impulse to like researchers in other parts of Italy. TOWNELEY caught the contagion, and was backed by large resources to aid him in the pursuit.

His first important purchase was made in 1765. It was that of a work already famous, and which for more than a century had been one of the ornaments of the Barberini Palace at Rome. This statue of a boy playing at the game of tali, or 'osselets' ... was found among the ruins of the Baths of Titus, during the Pontificate of URBAN THE EIGHTH. During the same year, 1768, Mr. TOWNELEY acquired, from the Collection of Victor AMADEI, at Rome, the circular urn with figures in high relief – which is figured in the first volume of Piranesi's *Raccolta di Vasi Antichi* – and also the statue of a *Nymph of Diana*, seated on the ground. This statue was found in 1766 at the Villa Verospi in Rome.

Two years afterwards,[1] several important acquisitions were made of marbles which were discovered in the course of the excavations undertaken by BYRES, Gavin HAMILTON, and JENKINS, amidst the ruins of Hadrian's Villa near Tivoli. The joint-stock system, by means of which the diggings were effected, no less than the conditions which accompanied the papal concessions that authorised them, necessitated a wide diffusion of the spoil. But whenever the making of a desirable acquisition rested merely upon liberality of purse or a just discrimination of merit, MR. TOWNELEY was not easily outstripped in the quest. Amongst these additions of 1769–71 were the noble head of *Hercules*, the Head said, conjecturally, to be that of *Menelaus*, and the '*Castor*' in low relief ...

The terminal heads of the bearded *Bacchus* – both of them of remarkable beauty – were obtained in 1771 from the site of Baiae. These were found by labourers who were digging a deep trench for the renewal of a vineyard, and were seen by Mr. ADAIR, who was then making an excursion from Naples. In the same year the statue of *Ceres* and that of a *Faun* were purchased from the Collection in the Macarani Palace at Rome. In 1772 the *Diana Venatrix* and the *Bacchus and Ampelus* were found near La Storta. It was by no fault of TOWNELEY'S that the *Diana* was in part 'restored', and that blunderingly. He thought restoration to be, in some cases, permissible; but never deceptively; never when doubt existed about the missing part. In art, as in life, he clave to his heraldic motto '*Tenez le vrai.*'[2]

In 1771, also, the famous '*Clytie*' – doubtfully so called – was purchased from the Laurenzano Collection at Naples.

The curious scenic 'figure on a plinth' ... together with many minor pieces of sculpture, were found in the Fonseca Villa on the Cælian Hill in 1773. In the same year many purchases were made from the Mattei Collection at Rome. Amongst them are the heads of *Marcus Aurelius* and of *Lucius Verus*. And it was at this period that Gavin HAMILTON began his productive researches amidst the ruins of the villa of Antoninus Pius at Monte Cagnoli, near the ancient Lanuvium. This is a spot both memorable and beautiful. The hill lies on the road between Genzano and Civita Lavina. It commands a wide view over Velletri and the sea. To HAMILTON and his associates it proved one of the richest mines of ancient art which they had the good fortune to light upon. Mr. TOWNELEY'S share in the spoil of Monte Cagnoli comprised the group of *Victory sacrificing a Bull*; the *Actaeon*; a *Faun*; a Bacchanalian vase illustrative of the *Dionysia*; and several other works of great beauty. The undraped *Venus* was found – also by Gavin HAMILTON – at Ostia, in 1775.

In the next year, 1776, Mr. TOWNELEY acquired one of the chiefest glories of his gallery, the *Venus* with drapery. This also was found at Ostia, in the ruins of the Baths of Claudius. But that superb statue would not have left Rome had not its happy purchaser made, for once, a venial deflection from the honourable motto just adverted to. The figure was found in two severed portions, and care was taken to show them, quite separately, to the authorities concerned in granting facilities for their removal. The same excavation yielded to the Towneley Collection the statue of *Thalia*. From the Villa Casali on the Esquiline were obtained the terminal head of *Epicurus*, and the best thought to be that of *Domitia*. The bust of *Sophocles* was found near Genzano; that of *Trajan*, in the Campagna; that of *Septimius Severus*, on the Palatine, and that of *Caracalla* on the Esquiline. A curious cylindrical fountain ... was found between Tivoli and Praeneste, and the fine representation in low relief of a *Bacchanalian procession* at Civita Vecchia. All these accessions to the Towneley Gallery accured in 1775 or 1776.

Of the date of the Collector's first return to England with his treasures I have found no record. But it would seem that nearly all the marbles hitherto enumerated were brought to England in or before the year 1777. The house, in London, in which they were first placed was found to be inadequate to their proper arrangement. Mr. TOWNELEY either built or adapted another house, in Park Street, Westminster, expressly for their reception. Here they were seen under favourable circumstances as to light and due ordering. They were made accessible to students with genuine liberality. And few things gave their owner more pleasure than to put his store of knowledge, as well as his store of antiquities, at the service of those who wished to profit by them. He did so genially, unostentatiously, and with the discriminating tact which marked the high-bred gentleman, as well as the enthusiastic Collector.

A contemporary critic, very competent to give an opinion on such a matter, said of Mr. TOWNELEY: 'His learning and sagacity in explaining works of ancient art was equal to his taste and judgement in selecting them,'³ If, in any point, that eulogy is now open to some modification, the exception arises from the circumstance that early in life, or, at least, early in his collectorship, he had imbibed from his intercourse with D'HANCARVILLE somewhat of that writer's love for mystical and supersubtle expositions of the symbolism of the Grecian and Egyptian artists. To D'HANCARVILLE, the least obvious of any two possible expositions of a subject was always the preferable one. Now and then TOWNELEY would fall into the same vein of recondite elaboration; as, for example, when he described his figure of an Egyptian 'tumbler' raising himself, upon his arms, from the back of a tame crocodile, as the 'Genius of Production.'

During the riots of 1780,⁴ the Towneley Gallery (like the National Museum of which it was afterwards to become a part) was, for some time, in imminent peril. The Collector himself could have no enemies but those who were infuriated against his religious faith. Fanaticism and ignorance are meet allies, little likely to discriminate between a Towneley Venus and the tawdriest of Madonnas. Threats to destroy the house in Park Street were heard and reported. Mr. TOWNELEY put his gems and medals in a place of safety, together with a few other portable works of art. Then, taking 'Clytie' in his arms – with the words 'I must take care of my wife' – he left his house, casting one last, longing, look at the marbles which, as he feared, would never charm his eyes again. But, happily, both the Towneley house and the British Museum escaped injury, amid the destruction of buildings, and of works of art and literature, in the close neighbourhood of both of them.

Liberal commissions and constant correspondence with Italy continued to enrich the Towneley Gallery, from time to time, after the Collector had made England his own usual place of abode. In 1786, Mr. JENKINS – who had long established himself as the banker of the English in Rome, and who continued to make considerable investments in works of ancient art, with no small amount of mercantile profit – purchased all the marbles of the Villa Montalto. From this source MR. TOWNELEY obtained his *Bacchus visiting Icarus* (engraved by BARTOLI almost a century before): his *Bacchus and Silenus*; the bust of *Hadrian*; the sarcophagus decorated with a *Bacchanalian procession* … and also that with a representation of the *Nine Muses*. By means of the same keen agent and explorer he heard, in or about the year 1790, that leave had been given to make a new excavation under circumstances of peculiar promise.

Our Collector was at Towneley when the letter of Mr. JENKINS came to hand. He knew his correspondent, and the tenour of the letter induced him to resolve upon an immediate journey to Rome. The grass did not grow under his feet. He travelled as rapidly as though he had been still a youngster, escaping from Douay, with all the allurements of Paris in his view.

When he reached Rome, he learnt that the promising excavation was but just begun upon. Without any preliminary visits, or announcement, he quietly presented himself beside the diggers, and ere long had the satisfaction of seeing a fine statue of Hercules displayed. Other fine works afterwards came to light. But on visiting Mr. JENKINS, in order to enjoy a more deliberate examination of 'the find', and to settle the preliminaries of purchase, his enjoyment was much diminished by the absence of Hercules, JENKINS did not know that his friend had seen it exhumed, and he carefully concealed it from his view. Eager remonstrance, however, compelled him to produce the hidden treasure. TOWNELEY, at length, left the banker's house with the conviction that the statue was his own, but it never charmed his sight again until he saw it in the Collection of Lord LANSDOWN. He had, however, really secured the *Discobolus* or Quoit-throwers, – perhaps, notwithstanding its restored head, the finest of the known repetitions of MYRO'S famous statue, – as well as some minor pieces of sculpture.

Other and very valuable acquisitions were made, occasionally, at the dispersion of the Collections of several lovers of ancient art, some of these Collections having been formed before his time, and others contemporaneously with his own. In this way he acquired whilst in England (1) the bronze statue of *Hercules* found, early in the eighteenth century, at Jebel or Gebial (the ancient Byblos), carried by an Armenian merchant to Constantinople, there sold to Dr. SWINNEY, a chaplain to the English factory; by him brought into England, and purchased by Mr. James MATTHEWS; (2) the Head of *Arminius*, also from the Matthews Collection; (3) the *Libera* found by Gavin HAMILTON, on the road to Frascati, in 1776 and then purchased by Mr. GREVILLE; (4) Heads of a *Muse*, an *Amazon*, and some other works, from the Collection of Mr. Lyde BROWNE, of Wimbledon; (5) the *Monument of Xanthippus*, from the Askew Collection; (6) the bust of a female unknown (called by TOWNELEY 'Athys') found near Genzano, in the grounds of the family of CESARINI, and obtained from the Collection of the Duke of ST. ALBANS; (7) many urns, vases, and other antiquities, partly from the Collection of that Duke and partly from Sir Charles FREDERICK'S Collection at Esher. The bronze *Apollo* was bought in

Paris, at the sale, in 1774 of the Museum formed by M. L'ALLEMAND DE CHOISEUL.

Some other accessions came to Mr. TOWNELEY by gift. The *Tumbler and Crocodile*, and the small statue of *Pan* ... were the gift of Lord CAWDOR. The *Oracle of Apollo* was a present from the Duke of BEDFORD. This accession – in 1804 – was the last work which Mr. TOWNELEY had the pleasure of seeing placed in his gallery. He died in London, on the 3rd of January, 1805.

He had been made, in 1791, a Trustee of the British Museum, in the progress of which he took a great interest. Family circumstances, as it seems, occurred which at last dictated a change in the original disposition which he had made of his Collection. By a Codicil, executed only twelve days before his death, he bequeathed the Collection to his only brother Edward TOWNELEY-STANDISH, on condition that a sum of at least four thousand five hundred pounds should be expended for the erection of a suitable repository in which the Collection should be arranged and exhibited. Failing such expenditure by the brother, the Collection was to go to John TOWNELEY, uncle of the Testator. Should he decline to fulfil the conditions, then the Collection should go, according to the Testator's first intent, to the British Museum.

Eventually, it appeared, on an application from the Museum Trustees, that the heirs were willing to transfer the Collection to the Public, but that Mr. TOWNELEY had left his estate subject to a mortgage debt of £36,500. The Trustees, therefore, resolved to apply to Parliament for a grant, and this noble Collection was acquired for the Nation on the payment of the sum of £20,000, very inadequate, it need scarcely be added, to its intrinsic worth.

Source

Edwards, E., 1870, *Lives of the Founders of the British Museum*, Vols 1 and 2, London, Macmillan: 372–8.

Notes

1 That is, 1770.
2 'Hold to the Truth'.
3 This was in the Preface (paragraph 61) to *Specimens of Ancient Sculpture*, published by the Society of Dilettante.
4 These were the Gordon Riots which raged in London in the days following 2

June 1780. The rioters were instigated by Lord George Gordon (1751–93), third son of Cosmo, Duke of Gordon, who was a member of Parliament and from 1779 head of the Protestant Association aimed at repealing the Catholic Relief Act of 1778. The riots destroyed the property of Roman Catholics, and were put down by the military with 450 killed or wounded. Lord George seems to have been, or became, insane, and in 1788 he was sentenced to five years' imprisonment in Newgate for libel. He died in prison.

References

Cook, 1985
Cooke, 1977

40

Henry Blundell forms his collection of marbles

The Blundell family, like the Towneleys, were important members of the Lancashire landed class, and Catholics. Their home was at Ince, known as Ince Blundell, near Burnley, and the marbles collected by Henry Blundell remained intact as a group at Ince Blundell Hall until 1959 when they were presented to Liverpool city to be part of the collections of the (then) Liverpool City Museum (now part of the National Museums on Merseyside).

Late in 1776 Henry Blundell joined Charles Townley in Rome and they began to visit museums and antiquities together: Blundell made his first purchase in 1777 of a statuette of Epicurius. Soon after, the important collections of sculpture at the Villa D'Este and the Villa Matei came onto the market and Blundell was able to make large acquisitions, followed through the years up to 1810 by material from other famous collections like the Villas Altieri and Borioni, and from dealers and restorers like Albacini, Cavaceppi, Gavin Hamilton, Thomas Jenkins and Piranesi. In 1800 he also bought from Christie's auction of pieces pillaged by the French from the papal apartments and captured on their way to France by the British.

By the time of his death in 1810 he had over 400 ancient sculptures, although he had some modern pieces also. Eighteenth-century connoisseurs and collectors viewed material in a way different to that which developed in the nineteenth century. Carved pieces from the ancient world were 'improved' to bring them in line with contemporary ideas of the ideal and the seemly, while often no particular distinction was made between ancient pieces and contemporary copies or pieces in the classical taste, since what mattered most was the spirit of the piece rather than the detail of its historical provenance.

At first at Ince Blundell Hall the sculptures were mainly embedded in walls in the house, but when the collection outgrew the space, Blundell built the Garden Temple, a neo-classical building, to display the material. This in its turn was superseded by a small version of the Roman Pantheon, a circular, domed building started in 1802 and finished shortly before his death. The internal exhibition of the sculptures here remained virtually as he had arranged it through the nineteenth and twentieth centuries.

It is this unity which gives the collection a particular importance, as the collection of a late eighteenth-century gentleman
whose taste in, and approach to, the antique was very characteristic of his generation.

LETTER FROM HENRY BLUNDELL TO CHARLES TOWNELY, 23 MARCH 1801

In your late letter you say you shd judge better what marbles out of Lord
Besboroughs collection wd best suit, if you know the size, plan and
situation of my intended room; it about 37 feet inside diameter, circular,
lighted from the top, as the Pantheon ...; the walls 6 feet thick to get
room for 4 large recesses, so as to be able to see round the principal
statues; nothing is yet done about it, but on paper except a model in wood
just put in hand. In the 4 other smaller recesses I shall place the 4 tables I
bt last year at London and placed on them smaller statues etc. ...

Source

Letter from Henry Blundell to Charles Townley, 23 March 1801, quoted in
Fejfer, J. and Southworth, E., 1991, *The Ince Blundell Collection of Classical
Sculpture*, Vol. I, Part I, The Female Portraits, London, HMSO: 18.

HENRY BLUNDELL DESCRIBES HOW A HERMAPHRODITE STATUE WAS TURNED INTO A SLEEPING VENUS

Bought at Roehampton, at a sale of Lord Besborough's,[1] by a friend with
a deal of erudition about it. When bought, it was in the character of a
Hemaphrodite,[2] with little brats crawling about its breast. The figure was
unnatural and very disgusting to the sight; but by means of a little
castration and cutting away the little brats, it became a sleeping Venus
and as pleasing a figure as any in this Collection ...

Source

Henry Blundell's *Engravings and Etchings of the Principal Statues, Busts,
Bass-reliefs, Sepulchral Monuments, Cinerary Urns etc. in the Collection of
Henry Blundell Esq. at Ince*, Vols 1–11, Liverpool 1809–10, p. 41, quoted in
Fejfer and Southworth, 1991: 22.

HENRY BLUNDELL'S ACCOUNT OF A STATUE BELIEVED TO BE OF JULIA PIA[3]

7. Julia Pia. Was a lady from Phoenicia, celebrated for her great talents and learning. She came to Rome and by her personal charms, the emperor Septimius Severus[4] became so enamoured, that he married her, and by her had Caracalla and Geta. She applied much to the study of geometry and astronomy, in which she made such proficiency that she was mostly represented, as in this statue, in the character of the muse Urania, with a globe in one hand, and a style in the other. This statue displays a beautiful drapery, and elegance in the whole figure. It was bought from the Duke of Modena, out of his Villa d'Este at Tivoli, where it always attracted the notice of the intelligent antiquarians who visited that place. This statue, as well as most of the marbles at that villa, were collected by Cardinal Hippolito, and were mostly found in the ruins of Adrian's villa. As that emperor was two years in Greece, it is supposed they were brought over by him, to ornament his villa, the greater part of them being in fine Greek marble.

CATALOGUE 10: INCE NO. 115. MODERN? PORTRAIT OF A WOMAN WITH DIADEM

Total height: 0.325m.; height of head and bust(?) 0.25m.; height from chin to hair-line 0.106m(?).
Marble: large-crystalled, probably Eastern.
Restored: nose, left ear, part of rim of right and base with index plaque. Damage: slight(?) of diadem. Surface: soap-like and highly polished except for the back which is left rough.
Lit.: Blundell Acc. 115; Michaelis, *Priv.* p. 2(?) Michaelis p. 369 no. 167; Ashmole p. 67(?); Howard p. 82.

Source

Henry Blundell's *Account of the Statues, Bust, Bas-reliefs, Cinerary Urns and other Ancient Marbles and Paints at Ince. Collected by Henry Blundell*, Liverpool, 1803, quoted in Fejfer and Southworth, 1992: 43–4.

Notes

1   Lord Besborough was a contemporary collector whose material was housed at Roehampton; Blundell bought twenty-two pieces from it at the Christie auction of the collection on 7 April 1802.
2   'Hermaphrodites' were classical pieces with the sexual characteristics of both sexes. A drawing of this piece before the 'castration' exists in the Townley collection in the British Museum.
3   Julia Pia was born the daughter of a priest of Baal in Emesa, Syria. In about 187 she married L. Septimius Severms, emperor 146–211, and had two sons, Caracalla and Geta. She had an intellectual circle in her own right which included the doctor Galen, the lawyer Ulpian, the historian-philosopher Diogenes Laertius, and a number of proponents of Eastern mysticism.
4   The statue, in fact, is unlikely to be of any Severan empress, although it does seem to date to the Severan period, perhaps during AD 210–38. It may represent an important private person. Similarly, the interpretation of the stylus and orbit in the statue's hands as a representation of the muse Urania is unjustified.

References

Fejfer and Southworth, 1991
Southworth, 1992

41

Sir Richard Worsley collects on a Grand Tour

In 1690 Sir Robert Worsley, then aged twenty, returned from his Grand Tour and made a financially advantageous marriage to Frances Thynne, daughter of the 1st Viscount Weymouth of Longleat. Sir Robert's estate was at Appuldurcombe on the Isle of Wight, with a Tudor house by then considered unfashionable. In 1701 Sir Robert began to build a new house in the modish style known as English Baroque, an exuberant neo-classical style with external columns running two storeys high, triangular pediments and lavish ornament around doors and windows. The building was completed by Sir Richard, Robert's descendant, who returned from his own Grand Tour in 1772 aged 21. Richard employed 'Capability' Brown to design the grounds and Thomas Chippendale to produce the furniture.

All male members of the eighteenth-century Worsley family, like most of their peers, experienced the Grand Tour as the final phase of their polite education. The tour usually meant a spell in Paris, followed by a movement down through France and over the Alps into Italy. Considerable time was spent in the Italian towns looking at art and antiquities and making acquaintances. Rome was a major goal, but many went on to Naples, and to Greece and beyond. The object was to give young gentlemen good taste and social polish. Most men brought back some artwork and classical antiquities. As the eighteenth century progressed, the whole apparatus of the Tour developed into a major tourist industry.

In 1775 Richard married Seymour Dorothy Fleming and Appuldurcombe became the setting for lavish house parties. But the marriage was disastrous – Lady Worsley admitted to twenty-seven lovers, and Richard's lifestyle was no less flamboyant – and ended in public scandal and a very messy divorce, a rare event at that time. Richard found it necessary to leave the country for a long period, and embarked on a second tour, which embraced the Mediterranean, Asia Minor and the Near East. During this time he made a very large collection of art and antiquities, an activity in part, at least, intended to rehabilitate his reputation in the eyes of English society. Not for the first (or last) time, art collecting had the capacity to turn a tarnished reputation into a golden one.

The collection included an important group of Greek marbles, a collection of antique gems acquired from Sir William Hamilton, and paintings by both Old Masters and the masters of the day. The

material was housed at Appuldurcombe where it was known as the
Museum Worsleyanum and was open to the (genteel) public. Richard published a two-volume catalogue of the museum, and it
remained there intact until the mid-nineteenth century. What follows is taken from the catalogue of the collection drawn up in
1806.[1]

APPULDURCOMBE HOUSE, ISLE OF WIGHT

Catalogue of Antique Marble Statues, Busts, Baso relievos, Vases and
Fragments at Appuldurcombe House with the Valuation
April 12th 1806.

At the entrance to the House
Two statuary marble chairs and a bronze knocker.

In the Colonnade Room
— Head of a young Hercules, head of Achilles,[2] head of Niobe, and a
  small bust of a faun
— Two truncated columns of veined Cipoline and a fluted vase of Greek
  saline marble.
— A group, size of life, of Bacchus and Acratus,[3] in the pedestal is
  inserted a mask of Silenus.
— Head of Alcibiades, a small figure of a Genius, and a small draped
  figure of Venus.
— A large Baso-relievo of a Bull, also two small Baso-relievos inlaid in
  the frame.[4]
— A small draped figure of a priestess of Diana with an inscription.
— Three truncated columns of veined cipoline marble.
— A small figure of Cupid, a head of Sophocles, and a truncated column
  of grey granite.
— The half figure of a draped female on a modern marble pedestal in
  which are inlaid three fragments of a baso-relievo and two alabaster
  pateras.
— Head of Demosthenes, a truncated column of granite, a young
  Britanicus, a truncated column of granite, and a small head of a
  Venus.
— An alabaster vase on a plinth of white marble.
— A head of Attilius Regulus forgery.[5]
— Fragment of two small feet on a plinth of statuary marble, also two
  feet in black Egyptian marble.
— A bronze tripod.

– In the tripod a fine specimen of rock crystal...

The whole of the foregoing statues, busts, baso-relievos and fragments are valued by me at the sum of One thousand six hundred and twenty-two pounds, five shillings.

Henry Tresham
Lower Brook Street[6]

Source

Manuscript entitled 'Correspondence and enclosures relating to Sir Richard Worsley's administrators, to estates in the Isle of Wight, to settlement with the Flemings and the Simpsons' (Earl of Bradford Archives). Deposited in Lincolnshire Archives, Lincoln.

Notes

1 Sir Richard was succeeded in 1805 by his niece Henrietta Simpson, who married the eldest son of the 1st Earl of Yarborough. This catalogue was part of the documentation of the estate at the time of Richard's death.
2 Marginal note in the same hand says, 'a forgery'.
3 Worsley describes Acratus as Bacchus' 'favorite genius'.
4 Marginal note says, 'This is inlaid in the wall and very massive'.
5 Presumably of M. Atilius (here spelt with two t's) Regulus, famous for keeping his integrity and returning into captivity during the First Punic War (264–241 BC) between Rome and Carthage.
6 Member of the firm employed to list and value the collection. Lower Brook Street is in Central London.

References

Haskell and Penny, 1981
Worsley, 1782
Worsley, 1794

42

Robert Wood, explorer of Palmyra, muses on ancient architecture and sculpture

Robert Wood was born in County Meath, Ireland, in about 1717. During the early 1740s he travelled extensively in the eastern Mediterranean, and in about 1749 agreed to visit mainland Greece with two friends, James Bouverie and John Dawkins, Bouverie died in September 1750, but Wood and Dawkins visited Greece, the Greek islands, the Black Sea, Palestine, Syria and Egypt.

They came to Athens in May 1751, and there found Nicholas Revett and James Stuart busy making drawings of the city's antiquities, having been commissioned by the Society of Dilettante. This society had been founded in London by Leonard Cust, probably in 1734, originally as a dining club for aristocrats who visited Italy. In 1751 the society funded Revett and Stuart to go out to Athens and there produce a scholarly record of the ancient buildings and their sculptures (as Antoine Desgodetź had done for Rome in *Edifices Antiques de Rome*. They published four volumes, the first in 1762, which set patterns of taste for the subsequent Greek revival. Dawkins and Wood provided considerable help towards the work for the first volume.

By March 1751 Dawkins and Wood had reached Palmyra in the Syrian desert, and on 1 April they reached Baalbec. Palmyra was an oasis city in the desert at the crossroads of the luxury trades which ran east to China and south to Arabia. It seems to have been in existence by 1100 BC, and throughout the Roman empire operated as a client state and a buffer against the Persian empire to the east. The famous Queen Zenobia made a bid for independence in AD 269 and as a result the Emperor Aurelian destroyed the city and massacred its population (AD 273). Palmyra declined to a ruined state. Its chief building was the famous Temple of the Sun, which Wood explored. Baalbec, known as Heliopolis from its great temple to the sun, is situated in east Lebanon. Augustus (31 BC–AD 14) made it a Roman colony. Its ruins are still very extensive.

Once back in Britain, Wood published his *The Ruins of Palmyra* in 1753, and his *The Ruins of Baalbec, Otherwise Heliopolis in Coelosyria* in 1757. These were both major works, containing plans and engravings of the monuments of the two cities executed to a high standard. In the later part of his life, Wood entered politics, and died in 1771.

The piece from *The Ruins of Palmyra* chosen here comes from the introduction, and shows how Wood was able to distinguish the phases of ancient classical architecture as early Greek Doric, succeeding Greek Ionic, later Greek Corinthian, and decadent Roman. This framework, and its aesthetic elevation of Doric and Ionic at the expense of later styles, was to be enormously influential.

CLASSICAL ARCHITECTURE

HOW far the taste and manner of the architecture may give any light into the age which produced it, our engravings will put in every person's power to judge for himself; and in forming such judgement, the reader will make what use he thinks proper of the following observations, thrown together, without any view to order.

We thought we could easily distinguish, at Palmyra, the ruins, of two very different periods of antiquity; the decay of the oldest, which are mere rubbish, and incapable of measurement, looked like the gradual work of time; but the later seemed to bear the marks of violence. ...

There is a greater sameness in the architecture of Palmyra, than we observed at Rome, Athens, and other great cities, whose ruins evidently point out different ages, as much from the variety of their manner, as their different stages of decay. The works done during the republican state of Rome are known by their simplicity and usefulness, while those of the emperors are remarkable for ornament and finery. Nor is it less difficult to distinguish the old simple dorick of Athens from their licentious corinthian of a later age. But at Palmyra we cannot trace so visible a progress of arts and manners in their buildings; and those which are most ruinous seem to owe their decay rather to worse materials, or accidental violence, than a greater antiquity. It is true, there is in the outside of the sepulchral monuments, without the town, an air of simplicity very different from the general taste of all the other buildings, from which, and their singular shape, we at first supposed them works of the country, prior to the introduction of the Greek arts; but we found the inside ornamented as the other buildings.

It is remarkable, that except four ionick half columns in the temple of the sun, and two in one of the mausoleums, the whole is corinthian, richly ornamented with some striking beauties, and some as visible faults.

In the variety of ruins we visited in our tour through the east, we could not help observing, that each of the three Greek orders had their fashionable periods: The oldest buildings we saw were dorick; the ionick succeeded, and seems to have been the favourite order, not only in Ionia, but all over Asia Minor, the great country of good architecture, when that art was in its highest perfection. The corinthian came next in vogue, and most of the buildings of that order in Greece seem posterior to the Romans getting footing there. The composite, and all its extravagancies followed, when proportion was entirely sacrificed to finery and crowded ornament.

Another observation we made in this tour, and which seems to our present purpose, was, that in the progress of architecture and sculpture towards perfection, sculpture arrived soonest at it, and soonest lost it.

The old dorick of Athens is an instance of the first, where the bas-reliefs on the metopes of the temples of Theseus and Minerva,[1] (the first built soon after the battle of Marathon,[2] and the later in the time of Pericles[3]) shew the utmost perfection that art has ever acquired, though the architecture of the same temples is far short of it, and in many particulars against the rules of Vitruvius,[4] who appears to have founded his principles upon the works of a later age.

That architecture out-lived sculpture we had several instances in Asia Minor, and no where more evident proofs of it, than at Palmyra.

This observation on the different fates of those sister-arts, which I have attempted to support by facts, has appeared a little extraordinary to some persons, who very justly consider architecture as the mere child of necessity, a discovery which our first wants must have pointed out, and employed using long before we could have thought of sculpture, the work of luxury and leisure. How comes it about then, say they, that it should be left so far behind by an art much later thought of? Perhaps my having had ocular demonstration of the fact, may induce me to think too favourably of the following manner of accounting for it.

The sculptor having for his object the human figure, has in his first, and most rude essays, the advantage of a model in nature, the closest imitation of which constitutes the perfection of his art. But the architect's invention is employed in the search of proportions by no means so obvious, though when once established they are easier preserved and copied. The first part of this remark perhaps accounts for the quicker progress of sculpture, from the infancy of arts to their happiest state, as the latter part of it attempts to reason why architecture should not so immediately feel the decline of good taste.

Source

Wood, R., 1753, *The Ruins of Palmyra, otherwise Tedmor in the Desert*, London: 15–16.

Notes

1 Minerva, that is, temple of Athene Parthenos, the Parthenon.
2 Battle of Marathon (490 BC) fought 24 miles N.E. of Athens between the Greek cities of Athens and Plataea and the Persians; the Greeks held the passes against the Persians and prevented their further penetration into the Greek mainland. Pheidippides ran the 24 miles to Athens with news of the victory, and died telling it.
3 Pericles (c. 490–429 BC) from 443 leader of Athens during the period (eventually unsuccessful) of Athenian expansion in Greece. He initiated the building of the Parthenon.
4 Vitruvius (active c. AD 10) Roman architect and engineer, author of *De Architectum Libri Decem* (*'Ten Books on Architecture'*), which the eighteenth-century classical revival treated as inspiration and example.

References

Shanks, 1996

43

Sir William Hamilton and his collecting

Sir William Hamilton (1730–1803) may be best remembered in popular legend as a member of the most famous *menage à trois* in English history, composed of himself, his wife Emma and her lover Horatio Lord Nelson, but in his own day he was known as a noted connoisseur and collector. He was the British Minister to the Neapolitan court for over thirty-five years, during the period when Herculaneum and Pompeii were being excavated, and his home, the Palazzo Sessa, was a major meeting place of antiquaries and those undertaking the Grand Tour.

The sites in the area of Naples, and those relating to cities further south in Italy offered at the time excellent opportunities for acquiring classical antiquities, and Hamilton accumulated important collections of sculpture, bronzes, gold jewellery and carved gemstones, and two collections of the famous vases, painted usually with black drawings of mythological subjects on the rich terracotta of the fired clay. Hamilton was acquainted with Winckelmann, who visited him in Naples.

Hamilton collaborated with the self-styled Baron d'Hancarville in the publication of his first vase collection. D'Hancarville was 'at best, an adventurer, and at worst a swindler' (Jenkins and Sloan, 1996: 45), and the publication eventually appeared, after much confusion and financial difficulty, in four volumes in 1767, 1770 and 1776 (2 volumes) under the title *Antiquités Etrusques, Grecques et Romaines*. The descriptions and illustrations of the vases had a massive impact upon fashion and design, being drawn upon, among others, by Josiah Wedgewood. By the time the books appeared, fully illustrated but with the pieces poorly catalogued, the original sources of the vases had been exhausted. Hamilton sold his first vase collection to the British Museum in 1772.

In 1789, however, new sites became known, and in that year Hamilton began collecting afresh what is known as the Second Vase Collection, so that by 1790 he had another major accumulation. The publication of this collection was edited by Wilhelm Tischbein, who supervised the preparation of the vase drawings. The first volume, dated 1791, probably did not appear until 1793, and the second and third were available in 1796 and 1800 (Jenkins and Sloan, 1996: 56). A fourth volume was published later, and further volumes were planned.

Hamilton intended to sell this second collection, and in 1798 with this in mind loaded much of the material on board HMS *Colossus*, bound for England. Unfortunately, she was wrecked off the Scilly Isles and her cargo lost, although some of it has been recovered in recent years. However, the best pieces seem to have been left behind in Naples, by a happy accident. Hamilton sold what he had to Thomas Hope, arbiter of fashionable interior decoration.

In Hamilton's day all the black and red figure vases known had been found in Italy, and were generally assumed to be the work of Etruscan craftsmen. However, connoisseurs in Naples were already asserting their Greek character, and Hamilton himself took this view, believing that they had been made in Italy by Greeks. It was not until excavations began to be undertaken in Greece itself, later in the nineteenth century, that the Greek mainland production of many of them became clear.

LETTER FROM HAMILTON TO CHARLES GREVILLE,[1] WRITTEN IN THE SPRING OF 1789, REFLECTING ON HIS FIRST VASE COLLECTION, BY THEN IN THE BRITISH MUSEUM

The value of my collection in the British Museum is immense, if you was to value it at the present price of antiquities in this country; and be assured that never such another collection will be made, considering the variety of the subjects and the beauty of the forms.[2] I have two or three very extraordinary, indeed, but the Museum shall not have them till I can see no more, for they beautify my new apartment. Emma often asks me, do you love me? ay, but as well as your new apartment ...

Source

Hamilton to Greville, 26 May 1789, Morrison, 1893–49, no. 117, quoted in Jenkins, I. and Sloan K., 1996, *Vases and Volcanoes, Sir William Hamilton and his Collection*, London, British Museum Press: 52

LETTER FROM HAMILTON TO CHARLES GREVILLE, 2 MARCH 1790

A treasure of Greek, commonly called Etruscan,[3] vases have been found within these twelve months, the choice of which are in my possession, tho' at a considerable expense. I do not mean to be such a fool as to give or leave them to the British Museum, but I will contrive to have them published without any expense to myself, and artists and antiquarians will have the greatest obligation to me. The drawings on these vases are the most excellent and many of the subjects from Homer. In short it will show that such monuments of high antiquity are never insignificant as has been thought by many, and if I choose afterwards to dispose of the collection (of more than 70 cases vases) I may get my own price ...

Source

Morrison, 1893–49, no. 180, quoted in Jenkins and Sloan, 1996: 53.

THE FRONTISPIECE ILLUSTRATION TO THE FIRST VOLUME OF THE PUBLICATION OF THE SECOND COLLECTION SHOWED WILLIAM AND EMMA STANDING BESIDE AN OPEN TOMB ADMIRING NEWLY DISCOVERED VASES. IN THE RELATED TEXT, HAMILTON EXPLAINS THE PICTURE.

I have been present at the opening of many of those ancient sepulchres, in which, and no where else, such vases are found; both in the neighbour-hood of Capua, at Nola, in different parts of Puglia, and in Sicily. I have constantly observed that those sepulchres were placed near, and without the walls of the town; under ground and at no great depth from the surface, except at Nola, where the volcanic matter issued from the neigh-bouring mountain of Vesuvius, seems to have added much to the surface of the soil since those sepulchres were made; so that some of the sepul-chres, which I saw opened there, were six and twenty palms beneath the present surface of the earth. The most ordinary sepulchres,[4] are con-structed of rude stones or tiles, and are of a dimension just sufficient to contain the body, and five, or six vases, a small one near the head, and the others between the legs, and on each side, but oftener on the right side, than on the left.

Source

Hamilton's 'To the Reader' in Tischbein, 1793–1803, Vol. 1: 22–4, quoted in Jenkins and Sloan, 1996: 144.

LETTER WRITTEN BY MAJOR BOWEN, COMMANDER OF THE ARMY DETACHMENT ON THE SCILLY ISLANDS, TO CHARLES GREVILLE, 1799

I feel there is no reasonable ground to hope that another article of Sir William Hamilton's interesting collection of antiquities will be recovered from the wreck of the Colossus. You will be sensible of this from the following statement of facts.

The Colossus being, as is generally thought here, in a very weak state, broke up uncommonly soon after striking on the rocks. The people of St. Martin's Island met several packages drifting out at Crow Sound, among the rest those described to them as Sir W. Hamilton's. They assert that, anxious to fulfil Captain Murray's and my earnest injunctions, they used the utmost efforts for recovery of the latter; but that the sea running very high and the wind blowing a storm, they found it impossible to lift the packages which were very large into their boats. They then tried to disengage the contents. Unfortunately, in this also they failed. Their solemn declaration to me is, in their own words, that they saw on opening the canvass cases, 'several large pieces of most beautifully painted clome' (the name for all earthen ware here) 'but that, on their trying to lift them, whether from the effect of seawater on them, or a cement used in joining them, a single piece could not be taken into a boat, each giving way in their hands like wet dough'.[5]

It will be evident to you Sir, that if articles of this, or even of a much more substantial nature, had remained in the hull when the guns shot, and ballast fell together in a mass, they must have been utterly demolished.

The few articles that were recovered were thrown on St. Martin's Island by the sea. I had early intimation of it; and, though they were divided amongst the women of the island, to whom this part of the spoil was left, I succeeded after much toil and the distribution of four guineas in obtaining every piece saved. They were then carefully packed in a large cask of mine, and sent to my friend, William Augustus Pitt, who, having a particular regard for Mr. Greville and Sir William Hamilton expressed great satisfaction in being ... the conveyor of them to the former.

Source

Hamilton's 'To the Reader' in Tischbein, 1793–1803, Vol. I: 22–4, quoted in Jenkins and Sloan, 1996: 144.

LETTER FROM HAMILTON, 25 JANUARY 1800, FROM PALERMO

As to my vases, that is a sore point. They had better be at Paris, than at the bottom of the sea. Have you no good news of them? They were excellently packed up, and the cases will not easily go to pieces, and the sea water will not hurt the vases. All the cream[6] of my collection were in those eight cases on board the Colossus, and I can't bear to look at some remaining cases here in which I know there are only black vases without figures. However, drawings were made of all and the prints for the fourth volume were engraved and are with Tischbein, who I hear is in Germany.

Source

Morrison, 1893–94, no. 444, quoted in Jenkins and Sloan, 1996: 59.

Notes

1 Charles Greville was Hamilton's nephew.
2 This was written just before Hamilton started the Second Collection. He felt he had not received enough from the British Museum for the First Collection.
3 Note 'Greek, commonly called Etruscan'.
4 Hamilton refers to this as 'an ordinary sepulchre found lately at Nola', in contrast to the major, elaborate tombs. It was this kind of site from which the Second Vase Collection came.
5 Captain George Murray commanded *Colossus*. St Martin's island is one of the Scilly group. The description of the painted pottery as 'wet dough' is odd, because skin diving during the 1970s brought up many sherds broken and weathered, but not soft.
6 In fact, the cream had been left behind in Naples.

References

Burn, 1997
Jenkins and Sloan, 1996

44

Plaster shops in Britain, 1760–1820

Plaster shops, mostly but by no means exclusively in London, grew up to supply figures and decorative pieces for collectors and for interior decoration of all kinds. This seems to have been a British phenomenon, linked in its later stages with the Napoleonic Wars which denied access to Continental sources, especially the metal traders of and around Paris, to British collectors and householders.

The plaster shops made mass-production sculpture, from varieties of plaster treated superficially in various ways to resemble bronze, gold and marble. The production seems to have been started around 1738 by John Cleere (1709–87) who had a yard at Hyde Park Corner. He used models by established sculptors like Rysbrack, and also supplied models to Wedgwood and Bentley for use in ceramic manufacture. By the 1780s there were a large number of figure businesses, a number of them featuring business women as well as men. Plagiarism of designs was a major problem, and inspired the so-called Garrard's Act of 1798 which created a copyright in such work. It was not, however, particularly effective.

A good deal is beginning to be known about the operation of the plaster trade. The Bullock brothers, William and his younger brother George, were both involved in it, George particularly. George (?1783–1818) specialised in selling furniture and plaster artwork, first in Birmingham, then Liverpool, and finally London: he seems to have committed suicide in 1818. One of the most famous establishments was that of Coade and Sealy (operating 1769–1820) in Pedlar's Acre, Lambeth. The firm produced a very famous artificial stone known as Coadestone, the recipe for which was carefully guarded, and which could be used to make very good fine detail on decorative and monumental pieces.

Wedgwood and Bentley were substantial buyers of plaster busts, figures and reliefs, using them as the basis from which to produce their famous (and very profitable) ceramic goods. Among others, they bought plaster material from Coade and Sealy (who worked in plaster as well as Coadestone), Mary Landres, and Flaxman, the father of the major artist John Flaxman.

As contact with the Continent was re-established after 1815, and tastes changed, the plaster shops went out of business. However, their products are still extant in the substantial town and country houses of Britain, and their products are a subject of contemporary collection.

COADE AND SEALY SALES LITERATURE

... we must confess, that as Plaster-Casts are so liable to be injured and defaced from the slightest touch, and even by long continuance in damp rooms, they are found in time very expensive, so that (notwithstanding it forms a branch of our business) we can seldom recommend them, for though it may appear to be saving of expense at first, yet it frequently happens, either through the carelessness of servants, accidents by carriage, or otherwise, they have been rendered unfit for their situation, and ARTIFICIAL STONE have at last been substituted in their stead.[1]

Source

Coade's Gallery, 1799.

BUSINESS BETWEEN MRS MARY LANDRE,[2] WHO RAN A PLASTER FIRM, AND JOSIAH WEDGWOOD, IN THE FORM OF TWO INVOICES DATED 1769 AND 1774

London 21 Jan: 1769/Mr. Bentley/Bot of Mary Lands/

4 quarts of the Earth	1. 1. 1
History of Apolow	1. 1. 0
6 passions or Vices	2. 2. 0
4 Groups of Boys	1. 1. 0
3 Female Virtues	1. 1. 0
Antique Baccanalians	7. 6
The Drunken Sylenus	5. 0
The English Poets	1. 1. 0
4 Scripture pieces	8. 6
Moses & the Serpents	1. 1. 0
Joseph	1. 1. 0
The Lords Supper & Company	2. 2. 0
A Battle piece	7. 0
3 pieces of Vintage	15. 0
Apolow & Dafnee	10. 0
A Baccus & Boys	5. 0

Antique figures	8. 0
6 Fryers	6. 0
Antique heads the 12 Caesars & 6 Empresses	18. 0
A large Horse	5. 0
A Magdalen	7. 0
A Baccus & Boys	16 9. 0
A packing case 2.9	2. 9
	16 11. 9

25 Mar. 1769 Rec[d] the above/contents in full/Mary Landre

Wedgwood an Bentley,/Bo of Mary Landre

Christ & the Virgin	0. 10. 6
12 signs of the Zodiak	1. 4. 0
4 plaister Casts	0. 2. 0
4 Medals &c.	0. 5. 6
Horse	0. 5. 0
Bas-relief cast	0. 8. 0
2 round Medals in Brass	0. 4. 0
4 Boys in metal, 7/-	1. 8. 0
Long Bas-reliefs, 15/-	3. 0. 0
	7. 7. 0

Rec[d] June 15 the contents in full/Mary Landre.

Source

Meteyard, E., 1865–66, *The Life of Josiah Wedgewood*, Vol. 2, London: 89, 326.

LETTER FROM JOSIAH WEDGWOOD TO BENTLEY, 16 FEBRUARY 1771

I wrote to you in my last concerning Busts. I suppose those at the Academy are less hackney'd & better in General than the Plaisters Shop can furnish us with; besides it will sound better to say – This is from the Academy, taken from an Original in the Gallery of &c &c than to say, we had it from Flaxman[3] & I suppose you must have these in moulds or not at all; so we must be content to have them as we can, & as Oliver,[4] as a plaister figure maker, in selling the moulds, transfers his business likewise to us he must be pd handsomely for them. I shod like to keep one hand constantly at Busts if you could dispose of them.[5] The Marquis of Rockingham[6] has some divine Busts, one you may remember is actually speaking. If he wod lend you some either to mold in Town or send down here. I think M. Olivers method is to take a mold, then prepare that mould & cast a plaister one out of it, from which he makes what *shod be* a working mould for us, & this long process makes them come so dear. When he takes any casts from Busts for us, let us have the original mould, & that shod not often be more than from 10.6 to a Guinea, & pay him well too.

LETTER FROM JOSIAH WEDGWOOD TO BENTLEY, JULY 1775

I wish you to see Mr. Flaxman before you leave London, & if you could prevail upon him to finish Mr. Banks & Mr. Solander they would be an acquisition to us, & as we shall now make *with tolerable certainty* any moderate sized Bass reliefs of the Composition sent you last in a Conquer'd Province & Composition, I submit it to you whether we should not have some of the finest things that can be modeled, and Original which have not been hackney'd in Wax and Plaister for a century past, & if you think we should, would it not be saving time to set Mr. Flaxman upon some business before you leave him? Mr. Grenville [at Stow][7] you know give us permission to copy or mould from any of the fine things in this possession.

Source

Two letters from Josiah Wedgwood to his partner Bentley, dated from Eturia, 16 February 1771 and July 1775 (Wedgwood Archives at Barlaston, quoted in Clifford, T. 1992 'The plaster shops of the rococo and neo-classical era in Britain', *Journal of the History of Collections*, 4, 1: 44, 54).

Notes

1   Eleanor Coade and her partner John Bacon ran what became the firm of Coade and Sealy, and circulated several pattern books and catalogues, including *Coade's Etchings* circulated with plates from c. 1773–77, *Coade's Descriptive Catalogue* (1784) and *Coade's Gallery* (1799). She and Mary Landre were two of the women influential in the trade.
2   Not much is known about Mary Landre (or Lands), but as these texts show, she was supplying plaster material to Wedgwood and Bentley for use in their ceramic business at Eturia. However, copyright was a difficulty. 'Bot' means 'Bought'. Landre seems to have been working in London around 1768–74.

Wedgwood and Bentley did not use all her plaster figures as bases for ceramic production and they may have favoured her competition.

3   'The Academy' is the Royal Academy, Burlington House, Piccadilly, London. Flaxman is John Flaxman senior (1726–95), the father of the sculptor John Flaxman (1755–1826), his second son. Flaxman senior ran a plaster shop in New Street, Covent Garden. Matthew Boulton of Soho, Birmingham, also bought Flaxman's plasters for his ormolu ornament production.

4   Samuel Euclid Oliver (working 1769–74) worked from St Martin's Lane, London, from which he ran a plaster shop with his partner James Hoskins.

5   Flaxman senior was evidently preparing busts – presumably plaster – of Joseph Banks and Daniel Solander, as well as other subjects, all of which Wedgwood intended to reproduce to reproduce in ceramic and sell.

6   The second Marquis of Rockingham, Charles Watson-Wentworth (1730–82). He was a Fellow of the Royal Society and of the Society of Antiquaries, and a leading Whig politician.

7   Richard Temple Grenville (1711–79) succeeded to his mother's estate of Stowe in Buckinghamshire in 1752, and her title as Earl Temple. He spent much time and money 'improving' the house and gardens at Stowe. He was succeeded by his nephew, who in 1822 was created 1st Duke of Buckingham and Chandos (1776–1839). He was a major collector.

References

Clifford, 1992
Kelly, 1990
Meteyard, 1865–6

45

Correspondence between Charles Tatham and Henry Holland

In May 1794 Charles Heathcoate Tatham, former architectural pupil of Henry Holland, and Joseph Gandy, former pupil of James Wyatt and John Soane, arrived at Livorno (which the English knew as Leghorn), the main port of Tuscany; Tatham was charged with acquiring a collection of artefacts for Henry Holland.

Tatham (1772–1842) was able to fund his Italian tour from a loan of £100.00 made by John Birch, the Prince of Wales's Surgeon-Extraordinary, and by an allowance from Holland of £60.00 per year for two years as recognition of his work as a purchasing agent for casts and antiquities which Holland intended to make use of in his contract to furnish Carlton House, the home of the Prince Regent. The two young architects reached Rome in July 1794 and Tatham set about his twin goals of purchasing material for shipment to London, and organising his election to the prestigious Accademia di S. Luca in Rome, a good career move. In Rome, Tatham and Gandy moved among an artistically influential Anglo-Italian circle which included Canova, Sir William and Lady Hamilton, Tischbein, who was responsible for the publication of Hamilton's Second Vase Collection, Carlo and Joseph Bonomi, and the Earl of Carlisle.

In later life Tatham went on to become a successful architect and furniture designer. He completed the interior of the west wing at Castle Howard for Lord Carlisle as a gallery and museum, with chimney pieces in an Egyptian style, and worked on Cleveland House, Trentham, again with an Egyptian style appearing in his Mausoleum there, and at Wilton Park, among many other British country houses. However, he had a difficult temperament, and engaged in lawsuits with his employers. As a result, he suffered a financial crash in 1834 when his house and personal collection had to be sold. He died four years later in 1842.

A number of letters survive of the correspondence that passed between Tatham and Holland between September 1794 and July 1796, mostly from Tatham but with some copies of Holland's replies; there are also a few pieces from other people on the same topic. From these a feasible account of the acquisition can be put together.

The letter of July 1794 from Richard Westmacott to Holland gives general reassurance that Tatham is operating well in Rome, and has the advice of two such experts as Canova and Westmacott himself. One case of gesses (plaster casts) had already been purchased and despatched, of (we may guess) relatively minor and inexpensive pieces. The letter of 15 February 1795 describes the purchase of an important piece of antique sculpture.

The letter from Holland of 19 May 1795 refers to sketches of possible candelabra, to be made up by local artists, which he had received from Tatham, and returned to him with additions. 'No. 1' referred to is in the form of an Egyptian male figure with kilt and headdress, with a three-branched candelabra on its head, and with a base carrying two winged sphinxes, price £10. Tatham's letter to Holland of 10 July 1795 proceeds with the business of the candelabra by giving the cost of having them made by various artists in the city.

Tatham was still acquiring both casts from the antique and antique pieces as the material for July 1795 shows, and was benefiting by his friendship with Canova. In October 1795, Tatham describes the three pairs of decorative animals he had ordered, copied from the antique. He had made a pen and wash drawing 'copied from the celebrated Egyptian lioness in basalt placed at the foot of the balustrade adjoining the steps leading to the Capital at Rome' as early as May 1795 and had discussed such an acquisition with Holland. Some of the material was despatched to London in October 1795. As the letter of April 1776 shows, Tatham was still interested in buying antiquities.

It will be seen that the material fell into three groups – ancient stone fragments, plaster casts from the antique, and artist-made pieces. Tatham included a copy of the sales catalogue of Jean Volparto, then working in Rome. He also included sketches of two designs by Boschi for candelabra, one mummiform with headdress and mock hieroglyphs, the other human with a single mummy foot running into the pedestal, with kilt and Egyptian headdress; the candle-holder on the head was in the lotus style. The sense suggests that Holland had seen these sketches a little earlier, and the sketch page was added later to the correspondence here.

Tatham made copies of the correspondence for Sir John Soane, and Soane acquired the collection itself in about 1821. It was displayed in a tiny study and dressing room leading out of the dining room.

LETTER TO HENRY HOLLAND, SLOANE SQUARE, LONDON FROM RICHARD WESTMACOTT,[1] FLORENCE, 7 JULY 1794

Mr John Holland without doubt has informed you that your case of gesses is shipped for England and which I hope will arrive safe and sound to your satisfaction ... Signor Canova,[2] a friend of mine in Rome has promised his assistance in procuring antique fragments.

LETTER FROM CHARLES TATHAM TO HENRY HOLLAND, ROME, 15 FEBRUARY 1795

[T dispatching to H] part of the Cima Recta of the cornice from the Temple of Neptune, very large (of the same design you have appropriated to the frieze of Brooke's in St James Street), a very scarce fragment, no one here having its duplicate.

LETTER FROM HENRY HOLLAND TO CHARLES TATHAM AT ROME, 19 MAY 1795

Dear Sir
On the other side you have the sketches you sent me returned in order to show what I mean by marble bases and the omission of the gilding ... I am still at a loss to know whether the prices you sent in the margin of the sketches is for the pair of each; in the one case they are cheap, in the other so high that they will not find many purchases here. At all events I wish to have the pair of No 1.

CHARLES TATHAM TO HENRY HOLLAND, ROME, 10 JULY 1795

The articles you have fixed upon viz. the Egyptian figure, the caryatids and the candelabra were obtained from Guiseppe Boschi, an obscure artist here.

CHARLES TATHAM TO HENRY HOLLAND, ROME, 10 JULY 1795

[The collection] fell into my hands at a very cheap rate through the interference of Canova the celebrated sculptor, several of the articles [in which] ... decorated formerly the museum of the late Piranesi[3] and from some of the same and others of the like nature he composed many of his works. The whole collection No. sixty-four altogether with the sixteen gesses cost me Scudi Romani 110 equal to about £27 sterling.

CHARLES TATHAM TO HENRY HOLLAND, ROME, 10 JULY 1795

List of Antique fragments and gesses sent from Rome. The list includes 64 fragments of stone work and statuary and 16 gesses, including two of Egyptian hieroglyphs from the obelisk of Monte Citorio, Italy.

CHARLES TATHAM TO HENRY HOLLAND, ROME, 25 OCTOBER 1795

I have ordered ... one pair of the Egyptian lioness copied from the famous antique over the fountain of Termoni here. Another pair from the Egyptian lions of basalt at the Capital, and have exceeded your order by another pair, making up the complete collection, copied from the five Egyptian sphinxes in the Museum of the Vatican. The animals to be bronzed casting upon gilt bases, enriched with Egyptian hieroglyphics. The whole will additionally have been placed upon granite and other plinths.

CHARLES TATHAM TO HENRY HOLLAND, 25 OCTOBER 1795

List of antique fragments and gesses sent to Holland. This includes five heads of sphinxes in Greek marble, and part of a sphinx wrought in Egyptian speckled granite, entirely polished.

CHARLES TATHAM TO HENRY HOLLAND, ROME, NOVEMBER 1795

[Cardinal Borgia at Velletri] has in the course of 30 years, made the most rare and extensive collection of Egyptian antiquities of any individual throughout Italy.

CHARLES TATHAM TO HENRY HOLLAND, ROME, 4 APRIL 1796

Such a duo of votaries as Mr Townley[4] and Mr H may form no very inconsiderable heads to establish the merits of the antiquities in question.

Source

Tatham–Holland correspondence, Victoria and Albert Museum, bound folio of letters and drawings, Department of Prints and Drawings, D. 1479. 13.

Notes

1   Richard Westmacott (1775–1856), sculptor and pupil of Canova, carved pedimental figures over portico of British Museum (finished 1847).
2   Antonio Canova (1757–1822). See Chapter 49, this volume.
3   Giovanni Battista Piranesi (died 1778) was a Venetian who settled in Rome. He engraved the ancient monuments and his work was published in a number of volumes before and after his death. He published series of drawings in his *Opere Veria di Architettura* in 1750 and his famous *Carceri* ('*Prisons*') in 1750: this showed sinister arches, staircases and geometrically poised buildings, and was one of the inspirations behind the development of the Gothic taste. He was proprietor of the Cafe Inglese in Rome (from about 1760) and its walls were decorated with Egyptian motifs, one of the inspirations behind the later eighteenth-century Egyptian taste.
4   This is, of course, Charles Townley, see Chapter 39, this volume.

References

Honour, 1955
Proudfoot and Watkin, 1972b
Proudfoot and Watkin, 1972
Salmon, 1998

46

The Edinburgh Trustees buy classical plaster casts for their academy

In 1798 the Board of Trustees for Manufactures in Scotland began to buy figure casts for their academy, or drawing school, in Edinburgh. These were intended to act as a teaching resource in the training of artists, designers and tradesmen. In 1838 they made a major purchase of 255 plaster casts of Greco-Roman portrait busts from Filippo Albacini (1777–1858) of Rome, the son of the sculptor-restorer Carlo Albacini. All these pieces were collected together in what was known as the Sculpture Gallery.

The collection arrived at the Port of Leith in March 1839 in seventeen packing cases, but there proved to be difficulties in the identification of individual pieces, and the compilation of a complete catalogue was abandoned in 1843 when C.H. Wilson, who had been engaged in the work, left Edinburgh.

The Albacini purchase was the last major cast acquisition by the trustees, and thereafter the role of the gallery gradually declined, and the Statue Gallery, having been through many vicissitudes and changes, was finally closed in 1904. Today, 154 of the original 255 busts survive.

The casts, in the form of busts on pedestals or of herms (head on stylised upper body) are taken from classical originals, presumably in Italy during the broad period 1750–1800. The originals are today concentrated in a small number of important collections in Naples, the Prado (Madrid), the Vatican and the Capitoline (both in Rome). The basis of the cast collection seems to have been those pieces made available to the Albacinis during the course of their restoration business: while working on antique (and sometimes modern) material, they took moulds of the portrait sculptures from which casts were made. There was a steady market during the period for such casts, not only as one-off major acquisitions by public bodies like the trustees, but also by private collectors who wished to enrich their libraries and reception rooms. Carlo Albacini also worked as a restorer for, and helped supply statuary to, Charles Townley and Henry Blundell.

REPORT TO THE TRUSTEES OF THE AVAILABILITY OF THE ALBACINI CAST COLLECTION FROM ANDREW WILSON, THEN IN FLORENCE

The collection of busts at present belonging to Sigr. Albigini [*sic*] *could* be got cheap. It is a pity but that the University of Edinr. or the British Museum would take it, as it never can be formed again, the originals having been dispersed all over Europe. This collection has the whole series mentioned by Visconti of Paris, and he refers to two busts at Albigini's as the only place where they are to be found. The collection would be sold at the price or under that of the Roman shops. To a society that would mould them, being all casts in prime order, they would produce an ample return. In *no* part of the world is there such a collection or so authentic. Most of the Greek ones have the artists names upon them and as they have been illustrated by Visconti the possession of them would be a great asset to the learned. In the Louvre they have only a selection of busts for the use of artists, but to see the originals of Albiginis collection it is necessary to visit the Vatican, the collections of the nobility in and around Rome, Florence, Paris, Berlin, Vienna, Munich and even Petersburgh besides London, and many of the originals having fallen into the hands of private individuals, it would be impossible again to do what has been done by Albigini and his father. Considering all this it would be a great object the getting this unique collection to England and, as it would not cost more than 3 or 400 pounds including transport ...

MATERIAL IN THE ALBACINI CAST COLLECTION REPRESENTING ORIGINALS ACQUIRED BY POPE PIUS VI (POPE 1775–99) FROM ITALIAN EXCAVATIONS

A bust of an anonymous Roman of unknown provenance.

A bust of Sabina, the wife of the emperor Hadrian, found by Gavin Hamilton at a villa at Lanuvium owned by the family of the Antonine emperors.

A double herm of Homer and Aeschylus, also acquired via Gavin Hamilton.

The statue of Posidippus, now in the Galleria delle Statue, from which the bust-shaped cast was taken for the Albacini collection. This was discovered in the sixteenth-century, but subsequently acquired by Thomas Jenkins, and then by Pius VI.

A bust of Euripides bought by Pius VI from Carlo Albacini before 1792. This last piece is particularly interesting because in fact only the upper part of the face is original – the rest was restored after the head of Euripides from the Farnese collection (now in Naples). This is on record as being in Albacini's care between June 1786 and 1798 – conveniently close to the 1792 date by which the Vatican piece had entered the collection.

Source

Wilson, C.H., 1837, *Descriptive Catalogue of the casts from Antique Statues in the Trustees' Academy*, Edinburgh: 34.

de Franciscis, A., 1949, 'Restauri di Carlo Albacini a statue del Museo Nazionale di Napoli', *Saurium* 1: 96–110.

References

Davies, 1991
de Gummond, 1991
Howard, 1991
Smailes, 1991
Vaughan, 1991

47

Captain Francis Beaufort, Royal Navy, surveys the coastal lands of Asia Minor

The Royal Navy had an important role in the creation of the great collections of classical sculpture, particularly those from Greece, Asia Minor, and elsewhere in the Mediterranean. The Navy provided the ships, the men and the expertise with difficult and dangerous cargoes, to transport large marble pieces to London, and it also provided the technical skills to produce the hydrographic surveys from which came the first detailed charts of the shorelines on or near which lay the great Greek and Roman cities.

One of the most important of these Navy men was Captain (later Admiral) Francis Beaufort, who first surveyed the coast of Asia Minor between 1811 and 1812. At this time the war with Napoleonic France was still in progress, but the victory of Admiral Howe off Ushant in June 1794, and Nelson's victories of the Nile in 1798 and Trafalgar in 1805, had established the supremacy of the Royal Navy and, among other things, meant that surveys of archaeologically significant areas, and carriage of cargoes from them, had become realistic possibilities.

The excerpt from Beaufort's account of this voyage of 1811–12 given here describes the remains of ancient Seleucia, a late Greek city on the south coast of Asia Minor. Beaufort also mentions 'Boodroom', which is the old Crusader Castle of St Peter at Bodrum, into the walls of which the Hospitaller Knights of St John had inserted a number of bas-reliefs and other marble pieces, probably around 1500. It was gradually realised that these must be some of the sculptured material from the frieze of the Mausoleum of Halicarnassus, one of the ancient Wonders of the World. The tomb had been constructed around 350 BC to house the body of Mausolos, King of ancient Caria. Various efforts were made to acquire these sculptures, particularly those described in a letter from Captain Jones Mangles RN to Beaufort dated 1 December 1840:

> In 1816 Mr. Bankes obtained a firman to have the sculpted marbles removed from the castle walls ...
> The order, however, was so vaguely worded that the Pasha who commanded at Bodroume refused to permit the marbles to be removed. In 1818 Capt. Irby and I, being at Constantinople, offered to Sir Robert

Listor, our ambassador (provided he provide a firman) to remove those marbles at our own expense and to present them gratuitously to the British Museum. We could not, however, persuade Sir Robert to comply ...

(quoted in Jenkins, 1992: 169)

In 1844, Sir Stratford Canning, the British Ambassador at Constantinople, was able to secure the marbles from the castle site and present them to the British Museum. In 1856 Charles Newton (1816–94), Keeper of Greek and Roman Antiquities at the British Museum 1860–86) claimed the credit for finding the site of the Mausoleum itself, and excavated there, finding more pieces of the frieze, and figure sculptures, all of which went to the museum. Newton was later to say that Beaufort's *Karamania* had been his inspiration in the search for the Mausoleum (Jenkins, 1992: 174).

ANCIENT SELEUCIA

The remains of *Seleucia* are scattered over a large extent of ground, on the west side of the river. This river, formerly the *Calycadnus*, and now called Ghuik-Sooyoo, or Heavenly river, is about 180 feet wide abreast of the town; where a bridge of six arches still exists in tolerable repair. They found the remains of a theatre partly cut out of the side of a hill, and facing the south-east; and in front of it, a long line of considerable ruins, with porticoes and other large buildings: farther on, a temple, which had been converted into a Christian church, and several large Corinthian columns, about four feet in diameter, a few of which are still standing. A quarter of a mile to the southward of the theatre, near a marble quarry that seems to have supplied all the materials for the town, there is an extensive cemetery, containing several sarcophagi of coarse workmanship; and in a vein of soft stone on the northern side of the hill, they discovered some catacombs; both, as usual, had been opened and emptied. At these two places they collected a variety of inscriptions; most of them have a cross at the east end, and, therefore, cannot be of great antiquity; and it is remarkable that four differently shaped alphas are promiscuously used. ...

Near the catacombs there is an enormous reservoir, hewn out of the same soft stone; the roof is supported on parallel rows of square pillars, and the sides and bottom are covered with very hard stucco, or terras. Its dimensions are 150 feet by 75, and 35 in depth.

On a hill, west of the town, are the remains of the citadel, of an oval form, surrounded by a double ditch, and a well built wall with numerous towers: the interior is full of ruined houses, among which are many fragments of columns. De Jauna asserts that Selefkeh[1] was given to the knights of Rhodes,[2] by the King of Armenia, as a recompense for their services; and, in proof of this fact, he quotes a brief of Innocent III. deposited in the Vatican. We had seen abundant evidence in the walls of Boodroom castle, of that place having once been in their possession; but, in the walls and towers of this citadel, no such traces were observed by our party.

Two remarkable inscriptions were found here, one in the interior, and the other on a tablet over the outer gate: the former is engraved in the stone, and appears to be the common Armenian of the books; but there was no person on board who understood that language ...

Source

Beaufort, F., 1817, *Karamania, or, a Brief Description of the South Coast of Asia Minor and the Remains of Antiquity*, London.

Notes

1   Selefkeh was the local name of the area.
2   The Knights of Rhodes were Hospitallers.

References

Jenkins, 1992

48

Charles Robert Cockerell travels to the temple at Bassae in Arcadia

The knowledge that Greece contained many more or less unexplored (by Europeans) temple sites, where sculptured works remained, worked powerfully upon the minds of many in Germany and Britain. Greece was during this period a part of the Ottoman (Turkish) empire with its capital at Constantinople (or Istanbul), and was ruled by a network of Turkish officials with whom explorers and collectors had to work. Relationships were often strained, a reflection of the overall political situation in which, at different times, various tensions developed between the government of the Sultan and the Western powers. The Greeks eventually fought a successful war which brought them independence from Turkey in 1827: this was regarded in the West as a deeply romantic event.

This is the background to the collecting career of Charles Robert Cockerell, who was born in 1788, the son of a London architect. He entered his father's practice in 1806, and in May 1810 he embarked on a tour of Greece and the ancient Greek lands of Asia Minor and Sicily, in order to see classical architecture at first hand as part of his professional studies. He spent the winter of 1810–11 in Athens, in a glittering social group which included Lord Byron.

By April, a party to explore temple sites had been made up which included Cockerell and von Hallerstein, the architect to the King of Bavaria. The party travelled to Aegina, an island in the Saronic Gulf, some twenty miles from Piraeus, the port of Athens. Here, they explored the ruins of the famous temple of Jupiter Panhellenius ('of all the Greeks') and stripped away or dug out a very important group of marble sculptures from the site. These were in the early classical Greek style, and probably date from around 500 BC.

These pieces, known as the Aegina Marbles, became the subject of intense international rivalry between the British and the Germans. The sculptures were sold in Zante (modern Zakynthos) when an effort at purchase on the part of a consortium of English bankers was unsuccessful, and the group was purchased by the Crown Prince of Bavaria and taken to the Munich Museum, where they remain.

Meanwhile, later in 1811, Cockerell had moved on to the temple of Apollo Epicurius at Bassae (ancient Phigleia) in Arcadia. Here were found the reliefs forming the frieze around the temple. These are, however, by several hands, and differ in competence; much of the frieze is rather roughly done and overall the artistic merit of the marbles is not much regarded. They are reckoned to belong to the later fifth century BC, and show two mythical battles depicting hoplites fighting the part-horse part-man centaurs, and Greeks fighting Amazons, the tribe of women-warriors. Both were favourite Greek themes, and represent the victory of goodness and normality (that is, the mindset of the Greek male citizen) over the doubtful and monstrous. The temple is situated on a rocky ridge beneath Mount Kotylion, and was built around 430 BC, in the Doric style, reputedly to a design by Ictinus, one of the architects of the Parthenon at Athens.

The digging out of the frieze sculptures, together with some other pieces, took two years, 1811 and 1812. Like the Aegina Marbles, the Bassae sculptures were shipped to Zante for sale, and this time the British were determined to secure the group: an English agent, Mr Taylor Combe sanctioned by the Prince Regent, was sent out, and he purchased the pieces for about £19,000, a very considerable sum. The sculptures arrived in England on 20 October 1815, and were deposited in the British Museum. An extra piece of frieze turned up in 1816 when it was found near the temple site by Mr Spencer Stanhope, and further fragments were presented by the Chevalier Bronstred in 1824; only one slab is now missing. The sculptures were put on display in the museum, in a room adjoining the Elgin Room where the Parthenon Marbles were exhibited.

Cockerell himself had continued his travels in Asia Minor and Sicily, and finally returned to London in 1817. Thereafter, until his death in 1863, he operated as a successful architect. He worked upon designs for Cambridge University Library, the Bank of England, the Ashmolean Museum at Oxford, the Fitzwilliam Museum at Cambridge, the Taylor Building at Oxford and St George's Hall, Liverpool. In 1840 he became Professor of Architecture at the Royal Academy. He was finally buried in St Paul's Cathedral. His *Journal* of his eastern Mediterranean travels was edited by his son, and finally published in 1903; it is included here as the typical product of the travellers and collectors of Cockerell's generation, of whom he was a distinguished, but characteristic member.

BASSAE

HITHERTO we had had an anxious time, but once they were landed we felt at ease about the marbles.[1] Henceforth the business is in Gropius' hands. The auction had been announced in English and continental papers to take place in Zante on November 1, 1812. It took us some time to install them, and altogether we passed an odious fortnight on the island. The Zantiotes, as they have been more under Western influence – for Zante belonged to Venice for about three centuries – are detestable. They are much less ignorant than the rest of the Greeks, but their half-knowledge only makes them the more hateful. Until the island was taken in hand by the English, murder was of constant occurrence, and so long as a small sum of money was paid to the proveditor no notice was taken of it. For accomplishing it without bloodshed they had a special method of their own. It was to fill a long narrow bag with sand, with which, with a blow on the back scientifically delivered, there could be given, without fuss or noise, a shock certain sooner or later to prove fatal. Socially they have all the faults of the West as well as those of the East without the virtues of either. But their crowning defect in my eyes is that they have not the picturesque costumes or appearance of the mainland Greeks.

The most interesting thing in Zante for the moment is Major Church's[2] Greek continent. He has enrolled and disciplined a number of refugee Greeks, part patriots, part criminals, and generally both, and has taken an immense deal of pains with them. He flatters them by calling them Hellenes, showing them the heads of their heroes and philosophers painted on every wall in his house, and endeavours generally to rouse their enthusiasm. He himself adopts the Albanian costume, to which he has added a helmet which he fancies is like that of the ancient Greeks, although it is certainly very unlike those of the heroes we brought into Zante. Altogether, with a great deal of good management and more fustian, he has contrived to attach to himself some thousand excellent troops which under his command would really be capable of doing great things.

At last, on the evening of the 18th of August, we considered ourselves fortunate in being able to get away, and we started to make the tour of the Morea. Gropius, Haller, Foster, Lincke, and I left Zante in a small boat and arrived next morning at Pyrigi, the port of Pyrgo, from which it is distant two hours and a half. We obtained horses at a monastery not far from where we landed, and rode through a low marshy country, well cultivated, chiefly in corn and melon grounds, and fairly well peopled up to the town.

Pyrgo itself lies just above the marshes which border the Alpheus, and, as it happened to our subsequent cost, there was a good deal of water out at this moment. We ordered horses, and while they were being brought in we entered the house of a Greek, a primate of the place. I have been so disgusted with the thinly veneered civilisation of the Zantiotes and bored with the affectations of our garrison offers there, that I was congratulating myself on having got back to the frank barbarism of the Morea, when my admiration for it received a check. The old Greek in whose house we were waiting seemed anxious to be rid of us, and, the better to do so, assured me that Meraca, or Olympia, was only 2½ hours distant, equal to the ordinary rate of Turkish travelling, which is 3 miles an hour, to 7½ miles. The horses were so long in coming, on account of their being out among the marshes and the men having to go up to their knees to get them, that Haller and I got impatient and resolved to go on foot as the distance was so little. It turned out, however, to be 7 hours instead of 2½, and at nightfall we arrived deadbeat at a marsh, through which in a pitch darkness, I may thank my stars, although invisible, for having struggled safely. We wandered about, lost our way, waded in pools to our knees, and finally took 8 hours instead of 2½ to get to our destination.

It was two o'clock in the morning when we got to Meraca, utterly tired out, and with our lodging still to seek. We were directed to a tower in which lived an Albanian aga. The entrance was at the top of a staircase running up the side of the house and ending in a drawbridge which led to the door on the first floor. Once inside we went up two other flights of stairs to a room in which we found two Albanians, by whom we were kindly received. When they heard how tired we were they offered us some rasky. Besides that there was some miserable bread, but no coffee or meat to refresh us. We had to lie down and go to sleep without.

There are few visible remains of the once famous Olympia,[3] and not a trace of stadium or theatre that I could make out. The general opinion is that the Alpheus has silted up and buried many of the buildings to a depth of 8 or 10 feet, and our small researches point in the same direction. We dug in the temple, but what we could do amounted to next to nothing. To do it completely would be a work for a king. I had had some difficulty with the Greek labourers at Aegina, but the Turks here were much worse. In the first place, instead of one piastre apiece per day they asked 2½, and in the next they had no proper tools. The earth was as hard as brick, and when with extreme difficulty it had been broken up they had no proper shovels; and when the earth, which they piled along the trenches as they dug it out, ran into the hole again, they scooped it out with their hands. The thing was too ludicrous. Worst of all, as soon as we turned our backs for a moment they either did nothing or went away. This happened when we left them to cross the river and try for a better view of the place. We got over in a caique, which the aga himself from the village across the water, punted over to us; but the view over there was disappointing, and we came back to find, as I say, our workmen all idling. The long and short of our excavations was that we measured the columns of the temple to be 7 feet in diameter, and we found some attached columns and other fragments of marble from the interior, the whole of which I suppose was of marble, that of the pavement being of various colours. Such stone as is used is of a rough kind, made up entirely of small shells and covered with a very white and fine plaster. And that is about all the information we got for a largish outlay.

From Meraca we rode through romantic scenery to Andritzena, a charming village in a very beautiful and romantic situation; and next morning we settled to go on to the Temple of Bassæ – the stylae or columns, the natives call it. But before we started the primates of Andritzena came in, and after turning over our things and examining and asking the price of our arms, they began to try and frighten us with tremendous stories of a certain Barulli, captain of a company of *klephts* or robbers who haunted the neighbourhood of the stylae. They begged us to come back the same evening, and to take a guard with us. As for the first, we flatly refused; and for the second, we reflected that our guards must be Greeks, while the *klephts* might be Turks, and if so the former would never stand against them, so it was as well for us to take the risk alone. We did, however, take one of their suggestions, and that was to take with us two men of the country who would know who was who, and act as guides and go-betweens; for they assured us that it is not only the professional *klephts* who rob, but that all the inhabitants of the villages thereabouts are dilettante brigands on occasion.

Our janissary Mohomet also did not at all fancy the notion of living up in the mountain, and added what he could to dissuade us. However, we turned a deaf ear to all objections and set out. Our way lay over some high ground, and rising almost all the way, for 2½ hours.

It is impossible to give an idea of the romantic beauty of the situation of the temple. It stands on a high ridge looking over lofty barren mountains and an extensive country below them. The ground is rocky, thinly patched with vegetation, and spotted with splendid ilexes. The view gives on Ithome, the stronghold and last defence of the Messenians against Sparta, to the south-west; Arcadia, with its many hills, to the east; and to the south the range of Taygetus, with still beyond them the sea.

Haller had engagements, which I had got him, to make four drawings for English travellers. I made some on my own account, and there were measurements to be taken and a few stones moved for the purpose, all of which took time. We spent altogether ten days there, living on sheep and butter, the only good butter I have tasted since leaving England, sold to us by the few Albanian shepherds who lived near. Of an evening we used to sit and smoke by a fire, talking to the shepherds till we were ready for sleep, when we turned into our tent, which, though not exactly comfort-able, protected us from weather and from wolves. For there are wolves – one of them one night tore a sheep to pieces close to us. We pitched our tent under the north front. On the next day after our arrival, the 25th, one of the primates of Andritzena came begging us to desist from digging or moving stone, for that it might bring harm on the town. This was very much what happened at Aegina. He did not specify what harm, but asked who we were. We in reply said that we had firmans,[4] that it was not civil, therefore, to ask who we were, and that we were not going to carry away the columns. When he heard of the firmans he said he would do anything he could to help us. All the same, he seemed to have given some orders to our guide against digging; for the shepherds we engaged kept talking of the fear they were in, and at last went away, one of them saying the work was distasteful to him. They were no great loss, for they were so stupid that I was obliged to be always with them and work too, in doing which I tore my hand and got exceedingly fatigued. I was repaid by getting some important measurements.

In looking about I found two very beautiful bas-reliefs under some stones, which I took care to conceal again immediately.

This incident is described in greater detail by Stackelberg in the preface to his book. The interior of the temple – that is to say, the space inside the columns – was a mass of fallen blocks of some depth. While Haller and Cockerell with the labourers were scrambling about among the ruins to get their measurements, a fox that had made its home deep down amongst the stones, disturbed by the unusual noise, got up and ran away. It is not quite a pleasant task to crawl down among such insecure and ponderous masses of stone with the possibility of finding another fox at the bottom; but Cockerell ventured in, and on scraping away the accumulations where the fox had its lair, he saw by the light which came down a crack among the stones, a bas-relief. I have heard this story also from his own lips. Stackelberg further says that the particular relief was that numbered 530 in the Phigaleian Marbles at the British Museum, and naively adds, 'indeed one may still trace on the marble the injuries done by the fox's claws.' He managed to make a rough sketch of the slab and carefully covered it over again. From the position in which it lay it was inferable that the whole frieze would probably be found under the dilapidations.

Early one morning some armed shepherds came looking about for a lost sheep. They eventually found it dead not far from our tent, and torn to pieces by a wolf – as I mentioned before. The day being Sunday we saw some grand specimens of the Arcadian shepherds. They stalk about with a gun over their shoulders and a long pistol in the waist, looking very savage and wild – and so they are: but, wild as they may be, they still retain the names which poetry has connected with all that is idyllic and peaceful. Alexis is one of the commonest.

As our labourers had left us, there was nothing for it but to work ourselves. We were doing so and had just lit upon some beautiful caissons, when a man on horseback, Greek or Turk (they dress so much alike there is no distinguishing them), rode up accompanied by four Albanians all armed. He told us he was the owner of the land, and, although he was very civil about it, he forbade our digging any more. We asked him to eat with us, but being a fast day in the Greek Church, he declined. Finally, after writing to Andritzena, he left us.

After so many objections being made to our excavations we felt it would be too dangerous to go on at present, and promised ourselves to come against next year in a stronger party and armed with more preemptory and explicit authority to dig, and in the meantime there was nothing to do but to get through our drawings and studies as quickly as we could.

The uneasiness of our janissary Mahomet, since our camping out began, gave us serious doubts of his courage, and a plan was invented for testing it. This was to raise an alarm at night that we were attacked by *klephts*. Our Arcadian shepherds entered into the joke with surprising alacrity and kept it up well. Just after supper a cry was heard from the mountain above that robbers were near. In an instant we all sprang up, seized pistols and swords, and made a feint as though we would go up the hill. Our janissary, thunderstruck, was following, when we proposed that he should go on alone.

But he would not do that. In the first place he was ill; in the next place, Would it not be better to go to Andritzena? He begged we might go to Andritzena.

Source

Cockerell, S.P., 1903, *Travels in southern Europe and the Levant 1810–1817. The Journal of C.R. Cockerell RA*, London, Longmans, Green & Co.: 68–78

Notes

1   That is, the Aegina Marbles.
2   Afterwards Sir Richard Church, and Commander-in-Chief of the Greek forces until his death in 1872.
3   Olympia was excavated by the Germans in 1875–76, when the famous statues of Hermes by Praxiteles and the Victory by Paeonios were found.
4   That is, formal permission from the Turkish authorities.

References

Jenkins, 1992

49

Lord Elgin acquires the Parthenon Marbles

Elgin's name is indissoluably connected with the sculpture from the site of the temple of Athene Parthenos ('Maiden') which crowns the hilltop Acropolis at the centre of Athens; the Parthenon Marbles have been constructed into the extreme expression of the Classical Greek genius with a political importance which transcends their archaeological or art-historical importance. The Parthenon was begun in 447 BC on the initiative of Pericles who dominated Athens, in order to mark the city's victory against the Persian empire in wars which had dominated the first half of the century. It was designed by Ictinus and Callicrates, and the sculpture was under the overall control of Pheidias, who probably worked on some of it himself. The temple, which was dedicated in 438, held the famous ivory and gold statue of Athene, which was by Pheidias. Work on the sculpture was, however, still going on in 433.

Thomas Bruce, Earl of Elgin and Kincardine (1766–1841) succeeded his brother in 1771 and in 1799 he went out to Constantinople as Ambassador Extraordinary to the Sublime Porte, the government of the Sultan. Elgin carried out his original intention of establishing artists in Athens to make drawings and casts of the marbles, but when he visited Athens himself he found considerable destruction proceeding and obtained permission not just to make copies but also to remove carved stone.

By 1803 all the available sculptured marbles from the Parthenon had been prepared for embarkation, having been either removed from the site of the temple building or excavated. Of the temple frieze, showing a procession, a length of 80 metres was acquired, the rest (90 metres) having been destroyed; of the statues and fragments of statues, 17, and of the high relief carvings above the frieze, 14. These carvings (metopes from their position in the building) feature the battle of the gods and giants, that of the Greeks and Amazons, and that of the Greeks and centaurs. Of this material, some was lost in a shipwreck near Cerigo and had to be salvaged, with further delay and cost: by 1805 Elgin had spent £40,000 of his own money on the project.

Once they had reached England, the marbles were put on display, in 1807 first in Elgin's own house in Park Lane, and then publicly in Burlington House, Piccadilly. Elgin was met with a storm, which attacked both his actions and the quality of the

works, although he had some powerful supporters. To a generation reared largely on late Greek works, Roman copies of Greek
originals, and sculpture created during the Roman empire, which
tended to be idealistic in concept and rather soft in style, works
from the Greek early classical period, especially of the fifth century BC, with their great naturalistic and individualistic qualities,
seemed at first sight dauntingly vigorous and demanding. In 1810
Elgin published his *Memorandum on the Subject of the Earl of
Elgin's Pursuits in Greece* to justify the quality of the sculptures
and the legitimacy of the circumstances in which he had acquired
them. More significant was the fact that Bavaria had acquired the
Aegina Marbles rather than Britain (see Chapter 48, this volume,
discussing Cockerell) and was showing interest in purchasing those
from the Parthenon. National rivalry, together with the change in
taste which the Aegina Marbles themselves had wrought, brought
into being a Select Committee of the House of Commons, and this
recommended acquisition for the nation at a cost of £35,000. The
marbles were purchased in 1816, and in 1817 went on show in the
British Museum where – controversially – they have been ever
since.

LETTERS RELATING TO THE SETTING UP OF A SELECT COMMITTEE OF THE HOUSE OF COMMONS TO CONSIDER THE PUBLIC ACQUISITION OF THE MARBLES

LONDON, *June* 8th 1815

Sir,[1]

You are, I believe, fully acquainted with the reasons which induced me in
the month of April last, to apply for permission to deposit my collection
of Athenian Sculpture in the British Museum. And I presume that it has
been intimated to you, that this application, for reasons which it is unnecessary for me to detail, was not accepted by the Trustees.

This circumstance, however, has, I am informed, induced the Trustees
to express their desire that the collection should be constituted national
property; and I have accordingly come to London for the purpose of
assuring His Majesty's Government of my readiness to make over my
Collection to the Publick whenever it may be convenient to receive it –
and to enter on the consideration of the transfer in the way that may be
the best adapted to appreciate the value of it, in a satisfactory manner, to
all parties.

When in the year 1811, the Speaker of the House of Commons made a
similar suggestion to me, he desired me to point out what had been my
expenditure in procuring these marbles, his idea being as he stated to me,

that such expenditure, together with interest upon it from the time of the outlay, ought to be reimbursed to me, in addition to any further acknowledgements of the merit which might be attached to the service I had rendered to my country, in securing to her the possession of the best remains of Grecian Sculpture.

I certainly at first felt a good deal of reluctance to produce the details of my expenditure, many particulars of which (however necessary in my own apprehension at the time) might be but little intelligible to others, without more knowledge of local circumstances, than could be entertained by the generality of persons in this Country. And I conceived it to be more eligible for all parties, to endeavour to fix a value on the collection, by aid of the most eminent artists and connoisseurs.

Still however I did prepare as accurate a view as the materials I had could furnish, of my actual disbursements. This paper is still in my possession, and I shall be happy to submit it to examination whenever called for.

But whilst I was engaged with this object, Mr. C. Long, having learnt from the late Mr. Perceval[2] that the sum of £30,000 was the amount beyond which he could not then recommend any appropriation of publick money for similar subjects, desired by immediate determination, on the supposition of such offer being proposed.

Mr. Perceval at the same time, did not hesitate to profess that this limit was in no ways calculated in any reference either to the *real value* of the marbles, or to the expence I had incurred. He acknowledged the matter to be one on which he had personally no opinion, or judgement whatever – and he admitted that he was actuated in regulating the amount, by the consideration of a grant at that moment in agitation in aid of the Sufferers in Portugal.

I am besides given to understand that Mr. Perceval did not think the House of Common would, under any circumstances grant for any one Collection of Objects of Art or Curiosity (wheer might be its intrinsick value) a larger sum than £30,000. I could not therefore but decline to continue the negotiation on these terms, the sum proposed by Mr. Long being wholly inadequate.

Since that time, a very considerable and valuable addition has been made to my Collection. And further opportunity having been afforded both to persons in England, and to foreigners to become acquainted with this series of Athenian sculpture, and to compare it with other collections in Europe, I may venture to assert on the testimony of the Highest Authorities here and abroad that the Collection which I now offer to the Publick, contains better materials in point of originality, variety, and intrinsick merit for forming a national school for the improvement of the fine arts (towards which the liberality of Parliament has already of late years afforded great advantages) and as a general standard of taste, than is known to exist elsewhere.

I take the liberty of stating this much, in explanation of the request which I have now the honor of communicating to you, that a Committee of the House of Commons may be appointed to acquire into the value of this collection.

I solicit this tribunal as offering the most unexceptionable, and the most honorable mode of ascertaining, by an impartial examination of persons, the best qualified to give an opinion on the subject, the real value of what I offer; the difficulties of all kinds which I had to encounter; and the true character of the service I have endeavoured to render to my country. I have no hesitation in declaring to you that I shall chearfully abide by whatever decision the House of Commons may please to come to, (on the report to be made by their Committee on the evidence adduced,) with regard to the extent of the indemnification I am entitled to receive.

Meanwhile, as I may be expected even in this stage of the business to name to His Majesty's Government, a sum, which would satisfy what I conceive to be my just expectations, I have only to premise, that I feel the most sincere regret and concern, that the circumstances of my private fortune, which has been far from being improved by a life spent in His Majesty's foreign service, do not enable me in justice to my family, to indulge the very high gratification of presenting my Collection gratuitously to the Publick. As it is, the only scale of value, which I invidually can give to the Collection, is, the amount of my Expenditure. This, including the preparations made for the undertaking; the artists employed; the obtaining and removing the marbles &c; the loss by sea, and expenses in England; in short the expenses incurred during sixteen years that these operations have been in progress, I may safely state not to have been less than £46,000, on which twelve years interest, on the best average, I can form, has already accrued, making the amount of the whole £73,600 St.

Supposing therefore, no specific enquiry to be made into the value of the collection, which (with very few individual exceptions) I am authorized by the voice of the publick, and by the declared opinion of competent Judges to set at a much higher sum, I profess myself ready, at the present moment, to dispose of my marbles, drawings, vases, casts, etc. etc. being the result of my pursuits in Greece, for the reimbursement of my expenses as above stated.

But if His Majesty's Government think proper to accept of my proposal for an examination into the merits, and value of this collection, before a committee of the House of Commons, I shall be equally ready to abide by their decision. I have only further to assure you, for the information of His Majesty's Ministers that I shall be at all times willing and anxious to offer them any further explanation, which may be required from me, on any of the subjects touched upon in this letter.

I have the honour to be, with the highest respect,
Sir, Your very obedient humble servant
ELGIN.

NOTE It is well known that larger sums have been given, even in this country, by private individuals for other collections of art. £12,500 were given for the Orleans Collection many years ago. £31,500 for the Agar Collection, and as far as £8,000 has been given for a single picture. The entire Orleans Collection was sold at Paris for £60,000. What was sold in England was exclusive of the Flemish School.

DOWNING STREET
10th June 1815

MY LORD
I have taken an early opportunity of communicating with Lord Liverpool[3] upon the subject of the letter which I have had the honor of receiving from your Lordship respecting the Transfer of your Collection of Marbles to the public, and I beg leave to acquaint you that we both coincide in opinion that the most eligible course of proceeding will be that the Subject should be fully enquired into before a Committee of the House of Commons, to which report Government would feel disposed to give the greatest weight, and under whose recommendation a Proposition for the Purchase might be made to Parliament with the greatest advantage. If this should meet your Lordship's views, as I should infer from the sentiments expressed in your letter, I take the Liberty of suggesting that there are two modes by which this subject might be regularly brought under the consideration of the House of Commons, either that a Proposal should be made by your Lordship to the Trustees of the British Museum, from whom an application might be made upon the subject to Parliament, or that Your Lordship should yourself petition Parliament, offering to dispose of your collection to the public. The former of these courses was adopted in respect to the Townley Collection, and the latter in respect to mr. Hargreave's Manuscripts, and it will be for your Lordship to decide which of the two it will be the most advisable to adopt in the present instance. I will only take the liberty of adding that in the present advanced Period of the Session, it is very desirable that no delay should arise in bringing the Subject under Consideration.

I have the honor to be
My Lord
Your Lordship's very obedient Servant
N. VANSITTART.

Source

Quoted in Smith, A.H., 1916, 'Lord Elgin and his Collection', *Journal of Hellenic Studies*, 36: 324–7.

CONTEMPORARY VIEWS OF ELGIN'S ACTIONS, AND THE QUALITY OF THE MARBLES

Entreaty to the British Government that the thorough exploration of the Peloponnesus, by the draughtsman and the modeller, should be made a national object, had been but so much breath spent in vain. Private resources had then been lavished, beyond the bounds of prudence, to confer a public boon. Personal hardships and popular animosities had been alike met by steady courage and quiet endurance. All kinds of local obstacle had been conquered. And now some of the most precious results of so much toil and outlay at the bottom of the sea. The chief toiler was a prisoner in France.

But Lord ELGIN was not yet beaten. He came of a tough race. He was –

> One of the few, the letter'd and the brave,
> Bound to no clime, and victors o'er the grave.

The buried marbles were raised, at the cost of two more years of labour, and after an expenditure, in the long effort, of nearly five thousand pounds, in addition to the original loss of the ship. Then a storm of another sort had to be faced in its turn. A burst of anger, classical and poetical, declared the ambassador to be, not a benefactor, but a thief. The gale blew upon him from many points. The author of the *Classical Tour through Italy* declared that Lord ELGIN'S 'rapacity is a crime against all ages and all generations; depriving the Past of the trophies of their genius and the title-deeds of their fame, the Present of the strongest inducements to exertion.' The author of *Childe Harold's Pilgrimage* declared that, for all time, the spoiler's name (the glorious name of BRUCE) –

> Link'd with the fool's who fired the Ephesian dome –
> Vengeance shall follow far beyond the tomb.
> EROSTRATUS and ELGIN e'er shall shine
> In many a branding page and burning line!
> Alike condemn'd for aye to stand accurs'd –
> Perchance the second viler than the first.
> So let him stand, through ages yet unborn,

Fix'd statue on the pedestal of scorn!

That the abuse might have variety, as well as vigour, a very learned Theban broke in with the remark that there was no need, after all, to make such a stir about the matter. The much-bruited marbles were of little value, whether in England or in Greece. If Lord ELGIN was, indeed, a spoiler, he was also an ignoramus. His bepraised sculptures, instead of belonging to the age of PERICLES, belonged, at earliest, to that of HADRIAN; far from bearing traces of the hand of PHIDIAS, they were, at best, mere 'architectonic sculptures, the work of many different persons, some of whom would not have been entitled to the rank of artists, even in a much less cultivated and fastidious age ... PHIDIAS did not work in marble at all'. These oracular sentences, and many more of a like cast, were given to the world under the sanction of the 'Society of Dilettanti.'

The equanimity which had stood so many severer tests did not desert its possessor under a tempest of angry words. When set at liberty, after a long detention in France, he resumed his journey. On his eventual arrival in England, in 1806, he brought with him a valuable collection of gems and medals, gathered at Constantinople. He also brought some valuable counsels as to the mode in which he might best make the Athenian Marbles useful to the progress of art, obtained in Rome.

For, at Rome, he had been enabled to show a sample of his acquisitions to a man who was something more than a dilettante. 'These', said CANOVA,[4] 'are the works of the ablest artists the world has seen.'

When consulted on the point whether restoration should, in any instance, be attempted, the reply of the great Italian sculptor was in these words: 'The Parthenon Marbles have never been retouched. It would be sacrilege in me – sacrilege in any man – to put a chisel on them.'

Lord ELGIN came to England with the intention of offering his whole Collection to the British Government, unconditionally. He was ready to forget the short-sightedness with which his proposal of 1799 had been met. He was prepared to trust to the liberality of Parliament, and to the force of public opinion, for the reimbursement of his outlay, and the fair reward of his toil. The ambassador was not in a position to sacrifice the large sums of money he had spent. He could not afford the proud joy of giving to Britain, entirely at his own cost, a boon such as no man, before him, had had the power of giving. There were conflicting duties lying upon him, such as are not to be put aside. That British artists – in one way or another – should profit by the grand exemplars of art which he had saved from Turkish musquetry and the Turkish lime-kilns, was the one thing towards which his face was set.

When first imprisoned in France, Lord ELGIN did actually send a direction to England that his Collection should be made over, conditionally, to the British Government. This order was sent, to guard against the possible effect of any casualty that might happen during his detention, the duration of which was then very problematical. He reached England, however, before the instruction had been carried into effect. In the mean time, the controversy about the real value of the Marbles, as well as that which impugned the Collector's right to remove them from Athens, had arisen, and had excited public attention. It became important to elicit an enlightened opinion on those points, before raising the question how the sculpture should be finally disposed of.

The ignorance of essential facts – which alone made such reproaches as those I have just quoted possible from a man devoid of malice, and gifted with genius – was a far less stubborn obstacle in Lord ELGIN'S intended path than was the one-sided learning (one sided as far as true art and its appreciation are concerned) which dictated the sneering utterances of some among the 'Dilettanti.' A BYRON, by his nature, is open to conviction, sooner or later, in his own despite. A connoisseur, when narrow and scornful, is above reason. And he is eminently repro-ductive ...

The self-conceit of the cognoscenti strengthened the too obvious par-simony of Parliament. Lord ELGIN made no direct overture to the Gov-ernment, but appealed to the great body of artists, of students, and of art lovers, for their verdict on his labours in Greece and their product. He arranged his marbles first in his own house in Park Lane, and afterwards – for the sake of better exhibition – at Burlington House, in Piccadilly, and threw them open to public view. The voice of the artists was as the voice of one man. Some, who were at the top of the tree, acknowledged a wish that it were possible to begin their studies over again. Others, who had but begun to climb, felt their ardour redoubled and their ambition directed to nobler aims in art than had before been thought of. Not a few careers, arduous and honourable, took their life-long colour from what was then seen at Burlington House. Some of the men most strongly influenced were not what the world calls successful, but not one of them ended his career without making England the richer by his work.

The eagerness of foreign artists to study the Elgin Marbles was equal to that of Englishmen. CANOVA, when on his visit to London in 1815, wrote: 'I think that I can never see them often enough. Although my stay must be extremely short, I dedicate every moment I can spare to the contemplation. I admire in them the truth of nature, united to the choice of the finest forms ... I should feel perfectly satisfied, if I had come to London only to see them.'

The most accomplished of foreign archaeologists were not less deci-sive in their testimony. VISCONTI, after seeing and studying repeatedly a small portion only of the Parthenon frieze, said of it: 'This has always seemed to me to be the perfect production of the sculptor's art in its kind.' When he saw the whole, his delight was unbound.

The Collector was not able to carry out his plan of exhibition, in any part of it, to the full extent which he had contemplated.

He was anxious that casts of the whole of the extant sculptures of the Parthenon should be exhibited, in the same relative situation to the eye of the viewer which they had originally occupied in the Temple at Athens. He was also desirous that a public competition of sculptors should be provided for, in order to a series of comparative restorations of the perfect work, based upon other casts of its surviving portions, and wrought in presence of the remains of the authentic sculpture itself.

Meanwhile, the chief of the artists employed in the work of drawing and modelling continued his labours at Athens, and in its vicinity, for more than twelve years after Lord ELGIN'S departure from Constantinople. Between the years 1811 and 1816, inclusive, eighty cases containing sculpture, casts, drawings, and other works of art, were added to the Elgin Collection in London.

In the year last named, when the question of artistic value had already been very effectively determined by the cumulative force of enlightened opinion, a Select Committee of the House of Commons was at length appointed, to inquire whether it were expedient that Lord ELGIN'S Collection 'should be purchased on behalf of the Public, and, if so, what price it may be reasonable to allow for the same.'

By this Committee it was reported to the House that 'several of the most eminent artists in this kingdom rate these marbles in the very first class of ancient art ... speak of them with admiration and enthusiasm; and, notwithstanding their manifold injuried ... and mutilations ... consider them as among the finest models and most exquisite monuments of antiquity.' It was also reported that their removal to England had been explicitly authorised by the Turkish Government. The Committee further recommended their purchase for the Public at the sum of thirty-five thousand pounds; and that the Earl of ELGIN and his heirs (being Earls of Elgin) should be perpetual Trustees of the British Museum. And the Committee expressed, in conclusion, its hope that the Elgin Marbles might long serve as models and examples to those who, by knowing how to revere and appreciate them, may first learn to imitate, and ultimately to rival them. On the 1st of July, 1816, the Act for effecting the purchase was passed by the Legislature. I do not know that any one member of the Society of Dilettanti really regretted the fact. But it is certain that by a very eminent connoisseur on the Continent it was much regretted. The King of Bavaria had already lodged a sum of thirty thousand pounds in an English banking house, by way of securing a pre-emption, should the controversy amongst the connoisseurs on this side of the Channel, of which so much had been heard, lead the British Parliament eventually to decline the purchase.

The nearest estimate that could be formed in 1816 of Lord Elgin's outlay, from first to last, amounted to upwards of fifty thousand pounds. And the interest on that outlay, at subsisting rates, amounted to about twenty-four thousand pounds. Upon merely commercial principles, therefore, the mark of honour affixed by Parliament to the Earldom of Elgin was abundantly earned. By every other estimate, Lord ELGIN had done more than enough to keep his name, for ever, in the roll of British worthies. And, as all men know, he had a worthy successor in that honoured title. The name of ELGIN, instead of ranking, according to BYRON's prophecy, with that of EROSTRATUS, has already become a name not less revered in the Indies, and in American, than in Britain itself.

Source

Contemporary views and other material in Edwards, E., 1870, *Lives of the Founders of the British Museum*, Vols 1 and 2, London: 388–96.

Notes

1   Addressed to N. Vansittart, a member of the government.
2   Previously Prime Minister.
3   Lord Liverpool was the Prime Minister.
4   Antonio Canova (1757–1822) regarded as perhaps the most important Italian sculptor of his generation. He registered a return to classic values and the 'pure' form of the antique: his statue *The Three Graces* has been the subject of much recent controversy.

References

Jenkins, 1992
Smith, 1916

50

'Ambulator' describes the New Gallery at the British Museum, opened in 1810

During the years either side of 1800 the British Museum had made an unprecedented series of acquisitions from those who had taken the opportunities the period offered to make major collections of Greek and Roman antiquities. But there was no adequate space in which to display those collections, and so it was clear that an extension was needed. Accordingly, a new gallery was built, projecting from the north-west corner of the old Montague House, which was in a restrained Palladian mode, and would blend in with Montague House. The work began in 1804 and the gallery was opened in 1810.

The anonymous correspondent ('Ambulator' – 'he who walks about') to the *Gentleman's Magazine* gives a description of the New Gallery. He mentions the displays of the Towneley and Hamilton Collections, and of the Barberini or Portland Vase (for all of which see previous chapters in this volume). His view of the Egyptian material as 'uncouth' in contrast to the 'elegant Greek and Roman sculptures' is an interesting comment. His reactions are probably fairly typical of most educated British people of his day.

MR. URBAN, TEMPLE,[1] 14 AUGUST

With the enclosed View of the New Gallery lately erected at the West side of the British Museum ... I think it likely that your Readers will be gratified to find some account of the dimensions and contents of the building, and of the easy manner in which the whole Museum is now made accessible to the publick.

The length of the whole building, as I was informed by one of the keepers, is 217 feet; the width of the main part, that next the eye in the print, is 46 feet; and its height 54 feet. The whole is divided into ten rooms or compartments, eight of which contain Mr. Townley's choice Collection of Greek and Roman Sculptures, which was purchased five years ago by Parliament for the sum of *20,000l.* and in the two others are deposited the Egyptian Antiquities, which were obtained from the French by the capitulation of Alexandria,[2] as also two Mummies, and a variety of small Egyptian Idols, and other curiosities. Over the Egyptian rooms is the Hamiltonian Collection of Greek vases, &c, as also a Medal-room, and a Print-room, to the latter of which strangers are not admitted, but by special leave of the Trustees, and only a few at a time.

The access afforded to the publick both to this Gallery, and to the other parts of the Museum, has of late been so much facilitated, as to be now, it may be justly said, incapable of farther extension. Three days in the week (the Mondays, Wednesdays, and Fridays) are now set aside for the free admission of all persons of decent appearance, from whom nothing is required, but their inscribing their names in a book. They are limited neither in number nor in time, except the shutting of the house at four o'clock. A compendious Catalogue, which is sold in the hall, points out the most remarkable objects contained in the Collections. I must own, that in my perambulations I was singularly gratified to find with what ease I could satisfy my curiosity, and by repeated and unrestrained visits, to have the means of examinging leisurely and attentively such articles as are the particular objects of my curiosity. Indeed, Mr. Urban, the publick must feel themselves very grateful for having such easy opportunities afforded them for improvement or rational entertainment.

Were an obscure individual like myself allowed to offer any strictures, I would venture to observe, that the Egyptian Collection, consisting chiefly of large stone coffins, and massive uncouth figures, ought never to have been placed on an upper story and among the elegant Greek and Roman sculptures. Besides, that their weight and huge bulk renders them only fit for a ground floor: their nature being chiefly sepulchral, it would be much more in character to see them in the solemn recess of a Cata-comb, which, in this instance, should be fitted up in the Egyptian style. I would likewise recommend that, if possible, sky-lights be opened over the Hamiltonian room, where the light at present is very defective.

I was informed in one of my visits, that the Duke of Portland had deposited the celebrated Barberini Vase in this now indeed splendid and well-conducted Repository; and that Mr. Greville's magnificent Collec-tion of Minerals, lately purchased by Parliament, is already removed to the Museum. These, however, are not yet exhibited to the publick.

I hope this slight piece of information will be acceptable to you from
    Yours, &c.   AMBULATOR.

Source

Gentleman's Magazine, September 1810, Vol. 80: 209.

Notes

1   The letter is dated from the Temple (although it does not specify whether the Middle or the Inner Temple is meant), so perhaps Ambulator was a lawyer. Silvester Urban was editor of the *Gentleman's Magazine*.

2   In 1803 Egyptian material captured from Napoleon's army at Alexandria had arrived in the British Museum. This included the Rosetta Stone with its multilingual inscription which greatly facilitated the translation of Egyptian hieroglyphics, and some thirty other pieces. More massive Egyptian pieces were soon to follow through Henry Salt.

References

Jenkins, 1992

Part V
Strange Voices

51

Collecting jewels from India

Until relatively recently, Indian culture was known in Europe only by the stories of its fabulous wealth, and by the material culture which was transported back to western Europe, especially Britain and Holland. The East India Companies of the two countries were in full operation by the end of the sixteenth century, and their officials were well placed to create private collections of Indian material. British power in India was established by Robert Clive, who in 1759 wrote to the British Prime Minister, William Pitt the Elder, extolling the wealth of India, and its availability, in the crudest terms (quoted in Ashton, 1988: 19). Clive himself had a collection of Indian material which featured pictures, swords and textiles. Particularly magnificent objects were gathered forty years later after the war in Mysore in southern India against Tipu Sultan, when the town of Mysore and the palace were sacked. The spoils included a superb jewelled throne, and two ivory thrones which survive at Kedleston Hall, the seat of the Curzon family.

Indian sculpture seems to have been first collected by Charles 'Hindoo' Stuart who served as a general in the East India Company Army between 1777 and 1828. Stuart appropriated pieces from Indian temples in much the same way as his contemporaries were doing from Greek temples, and his collection eventually found its way into the British Museum in 1872. He was one of the founder members of the Asiatic Society of Bengal (founded 1784). The society itself acquired a large collection, housed in the Leadenhall Street headquarters of the Company. It was transferred to the Victoria and Albert Museum in 1879.

A collection of thirty-three Indian jewels in the Rijksmuseum, Holland, has recently been identified as the group of jewels donated in 1754 by Julius Valentijn Stein van Gollenesse, Director-General of the Dutch East India Company in Batavia (now Jakarta in Indonesia). This identification was made by way of an inventory drawn up in 1760 for the director of the cabinet of art and curiosities owned by the then Stadholder of the Dutch republic, William V (of Orange): the collections in the cabinet were passed to the various museums in 1883. The jewellery was part of what was originally a much larger collection. This had been compiled originally by a Dutchman, possibly Jan Stuender, in the international port of Surat in north-west India not long before 1753 (Soheurheer, 1996).

SURAT CURIOSITIES

Memoir of Surat Curiosities sent by Director-General Julius Valentin Stein van Gollenesse to Mr. Van der Vorm and presented and handed over to Her Royal Highness[1] on 25 July 1754 by the same Mr. Van der Vorm

Ornament of a Heathen Woman

1. A *Daminie* or gold head ornament decorated with fine pearls and red stones...
2. A pair of *jaal* or large gold ear-rings set with fine pearls, red and green stones...
6. A *Tullie* or gold tablet round the neck. (lost)
7. A *Hansilie* or gold collar decorated with fine pearls, red, green and white stones...
8. A *kallyantie*, a sort of necklace consisting of fine pearls, red and green stones set in gold...
12. A *jung-malha*, or elongated gold beads, one string three deep.
13. Some rings with chains on them, being four gold rings hanging from a gold roundel with six chains for the right and four ditto for the left hand with green, red and other stones...
17. *Tsjenden tsurie* or bangles, silver covered with gold.
18. *Tsurie rhebbedaar* or bangles, silver coveted with gold, the upper edge with golden clusters...
20. Fourteen *tsuries* or bangles of tortoise-shell set in gold...
21. *Haersankel* or silver chain for the legs...

Ornament for a Moorish woman

24. A *schesful* or gold hair-disc, ornamented with fine pearls, red and green stones...
25. A pair of gold ear-rings with fine pearls and red stones...
26. A *toesie* or necklace of octagonal gold beads two deep (lost)
27. A *dugdughie* or gold breast-roundel with a pearl, red and green stones...
28. *Bedie malla*, or gold strung beads, four deep (lost)
29. Eight gold rings; one with a mirror; one with three red and two green stones; one with four red and one green stone; one with a green stone; one with three red and one green stone; one with a purple stone; and two each with a red stone...
30. A pair of gold *sjuries*, or bangles on silver plates...
31. A set of glass bangles, which were worn by the Moorish-women

rich though they might be, namely 15 green with gold: 4 gilt and 9 black with silver. (lost)

Ornament of both a Heathen and a Moorish women

3. Three pairs of gold ear-rings with fine pearls, red and green stones...
4. A *thica* or gold disc to be worn on the forehead, with fine pearls, some red, three green and a white stone...
5. *Nith* or nose-ring with two fine pearl and one red bead. (lost)
9. *Tien malha* or esclavage (necklace), consisting of seven strings of round gold beads, seven discs with red and green stones and on each disc a fine pearl...
10. *Tsjampakkelly* or a gold chain with red stones and on it a heart with red and green stones and a pearl...
11. *Tjenden haer* or necklace of gold spangles, five deep...
14. A *poensje* with a roundel, or two gold bracelets, each with a roundel of red and green stones with a white one in the centre...
15. A *poensje joewisa*, or two gold chain bracelets...
16. A *kangen*, or two gold bangles...
19. *Baja baanth*, or two gold arm ornaments strung on two purple silk strings with black tassels...
22. Long *haersenkel*, or two silver leg chains with silver bells...
23. Ten enamelled silver toe-rings with bells and chain...

Ornament of a Moor (lost)

1. A sword with a silvered and gilt hilt.
2. A *katherie* or dagger worked as before.
3. A shield complete with strap and mount.
4. A spear with silver mounts at the top and bottom.
5. Two buck horns with silver mounts, serving as a shield and also, if necessary, a dagger.
6. A bow with a red velvet quiver, embroidered with silver.
7. A red velvet quiver embroidered with silver and the 50 arrows belonging to it.
8. A matchlock with a barrel inlaid with silver.
9. A cartridge bag for two cartridges of red velvet embroidered with gold, a mother of pearl and an ivory powder-horn.
10. A set of man's clothing for a Moor.
11. A set of woman's clothing for a Mooress.
12. A set of man's clothing for a Heathen.
13. A set of woman's clothing for a Heatheness.

14.   Two stone figures representing a Heathen and a Heatheness in their costumes.

A Moorish garden with ivory figures, representing a Moorish king with his ministers in a pavilion surrounded by musicians.

Total amount

Of pages, 3, 4, 5, 6 the jewels of the Heathen and Moorish women	fl. 2065
Of pages 7, 8 the weapons, clothing etc.	fl. 110
Of pages 1, 2 the weapons & curiosities of the hereby attached list	fl. 1105
Total	fl. 3280

The undersigned declares that he has estimated the Curiosities mentioned herein (excluding gold, silver, stones and pearls) to the best of his knowledge and in good conscience, Done at The Hague 19 January 1760
A. Vosmaer

The undersigned declare that they have evaluated all the wrought work in gold, silver, stones, etc. likewise to the best of their knowledge and in good conscience Done at The Hague 19 January 1760
Johann Balthasar Krauth
F. Potier

Source

Scheurleer, P., 1996, 'Rich remains from social anthropological fieldwork in eighteenth century India', *Journal of the History of Collections* 8, 1: 71–92.

Notes

1   She was Princess Anna, widow of William IV and Regent for her son, the young Stadholder William V, since 1751.

References

Ashton, 1988
Nicholson, 1987

Smith, 1991

52

Exotic collectibles come back from Captain Cook's voyages of discovery

James Cook was born near Cleveland, Yorkshire, and acquired his seamanship in the Merchant Marine. He joined the Royal Navy and commanded a series of voyages which carried out surveys of the eastern Canadian coast. He also developed an expertise in mathematics and astronomy which made him the obvious choice to command the planned voyage to the southern Pacific to carry out astronomical observations and look for the supposed major southern continent.

Cook set sail for his first voyage in the *Endeavor* in 1768, accompanied by Joseph Banks. By April 1769 the ship reached Tahiti, and cruised on to New Zealand, New Holland and New South Wales (Australia), returning to England via the Cape of Good Hope in June 1711. The success of this voyage prompted the second, with the *Resolution* and the *Adventure*, which set out in July 1772 and crossed the Antarctic Circle to explore the southern seas. The ships also visited Easter Island, the Marquesas group, Tonga and the Friendly Islands, Tahiti, New Hebrides, New Caledonia and New Zealand, returning to Plymouth in July 1775. The third voyage, with the *Resolution* and the *Discovery*, was designed to search for a north-west passage through the Arctic islands from the Atlantic to the Pacific. Cook approached the problem from the Pacific side and on the way explored the Cook Islands, the Hawaiian Islands, and the coast of north-west America (Nootka Sound, Prince William Sound, Cook Inlet and up to the Bering Straits). On the way back, Cook was killed on Hawaii on 17 January 1779. The ships returned to England in 1780.

The avowed object of these voyages was exploration and the collection of scientific data and material, but the officers and men knew that what the age called 'curiosities', that is, material from non-European cultures, had financial value in England. A number of collections were made for this reason, from most of the virtually complete range of Polynesian islands which were visited in the course of the three voyages. This material found its way into many major contemporary collections, including that of Sir Ashton Lever, and so into the Bullock Museum and hence into a wide range of later collections, including the British Museum, the

Cambridge University Museum of Archaeology and Anthropology and the Royal Albert Museum, Exeter.

The Cook voyages material contributed considerably to the growing sense of the exotic and its role as the 'other', in contrast to Britain or Europe.

COOK MATERIAL IN THE BRITISH MUSEUM

When the objects[1] were placed on exhibition in the British Museum, the donors – and especially Joseph Banks[2] – were noted, but apparently the objects were given no labels. In comparing the British Museum to the private museum of Sir Ashton Lever, a German preacher in 1785 made the following remark:

> What I like about it [the Leverian Museum[3]] is, that one can walk around for hours without the need of a guide, because every case contains the name of the article on a small printed label stuck to the glass. I am surprised that the British Museum with all its natural rarities does not follow this example at least with major objects. It would be a great help to the guides and a great service to the public.

If the treatment by the British Museum of the artificial curiosities from the first two voyages was cavalier, that given to objects from the Third Voyage is even more surprising. On 10 November 1780, an entry in the British Museum register reads:

> A collection of artificial curiosities from the South Seas Islands, the West Coast of North America and Kamchatka; lately brought home in His Majesty's ships "Resolution" and "Discovery": from Joseph Banks, Esq.

A second entry for the same day reads:

> Several natural and artificial curiosities from the South Seas: from John Gore, Esq. Commander of the "Resolution," James King, esq. Commander of the "Discovery," James Burney, Lieut. Phillips, Lieut. Roberts, Mr. William Peckover and Mr. Robert Anderson gunners, and Mr. Thomas Waling, quartermaster.

And on November 24th, 1780, is entered:

Several artificial curiosities from the South Sea, from Captain Williamson, Mr. John Webber, Mr. Cleveley, Mr. William Collett and Mr. Alexander Hogg.

... There are two series of objects that one might expect to be composed of specimens from Cook's voyages. One series, known as the 'Cook Collection' is distinguished by labels pasted on the objects. In this 'Cook Collection' series the highest number that is noted on a label is 73, but there are only 12 objects that have such numbered labels. In addition, there are a number of pieces that have similar labels and are designed 'Cook Collection' but the labels do not include numbers. The objects with this series of old labels ('Cook Collection' either with or without a number) are probably authentic Cook voyage pieces – but not necessarily collected by Cook. For example, in this series is the Tahitian mourning costume ('Cook Collection No. 3: (TAH 78) that Cook gave to the British Museum after the Second Voyage. There is also a New Zealand cloak ('Cook Collection No. 1: [NZ 137]), the *taniko* border of which is similar to the cloak that Banks wears in his portrait by Benjamin West. Also in this series is a Hawaiian feather standard (*kāhili*) which may have been collected by Captain Clerk on Kauai in 1779 ..., that is, it was not collected by Cook himself.

A second series of objects is designated 'Banks Collection'. Most of the objects so noted which can be found with such a label or number, are from the Northwest Coast of America. In spite of circumstantial evidence which suggests that these pieces might be from Cook's voyages, it is equally likely that they came from Menzies, botanist on Vancouver's[4] voyage.

Imagine, then, the difficulty and frustration encountered in trying to identify Hawaiian objects in the British Museum that might have come from Cook's voyage, especially when the most obvious piece – a Hawaiian feather image that is with little doubt the one depicted by Webber from Cook's Third Voyage – is catalogued as having come from the voyage of Vancouver, acquired from the descendants of Jewett, surgeon's mate on Vancouver's voyage. In the 'Cook Collection' series only two Hawaiian pieces are included with assigned numbers: a feather standard, 'Cook Collection No. 23' ... and a boar tusk bracelet, 'Cook Collection No. 26' ... One other piece has a matching label but without a number, a gourd water container ...

In 1961 a list of Cook voyage artefacts in the British Museum was made at the request of Ernest Dodge, who was compiling an inventory of Pacific Islands specimens from the voyages of Cook. The list for Hawaii included some thirty-two pieces. If one checks the evidence for the attributions for these objects, however, only six have convincing documentation. These include the three listed above (feather standard, boar tusk bracelet, and gourd water container), two pieces of bark cloth, and a spear. Not very impressive for the National Collection. Also included in the list were two pieces from the 'Banks Collection' series – feather helmet and a feather *lei* (ornament for neck or hair). We will give these two latter pieces the benefit of the doubt, for the moment, because it is possible that they came to Banks from Clerk, but the evidence can only be considered circumstantial. Clerk certainly would have been a likely recipient for a helmet and *lei* and none are included in the 'Cook Collection' series. Further, even the rest of the list that cannot be documented as having an association with Cook's Third Voyage, is not very impressive – fragments of bark cloth, cord, basket, another gourd water container, a dagger, a gourd rattle, but no feather cloaks, no feather images, no wooden images, no bowls with human images, no shark tooth weapons, or other objects characteristic of Hawaiian Cook voyage collections.

On this 1961 list is a barbed wooden spear (1946. Oc.I.I.) ... It bears the note, 'Thrown into the boat when Captain Cook was murdered, brought to England by Thomas Bean, whose wife was nurse to Thomas Green, and gave it to her master'. From the Beasley collection, but not on the 1961 list, is a Hawaiian hook ornament of shell and turtle shell (1944. Oc.2.715) ... which has an old label that reads, 'This fishhook was brought from the South Seas by Mr. Alex Dewar, who accompanied Cap. Cook as clerk to the ship, on two voyages and witnessed his death at Owhyee, 14 Feb. 1779'. Since both of these individuals were on the voyage, there is no reason to doubt this information.

In short, if we depend on British Museum documentation, six, or at the most eight, pieces from Hawaii can be attributed to Cook's voyage. Could it be that only a few relatively minor pieces are really all the Hawaiian objects included in the 'collection' given by Banks and the 'several' given by others in November of 1780? The collection given by Banks probably included the things he inherited from Captain Clerk and from William Anderson, surgeon on the *Resolution* who died on the Northwest Coast of America between Cook's visit to Hawaii in 1778 and 1779. ...

Source

Kaeppler, A., 1979, 'Tracing the History of Hawaiian Cook Voyage Artifacts in the Museum of Manking', *British Museum Yearbook*, 3, 1979: 170–72.

COOK MATERIAL IN THE ROYAL ALBERT MEMORIAL MUSEUM, EXETER

Copies exist of the catalogue of what is known as the Leverian sale, annotated in some cases with the name of the buyer of individual lots, which are described in some detail. It must be remembered also, that many purchases were made by agents, so that a name written into a Leverian catalogue may not be that of the actual purchaser. While the material was still in the possession of Sir Ashton Lever, and no later than 1783, he had commissioned a water-colourist, Sarah Stone, to illustrate some of the exhibits in his museum. The drawings in two of her sketch books were published in 1968 as *Art and Artefacts of the Eighteenth Century* by Roland and Maryanne Force.

Where extant specimens can be matched with these drawings, and where their ownership can be traced back to a lot description and a purchaser at the Leverian sale, then there is every reason to think that the specimen formed part of the material originally acquired in the Pacific by Cook. Among the purchasers at the Leverian sale were a Rev. T. Vaughan of Exeter, a Capt. Cook (alias Smith) of Wortham Manor House near Okehampton, a Mr. Rowe who certainly bought on behalf of a Devon family (*Catalogue of Sale of Important Works of Art and Artifacts*, March 16th, 1971. Bearns Salesrooms, Torquay), and a Mr William Bullock, who bought a sufficient quantity of the material to open a museum of his own, also in London. The Accession Registers of the Exeter City Museums record a series of objects from Melanesia, the North West Coast of America, and Polynesia (cat. nos. 1, 10, 1, 133–5, 186, 195) presented in 1869 by Henry Vaughan, together with a note to the effect that the objects had been in the possession of his family for fifty years. Since some of these specimens have been identified with drawings made by Sarah Stone, it seems certain that the objects presented by Henry Vaughan are those purchased by Rev. T. Vaughan in 1806.

The Accession Registers also record a long series of donations made to the City Museum by the Devon and Exeter Institution including their collection of material from the Pacific and the North West coast. At least some of this material, including the feather cape and the feather helmet from Hawaii (cat. nos. 20, 21) and the gorget and the mourning dress from Tahiti (cat. nos. 153, 155) appear to be of eighteenth century date. The *Western Luminary* for Sept. 28th, 1813, describes a sale at the White Horse Hotel, Lifton, of material which had until shortly before 1813 been in the possession of the Capt. Cook who had bought at the Leverian sale. The material sold at the White Horse included what is described as ·'a dress made of the bark of trees ornamented with feathers and sharks' teeth, worn by the King of Otaheite (Tahiti) ... with the priest's neck and headdress who attended' (I am indebted for this reference to Mr H. L. Douch, Curator of the County Museum and Art Gallery, Truro). These descriptions roughly fit the gorget and the mourning dress parts now in the Exeter collections, and since the Devon and Exeter Institution was founded in 1813 with the avowed intention of establishing a museum, it seems likely that these two pieces, probably together with some others, were purchased at the White Horse sale for the new Institution. Equally, it may be that some of the pieces bought at the Leverian sale by Mr. Rowe on behalf of the Devon family were eventually deposited in the Institution, and so came to the City Museum. The Mr Bullock who had opened his own museum after the Leverian sale was also forced to sell up his collection in 1819. The short *Account of the Origin and Progress of the Devon & Exeter Albert Memorial Museum* by G. T. Bonisthorpe (1868) says 'at the sale in London of Mr. Bullock's noted collection, Sir Thomas Acland made purchases amounting to several hundred pounds, and presented what he had thus acquired to the Institution'. A sad note is added to the effect that most of the specimens have been destroyed by insects, a few only remaining. There are then, three sources by which material from Cook's voyages may have reached the City Museum via the collection of the Devon and Exeter Institution, although, with the probable exception of the gorget and mourning dress, exactly what specimens belong to which source, and which belong to none of them, remains at present in doubt. Some material was presented to the Institution, and then to the Museum, by a Capt. Bond, and these are indicated in the catalogue ...

Easter Island

1. A STAFF, the terminal carved on both sides with a human head, the cheeks pouched, the long ears carved with fine detail, the domed forehead 410 × 20 H. Vaughan E1216 (1868) ...

Hawaiian Islands

10. AN ADZE, having a wooden shaft and a blade of finely polished black basalt, the upper surface of the cutting edge flat, the lower surface gently curved, lashed to the shaft with platted fibre 460 × 160 H. Vaughan E1224 (1868) Force (1868) p. 109 ...

11. A WEAPON with slender handle pierced at the butt, broadening into a wide spatulate blade, the blade edge having twenty-one sharks' teeth (three missing) lashed to it with twisted fibre 290 × 70 H. Vaughan E1226 (1868) ...

15.   AN ARMLET of twenty-three boars tusks, each pierced twice. It has been re-strung on modern wire
82 × 111 H. Vaughan E1278 (1868) ? Force (1968) p. 89, centre

20.   A FEATHER CAPE, of semi-circular shape. The ground work is constructed of sennit, knotted in a diamond pattern, edged along the back across the top and sides, and for a short distance along each side of the bottom with a plaited border of sennit. This ground work is sewn overall with feathers, red feathers forming the background of the design, which comprises two triangles of red and predominantly yellow feathers, both 360mm along the base, each flanked by two triangles one above the other, of predominantly yellow feathers, the lower pair being 150mm across the base, and the upper pair being 100mm. There is a lower border, approx 60mm deep, of predominantly yellow feathers. The cape bears the number 105, which may be an old sale number
435 × 1035 Devon and Exeter Institution E1824 (1875)

21.   A CHIEF's HELMET, having a rounded head-piece with scallops cut out over the ears, and a crest 90mm broad and 80mm high at its highest, extending from the centre front to the centre back. The helmet is constructed of an internal central strip of women aerial roots. On either side the head and cheek pieces of woven roots have been fastened with fibre. The hollow crest, made in the same manner, has been fastened to the top of the central panel. The head pieces and the sides of the crest have been sewn with red feathers, while the top of the crest has been sewn with yellow feathers
302 × 244 Devon and Exeter Institution E1775 (1872) ...

Tahiti

153.   A CEREMONIAL GORGET of crescent form. The framework is of thin strips of wood, lashed together with twisted fibre. Onto the front of this has been bound with twisted fibre a fabric of loosely woven plaited sennit which is turned over onto the back at the neck. A length of the same fabric has been fastened to the front of the neck, and beneath this is bound on with twisted fibre a row of sharks' teeth. Under these, and over-lapping them, are a row of feathers. Beneath these again are a second crescent of sharks' teeth and feathers, bound with twisted fibre to a strip of wood, which is bound to the fabric in the same way. Beneath these, fastened in the same way, is a row of feathers, some red and yellow, and beneath these a third row of sharks' teeth and feathers. Finally, there is a

row of feathers. The outer edge of the gorget is trimmed all round with tassels of dogs' hair, each tassel bound with fibre, and fastened onto the back of the framework with fibre and two further strips of wood. The upper ends of the crescent bear three rosettes of feathers bound onto wooden trips and fastened to the fabric.
586 × 505 Devon and Exeter Institution E1769 (1872) ...

155. Five associated pieces forming the greater part of a MOURNING DRESS. The headdress is composed of eleven pieces of pearl shell, drilled and bound together with fibre, to mask the face. The upper part of the mask is of eight trimmed sections of shell fastened to a rectangular piece, to the lower edge of which are fastened side by side complete half shells. The upper edge of the mask is surmounted by a plume of feathers.
1.160 × 910 E1776
The crescentic board is of wood. Three complete half shells, drilled around the edges and twice at the top, are fastened to its centre portion by fibre, and at each of the crescent tips is a further trimmed shell drilled and fastened in the same way, and decorated with small black feathers. From the crescentic board falls the pendant, now incomplete. This is fastened to the lower edge of the board with fibre, and is composed of rectangular pieces of pearl shell, the pieces largest towards the two sides, but all approx. 30 × 10. The shell rectangles are drilled twice at each end, and are threaded together vertically to form a flexible chest covering.
850 × 85 (board), 740 x 220 (pendant) E1777
A piece of pale brown tapa cloth, bearing five horizontal panels of decoration. The first is of vertical strips of dark tapa overlaying the pale, and overlaying these are strips of black tapa cut with dentate edges. At the end of the panel the strips are confused. The second panel is of three horizontal strips of dark tapa with dentate edges overlaying the pale, and the third is similar, but with black tapa strips. The fourth has alternate panels of horizontal and vertical dentate-cut tapa overlaying the pale, which does not extent quite across the width of the piece, and the fifth is like the third.
1,110 × 1,020 E1778a
The foundation layer piece is of several thicknesses of brown tapa cloth. It has a vertical slit for the head at the top, and 265mm below the end of this are coconut shell pieces fastened in ten vertical rows, each row having fifteen pieces. The pieces are chiefly of plain oval form, but eleven are cut into double-sided dentates. (six pieces are missing) ...
1,150 × 230 E1778b

Tonga

186. A CLUB of lozenge section, the blade carrying four carved bands comprising ribs, enclosing two bands of ribbed triangles, placed to form a double chevron. The butt is partially pierced.
1,160 × 130 H. Vaughan E1205 (1868) fig 7

187. A CLUB of lozenge section, carrying fifteen principal bands of dentate, linear, and lozenge ornament. The butt has a pieced tongue.
1,080 × 120 H. Vaughan E1206 (1868) fig 7

188. A CLUB of lozenge section, bearing eleven bands making up a lozenge and herring bone design. The butt terminates in a small knob.
905 × 130 H. Vaughan E1207 (1868) Force (1968) p. 123, far fight, fig 8

189. A CLUB of lozenge section, bearing six rounds of carving, which are all of linear designs, but the third carries four figures of pigs, the fourth four fish, the fifth four stylised human figures, and the sixth the same, the figures the other way up. The butt terminates in a pierced tongue.
865 × 70 H. Vaughan E1208 (1868) fig 4

190. A CLUB of triangular section, carrying five bands of linear and chevron designs. The butt terminates in a pierced tongue.
930 × 78 H. Vaughan E1209 (1868) fig 9

191. A CLUB of lozenge section, the handle terminating in a pyramid-shaped butt
976 × 73 H. Vaughan E1210 (1868)

192. A CLUB, the head swelling into a mushroom shape, with carved bosses. The butt has a loop pierced for suspension.
1,100 × 102 H. Vaughan E1211 (1868)

193. A CLUB of lozenge section, having a spatulate blade, the tip carrying an irregular pattern of round indentations. The blade is carved with very fine lines, and the handle is bound with strands of plaited fibre to form a diamond pattern.
1,160 × 104 H. Vaughan E1217 (1868) fig 5

194. A NECK-REST, supported on three feet by a centre rib passing under the head piece. The two feet at one end have inturned base supports, and the single foot at the other has the base turned out in front and on both sides.
651 × 75 H. Vaughan E1227 (1868) fig 14

Source

Pearce, S., 1973, *Arts of Polynesia*, Exeter City Museum: 1–3.

Notes

1 From the first and second voyages.
2 For Banks, see Chapter 27, this volume.
3 See Chapter 54, this volume.
4 For Vancouver, Chapter 53, this volume.

References

Force and Ward, 1968
Kaeppler, 1978a
Kaeppler, 1978b

53

George Vancouver sails up the north-west coast of America

George Vancouver (1757–98) joined the Royal Navy aged thirteen, and sailed with Captain James Cook on his second and third voyages. In 1791 he left in command of his own expedition comprising two ships, the *Discovery*, under his own command, and the *Chatham*, with orders to explore the north-west coast of America. Vancouver sailed by way of Australia, New Zealand, Tahiti and Hawaii and then up the north-west coast. He discovered and sailed all round Vancouver Island, demonstrating that it was indeed an island. He arrived back in England in 1795.

Vancouver's career shows the personal links between the officers of the Royal Navy which parallel those between contemporary collectors, and demonstrate how small and interconnected the world of British science, exploration and conoisseurship was. Vancouver's officers and men brought home material, as those of Cook had done, and it similarly reached a range of collections.

The group of material described here was presented to the Royal Albert Museum, Exeter in 1869 by Mr W. Bower Scott. The museum catalogue describes them: 'these specimens were brought home by an uncle of Mr Scott who was a midshipman with Vancouver on his voyage of discovery'. James Scott seems to have served for most of the voyage on the *Chatham*, but to have transferred to the *Discovery* for the last four months. In the Exeter Catalogue, the Scott north-west coast material, printed here, is catalogued under one section, and his Pacific material in another.

MATERIAL COLLECTED ON THE VANCOUVER VOYAGE BY MIDSHIPMAN JAMES SCOTT

North America West Coast
20 April 1869

E788   Harpoon head of bone. 3. Cook's Inlet or River.
E789a   Gigg Spear heads. 2 with slits [flint crossed out] points. Cook's Inlet or River.
E789b   Harpoons. 3 with slits for shell points. Cook's Inlet or River.

E790   Harpoon & Line [with point of slate crossed out]. Nootka Sound.
E791   Harpoon & Line with mother of pearl point. Prince William Sound.
E792   Bears teeth (one carved) 2 N.W. Coast of America.[1]
E1273   Platted lines made from the Sinews & Hair of animals (5). N.W. Cost of America?
E1274   [Knife sheath (2). Crossed out]
E1275   Club of a Whalebone? inlaid with Mother of pearl. North West Coast of America. ...

South Sea Islands
20 April 1869

E1267   Stone Adze in wooden Handle. Otaheite
E1268   Fish hooks made from fish or spines? (4). Sandwich Islands.
E1269   Fish hooks made from Hog bone (6). Sandwich Islands.
E1270   Fish hooks made from Mother of pearl (4). Otaheite
E1271   Fish hooks made from Turtle Shell? (I). Sandwich Islands
E1272   Fish hooks [made from] Human bone (6). Sandwich Islands.

Source

Royal Albert Memorial Museum (Exeter City Museum) Accessions Catalogue.

Notes

1   The carved bear's tooth is very fine and shows a crouching animal with the skeletal details emphasised. It is catalogued as representing a killer whale, but may in fact represent a bear.

References

King, 1994

54

Sir Ashton Lever collects, and then organises a lottery

Ashton Lever came of a rich merchant family whose successful social aspirations were shown by the family's country house, Alkrington Hall, built soon after 1735, just outside Manchester. He was born in 1729, and inherited in 1742, on his father's death. He was collecting in earnest by the 1760s, when he issued leaflets requesting material, and the museum at the hall was opened to the public in 1773. The attendances were huge – more than 1,000 on a single day sometimes – and Lever had to restrict entry to ticket holders, who had, in effect, introductions from one of his own friends.

In 1775 he moved the collection to Leicester House, formerly a royal palace, in London, where he opened a twelve-room museum, the Holophusicon. Lever was clearly an eccentric, but he was a genuinely great collector of natural history, who was made a Fellow of the Royal Society, and was a friend of Captain James Cook (1728–79), from whose second and third voyages Lever was able to gain additional material. By the 1780s the museum was said to contain more than 26,000 items, mostly natural history, but also ethnography from the Pacific, and some European and classical antiquities. There were also some North American and Asian collections.

By the late 1770s Lever seems to have been in financial difficulties, although he retained possession of Alkrington Hall and it is difficult to assess the true state of his affairs. The museum seems to have been available for sale from perhaps 1783, but no one came forward, and so Lever obtained permission (an Act of Parliament was required) to dispose of the collection by lottery. The tickets were sold at a guinea (£1 1s) each, and the draw was made on 22 October 1786. The winning ticket was held by James Parkinson, the proprietor of Ranelagh Pleasure Gardens in London. Lever died in 1788.

Parkinson moved the museum from Leicester Square in 1787 and rehoused it on the south side of the Thames near Blackfriars Bridge in 1788, but he continued to operate the museum as a going concern and added innovative explanatory material in the displays. Also, he maintained a very active programme of additional acquisitions, mostly of natural history material with a strong emphasis on imposing and interesting appearance. However, as a financial venture it does not seem to have been successful, and in 1806 Parkinson disposed of it at auction, the whole being divided into nearly 8,000 lots. The sale catalogue is an exceptionally important source of information relating to the provenance of material still in various collections, which can be traced back to it. The material in the Lever collection had also been recorded in an important series of watercolours by Sarah Stone; some 700 of these pictures survive, a number in the British Museum.

A LETTER BY SUSAN BURNEY TO HER SISTER MADAME D'ARBLAY (FANNY BURNEY) 16 JULY 1778

Saturday morning we spent extremely well at Sir Ashton Lever's Museum. I wish I was a good Natural Historian, that I might give you some idea of our entertainment in seeing birds, beasts, shells, fossils, etc. but I can scarce remember a dozen names of the thousand I heard that were new to me. The birds of paradise, and the humming-birds, were I think, among the most beautiful. There are several pelicans, flamingos, peacocks (one quite white) a penguin. Among the beasts a hippopotamus (sea horse) of an immense size, an elephant, a tyger from the Tower, a Greenland bear and its cub – a wolf – two or three leopards – an Otaheite dog (a very coarse ugly-looking creature) – a camelion – a young crocodile – a roomful of monkeys – one of them presents the company with an Italian song – another is reading a book (are these alive perhaps?) – another the most horrid of all, is put in the attitude of Venus de Medicis, and is scarce fit to be looked at.[1] Lizzards, bats, toads, frogs, scorpions and other filthy creatures in abundance. There were a great many things from Otaheite – the complete dress of a Chine Mandarine, made of blue and brown sattin – of an African Prince. A suit of armor that they say belonged to Oliver Cromwell – the Dress worn in Charles 1st's time etc.etc.

ADVERTISEMENTS AND REPORTS FROM THE *MORNING POST AND DAILY ADVERTISER*

7 April 1785, p. 1
The collection is allowed to be infinitely superior to any of the kind in Europe, the very large sum expended in making it, is the cause of its being thus to be disposed of, and not from the deficiency of the daily receipts (as is generally imagined), which have annually increased, the average amount for the last three years being £1833 per annum.[2]

22 December 1785, p. 1
SIR ASHTON LEVER'S LOTTERY TICKETS are now on sale at Leicester-House every day (Sundays excepted) from nine in the morning till six
in the evening, at One Guinea each: and as each Ticket will admit four
persons, either together or separately, to view the Museum, no one will
hereafter be admitted but by the Lottery Tickets, excepting those who
have already annual admission.

9 January 1786, p. 1
From the quantity of Tickets already sold, in all probability this Collecton
will either become a private Cabinet, be taken abroad, or fall into hands
that will directly sell it in lots, by which means the public may be for ever
deprived of an opportunity of seeing it after the Lottery is drawn. Therefore it is earnestly requested of those who have already purchased, as
well as those who intend to purchase tickets, to be as early as possible in
visiting Leicester-House, to view the Museum before the day of drawing
the Lottery becomes too near, that they may not be inconveniently crowded,
but have every opportunity of seeing the collection to advantage ...

24 January 1786, p. 2
But should this Collection be kept together in any part of these kingdoms,
fortunate it will be for the Town and neighbourhood, where it may be
fixed; for when in Lancashire, the Inns in and near Manchester were
constantly filled with company from all parts, who came on purpose to
view it; and Sir Ashton admitted above 18,000 persons the summer
before he brought it to London. From the above circumstance, is it not of
great moment to every City, Town Corporation, or otherwise, to have a
Subscription by the inhabitants in each City, conjointly for the purpose of
having so valuable a Museum, which will be a lasting monument of
fame, and benefit to the place and possessions thereof.

23 October 1786, p. 1
Yesterday exactly five minutes before Three o'clock at Guildhall, the
holder of No. 34,119, was announced the proprietor of the *Holophusikon*.
Enquiry has in vain been made to ascertain the individual who is hence-
forward to possess this philosophic treasure. The whole that can be
collected even from Sir Ashton Lever himself, is, that the fortunate
number was disposed of at his house in Leicester-fields, so far back as
Dec. 1784, but to whom he cannot at this time recollect ...

13 December 1786, p. 1
[Parkinson publishes the following advertisement in which he] ... begs
leave to subjoin the opinion of Sir Ashton Lever concerning it, who has

lately visited the Museum, and not only commissioned, but even importuned the present Proprietor to make known such his opinion to the public. He avers that he never before saw it in such perfect and improved condition, or made altogether that superb appearance it now does; and added he was happy in the idea of its being continued, what the ultimate object of his wishes ever was to make it – a public ornament, a national honour, and one of the most august and dignified spectacles in the universe.

20 February 1787, p. 1
THIS admired Assemblage for the Productions of Nature and Art, will be again opened for public inspection, on Monday next, at the New Building lately constructed for its reception; and considering the difficulties that must necessarily attend the projecting of a new edifice for this Collection, and the removal and distribution of the various articles which compose it, the Proprietor flatters himself with the hope that his unremitting exertions will meet with the approbation of all persons of taste and science; to whom, and to whose candour, as the natural guardians of a polite, elegant, and rational entertainment, calculated to exercise and strengthen the powers of the human mind, to give pleasure to the imagination, and to excite the most sublime and delightful sensations, he submits his ardent endeavours to please, and to oblige the public.[3]

6 March 1787, p. 1
MR. PARKINSON takes this method of paying his acknowledgements to three several Gentlemen, for presents already lent to his Museum, and assures not only those who are thus early intitled to his gratitude, but ladies and gentlemen in general, who may be disposed to augment and enrich this distinguished collection; and in particular such persons as by accident, profession or inclination, are led to visit foreign parts, where opportunities occur of obtaining uncommon or unknown productions in the animal, vegetable, and fossile kingdoms; that whatever presents he may be favoured with, shall be respectfully received, and carefully preserved by him, as articles of public curiosity, and public amusement; and in case the present collection should ever be sold, of which there is not any intention (unless the now Proprietor should be called upon to fulfil an engagement entered into by him at the instance of a gentleman residing in this metropolis, to sell the same to a great Personage abroad on certain stipulated terms), then such presents shall become liable to the future disposition of the Donors; as likewise all rare and estimable works of art, or either curious subjects, antique or modern.

30 August 1787, p. 1

MUSEUM, at LEICESTER HOUSE, (Late Sir ASHTON LEVER'S) Mr. Parkinson, the present Proprietor, respectfully acquaints the Nobility, Gentry, and Public, at large, that The Exhibition of the INTIRE MUSEUM, Which constituted the LOTTERY PRIZE, Will be continued This and every other Day ...

1 December 1787, p. 1

Mr. Parkinson proposes, in the ensuing spring, to introduce a course of Lectures on Natural History, which will be read at his Museum, by a gentleman of the most respectable character, and of known literary abilities. As the plan of these lectures is yet in its infancy, it is impossible at present to describe it with precision; but Mr. Parkinson wishing to know how far this proposal meets the approbation of the public, intreats the favour, that such Gentlemen who may be inclined to attend the above Lectures, will be pleased to send their names and addresses to Leicesterhouse, before the 20th of March instant, where the terms may be known.

2 September 1788, p. 1

An idea having gone abroad, that the columns, frieze, cornish, and balustrades, in the Rotunda, are only an artificial composition, it may be a Satisfaction to the Public, as they are extremely beautiful, to mention that they are fossil substances, usually known by the name of GYPSUM, and the very substances particularly noticed by the Right Reverend the Bishop of LANDAFF, in his Chemical Essay, Vol II page 306, and Mr. WHITEHURST, in his Enquiry into the Nature and Formation of the Earth, page 224, last edition.[4]

20 May 1788, p. 1

ARTICLES recently added to the MUSEUM, ANIMALS. A creature of the ape species, strongly impressed with the human similitude, being when living, nearly five feet in height, a Unique. A curious Partridge (variety). A beaut'ful Ring Pheasant. Also a remarkable fine Blue and Yellow Maccaw, brought from the Havannah, by General Keppel, in 1762, all presented by very respectable persons. FOSSILS. Some very elegant varieties of Spas, &c.

26 June 1788, p. 1

RECENTLY added to the MUSEUM, A BEAUTIFUL MALE ELK. This noble creature is the most lofty of all European quadrupedes, and may be considered as the first ornament of the forest. It is a perfect, grand, and stately figure, and appears with an inexpressible animation. The curious in Natural History will now have an opportunity of determining whether this is of the same species with the American Elk figured and described by Mr. Pennant. The Natural History of this animal in manuscript, by Dr. Peter Gastavus Lindroth, of the Grilianum Museum in Sweden, First Physician and Surgeon to his Swedish Majesty's Upland Legion (from whom Mr. Parkinson obtained this admirable specimen) contains many curious particulars not generally known, and which may be read at the Museum ...

9 June 1789 p. 1
Recently added to the Museum, select Specimens of Ores, particularly Iron Ores, from the Electorate of Triers, of singular forms, and highly prismatic colours, of which Baron de Winckelman has favoured the present Proprietor with the following Account. 'The beautiful variety of this Iron Ore, which formed Part of the Cabinet of the late Baron de Krisst, Prime Minister to the Elector of Triers, merits attention, it is not being found in any other part of Europe – nor even so frequently now as heretofore; for which reason it is esteemed very rare in the Electorate; the mines appearing to be nearly exhausted of these choice productions.'

Source

Barrett, C. and Dobson, A. 1905: 16 July 1778; pieces from *Morning Post and Daily Advertiser* quoted in King, J., 1996, 'New Evidence for the Contents of the Leverian Collection', *Journal of History of Collections* 8, 2: 169–85.

Notes

1   This is interesting: in Victorian England there was a fashion for this kind of display, particularly for cats and mice.
2   Lever here is seen to be very optimistic about his museum.
3   This is the new museum near Blackfriars Bridge. It was designed by James Burton (1761–1837) a successful London builder, and had the front of a terraced house with a portico.
4   Ill-natured persons had alleged that the portico of the museum was only concrete; this is Parkinson's reply.

References

Force and Force, 1968
King, 1996

55

William Bullock's London museum

William Bullock's enterprises are an interesting mixture of popular entertainment and scientific enquiry. William and his brother George seem to have been born in Birmingham, but in 1799 William had a humble collection of curiosities on show in Sheffield, for which he published the first edition of his *Companion to the Museum*. By 1801 they were both in Liverpool, William and his museum first in Lord Street, then Church Street, and George nearby with his furniture design and production business. William added substantially to his collection by purchases made at the Leverian Collection sale in 1806, particularly in ethnographic material collected in the Pacific. In 1809, William finally moved the collection to London, on show at 22 Piccadilly.

In 1812 the Bullock Museum was installed in custom-built quarters at Piccadilly: this was the famous Egyptian Hall.[1] By 1811, when the tenth edition of the *Companion* was published, the collection included 'upwards of ten thousand Natural and Foreign Curiosities' and by 1818 this had increased to 32,000. Unlike Lever, Bullock was a good man of business, and there does not seem to have been any falling-off in visitors to the Egyptian Hall. However, in 1819 he decided to sell off the whole collection. The sale lasted twenty-six days, from 29 April to 11 June, with Bullock acting as his own auctioneer. Buyers included a number of Continental scholars, the British Museum, the Earl of Derby whose collection eventually went to the Liverpool City Museum, and Sir Walter Scott.

William himself was an ardent field collector, particular of birds, and visited the Firth of Forth (1807), Orkney (1812 and 1814) and Shetland (1814). After the auction of 1819, he began to mount a series of exhibitions at the Egyptian Hall which in February 1822 included the display of a family of Laplanders complete with a herd of living reindeer, and later that year involved two elks brought from North America. In December 1822, William sailed for Mexico, where he stayed for six months and made a substantial collection of ancient Mexican material and casts of antiquities, together with natural history material: these were displayed at the Egyptian Hall in 1825. Thereafter, he spent time in the United States, and the circumstances of his final years and death seem obscure.

CATALOGUE OF THE BULLOCK MUSEUM SALE

Part First, containing the first six days sale. Catalogue (*without which no Person can be admitted either to the View or Sale*) of the Roman Gallery, of Antiquities And Works of Art And the London Museum of Natural History: (unquestionable the most expensive and valuable in Europe) at the Egyptian Hall in Piccadilly; Which will be Sold by auction, Positively without the least reserve. by Mr. Bullock, on the premises, on Thursday, the 29th of April, 1819, and continue every Tuesday, Wednesday, Thursday, and Friday, till the whole is sold *To commence precisely at One o'clock*. The remaining Parts of the Catalogue, about Twenty Days, will be published with all possible speed; the Articles to be viewed Three Days previous to that on which they are respectively sold.[2] ...

From the great extent and variety of objects contained in the London Museum, the Proprietor feels it utterly impossible to publish the whole of the Auction Catalogue, with that descriptive accuracy which the subject requires, in time for the requisite circulation previous to the commencement of the sale, he is therefore under the necessity of circulating it in Parts (each Part Containing Six Days Sale), which will be published with all possible despatch, until the whole is complete.

In submitting the whole of this valuable Collection to the hammer without the smallest reserve or purchasing in, either directly or indirectly, Mr. Bullock trusts to the liberality of the Public, and confidently expects to receive a fair remuneration for the articles which now compose the London Museum; a Collection, which is the result of Thirty Years unremitting attention, under the auspices of the most scientific characters, not only in this country, but in various other parts of the world; and which has been formed at an expense considerably exceeding £30,000.

As many of the articles of Natural History in the Museum have been collected in several places, and under a variety of circumstances, by Mr. Bullock himself he trusts that his knowledge of many particulars, which may add interest or value to the articles themselves, will be a sufficient apology (if any be necessary for the manner in which a man chooses to dispose of his own property) for his appearing before the Public in the new character of an Auctioneer ...

Any Catalogue of a sale so various and complicated as this, must be necessarily incomplete ... The almost exclusive command of the seas, during a protracted war, successively filled this country from every part of the world with the most novel and extraordinary specimens in this branch (the Ornithological) of Natural History, which generally centred in this Museum, and formed an important part of its extensive attractions. There are many thousands of birds unknown to continental Naturalists, and for which names are not to be found in the Linnaean classification ...

The Proprietor, as they must see, availed himself of the great opportunities his Country possessed during the late war of enriching this branch of his Collection at a great expense. He now confidently relies that the result of his labour will not prove an eventual bar to the laudable enterprise of future collectors ...

Second Day's Sale
p. 9–16. Pictures; a few birds; and sundry property of Napoleon. The pictures include many attributed to various well-known artists, amongst them may be mentioned Lot 19, p. 9. Virgin and Child, and St. Anthony, by Corregio, against which is the following note in Professor Newton's copy: 'Cab hire, 10d. and 5d. carriage. Bought at Tivoli, near Rome, where he found it stopping the window of a Cow House, £16 Hume.' The highest price for a picture appears to have been £53 11s. given by an unrecorded buyer for a study of Rinaldo and Armida by Albano.

With Lot 45 p. 11, commenced the disposal of the 'Articles originally the property of the late Ruler of France.' These comprised his military saddle and bridle. Lot 18, £2 15s. various busts of Napoleon and members of his family, plate and glass with arms and initials of Napoleon, sword, orders and medals, pictures illustrating his victories, portraits, cases of arms. Lot 88, p. 16 'A case containing the "Double-barrelled Fowling Piece," with which Napoleon pursued the amusement of shooting down the last six years of his imperialism. This tasteful and highly finished Fowling Piece is ornamented with gold and silver, in various devices of classic and sporting allusion. It was made by Lepage, the gun maker to the Emperor, and bears the initial N. on the gold between the barrel.' £85 1s. (no name of purchaser).

Third Day's Sale
Pp. 17–21. Birds, p. 18, Lot 23. Larus Glaucus. White winged Gull: killed in Northumberland: and ditto of the first year. Lot 29, Ardea Garzetta, Little Egret: very rare, British. This was purchased by Dr. Leach for £1 2s., and presumably went to the British Museum, but Dr. Bowdler Sharpe's pencil note says 'not in Gray's Cat. 1863.' Lot 96, p. 21, Pava Muticus, cost Baron Logier £10 10s.

Fourth Day's Sale
Pp. 22. 28. British Land Birds, Lots 1, 2 and 3 – (1) Golden Eagle killed in Scotland, (2) Ditto Female, (3) the Young and Egg of Ditto, taken in the Orkneys, the only one known in any collection, were all purchased by Dr. Leach at £9 9s., £4 4s., and £1 15s, respectively.

Lot 4 Falco Ossifragus, Sea Eagle (Male) shot on the head of a deer in the New Forest. Dr. Leach, £5 15s. 6d.

Lot 5 Ditto (female) killed in the park of Sir Joseph Banks in Lincoln-shire [extent of wing 8ft 4in.] Leach, £9 9s.

Lot 65 Falco Albicilla. White-tailed Eagle. Dr Leach £3.

Lot 7 Diddo (female). Dr. Leach £3 8s.

Lot 8 Two young, taken in the Isle of Hoy, one of the Orkneys. Dr. Leach, £4 4s.

Lot 9 – Falco Leucocephalus, White-headed Eagle (male). Baron Logier, £5 15s.

Lot 10 Female ditto. These have been lately proved to be the Adult of Albicilla, by one in possession of Mr. Brookes, of Blenheim Street, having this season had the head completely white. Mr. Temminck, £7 5s. [The Mr. Brooks referred to was Joshua Brookes (1761–1823) the well-known Sur-geon and Anatomist of resurrectionist fame; his museum was sold by auction in August, 1828, he kept a menagerie in connection with it. – W.H.M.]

Lot 11 – Falco Fulvus, Ring-tailed Eagle (male). Mr. Sabine, £7 15s.

Lot 12 – Ditto (female). Dr. Leach, £5 5s.

Lot 13 – Two young of ditto. Ditto, £5 15s.

Lot 14 – Falco Haliacetus. The Osprey. Mr. Hamilton, £2 2s.

Lot 15 – Falco Haliacetus. The Osprey (female). Sir Thos. Ackland, £2 12s. 6d.

Lot 16 – Falco Apivorus. Honey Buzzard. £2 14s. (no purchaser recorded).

Lot 19 Lagopus. Rough-legged Falcon (male and female and young bird). £9 9s. (no purchaser recorded).

Lot 20 F. Islandicus Gerfalcon, rare, an adult male: very rare. Sir Thos. Ackland, £3 3s.

Lot 21 – Ditto, a young Bird, not having assumed the White Plumage. Ditto, £2 4s.

Lot 21 – F. Lanatens. Lanner (male and female). Lord Stanley, £2 12s. [Lord Stanley, afterwards Earl Derby, whose museum was given to Liv-erpool. – W.H.M.]

Lot 30 F. Palumbarius. Goshawk. £5 5s. (no purchaser recorded).

Lot 31 Strix Nyetea, Snowy Owl (male), killed in Britain. Dr. Leach, £26 5s.

Lot 32 Ditto ditto. Dr. Leach £9 10s. [Killed in Scotland by Mr. Edmondson.]

Lot 33 – Ditto (female). Dr. Leach, £10 10s.

Lot 34 Strix Bubo. Great eared Owl. Col. Bullock. £3 10s.

Lot 48 Coracius Garrula. The Roller: killed in the Orkneys, very rare. Lord Stanley. £1 2s.

Lot 52 Nondescript Cuckoo, perfectly white, less than half the size of the common : taken in Cornwall, and sent to Sir Joseph Banks ; the only one known. Mr. Sabine, £3 3s.

Lot 60. Upupa Epops. Hoopoe, beautiful male Bird, killed in the Isle of Wight. Sir Thomas Ackland, £1 16s.

Lot 66 – T. Roseus. Rose coloured Thrush (female), taken in the Orkneys, 1818: extremely rare. Lord Stanley, £3 3s. [Killed in the garden of Rev. Mr. Hamilton, Isle of Hoy.]

Lot 67 Diddo (male), very fine. Sir Thomas Ackland, £5 0s. [flew against the Lighthouse of Isle of Sanda and was killed; sent to Mr. B(ullock) by Mr. Strange.]

Lot 99 Great Bustard (male), shot near Ipswich: Otus Tarda: now nearly extinct in Britain. Col. Bullock, £10 10s.

Lot 101 Female ditto, shot near Newmarket. Col. Bullock, £11. (Query, Bustard?).

Lot 102 – Little Bustard, Otis Tetrax (male), extremely rare. Dr. Leach, £10. [Killed in Britain] (killed in Berkshire, see *Comparison* to Museum, ed. 1812, p. 84 and ed. 1813, p. 67, omitted in later eds. Query, Dorset? see *Zoologist*, 1850, p. 4253).

Lot 103 Female ditto. Mr. Brooks, £8 8s. (Prof. Newton notes O. Pickard Cambridge, says 2 Nov., 1877 that his father sent Bullock a female Little Bustard killed in Dorset in the late autumn or beginning of winter about or before 1818).

Lot 108 Crane. A. Grus: extremely rare. Mr. Sabine, £6. [Shot by Lord Gage in Britain.]

Lot 114 Little Bittern. A Minuta (male), extremely rare. Col. Buttock £2 10s. [Killed in the Isle of Sanda, one of the Orkneys.]

Fifth Day's Sale
PP. 29–34. British water Birds.

Lot 15 – Greenwich Sandpiper, T. Grenovicensis; very rare. Dr. Leach, £1 11s. 6d. [Shot near Edinburgh (supposed to have been a young Reeve.)]

Lot 32 Red Phalarope, Phalaropus Hyperborens (male and female). Nest and Eggs; very rare. Baroa Logier, £2 2s. [From Sanda Isle, Orkneys.]

Lot 42 Scooping Avoset, Recurvirostra Avocetta (male and female) and Young; in case. No purchaser recorded, £1 10s. [From the Estate of Lord Ravenshaw.]

Lot 43 – Great Auk, Alca Impennis (male); a very fine specimen of this exceedingly rare bird, killed at Papa Westra, in the Orkneys, the only one taken on the British Coast for many years; and an egg; in glass case. Dr. Leach, 15 1/2 guineas. [This was the bird after which Bullock in 1812 made his famous chase in a six-oared boat, without being able to kill it; *cf.* Montagu, *Ornithological Dictionary.* Supplement (1813) Appendix. It came into his possession in the following year. The bird and egg are now both in the British Museum, South Kensington. – W.H.M.])

Lot 59 Arctic Gull, Larus Parasiticus (male and female) variety, and Egg taken in the Orkneys; rare. Mr. Winn, £3 3s.

Lot 60 Black toed Gull, Larus Crepidatus, shot in Lincolnshire, ditto, £1 2s.

Lot 62 An undescribed Gull, much allied to the Arctic but greatly superior in size, killed at Brighton. Dr. Leach, £3 15s.

Lot 63 Brown-headed Gull, I. Erythropus (male and female), Young and Eggs: taken at Westra, in the Orkneys. Dr. Leach, £2 2s.

Lot 73 Little Gull, Larus Minutus: very rare, Mr. Sabine, £5 5s. [One shot on Edin. Links, other in Lincolnshire.]

Lot 78 An undescribed Petrel with a forked tail, taken at St. Kilda, in 1818; the only one known (with eggs). Dr. Leach £3 15s.

Lot 79 Glariola Austriaca, Austrian Pratincole (male), killed in Shetland in 1812; the second specimen killed in Britain. See Montague and Linnaean Transactions. [Shot on Island of Unst.] Dr. Leach, £8 8s.

Lot 83 Red breasted Goose, Anas Ruficollis (male), shot near Berwick, the only one recorded to have been killed in Britain for upwards of forty years. Dr. Leach, £27. [Shot by Mr. Innes, of Berwick.]

Lot 90 – Round-crested Duck, killed in Norfolk; extremely rare. Lord Temple, £3 3s (*cf.* Hunt *Brit. Birds*). [This may possibly be the Red crested Duck mentioned in Hunt's British Ornithology (1815), Vol. III., page 331, as follows: 'We are informed that a specimen of the male (red crested Duck) was killed in Norfolk, a few years since, and was preserved in the London Museum, – W.H.M.']

Sixth Day's Sale
Pp. 35–40 consists of Foreign Dresses, Arms, Quadrupeds, &c.

Lot 37 – Large superb green Feather Cloak, of the finest workmanship; it was the most beautiful in the Leverian Museum, and esteemed the most valuable ever brought from the Sandwich Isles. Mr. Brettal £13 2s. 0d.

Lot 106 – A small full grown undescribed Animal of the Opossum genus, from New Holland; about one inch in length, by far the least quadruped known; the perfect formation of the teeth proved it to be in adult state. Lord Stanley, £1 1s.

At the end of this day's sale is recorded in MS, the names of the buyers for the principal museums as follows. Lichtenstein, for Berlin, Prussia; Teminick, or Temminck, for Amsterdam; Logier for Paris.

Professor Newton has added: Proctor, for Vienna; Leach, British Museum; Adams, Edinburgh.

Seventh Day's Sale
Pp. 41–50. Shells. Lot 6 A fine stellated branched Coral (variety of Madrepora, Virginia), having a few cells or stars. West Indies, Captain Brown, £1 10s.

Lot 35 A fine Flambeaux Cone, the Striated Cone, and a Tortoiseshell Harp. Count Brenner, £1. 7s.

Lot 76 A large and fine Voluta Fluctuata, from Van Diemen's Land. Count Brenner, £1 10s.

Lot 104 – A pair of the Brown variety of Turbo Scalaris, from Ceylon; very rare. Count Brenner, £2 10s.

Eighth Day's Sale
Pp. 50–58. Shells.

Lot 41 Balanus Gigas, with the Teeth, from California; very scarce. Dr. Goodall £3.

Lot 65 – A large and fine clouded Persian Crown Volute, from the Moluccas; very rare. Mrs. Warner, £2 9s.

Lot 74 – A very uncommon Spiral Terrestrial Helix, from the East Indies, Mrs. Warner, £4 18s.

Lot 106 The Wenteltrap, Turbo Scalaris. The magnificent and well known specimen from the late Mr. Webber's Museum, unquestionably the first example of this rare Shell, known in any collection. Mrs. Warner, £22 11s.

Nineth Day's Sale
Pp. 59–65 – Shells, Fossils

Lot 89 A most splendid specimen of Fossil Crabs, from Sheepy Island; this and the last lot [described as "A Crab from Ceylon; a magnificent Fossil," bought by Mr. Lönig for £21] are absolutely unrivalled in their kind. Lord Stanley, £8 18s. 6d.

Lot 152 The finest example of a Fossil Tortoise known in any collection, found in the Isle of Portland, presumed to be unique; with the case [and a beautiful specimen of the Head from Sheepy Island. 25 guis. Mr. König].

Tenth Day's Sale
Quadrupeds.

Lot 98 A most superb and finely prepared specimen of the Royal or Bengal Tiger, seized by the Boa Constrictor [from Ceylon]. The beautiful manner in which the group is preserved, render it worthy of a place in the first museum in the world. A fine picture, copied from it by the Chevalier de Barde, is now in the Louvre. Mr. Cross, £38 17s.[3] [On the twenty-second day of the sale there was sold as Lot 111. The great Boa Constrictor, twenty-two feet long, in the act of seizing a Deer, most beautifully set up and considered as the finest subject in the Museum; this was purchased by the Marquis Buckingham for £47 5s., and the MS, note against it says. The Boa with Tiger (*i.e.* Lot 98) only twenty feet long but much thicker. W.H.M.]

Lot 109 – The Black Ourang Outang, Simia Satyrus (from Africa), a very finely prepared specimen which died at Liverpool. Dr. Adams, £12 12s.

Eleventh Day's Sale
Pp. 72–76. Birds.

Lot 26 Grand Hoopoe, Upupa Superba; very fine specimen. Prof. Lichtenstein, £4 15s.

Lot 42 – Black Petrel, Acquinoctalis, Dr. Leach, £6 16s. 6d.

Lot 61 – The Tailor Bird, with its curious Nest, from the Leverian Museum; the only ornithological specimen from that collection in the sale. Mr. Ledbrook. £2 7s. [This somewhat conflicts with Lot 91 sold on the seventeenth day, which is described as 'The Tailor Bird, Motacilla Sutoria (male and female), with their highly curious nest, from the East Indies; the only specimen known in Britain.' It was brought by Lord Stanley for £3 15s. – W.H.M.]

Lot 94 – The Ostrich, S. Camelus (a fine fully-grown male), 10 feet high, beautifully preserved, and in the highest preservation. Prof. Temminck, £38 6s. 6d.

Twelth Day's Sale
Pp. 77–80. Birds

Lot 23 – Antigua Yellow Oriole, Oriolus Flavus, and next. Prof. Temminck, £1 4s. [See Hunter's Museum.]

Lot 70 – Le Coucou Geant, Le Valliant, Vol. V., P. 223. Baron Logier, £3 13s.

Lot 111 – Beautiful Blue Crow, from Mexico, undescribed. Lord Stanley, £16 5s. 6d.

This completes the first Two Parts of the Catalogue, and here follows the title page of Part III., the sale thereon being announced for Thursday the 24th of May, 1819.

Thirteenth Day's Sale
Pp. 81–85. Birds of Prey, Toucans and Hornbills.

Lot 4 – Black Hawk, American Ornithology, Vol. VI., p. 82. Very rare, only known in Peale's Museum. Prof. Temminck, 12s.

Lot 25 – Sooty Owl, Strix Fuligonosa; very fine. Prof. Temminck, £11.

Lot 64 A splendid nondescript species of Lanius [altered in MS, to Corvus] sent to Europe by Perouse, and perhaps the only remaining memento of his voyage. Mr. Leadbetter, £7 17s. 6d.

Lot 105 – Imperial Eagle, Falco Imperialis, a very fine example of this noble bird, preserved in the act of seizing a large nondescript serpent of South America: with the Glass Case. Col. Bruen, £27 6s.

Lot 121 – White Jer Falcon, Falcon Islandicus; a beautiful specimen of this exceeding rare British bird, in its snow white plumage. Dr. Leach, £10. [Prof. Newton's note against this item runs, 'Not included in list of Birds in Brit. Museum. Hence Dr. Leach may have bought other things not for the Mus. or some may have been destroyed since, *i.e.*, the Aust. Pratincole.' (This was Lot 79 on the fifth day's sale).]

Fourteenth Day's Sale
Pp. 86–90. Birds.

The whole of this Day's Sale consists of Birds of the Psillacus, or Parrot Genus, of which this Collection contains perhaps greater Variety and more undescribed Species, than any other; many of them were bought by Sir Joseph Banks in his Voyage of Discovery with captain Cook: and are in no other Collection.

Lot 19 Horned Parakeet, P. Cornatus: brought by Sir Joseph Banks from the South sea: the specimen described by Dr. Latham. Very rare Dr. Leach, £5 12s [Prof. Newton's note, 'In Gray's list, 1859 (p. 7), but not now in Brit. Mus.'.]

Lot 93 Pair of beautiful Yellow Macows (male and female), from the Spanish main; undescribed. Lord Stanley, £21.

Lot 113 Black Parrot, P. Niger, Baron Logier. £5 10s. [Prof. Newton's note – Probably P. Vasa, see Vigor's Zool. Jour. iii. p. 242.]

Fifteenth Day's Sale
Pp. 91–95. Herons, Ducks, Wood Peckers, Bee Eaters, etc.

Lot 59 Harlequin Duck, A Histronica, Dr. Adams (Edinburgh) £1 1s. (Killed in Orkneys).

Lot 102 Red throated Bee eater, Mr. Gularis. Baron Logier, £15 15s. 0d.

Lot 123 – Rose-coloured Spoonbill. Platelea Ajaja: a most splendid specimen of this beautiful bird, in its adult plumage. Mr. Fector, £8.

Sixteenth Day's Sale
Pp. 96–100. Pigeons, Grouse, Chatterers and Manakin.

Lot 35 – Bronze-winged Pigeon, C. Chatcoptera, Coil. Bruen. £1 [Bred in England by Duke of Northumberland.]

Lot 70 – Puff-breasted [*i.e.* Bull breasted] Partridge, I. MS. Prof. Temminck, £1 (also in his work).

Lot 89 – The whole Collection of Swallows, Hirundo: consisting of eighteen different species, some of which are rare, and others new. Lord Stanley, £7 7s.

The remainder of this day's sale (after Lot 109) was chiefly devoted to serpents and lizards, it also contained some birds.

Seventeenth Day's Sale
Pp. 101–107. Tuesday, May 27th, 1819, – Tanagers, Humming Birds, Creepers, Birds of Paradise, etc., etc.

Lot 35 An undescribed Peacock from Java; the only one known. Baron Logier, £40 19s.

Lot 46 – Red-legged Partridge, T. Rufous. [Killed in Suffolk in grounds of Col. Rendlesham]. Mr. Ledbrook. £1 7s.

Lot 60 White Gallinule, F. Alba; New Zeland, rare (brot (*sic*) by J. Banks). Lord Stanley, £3 3s.

Lot 87 A magnificent species of turkey, from the Bay of Honduras, undescribed; it was sent as a present to Sir Henry Halford, and died on its passage: the only one known. Baron Logier, £54 12s.

Eighteenth Day's Sale
Pp. 108–114. Insects, Fishes, Shells, Corals, and Marine Productions.

Lot 40 – A fine Branch of Isis Hippuris, or Pied-jointed Coral; from the Straits of Sunda. Dr. Goodall, £6 10s.

Lot 105 A large Case of Exotic Fishes, containing seventy of the most interesting and curious inhabitants of the waters ... Mr. Ledbrook for Marquis of Buckingham, £31. 10s.

Source

Mullens, W., 1917–18, 'Some Museums of Old London, II. William Bullock's London Museum', *Museums Journal*, 17: 51–5, 132–7, 180–87.

Notes

1   Bullock opened the Egyptian Hall at 22 Piccadilly, London, in 1812. The architect of the facade was P. F. Robinson, and the scheme showed an Egyptian-style pillared entrance with above two large-size sculptures of Egyptian gods surrounded by a pediment, and with four windows of truncated triangular shape. After the sale in 1819, numerous exhibitions of a wide range of types were held in the hall up to 1905, when it was demolished.

2   Copies of the sales catalogue exist in the British Museum (Natural History), National Museums on Merseyside (old Liverpool City Museum), and the Newton Library, Cambridge. Mullens used the Newton copy, which seems to have belonged to George Caley (d. 1829), a zoologist sent out to Australia by the Linnaean Society. This copy has notes giving the names of purchasers and prices paid in Caley's handwriting, and is further annotated by Professor Newton who bought it in 1860. These notes had been cross-referenced with the British Museum copy by Dr Bowdler Sharpe.

3   This exhibition, and possibly the case too, survive in Rossendale Museum in Rawtenstall, Lancashire. Edward Cross (1774–1854), who bought the lot at the sale, was an active dealer with his own 'menagerie' at Exeter Exchange, off the Strand, London. The exhibit reappears as a donation of Lord Hastings to the Castle Museum, Norwich in 1893, and passed from Norwich to Rawtenstall in 1930. The snake is a fake, as Bullock himself admitted (it is two specimens joined, with a wooden head). See further Hancock, 1980.

References

Hancock, 1980
Mullens, 1917–18

56

Visitors see sensational collections at York

Scattered records make it plain that there were a number of collections available for viewing in popular, rather than elite, locations, and in the provinces rather than in London. The problem is that details of these collections seldom survive. They were accumulated and displayed in inns, or in various halls and salerooms, sometimes permanently, sometimes as a result of a tour organised by their commercially-orientated owner.

An insight into some of these collections – albeit one which in its own way was of particular importance – was that on show in the County Gaol housed in York Castle (and now the home of the York Castle Museum, the city's historical museum). The material was on show from at least the 1790s, by which time York had its own mythology of sensational murder and highway robbery. The exhibition seems to have been put together by the gaolers, who presumably used it as a supplement to their incomes.

The York display was very popular. By 1840, one of the gaolers was writing to a local magistrate complaining: 'I attend 7 days in the week, in summer from 6 in the morning until 10 at night, the number of visitors since the railroad commenced has increased to a great extent, in the first week in September last year I let in from 400 to 500 persons to see the curiosities alone' (quoted in Brears and Davies, 1989: 7).

When the prison closed in the late nineteenth century, most of the material was transferred to the Yorkshire Museum. Some of it was returned to the castle when the Debtor's Prison was opened to the public in 1952.

YORK COUNTY GAOL

… a small room adjoining the house of the governor [has] its walls covered with implements of crime, murder and robbery &c. Here are preserved the coining apparatus used by David Hartley; the razor with which Jonathan Martin, the incendiary, struck a light to burn the minister;[1] the bellrope by which he let himself down from the window; a part of the skull of Daniel Clark, the victim of Eugene Aram, dug up in Knaresborough; the strap with which one Holroyd hung his father on a cherry tree; the knife and fork with which the rebels were quartered,

1745; the fetters (24lbs) which confined Dick Turpin's[2] legs, and the belt which went round his waist, while in prison here ... and many other articles which would do substantial duty in a sensation novel ...

Source

Palliser, D. and M., 1979, *York as they saw it*, York: 45, 67, 75

Notes

1   This is York Minster, the cathedral of York and seat of the Archbishop of York, who is the senior Church of England clergyman in the Northern Province of England.
2   Dick Turpin was one of the most famous highwaymen of the eighteenth century, whose fast ride from London to York on his mare Black Bess was the stuff of street ballads and popular culture. The other men named were of more local interest.

References

Brears and Davies, 1989

57

William Beckford collects his fantasies

In 1786, when he was twenty-six, William Beckford published his novel *Vathek* which was to become one of the founding narratives of the Gothic imagination. It is a clearly autobiographical novel centring on the person of the Calif Vathek, who lived as an all-powerful oriental despot surrounded by a palace of treasures and with adoring multitudes at his feet. The same note had been struck in another unpublished autobiographical fantasy, *L'Esplendente*, written in 1780. The circumstances of Beckford's career, mixed with his particular temperament, united in an effort to bring these early fantasies to life in the world he constructed around himself.

Beckford was born in 1760, on his father's side the heir to a Jamaican sugar fortune, and on his mother's a member of the aristocratic Hamilton family.[1] He received a hothouse education, and inherited a fortune on his father's death in 1770. In 1779 he started an affair with the youthful William Courteney (later Earl of Devon), and was packed off on his Grand Tour as a result, but on his return resumed the affair with William, and the upshot was a major scandal centring upon 1784. He went to Europe again, but was forced to return when the war with France broke out. During his time aboard he had collected art and related objects steadily.

From about 1799 Beckford withdraw to his estate at Fonthill in Wiltshire, where there was already a gentleman's country seat, known as Splendens. He devoted himself to building a new house, Fonthill Abbey, within which he could preserve his solitary state and act out his inner imaginings. Fonthill was intended to create a theatrical effect, and became one of the first houses in what was to be the Gothic Revival style. It was planned between Beckford and the architect James Wyatt, and eventually evolved into a cruciform building with an octagonal main reception room and tower above at the crossing, and the Fountain Court in one of the angles. The doors and windows were arched, and the design included stained glass windows and fan vaulting. Beckford was able to move into part of it in 1807, but the whole building was not finished until 1813. In 1807 Splendens was pulled down. Fonthill was generally considered by the artistic taste of the day to be a building of sublime beauty, and in it Beckford lived the life described in the pieces given here.

Meanwhile, these expenses, the mismanagement of his Jamaica estates, and the general state of trade, were eroding Beckhill's fortune. By 1820, his affairs were desperate, and in 1822 Fonthill was put on the market and was bought by John Farquhar, a gunpowder millionaire. He did not enjoy it for long: in 1825 the central tower collapsed, and on Farquhar's death, the estate was broken up. Beckford, meanwhile, had moved to Lansdown Crescent in Bath, and while in Bath he bought land on Lansdown Hill and then built Lansdown Tower, a tower with a few small rooms at its base, this time in a classical style. Beckford died in Bath in 1844.

EXTRACT FROM *L'ESPLENDENTE*

The pride of Ancestry and a haughty consciousness of his descent (which he strove in vain to dissemble) rendered him obnoxious to the World in general. And finding himself disliked and dreaded, he had retired from court to the solitude of an ancient castle in the midst of his Duchy, where he employed himself in literary pursuits and forgot his ennuis and ill-humours in the cultivation of the arts and the sciences. He was surrounded by poets, musicians, sculptors and designers, who lost and gained by turns the empire of his mind. Sometimes he was enchanted by chemical researches; another moment, Architecture engaged his attention, and he built lofty towers in the morisco style, and added magificent corinthian porticos to the gothic abodes of his ancestors. When this rage was subsided, the fury of antiquities began to predominate. Every corner of his domain was first ransacked for medals and tesselated pavements; then collectors were sent out to explore the most remote provinces of the Kingdom in search of rusty helmets, tattered shields, inscriptions and broken milestones. Meanwhile, commissions being sent to Sicily and Greece, whole shiploads of mutilated figures were landed at Alicant, and these pagan images scandalously usurped the nitches of the best Saints in the Calendar. When this passion had worn itself out, a violent admiration of paintings succeeded. Nothing pleased the Grandee but the productions of the pencil. He filled his appartments with the works of Raphael, Titian and Julio Romano at an immense expense, and constructed whole suites of rooms purposely to display them.

Source

Unpublished autobiographical fantasy of Beckford's, published in Alexander, B., 1960, 'The decay of Beckford's Genius', in Mahmoud, F. (ed.), 1960, *William Beckford of Fonthill 1760–1844, Bicentenary Essays*, Cairo, Tsoumao and Co.

EXTRACT FROM *VATHEK*

Vathek, nineth Caliph of the race of the Abassides, was the son of Motassem, and the grandson of Haroun al Raschid.

He surpassed in magnificence all his predecessors. The palace of Alkoremi, which his father, Motassem, had erected on the hill of Pied Horses, and which commanded the whole city of Samarah, was, in his idea, far too scanty: he added, therefore, five wings, or rather other palaces, which he destined for the particular gratification of each of the senses.

In the first of these were tables continually covered with the most exquisite dainties; which were supplied both by night and by day, according to their constant consumption; whilst the most delicious wines and the choicest cordials flowed forth from a hundred fountains that were never exhausted. This palace was called *The Eternal or Unsatiating Banquet.*

The second was styled *The Temple of Melody, or the Nectar of the Soul.* It was inhabited by the most skilful musicians and admired poets of the time; who not only displayed their talents within, but dispersing in bands without, caused every surrounding scene to reverberate their songs, which were continually varied in the most delightful succession.

The palace named *The Delight of the Eyes, or the Support of Memory,* was one entire enchantment. Rarities, collected from every corner of the earth, were there found in such profusion as to dazzle and confound, but for the order in which they were arranged. One gallery exhibited the pictures of the celebrated Mani, and statues that seemed to be alive. Here a well-managed perspective attracted the sight; there the magic of optics agreeably deceived it; whilst the naturalist, on his part, exhibited in their several classes the various gifts that Heaven had bestowed on our globe. In a word, Vathek omitted nothing in this palace that might gratify the curiosity of those who resorted to it, although he was not able to satisfy his own; for, of all men, he was the most curious.

The Palace of Perfumes, which was termed likewise *The Incentive to Pleasure,* consisted of various halls, where the different perfumes which the earth produces were kept perpetually burning in censers of gold. Flambeaux and aromatic lamps were here lighted in open day. But the too powerful effects of this agreeable delirium might be alleviated by descending into an immense garden, where an assemblage of every fragrant flower diffused through the air the purest odours.

The fifth palace, denominated *The Retreat of Mirth, or the Dangerous,* was frequented by troops of young females, beautiful as the Houris, and not less seducing; who never failed to receive, with caresses, all whom the Caliph allowed to approach them and enjoy a few hours of their company.[2]

Source

First published (in French) in 1786, republished in Fairclough 1986: 151–3

THE VISIT OF THE POET SAMUEL ROGERS, A POET, TO FONTHILL IN 1817 IS DESCRIBED IN A LETTER BY HIS FRIEND LADY BESBOROUGH TO LORD GRANVILLE, 28 OCTOBER 1817

He was received by a dwarf[3] who, like a crowd of servants thro' whom he passed, was covered with gold and embroidery. Mr. Beckford received him very courteously, and led him thro' numberless apartments all fitted up most splendidly, one with Minerals, including precious stones: another the finest pictures: another Italian bronzes, china, etc. etc. till they came to a Gallery that surpass'd all the rest from the richness and variety of its ornaments. It seem'd clos'd by a crimson drapery held by a bronze statue, but on Mr. B's stamping and saying 'Open! the statue drew back, and the gallery was seen extending 350 feet long. At the end an open Arch with a massive balustrade opened on to a vast Octagon Hall, from which a window shew'd a fine view of the park. On approaching this it proved to be the entrance of the famous tower – higher than Salisbury Cathedral: this is not finished but great part is done. The doors, of which there are many, are violet velvet covered over with purple and gold embroidery. They pass'd from hence to a chapel, where on the altar were heaped golden candlesticks, vases and chalices studded over with jewels: and from there into a great musick room, where Mr. Beckford begg'd Mr. Rogers to rest till refreshments were ready and began playing with such *unearthly* power that Mr. Rogers says he never before had any idea how delighted one might be with him, that he thinks even Lady Douglas fails in the comparison. They went on to what is called the refectory, a large room built on the model of Henry 7 Chapel, only the ornaments gilt, where a Verdantique table was loaded with gilt plate fill'd with every luxury invention could collect. They next went into the Park with a numerous cortege, and horses and servants etc., which he described as equally wonderful, from the beauty of the trees and shrubs, and manner of arranging them, thro' a ride of five miles. They were met at the setting out by a flock of tame hares, that Mr. Beckford feeds: then pheasants, then partridges: and lastly came to a beautiful romantick lake, transparent *as liquid Chrysolite* (this is Mr. Rogers' not my expression), cover'd with wildfowl. Mr. R. was hardly arrived at the Inn before a present of game follow'd him, and a note beginning the unfortunate Vathek[4] was too sensible of the favour confer'd upon him by Mr. Roger's visit not to keep something back to allure him to a repitition of it, and then pressing him so strongly to return next day that he did so, and was shewn thro' another suite of apartments fill'd with fine medals, gems, enamell'd miniatures, drawings old and modern, curios, prints and manuscripts, and lastly a fine and well furnish'd library, all the books richly bound and the best editions etc. etc. An Old Abbé, the Librarian and Mr. Smith, the water-colour painter, who were there, told him there were 60 fires always kept burning, except in the hottest weather. Near every chimney in the sitting rooms there were large Gilt fillagree baskets fill'd with perfum'd coal that produced the brightest flame.

Source

Published in Chapman, G., 1940, *Beckford*, Oxford, Alden Press: 283–5.

DR G. WAAGEN DESCRIBES THE DINING ROOM AT 19 LANSDOWN CRESCENT

I shall never forget the dining-room, which taken all in all, is perhaps one of the most beautiful in the world. Conceive a moderate apartment of agreeable proportions, whose walls are adorned with cabinet pictures, the noblest productions of Italian art of the time of Raphael, from the windows of which you overlook the whole paradisaical valley of the Avon, with the city of Bath, which was not steeped in sunshine. Conceive in it a company of men of genius and talent, between the number of the Graces and Muses, whose spirits are duly raised by the choicest viands, the preparation of which the refined culinary art of our days has displayed its utmost skill, by a selection of wines, such as nature and human care produced only on the most favoured spots of the earth, in the most favourable years, and you will agree with me that many things here meet in a culminating point, which, even singly, are calculated to rejoice the heart of man.

Source

Waagen, G., 1838, *Works of Art and Artists in England*, Vol. 3, London: 119.

GEORGE RADFORD DESCRIBES THE FONTHILL ABBEY SALE

The sale we are now about to speak of was necessitated in consequence of the loss of two large estates in a lawsuit, the value of which may be inferred from the fact that in these West India properties no less than 1500 slaves were included. After having expended a large sum in his taste for the fine arts, Mr. Beckford decided to sell everything and quit Fonthill, notwithstanding that he had so provided for his seclusion as to build a wall 17 feet high, with iron spikes on the top, all round the domain, about seven miles in extent. It is recorded that he had consulted Mr. Christie, and intended that he should sell the collection. The catalogue was made, and 1500 sold at a guinea; but, before it was available an offer was made in 1822 by a Mr. Farquhar, to purchase the whole Fonthill property, with the collection for £350,000; and this was accepted. The sale by auction of the works of art, the library, and furniture, &c., being placed in the hands of Mr. Phillips, was conducted at the abbey during September and October. Accommodation was provided in a pavilion in the park, beds being charged 3d 6d single, and 5s double; and guinea tickets gave admission to the abbey for two persons, half-guinea for one, the catalogues being charged 12s, giving admission to the sale-room only. *The Times*, noticing the view before the sale said: 'He is fortunate who finds a vacant chair within twenty miles of Fonthill; the solitude of a private apartment is a luxury few can hope for ... Falstaff himself could not take his ease at this moment within a dozen leagues of Fonthill. The beds through the country are literally doing double duty: people who come in from a distance during the night must wait to go to bed until others get up in the morning. Not a farm-house, however humble, not a cottage near Fonthill but gives shelter to fashion, to beauty, and rank; ostrich plumes, which by their very waving, we can trace back to Piccadilly, are seen nodding at a casement window over a depopulated poultry yard.'

The books and prints occupied twenty days; the furniture and works of ornamental art, thirteen days; the pictures and miniatures, &c., four days: altogether there were forty-one days' sale producing £43,869 14s the 424 pictures amounting to £13,249 15s. Some very fine things of historic interest were amongst the furniture, such as the set of chairs of ebony which belonged to cardinal Wolsey, and came from his palace at Esher. A magnificent state bedstead, of ebony, with crimson damask hangings, and a rich purple silk quilt worked with gold, which belonged to Henry VII; a matchless state bed-quilt of Brussels point-lace over a damask ground and a toilette table-cover of similar work. Ebony tables with slabs of Verde antique: a table inlaid with precious marbles, jaspers, and oriental onyx, with arabesque border of costly marbles, from the Borghese Palace; cabinets of the time of Queen Elizabeth and James I; Japan cabinets, from the Collection of the Duc de Bouillon, and the Duchess of Mazarin; and a superb coffer of raised Japan work, with animals in gold and silver, which belonged to Cardinal Mazarin. Services of Sèvres and Dresden porcelain; silver-gilt and silver plate, of various designs, as a plateaux, candelbra and many fine candlesticks, caskets, toilette-services &c., &c. Amongst the objects of Oriental art was a matchless Hookah, carved in jade and set with jewels, mounted in silver-gilt, and the stand elaborately chased, which belonged to Tippoo Sahib, and was taken as plunder from his palace of Seringapatam. The bronzes were many of the size of the antique: The LAOCOON, cast and chased by Carbonneau, to which the gold medal of the Institute was awarded; the Medici Venus; a vase of the largest block of Hungarian topaz known, set with diamonds and gold mounts enamelled, made as a present to Catarina Cornaro, the work of Cellini; a commode and a secretaire, inlaid by Riesener, from the *Garde Meuble*, Paris, and bearing the cypher of Queen Marie Antoinette. These were, no doubt, those sold in the Hamilton Palace Sale, and were bought in at this sale, as were many other objects included in the catalogue. The pictures were sold on October 10, 11, 14, 15 – 385 lots, nearly all single pictures. The miniatures, only nineteen in number all French. The cameos and intaglios, twenty, with fifty-four cameos in oriental alabaster of large size, called antique, but no doubt of modern work from ancient sculptures at Rome. The noticeable pictures, as named in the catalogue were: COELLO, The Duke of Alva in a cuirass, with bâton. ORCAGNA, Crucifixion, on gold ground, from the Campo Santo, RUBENS, 'Le 'Chapeau de Paille' portrait. MANTEGNA, 'Christ in the garden', with figures in a landscape, and angel with the cup in the sky, VAN EYCK, 'Entombment of a Cardinal', from Lord Bessborough's Collection. G. JAMIESON, 'The Regent Murray in Highland dress'. METZU, Woman cleaning fish, a kitten on a brass kettle, from Collection of Duke d'Alberg. ANT. MORO, Portrait of St Catherine', from the Oratory of the Doge Loredano, P. DE HOOGE, Lady, with a spaniel, in white satin, a servant caressing a hound, in interior. Interior, woman weighing money. VAN HUYSUM, Vase of Flowers, from Duc de Praslin Cabinet. WOUWERMANN, Battle-piece, from the Collection of the P. of Orange. REMBRANDT, A Rabbi, from Vandergucht Collection; An Architect and his Wife. BONIFACCIO, Virgin and Child, St Catherine, St John, St Jerome, and Mary Madgalen, in a landscape – a gallery picture. TENIERS, A Village Fête, called 'Sign of the Teniers'. ALBERT DURER, Virgin with the Infant on a table, with the word '*Veni*' in gold before his extended hand, in a landscape; presented by Philip V to a convent at Saragossa. L. DA VINCI, 'The Laughing Boy with a Toy'. G.

DOW, 'The Poulterer's Shop', from the Choiseuil Collection. JAN STEIN, 'The Poultry Market', from the Aynard Collection. BERGHEM, A Sea Port, 'Embarquement des Vivres', Gold of Genoa, from Duc de Praslin Collection. P. VERONESE 'St. Jerome at Devotion', from the Monastery of St Benedict at Mantua, where it was the companion to the 'Communion of St Jerome' presented by the British Institution to the National Gallery. RUBENS, 'Holy Family, with SS John and Joseph', of gallery size. CUYP, Landscape with a camp, officer and other figures, soldiers playing cards. PALMA, 'Martyrdom of a Saint', large gallery picture. BONIFACCIO, 'Adoration of Magi', in a landscape, grand gallery picture. VAN EYCK, The Virgin, with the Infant on her lap, an angel presenting an apple, a saint kneeling, a landscape and fortified city in distance. K DU JARDIN, 'Le Menège', upright landscape, with horses exercising, from the Aynard Collection. GAINSBOROUGH, A grand Landscape woody scene, with cattle in distance; a girl with milkpail, and man on horseback refreshing his horse with water; shepherd and flock coming to the brook.

When this sale took place, Mr. Beckford was in his 63rd year; but he was not parting with his favourite pictures, for he reserved them at prices which were not nearly approached then; and in 1839 (as will be seen on referring to the catalogue of the National Gallery) he sold three pictures, one of which was the 'St. Catherine' by Raphael, which was not in the Fonthill Sale, to the National Gallery for £7350; and in 1841, three years before his death, the Perugino 'Holy Family' (No. 181) for £800. 'The Laughing Boy', by Leonardo, and other pictures, were long afterwards to be seen on the walls of Hamilton Palace, where they passed with the choicer part of his fine library as dowry of his daughter, who became the wife of the Duke of Hamilton, and were sold finally in 1882. Had the collection at Fonthill been sold at the present time, the prices would have been far higher than any then bid as was seen at the Hamilton Palace Sale.

Source

Redford, G., 1888, *Art Sales*, Vol. 1, London.

Notes

1   Beckford was obsessively proud of his Hamilton blood, which enabled him to claim descent from the English and Scottish royal families. Heraldic decoration played a considerable role in the scheme at Fonthill. This piece foretells Beckford's life and the creation of Fonthill.

2   The palace is laid out in ways which recall the notions of Bacon and other
    sixteenth- and seventeenth-century writers on collections; but adjusted to
    support Beckford's ideas of Vathek's sensuality.
3   The dwarf was called Perro, a Swiss from Evisen, who remained with his
    master for forty years.
4   This is, of course, a reference to the novel.

References

Chapman, 1928
Chapman, 1940
Fairclough, 1986
Lees-Milne, 1976
Mahmoud, 1960

58

Horace Walpole collects at Strawberry Hill

Forty-five years after Walpole's death in 1842, the contents of his villa at Strawberry Hill, Twickenham, London, was put up for sale. The sale, conducted by George Robins, the most famous auctioneer of the time, lasted twenty-four days and resulted in £33,450 11s 6d, excluding the prints and engravings. Many pieces were bought by the leading collectors of the day, including the Dukes of Bedford and Sutherland.

Horace Walpole (1717–97) was born the youngest child of the Prime Minister, Robert Walpole. His writings were enormous and included (like Beckford) a famous Gothic novel, *The Castle of Otranto* (1764), a book intended to rehabilitate the reputation of Richard III (1760), journals and an immense quantity of letters.

Walpole remained a bachelor, and in 1747 moved to the villa at Strawberry Hill, which he renovated in the Gothic taste. Here he devoted himself to his correspondence and his collecting. The biography of him by R.W. Ketton-Cremer is a classic of biographical writing, and the piece given here describes the villa and its contents.

DESCRIPTION OF STRAWBERRY HILL, FROM KETTON-CREMER 1964

The Gallery must have presented a noble spectacle when it was filled with all its treasures. Though not a remarkably large room (it was fifty-six feet by thirteen) it was the largest room at Strawberry Hill: and in it Walpole assembled many of his finest pictures, his most spectacular pieces of porcelain, his most precious marbles and bronzes. Light streamed through the five large windows in which Peckitt had depicted all the quartering of the Walpoles in painted glass. On the other side of the room were five deep canopied recesses, the middle recess containing a chimney-piece designed by Chute and Pitt. The furniture was covered with the same crimson damask as the walls; its woodwork was painted in black and gold. The walls were loaded with pictures, the recesses were filled with them – portraits of relations and friends, portraits of the celebrities of the sixteenth and seventeenth centuries, the painting by Mabuse of the marriage of Henry VII, landscapes and subject-pieces by an endless variety of artists. There was work by Cornelius Hansen, Rubens, Lely, Rosalba, Liotard, Reynolds – an extraordinary medley of period and styles. On an ancient sepulchral altar stood the famous Boccapadugli eagle, which had been dug up in the Baths of Caracalla in 1742, and which Walpole liked to think had inspired Gray with the line about the 'ruffled plumes and flagging wing'. And between two of the windows hung Van Somer's portrait of Henry Carey, Lord Falkland, all in white, a picture which haunted its owner strangely. It became a part of the fantasy which found expression in *The Castle of Otranto*,[1] and was transformed in that story into the portrait of Duke Manfred's grandfather, which sighed so deeply and descended from its frame, and 'marched sedately but dejectedly' along the gallery of the visionary castle.

The Round Tower was built at the end of the wing formed by the Cloister and Gallery and was the western termination of the house. It was a sturdy tower of three stories, batttlemented and machicolated, with a great bow-window (considerably later in style) overlooking the road to Hampton. Each floor contained one big circular room. The ground floor became the new kitchen; the first floor was called the Round Drawing Room, and was approached from the Gallery through a small lobby. Its main features were the bow-window, and chimney piece 'taken from the tomb of Edward the Confessor, improved by Mr Adam, and beautifully executed in white marble inlaid with scagliuola, by Richter'. Adam's 'improvement' amounted to a much-needed simplification of the Confessor's gaudy mosaic sarcophagus, and he also designed a pleasant frieze for the walls. The Round Drawing-Room was hung, like the Gallery, with crimson Norwich damask; the chairs were of aubusson tapestry, of flowers on a white background, with green and gold frames. It contained a few good pictures, and many of Walpole's larger books and volumes prints.

The Chapel, which later came to be called the Tribune, opened off the Gallery. It was a small room, square with a semi-circular recess in the middle of each wall; the roof vaulted in imitation of that of the chapter-house of York Minster, rose to an apex formed of a large star of yellow glass. The windows were entirely filled with ecclesiastical stained glass, and the dominant light of the room was the 'golden gloom' which filtered down through the great star. In one of the recesses stood an altar of black and gold, copied from a tomb in Westminster Abbey. 'The sable mass of the altar'. Walpole wrote, 'gives it a very sober air, for notwithstanding the solemnity of the painted windows, it had a gaudiness that was a little profane. The ecclesiastical atmosphere was, however, so successfully conveyed that the Due de Nivernais, the French ambassador, pulled off his hat when he entered the room; after which 'perceiving his error, he said, "Ce n'est pas une chapelle pourtant" and seemed a little displeased.

Walpole, of course, had never intended to distress the faithful by making a frivolous imitation of a chapel; he was growing ever more serious about his buildings, and in the construction of a Gothic castle the chapel held a very special place. Great hall, south tower, armoury, cloister, gallery, round tower, chapel – one after another they were coming into being. His fantasies found concrete form; the little house called Strawberry Hill was fast assuming the splendours of the Castle of Otranto.

It is possible that when Monsieur de Nivernais was shown the Chapel, quite soon after its completion, it still retained a degree of austerity which the ever-increasing pressure of Walpole's collections was soon to dispel. If he had inspected it in 1774, the date of Walpole's printed *Description of Strawberry Hill*, he would have found that its walls and niches were adorned with very secular objects indeed. Walpole never allowed any Gothic prejudices about uncrowded rooms or undecorated surfaces to interfere with his remorse-less and incessant accumulation of objects of art. He selected the Chapel as the repository of his smaller and more exquisite treasures; and, with cabinet-pictures and miniatures crowding the walls, and shelves and brackets loaded with trinkets extending in all directions, it must indeed have reverted to the gaudiness which he had originally felt to be 'a little profane'. In the niches were placed casts or bronzes of the Venus de Medicis, an Antinous, the Apollo Belvedere, the Farnese Flora, and his own mother. Above the altar was a cabinet which contained his marvellous collection of miniatures – the Olivers, the Coopers, the Hoskins – and his superb enamels by Petitot and Zincke. The antiques belonging to Conyers Middleton, which he had bought after the Doctor's death, were placed about the room. In two glass-cases were some of his supreme treasures – the bust of Caligula in bronze, with silver eyes; the missal 'with miniatures by Raphael and his scholars'; and the silver bell carved with miraculous ornament by Benvenuto Cellini. Jostling them were such curiosities as Henry VIII's dagger, a mourning-ring of Charles I, the great seal of Theodore, King of Corsica, and the cravat carved in wood by Grinling Gibbons. The entire room was an indescribable display of pictures, bronzes, carvings, ivories, enamels, faience, pot-pourri jars, snuff-boxes, kettles, tea-pots, cups and saucers, seals and rings.

Sources

Ketton-Cremer R. 1964, *Horace Walpole*, 3rd edn, London

FROM *THE CASTLE OF OTRANTO*

The company was assembled in the chapel of the castle, and every thing ready for beginning the divine office, when Conrad himself was missing. Manfred, impatient of the least delay, and who had not observed his son retire, dispatched one of his attendants to summon the young prince. The servant, who had not staid long enough to have crossed the court to Conrad's apartment, came running back breathless, in a frantic manner, his eyes staring, and foaming at the mouth. He said nothing, but pointed to the court. The company were struck with terror and amazement. The princess Hippolita, without knowing what was the matter, but anxious for her son, swooned away. Manfred, less apprehensive than enraged at the procrastination of the nuptials, and at the folly of his domestic, asked imperiously, what was the matter? The fellow made no answer, but continued pointing towards the courtyard; and at last, after repeated questions put to him, cried out, Oh, the helmet! the helmet! In the mean time some of the company had run into the court, from whence was heard a confused noise of shrieks, horror, and surprise. Manfred, who began to be alarmed at not seeing his son, went himself to get information of what occasioned this strange confusion. Matilda remained endeavouring to assist her mother, and Isabella staid for the same purpose, and to avoid showing any impatience for the bridegroom, for whom, in truth, she had conceived little affection.

The first think that struck Manfred's eyes was a group of his servants endeavouring to raise something that appeared to him a mountain of sable plumes. He gazed without believing his sight. What are ye doing? cried Manfred, wrathfully: Where is my son? A volley of voices replied, Oh, my lord! the prince! the prince! the helmet! the helmet! Shocked with these lamentable sounds, and dreading he knew not what, he advanced hastily – But what a sight for a father's eyes! – He beheld his child dashed to pieces, and almost buried under an enormous helmet, an hundred times more large than any casque ever made for human being, and shaded with a proportionable quantity of black feathers.

The horror of the spectacle, the ignorance of all around how this misfortune happened, and above all, the tremendous phaenomenon before him, took away the prince's speech. Yet his silence lasted longer than even grief could occasion. He fixed his eyes on what he wished in vain to believe a vision; and seemed less attentive to his loss, than buried in meditation on the stupendous object that had occasioned it. He touched, he examined the fatal casque; nor could even the bleeding mangled remains of the young prince divert the eyes of Manfred from the portent before him. All who had known his partial fondness for young Conrad, were as much surprised at their prince's insensibility, as thunderstruck themselves at the miracle of the helmet. They conveyed the disfigured corse into the hall, without receiving the least direction from Manfred. As little was he attentive to the ladies who remained in the chapel; on the contrary, without mentioning the unhappy princesses his wife and daughter, the first sounds that dropped from Manfred's lips were, Take care of the lady Isabella.

The domestics, without observing the singularity of this direction, were guided by their affection to their mistress to consider it as peculiarly addressed to her situation, and flew to her assistance. They conveyed her to her chamber more dead than alive, and indifferent to all the strange circumstances she heard, except the death of her son. Matilda, who doted on her mother, smothered her own grief and amazement, and thought of nothing but assisting and comforting her afflicted parent. Isabella, who had been treated by Hippolita like a daughter, and who returned that tenderness with equal duty and affection, was scarce less assiduous about the princess; at the same time endeavouring to partake and lessen the weight of sorrow which she saw Matilda strove to suppress, for whom she had conceived the warmest sympathy of friendship.

Sources

Fairclough, P. (ed.) *Three Gothic Novels*, Harmondsworth, Penguin Books 1986: 52–3.

Note

1   See next extract.

References

Herrmann, 1972
Praz, 1986

59

The Society of Antiquaries of London encourages the study of antiquity and the collecting of its remains

The background to the formation of the Society of Antiquaries of London was the interest in both the past in general, and the national past in particular, which had been a significant feature of the northern Renaissance, represented in England by figures like John Leland, William Camden and Robert Cotton. By about 1590, Camden, Cotton and a group of like-minded friends had formed the habit of meeting regularly to hold discussions on antiquarian matters, and this constituted the first effort towards a regular society, although it was relatively short-lived and had apparently ceased to meet by 1616.

The project was revived in the 1630s and by 1638 Sir Edward Dering, William Dugdale, Sir Christopher Hatton and Sir Thomas Shirley had banded themselves together for antiquarian study, but the political upheavals of the seventeenth century stifled development and it was not until 1707 that an Antiquarian Society was formed, meeting regularly at the Bear Tavern in the Strand, London, and after various fits and starts, the continuous records of the present Society of Antiquaries begin with the meeting in the Mitre Tavern, Fleet Street in July 1717. The Society's Royal Charter was granted on 2 November 1751.

After considerable debate, it was agreed by 1770 that the society should publish a volume of papers to be called *Archaeologia, or Miscellaneous Tracts relating to Antiquity*, and the volume duly appeared in the same year. A second volume appeared in 1773, and a third and fourth in subsequent years. The kind of antiquarian material, and the collecting associated with it, which was published in *Archaeologia* is represented here with the excerpt from the paper in the volume for 1779 by John Strange, which gives an account of Roman material from Brecknock in South Wales.

By the 1770s, the society was well enough established to be a target for satire. In 1772 Samuel Foote saw his comedy *The Nabob* put on at the Haymarket Theatre (a 'nabob' was a man who returned to England having made a large fortune in India; and the Haymarket is still a part of London's theatre quarter). The third act of the play is set in the rooms of the Society of Antiquaries, at

that time in Chancery Lane. The Nabob of the piece is Sir Matthew Mite, and the list of accessions is highly ridiculous: it represents the views of those for whom the collecting of British historical
material had little or no place, in comparison with that of classical
antiquity or European art.

AN ACCOUNT OF ANTIQUITIES IN AND NEAR BRECKNOCK, SOUTH WALES, PUBLISHED IN *ARCHAEOLOGIA* 1779.

From the evidence of Roman coins frequently found in and about the
town of Brecknock, Camden was of opinion, that this country was inhabited in the time of the Romans.[1] Lhwyd's[2] further enquiries confirmed
that opinion, for he particularly informs us of a Roman brick, stampt
LEG. II. AVG. dug up near Brecknock, and of a square camp at a place
called *The Gaer*, about three miles from the town. But as he only slightly
mentions this camp, and is mistaken in some particulars relating to it, I
shall endeavour to supply his omissions, by giving a more exact account
of a place which I think not undeserving the attention of a curious
traveller. It is superfluous to remark, that the very name of *The Gaer* is a
sufficient proof of its antiquity; the word itself importing a *round wall* or
fortification; and most of the places in that country, where such works
have been made, retain this name even at present. But *The Gaer* near
Brecknock seems to have been so called by way of distinction, as being
the most considerable fortification in that part of the country. As bricks
with the aforesaid inscription upon them are frequently found upon the
very spot, and considerable ruins of a Roman wall are still remaining, it
is probable that a detachment of the second Britannick legion, from
Caerleon in Monmouthshire, was stationed at this place. These bricks
even now are so common, that a servant in the family at *The Gaer* found
one for me upon a day's notice, which measured 8 inches square, and 2½
thick, and is stampt nearly in the middle in the same form with those dug
up at Caerleon. Since my return to London, I have been apprised by
Thomas Jones Esq. of the Exchequer, that other Roman bricks have been
dug up in the area of this camp, of an oblong square form, and with the
same inscription LEG. II. AVG. stampt across one of the corners. Mr
Jones saw one dug up at *The Gaer* about five years since; and likewise
assures me, that several of the same kind were found at this place some
years before.

But to bring those remains of antiquity more immediately under your
notice, let me observe, that the place, now called *The Gaer*, is a small
farm belonging to the widow of David Williams Esq. about three miles
North-west from *Brecknock*; within half a mile of the farm house, the

present road from *Brecknock* joins the old Roman causeway; which, though much broken and over-run with bushes, is still very discernible. It was originally a raised way near forty feet wide, and seems to have been chiefly made with large round pebbles of various sizes, collected probably from the bed of a neighbouring river. This causeway runs in a direction nearly at right angles with *The Eskir*, a small brook which joins the river *Usk* just below the *Gaer*. I could find no traces of it on the other side of the *Eskir*, nor signs of a Roman road any where in that neighbourhood, except near *Rhyd y Briw* bridge, about seven miles from *Brecknock* in the road to Trecastle, where there are very visible remains of one, which will be mentioned in a subsequent part of this letter. The causeway at *The Gaer* seems then to have conducted only to this station; and was, in all probability, a branch of the great Roman causeway leading from *Caerleon* in Monmouthshire through the vale of *Usk*, and the Eastern part of Brecknockshire to *Ariconium*, which is the 12th lter in Antoninus's Itinerary. In the middle of this causeway, about a quarter of a mile short of the farm house, is the monumental stone described and engraved by Mr. Lhwyd. It is called *Maen y Morinnion*, or the maiden stone; from a tradition prevailing among the common people in the neighbourhood, that it was erected to the memory of two virgins who were murdered there. It formerly lay by the road side, but was set up in the place where it now stands a few years ago, and is about six feet high from the ground, and three and a half wide. Mr. Lhwyd gives it only two feet in width, and doubts whether it be British or Roman. The bas relief upon it, representing probably a soldier and his wife, rude as it is, seems clearly of Roman sculpture. Had we, indeed, no other proof, there is such a precision in all their works, even of the most barbarous ages, as sufficiently distinguishes them from the unmeaning strokes of Gothicism. But there is likewise an actual inscription in good Roman characters upon the stone itself under the figures, not mentioned by Mr. Lhwyd; which, though in great measure effaced by time, yet manifestly appears to have consisted of four lines in a regular compartment; and the word CONIVNX,[3] which begins the last line, with several other letters, is still plainly legible.

Source

Strange, J., 1779, 'An Account of some remains of Roman and other Antiquities in and near the Town of Brecknock, in South Wales', *Archaeologia* 1779: 295–7

EXCERPT FROM THE PLAY *THE NABOB* BY SAMUEL FOOTE WHICH RAN AT THE HAYMARKET IN THE SUMMER OF 1772. ACT 3 IS SET IN THE ROOMS OF THE SOCIETY OF ANTIQUARIES AND PART OF IT IS GIVEN HERE.

Secretary. Sir Matthew Mite, preceded by his presents, will attend this honourable Society this morning.

1st Ant. Is he apprised that an inauguration speech is required, in which he is to express his love of vertu, and produce proofs of his antique erudition?

Sec. He has been apprised, and is rightly prepared.

2nd Ant. Are the minutes of our last meeting fairly recorded and entered?

Sec. They are.

1st Ant. And the valuable antiques which have happily escaped the depredations of time ranged and registered rightly?

Sec. All in order.

2nd Ant. As there are new acquisitions to the Society's stock, I think it right that the members should be instructed in their several natures and names.

1st Ant. By all means. Read the list!

Sec. 'Imprimis, In a large glass-case, and in fine preservation, the toe of the slipper of Cardinal Pandulpho, with which he kick'd the breech of King John at Swinstead Abbey, when he gave him absolution and penance.'

2nd Ant. A most noble remains!

1st Ant. An excellent antidote against the progress of Popery, as it proves the Pontiff's insolent abuse of his power – Proceed.

Sec. 'A pair of nut-crackers presented by Harry the eighth to Anna Bullen the eve of their nuptials; the wood supposed to be walnut.'

1st Ant. Which proves that before the Reformation walnut trees were planted in England.

Sec. 'The cape of Queen Elizabeth's riding-hood which she wore on a solemn festival, when carried behind Burleigh to Paul's; the cloth undoubtedly Kidderminster.'

2nd Ant. A most instructive lesson to us, as it proves that patriotic princess wore nothing but the manufactures of England!

Sec. 'A cork-screw presented by Sir John Falstaff to Harry the Fifth, with a tobacco-stopper of Sir Walter Raleighs, made of the stern of the ship in which he first compassed the globe; given to the Society by a clergyman from the North-Riding of Yorkshire.'

1st Ant. A rare instance of generosity, as they must have both been of singular use to the reverend donor himself!

Sec. 'A curious collection, in regular and undoubted succession, of all the tickets of Islington-Turnpike, from its first institution to the twentieth of May.'

2nd Ant. Preserve them with care, as they may hereafter serve to illustrate that part of the English History.

Sec. 'A wooden medal of Shakespeare, made from the mulberry tree he planted himself; with a Queen Anne's farthing from the Manager of Drury-Lane Playhouse.'

1st Ant. Has he received the Society's thanks?

Sec. They are sent.'

Source

The Nabob appears in Belden, M., 1929, *The Dramatic Works of Samuel Foote*, London, Dent: 147, quoted in Evans, J., 1956, A History of the Society of Antiquaries, Oxford University Press: 167–8.

Notes

1   The reference is to Camden's *Britannia*, Vol. 2: 705.
2   Edward Lhwyd or Lluyd (1660–1709) was born in Cardiganshire, West Wales, and went up to Jesus College, Oxford, in 1682. He became successively under-keeper (1684) and keeper (1690) of the Ashmolean Museum, and spent 1693 and 1697 in Wales collecting details of antiquities. Volume 1 of his *Archaeologia Britannica* was published in 1707 but contained speculations about the Celtic languages rather than antiquities; the projected Volume 2 was not published. He died at the Ashmolean in 1709.
3   'Coniunx' means 'wife'. The piece is a Roman tombstone.

References

Belden, 1929
Evans, 1965

60

Sir John Soane and his house of collection at 13 Lincoln's Inn Fields, London

Soane's house at Lincoln's Inn Fields, which still survives with its installations recognisably as he left them, represents a new departure in the collection of the past. Soane was born in 1753 near Reading, the son of a relatively poor background, and was largely self-educated. He attracted some attention with his drawings, and became the pupil of the architect George Dance. In 1777–80 he travelled in Italy, funded by a travelling studentship provided by the Royal Academy, and on his return to London set up a successful business as an architect, which in due course led him to design a number of country houses and to become architect to the Bank of England.

Meanwhile, he had acquired and started to develop his private house at Lincoln's Inn Fields in the legal quarter of London. Here he gathered and displayed in 'realistic' or 'impressionistic' style a large collection of classical, Egyptian and later antiquities, all disposed with an eye to effect in the various rooms of the house. The collecting of material of this broad kind had its roots partly in the long tradition of classical accumulation and partly in the more recent antiquarian mode stimulated by Scott in Britain and Alexandre Lenoir in France, who during the course of the French Revolution had preserved a large range of medieval religious material, politically unacceptable at the time, in the convent of the Petits-Augustins in Paris. In 1795 he opened the rooms here to the public: the objects were arranged chronologically to produce a sequence of period rooms, something which had not been done before. The exhibition was closed in 1816, but not before it had been very influential.

As early as 1812 Soane had written 'Some Hints towards a History of my House'. This was never published but became the first version of what were to be successive versions of his *Description of the House and Museum on the North Side of Lincoln's Inn Fields*, privately printed in London in 1830, 1832 and 1835. The *European Magazine* for July–December 1812 had published an account of the collection (pp. 381–7), so presumably by around that date the house and its installations were becoming known and visited by those to whom Soane permitted entry.

The collections were arranged in a number of rooms on several floors of the house, each of which was given a name which reflected its character. During their lifetimes, Soane and his family continued to live amongst the displays. In 1833, by Act of Parliament, the Soane house and collection was donated to the nation on Soane's death on condition that the arrangement left by Soane should not be altered. Soane died in 1837.

DESCRIPTION OF THE CRYPT FROM *DESCRIPTION OF THE HOUSE AND MUSEUM ON THE NORTH SIDE OF LINCOLN'S INN FIELDS* (1835): 34–6, 39–40

Leaving the Sepulchral Chamber, we enter the Egyptian Crypt, the ceiling of which is composed of massive blocks of stone, supported by stone pillars. On the south side is a Sleeping Cupid, opposite to which are cork Models of the Temple of Fortuna Virilis at Rome, and of the Druidical remains at Stonehenge. In the centre is Britannia Triumphant, holding in her hand the trident of Neptune, and pointing to the Dying Patriot of Banks,[1] and the Rostral Monument of Flaxman, in honour of the services rendered to their country by Captains Riou and Moss. To the right of the Britannia is a Cast of the Infant Hercules; and in another part of the Crypt is a Cast of a Female Torso, sculptured with hieroglyphics.

In this Crypt are also placed four Cork Models of ancient sepulchres, found at Capua and various parts of Sicily. The walls of these models are decorated with painting and sculpture; and in the body of the chamber are deposited the skeleton, a variety of Etruscan vases, and implements of sacrifice. They are, therefore, very interesting, as explaining the method of sepulture in use amongst the ancients, and accounting for the high state of preservation in which are found, from time to time, so many Etruscan vases, pateras, and other utensils of remote antiquity.

Another record of sepulture deposited in the Crypt reminds us of the monuments in the mountains of Telmissus. It is a Patina, presented to me by Dr. Moore, which was discovered, while searching for some strayed goats, in a cave situate in the Cañadas Del Chasma, at the Peak of Teneriffe. In the cave were thirteen mummies of the Guanches, aborigines of the island (twelve males and one female), arranged in a row on a kind of bier composed of stones, at one side of which was placed the above-mentioned Patina, which cannot be less than five hundred years old, and is probably much more ancient.

In a recess to the left is a monument to the memory of Mrs. Soane: and underneath it another to the memory of Mr. John Soane, jun., who departed this life on the 21st of October, 1823, in the 37th year of his age.

On leaving the Crypt, a passage to the right gives a view into the Corridor: beyond is an Equestrian Statue of King George the Third, by P.

Turnerelli; and opposite is the Model of a statue of his highly talented
and faithful minister, William Pitt, placed in the Town-hall at Glasgow.

This portion of the Museum is terminated by two antique truncated
columns, surmounted by two beautiful marble Capitals from the Villa
Adriana; and above these are two Pilaster Capitals of the Corinthian
order. To the right is a Cast from a Medallion by Banks, copied from the
Arch of Constantine at Rome; on the opposite side is a Cast of the Head
of Mary Queen of Scots, from her monument in Westminster Abbey; and
at the foot of the staircase is a Cast from the Venus de' Medici ...

... we enter the Crypt, which is also of an Egyptian character, and
may be termed a 'place of tombs,' for here hath memory poured its
tribute of the owner's affection as a husband and a father, and here placed
the tomb of the expiring patriot; and models of many an ancient sepulchre tell of those feelings which, in far distant ages, have hallowed the
remains of the beloved and the departed.

But even here the ameliorating effects produced by architecture and
sculpture are experienced – the fine model of the Roman temple con-
trasted with the rude erections of shapeless pillars congregated by the
Druids – the majestic figure of Britannia in the hour of naval triumph,
opposite to the statue of the expiring hero, alike shewn by subdued yet
sufficient light, – combine to produce an effect of pensive pleasure upon
the mind, suited to the objects by which it is excited, and to that exclu-
sion of light and extraneous matters so desirable in a scene where we
may exclaim with Milton; –

> "Hail, divinest melancholy!"

> Oh deem we not the Crypt resign'd to gloom,
> Since death's pale trophies mingle on the ground:
> True, 'tis the path that leads to many a tomb;
> Yet even here taste strews her wreaths around,
> And not one object speaks of man's dark doom,
> But shews his intellectual power profound,
> And from his very dust and ashes cries,
> "O heavenly gifted thing, that shall again arise!"

> Behold Britannia calmly potent stand,
> Mistress of every sea that laves the shore;–
> And shall not Art her empire here expand,
> And shew what Rome, Greece, Egypt, were of yore?
> Yes! from this fostering nest shall genius soar,
> And shed her rays o'er many a distant land
> That held our country but to commerce prone,

Reckless for others' good, resistless for her own.

> Bless'd is the power that to the few belong,
> Who join to worldly wealth the wealth of mind.
> Hence their ennobled spirits dwell among
> Those works that grace and dignify mankind; –
> For them the artist's lyre, the poet's song,
> The temple, statue, picture, are enshrined;
> Yet far more blest if they such gifts impart,
> To aid youth's struggling mind, and cheer its anxious heart.
>
> B.H.[2]

DESCRIPTION OF THE MONK'S PARLOUR AND ORATORY FROM *THE GENERAL DESCRIPTION OF SIR JOHN SOANE'S MUSEUM*

THE MONK'S PARLOUR, ORATORY, &c.[3]

The ceiling and walls of this room are covered with numerous Fragments and Casts in plaster of different parts of Ecclesiastical and other Structures of the Middle Ages, a variety of Carvings in Wood and Ivory, Metal Grave Plates, &c.

The large window, doors, &c., are filled in with specimens of ancient Painted Glass, the greater number being scriptural subjects.

From the window of this room a view is obtained of the Gothic Fragments which are arranged to resemble the remains of a ruined Cloister.

The Glazed Cases on the *east* side contain a collection of Vases brought from the interior of Peru, found in the tombs of the aboriginal Indians, and some other Antiquities. The *Cabinet* on the *south* side, and the Drawers on the *west* side are filled with Architectural Drawings.

In the small recess at the *north-east* angle, designated the ORATORY, is a fine specimen of ancient Flemish Carving in Wood, representing the Crucifixion …

DRESSING ROOM AND RECESS.

This room is lighted by two windows, that on the *west* side affords a View of the MONUMENT COURT; that on the *east*, of the MONK'S YARD, &c., in which is a Collection of Gothic Fragments, arranged in a picturesque form, so as to resemble the remains of a ruined cloister: these fragments are portions of the ancient Palace at Westminster, known of

late as 'the Old House of Lords,' and 'Prince's Chamber,' which being in
a very dilapidated and ruinous condition, were taken down in the year
1823, the site thereof being now occupied by the new Royal Gallery,
erected in the year 1823–4, from the designs, and under the superintendence of Sir John Soane; likewise some Models of capitals of columns,
and other portions of buildings erected from his designs.

Source

Soane, Sir John, *Description of the House and Museum of the North Side of
Lincoln's Inn Fields*, London, 1st extract, 1835 edition: 34–6, 39–40; 2nd
extract, 1844 edition: 15, 21–2

Notes

1 'This Model was presented to me by Dr. Pugh, to whom it had been sent by
   Mrs. Banks, in exchange for a bust of her deceased husband.' (Soane's note.)
2 BH is Soane's friend Barbara Hofland who wrote a kind of running com-
   mentary to Soane's own sparer description of the rooms; her thoughts were
   first added to the 1835 edition of the *Description*. Hofland's commentaries
   are effusive and poetic in tone in contrast to Soane's sparer style. Including
   her descriptions enabled him to achieve the best of both worlds: a straight-
   forward description for posterity, and an emotional flow which appealed to
   the obsessive collector in Soane, which he, as a professional man, found
   difficult to acknowledge directly.
3 The Monk's Parlour was created in 1824. It is in the Gothic mode but was
   evidently intended as a joke. The *New Description of Sir John Soane's
   Museum* published by the Museum in 1986 includes a question asked of
   Soane by those who visit the Museum – who the 'Monk' was and when he
   lived – and Soane's answer is a quotation from Horace that 'it is pleasant to
   be nonsensical in due place'. In other words, the Monk is Soane himself, in
   playful mood.

References

Bann, 1988
Elsner, 1994
Summerson, 1982
Thornton and Dorey, 1992

61

Sir Walter Scott describes a collector of antiquities

Walter Scott was born in Edinburgh in 1771, the child of an old Border family whose childhood was characterised by illness which freed him from formal school life and gave him the scope to follow his own interests in the history and traditions of the Border. Nevertheless, he became a member of the Faculty of Advocates. It has often been said that Scott's life was in many ways a tension between the heart of a romantic steeped in the lore of Old Scotland, and the hard head of an Edinburgh lawyer.

Scott's creative life was, of course, dominated by his heart. In 1802 he published the two volumes of *Minstrelsy of the Scottish Border*, a collection of folk ballads, somewhat 'improved' by their editor, and in 1805 appeared his best-selling and hugely influential poem *The Lay of the Last Minstrel*. His first novel, *Waverley*, begun in 1805, was published anonymously in 1814, and *The Antiquary* followed in 1816, with *Guy Mannering* in 1815. As Scott said in a later Preface, his 'Advertisement' to *The Antiquary*, 'The present work completes a series of fictitious narratives intended to illustrate the manners of Scotland at three different periods. *Waverley* embraced the age of our fathers, *Guy Mannering* that of our own youth, and *The Antiquary* refers to the last ten years of the eighteenth century.' The character of Jonathan Oldbuck of Monkbarns, the antiquary of the title, gives (among other things) a portrait of a collector of what we would call archaeological and historical material at the end of the eighteenth century.

Scott continued to produce a huge mixed output which included *Rob Roy* (1817), *The Heart of Midlothian* (1818) and *Ivanhoe* (1820). In 1820 he was made a baronet by George IV, as a reward for masterminding George's Scottish coronation as a *tour de force* of Scottish Antiquarian pageantry, and he acquired the estate of Abbotsford on the Tweed, where he lived in the style known to the later nineteenth and twentieth centuries as 'Scottish Baronial'. At Abbotsford, Scott made a substantial antiquarian collection of his own, which included material from the Jacobite risings of 1715 and 1745, and an important group of arms and armour.

From Abbotsford, Scott exercised a European-wide literary influence unequalled, probably, by any writer in English except

Shakespeare. He was the spearhead of the new medievalism and re-creative view of history which was to shape much nineteenth-century culture, including the arts and crafts movement, the museum movement and, indeed, the whole notion of heritage preservation and transmission. Unfortunately, unhappy publishing ventures left him, by 1825, deep in debt, and he worked himself hard in the effort to pay off what he owed. He died, exhausted, in 1832.

FROM *THE ANTIQUARY*, BY SIR WALTER SCOTT

It was, indeed, some time before Lovel[1] could, through the thick atmosphere, perceive in what sort of den his friend had constructed his retreat. It was a lofty room of middling size, obscurely lighted by high narrow latticed windows. One end was entirely occupied by book-shelves, greatly too limited in space for the number of volumes placed upon them, which were, therefore, drawn up in ranks of two or three files deep, while numberless others littered the floor and the tables, amid a chaos of maps, engravings, scraps of parchment, bundles of papers, pieces of old armour, swords, dirks, helmets, and Highland targets. Behind Mr Oldbuck's[2] seat (which was an ancient leathern-covered easy-chair, worn smooth by constant use), was a huge oaken cabinet, decorated at each corner with Dutch cherubs, having their little duck-wings displayed, and great jolter-headed visages placed between them. The top of this cabinet was covered with busts, and Roman lamps and paterae, intermingled with one or two bronze figures. The walls of the apartment were partly clothed with grim old tapestry, representing the memorable story of Sir Gawaine's wedding, in which full justice was done to the ugliness of the Lothely Lady ; although, to judge from his own looks, the gentle knight had less reason to be disgusted with the match on account of disparity of outward favour, than the romancer has given us to understand. The rest of the room was panelled, or wainscoted, with black oak, against which hung two or three portraits in armour, being characters in Scottish history, favourites of Mr. Oldbuck, and as many in tie-wigs and laced coats, staring representatives of his own ancestors. A large old-fashioned oaken table was covered with a profusion of papers, parchments, books, and nondescript trinkets and gew-gaws, which seemed to have little to recommend them, besides rust and the antiquity which it indicates. In the midst of this wreck of ancient books and utensils, with a gravity equal to Marius among the ruins of Carthage, sat a large black cat, which, to a superstitious eye, might have presented the *genius loik*, the tutelar demon of the apartment. The floor, as well as the table and chairs, was overflowed by the same *mare magnum*[3] of miscellaneous trumpery, where it would have been as impossible to find any individual article wanted, as to put it to any use when discovered.

Amid this medley, it was no easy matter to find one's way to a chair, without stumbling over a prostrate folio, or the still more awkward mischance of overturning some piece of Roman or ancient British pottery. And, when the chair was attained, it had to be disencumbered, with a careful hand, of engravings which might have received damage, and of antique spurs and buckles, which would certainly have occasioned it to any sudden occupant. Of this the Antiquary made Lovel particularly aware, adding, that his friend, the Rev. Doctor Heavysterne[4] from the Low Countries, had sustained much injury by sitting down suddenly and incautiously on three ancient calthrops, or *crawtaes*, which had been lately dug up in the bog near Bannockburn, and which, dispersed by Robert Bruce to lacerate the feet of the English chargers, came thus in process of time to endamage the sitting part of a learned professor of Utrecht.

Having at length fairly settled himself, and being nothing loath to make inquiry concerning the strange objects around him, which his host was equally ready, as far as possible, to explain, Lovel was introduced to a large club, or bludgeon, with an iron spike at the end of it, which, it seemed, had been lately found in a field on the Monkbarns property adjacent to an old burying-ground. It had mightily the air of such a stick as the Highland reapers use to walk with on their annual peregrinations from their mountains: but Mr. Oldbuck was strongly tempted to believe, that, as its shape was singular, it might have been one of the clubs with which the monks armed their peasants in lieu of more martial weapons, whence, he observed, the villains were called *Calve-carles*, or *Kolb-kerls*, that is, *Clavigeri*, or club bearers. For the truth of this custom, he quoted the Chronicles of Antwerp and that of St. Martin ; against which authorities Lovel had nothing to oppose, having never heard of them till that moment.

Mr. Oldbuck next exhibited thumb-screws, which had given the Covenanters of former days the cramp in their joints, and a collar with the name of a fellow convicted of theft, whose services, as the inscription bore, had been adjudged to a neighbouring baron, in lieu of the modern Scottish punishment, which, as Oldbuck said, sends such culprits to enrich England by their labour, and themselves by their dexterity. Many and various were the other curiosities which he showed : but it was chiefly upon his books that he prided himself, repeating, with a complacent air, as he led the way to the crowded and dusty shelves, the verses of old Chaucer

"For he would rather have at his bed-head,
   A twenty books, clothed in black or red,

Of Aristotle, or his philosophy,
Than robes rich, rebeck or saltery."

This pithy motto he delivered, shaking his head, and giving each guttural
the true Anglo-Saxon enunciation, which is now forgotten in the southern
parts of this realm.

The collection was, indeed, a curious one, and might well be envied
by an amateur. Yet it was not collected at the enormous prices of modern
times, which are sufficient to have appalled the most determined, as well
as earliest bibliomaniac upon record, whom we take to have been none
else than the renowned Don Quixote de la Mancha, as, among other
slight indications of an infirm understanding, he is stated, by his vera-
cious historian, Cid Hamet Benengeli, to have exchanged fields and
farms for folios and quartos of chivalry. In this species of exploit, the
good knight-errant has been imitated by lords, knights, and squires of our
own day, though we have not yet heard of any that has mistaken an inn
for a castle, or laid his lance in rest against a windmill. Mr Oldbuck did
not follow these collectors in such excess of expenditure; but, taking a
pleasure in the personal labour of forming his library, saved his purse at
the expense of his time and toil.

Source

Scott, W. Sir, 1816, *The Antiquary*, Chapter 3, Edinburgh.

Notes

1 Lovel is the young 'male lead' of the novel
2 The original of Mr Oldbuck, Scott's Antiquary, is often supposed to be
   Gordon Alexander (1692–1754) who in 1726 published his *Itinerarium
   Septentrionale*, an account of the antiquities of Scotland. In 1741 he went to
   South Carolina, and there acquired a land grant and became registrar of the
   province.
3 *genius loci*, 'the spirit of the place'; *mare magnum*, 'great sea', a reflection
   on the overflowing and chaotic nature of the arrangement of the antiquities.
4 'Heavysterne' is, of course, an invention.

References

Collon, 1985
Norman, 1963

62

Newcastle collects antiquities

Interest in the British past was by no means confined to London; indeed, a strong strand of regional regard to the past was significant not only in Scotland and Wales, but also in the individual English counties, and in the large northern shires of Yorkshire and Northumberland, which at different times in the pre-Norman period had been the Anglo-Saxon kingdom of Northumbria and the Viking kingdom of York.

Accordingly, the Society of Antiquaries of Newcastle upon Tyne was established in 1813, and obtained premises in part of the Castle Keep in Newcastle where material could be stored. The society published *Transactions* and held summer 'country meetings' through which members could visit the extremely significant and well-preserved Roman and medieval sites in the area, especially Hadrian's Wall.

The extract gives the list of pieces collected and donated to the Society's collection from its establishment in early 1813 to July 1814. Roman material occupies a significant place, but the general impression is of a very mixed group of material.

FIRST ANNUAL REPORT OF THE SOCIETY OF ANTIQUARIES OF NEWCASTLE

Date.	Donations.	Donors.
1813. March 3.	Eleven Coins and Medals.	R. Surtees, Esq. Mainsforth.
	Three Coins of English Silver; 51 of Roman Silver; 74 Roman third Brass; 14 Portuguese Silver; and 42 Portuguese Copper.	Mr. John Adamson, Secretary.
	Noble on the Mint and Coins of Durham; and Smellie's Historical Account of the Edinburgh Society of Antiquaries.	Mr. John Bell, Treasurer.
	A Fragment of a Roman Millstone, found on Carlisle Sands.	Mr. G. A. Dickson.
April 7.	A Roman Altar to Belatucader, found at Brougham Castle, in Westmorland, – see Appendix, No. 1.; a small votive Altar, uninscribed, found at Voreda, or Old Penrith, in Cumberland; a centurial Stone inscribed >CLAUDI; a Roman Millstone and the Head of a Roman Statue of	

Date.	Donations.	Donors.
	Stone, all found at Caervorran, on the Roman Wall; 2 Specimens of the Cement used in Roman Baths, found in Carlisle; and a Piece of Basalt, which, from its form, appears to have been Part of a Millstone.	Mr. G. A. Dickson.
	Eighty-eight Tradesmen's Tokens of the old issue, with a Manuscript Description of them; and 28 Impressions, and 5 Casts of ancient Seals, principally Scottish.	Thomas Davidson, Esq.
	Fifty Guineas.	His Grace the Duke of Northumberland.
	Nine Guineas.	Sir C. M. L. Monck, Bart. V. P.
June 2.	An ancient Urn, containing calcined Bones, and discovered in Lincolnshire; a centurial Stone, inscribed > OCTAVI SEBANI; a Roman Brick inscribed TIPRINUS; and a Fragment of an Amphora, and a large Iron Ring, both supposed to be Roman.	A. M. L. de Cardonnell, Esq. of Cramlington.
	A circular British Earthen Vessel, 3½ Inches high, and 6 Inches in diameter, found near Corbridge; – see Plate VI. fig. G.; Fragments of Pottery, &c.	Joseph Forster, Esq.
	A List of the Members of the Antiquarian Society of London.	William Radclyffe, Esq. Rouge Croix.[1]
	Thirty-three miscellaneous Coins, chiefly English.	Mr. J. T. Brockett.
July 7.	Three Brick Flues of a Roman Bath; 8 Copper and 4 Roman Silver Coins; 4 Fragments of an Amphora, one of them inscribed D. O. M. S.; 2 Pieces of a Dear's Horn, &c. all found at Corstopitum or Corchester, an ancient Roman Station, a little to the West of the Town of Corbridge.	Rev. S. Clarke, of Hexham.
	Addison's Dialogues upon the Usefulness of ancient Medals; and Bell's Rhymes of Northern Bards.	Mr. John Bell, Treasurer.
	New Agricultural and Commercial Magazine, Vol. I. and II.	Mr. John Clennell, Homerton, Middlesex.
	A Bottle of Roman Earthenware, found in digging a cellar in Carlisle; a Fragment of a Roman Amphora, found under the foundations of the Roman Wall at Stanwix; and another Fragment of Roman Earthenware, found at Benwell, in Northumberland.	Mr. G. A. Dickson.
	A Drawing of the Entrance of Voreda, as it appeared when cleared from Rubbish in 1812, – fig. A.; a Drawing of one of the Corners of the same place, with an Arch in the Foundations of its Wall, – fig. B.; and Drawings of two brazen Articles found in that station, – fig. C. and D. – see Plate IX.	James Losh, Esq. V.P.

Date.	Donations.	Donors.

August 4. A Copy of the Royal Charter and the Statutes of the Society of Antiquaries, London; four Plates of Roman Antiquities found near Capheaton. See Archaeologia, Vol. XV. p. 393. — Sir John E. Swinburne, Bart. President.

A Silver Ring, found at Towton Moor in 1770. — Rev. Wm. Turner.

Sept. 1. The Seal of the Society, designed by Mr. Howard of the Royal Academy, and engraved by Mr. Wyon, of the Royal Mint. — Sir John E. Swinburne, Bart. President.

A reversed Impression of the Inscription deposited in the Foundation Stone of the new County Courts of Northumberland. — Thomas Davidson, Esq.

Oct. 6. A Copper Styea of Eegfrith, one of the Saxo-Northumbrian Kings, – see Plate VI. fig. H. — Rev. J. Hodgson, Sec.

Nov. 3. Three Fragments of Roman Pottery; an ancient Iron Key found under the Foundations of St. Alban's Church in Carlisle; another Key of Brass found at York; and a Bronze Cast, bearing this Inscription, TIT. VESP. C. with the Head of that Emperor. — Mr. G. A. Dickson, Newcastle

Dec. 1. A Roman Copper Vessel, and some Pieces of Copper, which had apparently belonged to it, two Fibulæ and a Ring, all found in a tumulus near Capheaton. Also a Penny of Queen Elizabeth, dated 1575, found in Hill-Head-Bank New-Plantation-Fence; and a Counter found at Harnham. — Sir John E. Swinburne, Bart. President.

A Bottle of Black Earthenware from Pompeii; a small Etruscan Earthen Vessel from Herculaneum; an Etruscan Vase; a British Urn, with part of the calcined Bones it contained, found under a large Cairn, at Croglin, in Cumberland, – see Plate VI. fig. I. The Pedestal of the Pillar, converted into a Mortar, found at Caervorran; and Copies of two Roman Inscriptions, – see Appendix, No. II. — Mr. G. A. Dickson, Newcastle.

A curious Mortar found near Chester-le-Street. — Isaac Cookson, Esq. of Whithill, Durham.

A Copy of an Inscription on a Rock on Fallowfield-Fell, in Northumberland, – see Place VI. fig. E.; and a Copy of an Inscription found at Walwick Chesters, – see Plate VI. fig. F. — Rev. John Hodgson, Secretary.

1814. Jan. 5. An Engraving, framed, of the Herald's College, London, in 1768. — Thos. Davidson, Esq.

A Celtic Hammer of very hard granular stone, found near Kirkoswald Castle, in Cumberland; a silver Penny of Henry the Second, found with a great quantity of the same kind of coin, at Cutherston, near Bowes, in Yorkshire, about the year 1782; a Silver Penny of Edward the First, coined at London; a Silver Penny of Edward the Second,

Date.	Donations.	Donors.
	coined at Canterbury; a Swedish Copper Dollar, of Charles the Twelfth, date 1716.	Mrs. Atkinson, Temple-Sowerby.
	Six Copper Stycas of the Northumbrian Kings, Eanred and Ethelred.[2]	M. Atkinson, Esq. Carrhill, Durham.
Feb. 2.	Eighty-seven Copper Coins of various Nations; an Etching of two Roman Brass Vessels, with bas relief Handles.	Mr. G. A. Dickson.
	Potter's Greek Antiquities.	Mr. Thomas Hodgson.
	Forty Pounds.	Ed. Hussey Delaval, Esq.
March 2.	Ten Roman Silver Coins, and 8 English Silver Coins.	Mr. N. Naters.
	Eighteen English Copper Coins.	Mr. J. Bell, Treasurer.
	Chamberlayne's Magnæ Britanniæ Notitia.	Mr. G. A. Dickson.
	Two English Tokens	John Brumell, Esq.
April 6.	The "Testa de Nevill."	Sir C. M. L. Monck, Bart. V. P.
May 4.	A Silver Coin of Eugenius.	Mr. J. T. Brockett
	A Bronze Ax or Celt.	Mr. James Hawthorn.
	Twenty-four English Copper Local Tokens.	Mr. J. Bell, Treasurer.
	Four Roman Sepulchral Urns, and Fragments of several others, found in Auckland Park, and near the Roman Station at Binchester.	Anonymous.
June 1.	A Roman Lamp of red Earthenware; a Fragment of another, with the figure of Jupiter and the Eagle on its top; and 12 remarkably small Copper Coins, all found in removing a mound of earth in the Estate of J. J. Robinson, Esq. adjoining to Old Carlisle, in April, 1814. Also Kennett's Roman Antiquities, 8vo. 1769.	Mr. G. A. Dickson.
	The six first Parts of "The Border Antiquities of England and Scotland."	Walter Scott, Esq. of Edinburgh. [3]
	The upper and lower Stones of an ancient Quern, or Hand Mill, found on Gateshead Fell. This donation was accompanied by a Drawing of the Lines of a certain Enclosure or Camp, in which these and several fragments of mill-stones were found. The place was situated in a parcel of ground allotted to Mr. Henderson, at the time of the enclosure of Gateshead Fell. The west side of the entrenched ground measured 220 yards, the north end 66 yards, and the breadth of the area from east to west at the south end, and from the N. E. to the S. E. corner 33 yards. An oblong entrenched area, 30 yards long and 14 broad, was also formed on the east side of it; at its south end there was a circular enclosure, 14 feet in diameter, formed with stones, each 3 feet long, and set on edge; and at 21 yards from the west side an entrenched line led to a spring opposite the north west corner.	Mr. Joseph Henderson, Gateshead Fell.

Date.	Donations.	Donors.
July 6.	A small Vessel of Earthenware, in which several Copper Stycas of Ecgfrith, King of Northumberland, were found in the Chapel Yard of Heworth, Durham; and a Plan of an ancient Entrenchment at Wardley, in the Parish of Jarrow, Durham, – see Plate V.	Rev. John Hodgson, Secretary.
	A Stone Celt, found on Throckley Fell, Northumberland; a Pipe of red Earthenware, for conveying	

Source

First Annual Report, Society of Antiquaries of Newcastle upon Tyne, 1814: 1–4.

Notes

1 'Rouge Croix' is the title of one of the English heralds who make up the College of Heralds, in charge of matters relating to coats of arms and similar affairs.
2 'They were found a few years since, near Kirkoswald, in Cumberland, by the blowing down of a large tree, the roots of which had taken hold of, and brought up with them, a large earthen vessel, full of similar Coins.' (original note)
3 This is, of course, Walter Scott the novelist (see this volume, Chapter 61)

Bibliography

Alexander, B., 1960, 'The decay of Beckford's Genius', in Mahmoud, 1960: 17–29

Allan, M., 1964, *The Tradescants, their Plants, Gardens and Museum 1570–1662*, London, M. Joseph

Allen, D., 1978, *The Naturalist in Britain: A Social History*, Harmondsworth, London

Allen, P.S. (ed.), 1910, *Erasmus Epistelae*, Vols 1–10, London

Arnold, K., 1996, 'Trade, Travel and Treasures: 17th century Artificial Curiosities', in Chard C. and Langdon H. (eds), *Transports: Travel, Pleasure and imaginative Geography, 1600–1830*, Yale University Press: 263–86

Ashton, S., 1988, *Colonialism in British India*, London, British Library

Balsiger, B.J., 1970, 'The Kunst- und Wunderkammern. A catalogue raissoné of collecting in Germany, France and England 1565–1750.' PhD thesis, University of Pittsburgh

Bann, S., 1988 '"Views of the Past" – reflections on the treatment of historical objects and museums of history (1750–1850)' in Fyfe and Law, 1988: 39–64

Bann, S., 1994, *Under the Sign: John Bargrave as collector, traveller and witness*, Ann Arbor: University of Michigan Press

Bargrave, J., 1968, (written 1676) 'Catalogue of Dr [John] Bargrave's Museum', in Robertson J.C. (ed.), 1968, *Pope Alexander the Seventh and the College of Cardinals* by John Bargrave, London, Camden Society: 92

Barrett, C. and Dobson, A. 1905, *The Diary and Letters of Madame D'Arblay*, London, Macmillan

Beanglehole, J.C. (ed.), 1962 *The 'Endeavor' Journal of Joseph Banks 1768–1771*, 2 vols, Sydney, Public Library of New South Wales and Augus Robertson

Beaufort, F., 1817, *Karamania, or, a Brief Description of the South Coast of Asia Minor and the Remains of Antiquity*, London

Belden, M., 1929, *The Dramatic Works of Samuel Foote*, London, Dent

Benett, E., 1831, *A Catalogue of the Organic Remains of the County of Wilts*, Warminster, J.L. Vardy

Benjamin, M., 1991(ed.), *Science and Sensibility in Gender Enquiry 1780–1945*, Oxford, Blackwell

Bernal, M., 1987 and 1991, *Black Athene: The Afro-Asiatic Roots of Clasical Civilization*, Vols 1 and 2, London, Free Association Press

Birch, T., (ed.), 1756, *The History of the Royal Society*, Vol. 2, London

Blundell, H., 1803, *Account of the Statues, Busts, Bas-reliefs, Cinerary Urns and other Ancient Marbles at Ince. Collected by Henry Blundell*, Liverpool

Blundell, H., 1809–10, *Engravings and Etchings of the Principal Statues, Busts, Bass-reliefs, Sepulchral Monuments, Cinerary Urns etc. in The Collection of Henry Blundell Esq. at Ince*, Vols 1–11, Liverpool

Boyle, R., 1663, *Some Considerations touching the Usefulnesse of Experimental Natural Philosophy*, London

Bray, W., (ed.), 1889, *Diary and Correspondence of John Evelyn*, vols 1–3, London

Brears, P. and Davies, S., 1989, *Treasures for the People*, Yorkshire and Humberside Museums Council

Browne, T.M., 1978, 'The rise of Baconianism in seventeenth century England', *Studia Copernicana*, 16, 507–16, Wroclaw

Burn, L., (ed.), 1997, *Sir William Hamilton, Collector and Connoisseur:* special issue of *Journal of the History of Collections*, 9, 2

Butt, J., (ed.), 1963, *The Poems of Alexander Pope*, London, Methuen

Castellani, C., 1970, 'Aldrovandi, Ulisse' in *Dictionary of Scientific Biography*, ed.-in-chief Gillespie, C., New York, Charles Scribner's Sons: 108–110

Chapman, G., 1940, *Beckford*, Alden Press, Oxford

Chapman, G. (ed.), 1928, *The Travel Diaries of William Beckford of Fonthill*, Vols 1, 11, Cambridge University Press

Charleton, W., 1657, *The Immortality of the Human Soul*, London

Clifford, T., 1992, 'The plaster shops of the rococo and neo-classical era in Britain', *Journal of the History of Collections*, 4, 1: 39–68

Cockerell, S.P. (ed.), 1903, *Travels in southern Europe and the Levant 1810–1817. The Journal of C.R. Cockerell RA*, London, Longmans, Green and Co.

Cole, F.J., 1975, *A History of Comparative Anatomy*, New York, Dover Publications

Collon, D., 1985, *The Civilised Imagination: A Study of Anne Radcliffe, June Austen and Sir Walter Scott*, Cambridge University Press

Comenius, J.A., 1664, *Joh. Amos Comenius's Visible World*, '*Translated into English by Charles Hoole*', London

Comenius, J.A. 1938, *The Way of Light*, London, Hodder and Stoughton, (republication)

Cook, B., 1977, 'The Townley Marbles in Westminster and Bloomsbury', *British Museum Yearbook*, 2: 34–78

Cook, B., 1985, *The Townley Marbles*, London, British Museum

Crook, J.M., 1972, *The British Museum: A case-study in architectural politics*, London, Allen Lane

Dance, P., 1966, *Shell Collecting*, London, Faber & Faber

Daston, L., 1988, 'The Factual Sensibility', *Isis*, 37: 452–70

Davies, G., 1991, 'The Albacini cast collection: character and significance', *Journal of the History of Collections*, 3, 2: 145–66

de Beer, E.S. (ed.), 1955, *The Diary of John Evelyn*, Oxford, Clarendon Press

de Franciscis, A., 1949, 'Restauri di Carlo Albacini a statue del Museo Nazionale di Napoli', *Saurium* 1: 96–110

de Gummond, 1991, 'Portraits of Augustus and his family in the Albacini collection', *Journal of the History of Collections*, 3, 2: 167–82

de Renou, J., 1657, *Medicinal Dispensatory*, London

Dorey, H., 1992, 'Soane as a Collector' in Thornton and Dorey 1992: 122–6

Dury (or Durie), J., 1650, *The Reformed School*, London, [1650] A Scolar Press Facsimile. Scolar Press, 1972. pp. 74–6

Eamon, W., 1990, 'From the Secrets of nature to public knowledge', in Lindberg,

D. and Westman, R.S. (eds), *Reappraisals of the Scientific Revolution*, Cambridge University Press, 333–66

Edwards, E., 1870, *Lives of the Founders of the British Museum*, Vols 1 and 2, London, Macmillan

Elsner, J., 1994, 'A Collector's Model of Desire: The House and Museum of Sir John Soane' in Elsner and Cardinal, 1994: 155–76

Elsner, J. and Cardinal, R. (eds.), 1994, *The Cultures of Collecting*, Reaktion Books, London

English Heritage, 1987, *The Trial, a Facsimile of the Worsley v Bisset Trial, 1782*, London, English Heritage

Eri, I., 1985, 'A brief history of the show-case,' in *Museum*, 37: 4–7

Evans, J., 1956, *A History of the Society of Antiquaries*, Oxford University Press

Evelyn, J., 1697, *Numismata*, London

Fairclough, P., 1968 (ed.), *Three Gothic Novels*, Harmondsworth, Penguin Books.

Feinberg, M.S., 1987, *Sir John Soane's Museum*, Ann Arbor, University of Michigan Press

Fejfer, J. and Southworth, E., 1991, *The Ince Blundell Collection of Classical Sculpture* Vol. I, Part 1 *The Female Portraits*, London, HMSO

Findlen, P., 1996, *Possessing Nature: Museums, Collecting, and Scientific Culture in Early Modern Italy*, Berkeley and London, University of California Press

Force, R. and Force, M., 1968, *Art and Artefacts of the Eighteenth Century Objects in the Leverian Museum as painted by Sarah Stone*, Honolulu, Bishop Bernice Museum

Fyfe, G. and Law, J., 1988 (eds), *Picturing Power: Visual Depiction and Social Relations*, Sociological Review Monograph, 35

Galihard, J., 1678, *A Treatise Concerning the Education of Youth, 'The Second Part'*, London

Gloag, J., 1952, *A Short Dictionary of Furniture*, London, Cassell

Gordon, Mrs, 1894, *Mary Anning, the Heroine of Lyme Regis*, London

Grew, N., 1681, *Musaeum Regalis Societatis. Or a catalogue and description of the natural and artificial rarities belonging to the Royal Society and preserved at Gresham Colledge ...* , London.

Gunther, A.E., 1980, *The Founders of Science at the British Museum, 1753–1900*, Halesworth, Suffolk, Halesworth Press

Gunther, R.W.T., 1925–31, *Early Science in Oxford, Vols 1–8*, Oxford University Press

Gutfleisch, B., and Menzhausen, J., 1989, 'How a kunstkammer should be formed: Gabriel Kaltermarckt's advice to Christian I of Saxony on the formation of an art collection, 1587', *Journal of the History of Collections*, 1, 1... 3–32

Hadfield, M., 1960, *Gardening in Britain*, London, Hutchinson

Hale, J.R., 1963, *England and the Italian Renaissance*, revised edition, London, Arrow Books

Hall, A.R. and Hall, M.B. (eds and trans.), 1966, *The correspondence of Henry Oldenburg*, Madison, Milwaukee and London, University of Wisconsin Press

Hall, A.R. and Hall, M.B., 1970, *Correspondence of Henry Oldenburg*, Vols 1–7, Madison, University of Wisconsin Press

Hancock, E., 1980, 'One of those dreadful combats – a surviving display from William Bullock's London Museum, 1807–1818', *Museums Journal*, 74, 4: 172–5

Haraucourt, E., 1860, *Medieval Manners Illustrated at the Cluny Museum with a description of the Most Important Exhibits*, Larousse, Paris

Haskell, F. and Penny, N., 1981, *Taste and the Antique: the Lure of Classical Sculpture 1500–1900*, Yale University Press, New Haven

Hawkins, T., 1832, *Geological Sketches and Glimpses of the Earth*, London

Haynes, D.E.L., 1975, *The Arundel Marbles*, Oxford, Ashmolean Museum

Hemmings, F.W.J., 1987, *Culture and Society in France 1789–1848*, Leicester University Press

Herrmann, F., 1972, *The English as Collectors*, London, Chatto & Windus

Hibbert, C., 1969, *The Grand Tour*, London, Weidenfeld & Nicolson

Hill, C., 1965, *Intellectual Origins of the English Revolution*, Oxford, Clarendon Press

Hodgen, M.T., 1971, *Early Anthropology in the Sixteenth and Seventeenth Centuries*, Philadelphia, University of Pennsylvania Press

Honour, H., 1955, 'The Egyptian Taste', *Connoisseur*, 125, 546: 242–6

Hoole, C., 1913 (first published 1660), *A New Discovery of the old art of Teaching Schoole*, Liverpool

Houghton, W., 1942, 'English Virtuosi in the seventeenth century', *Journal of the History of Ideas*, 3: 51–73, 140–219

Howard, S., 1991 'Albani, Winckelmann and Caraceppi: the transition from amateur to professional antiquarian', *Journal of History of Collections*, 4, 1: 27–38

Howarth, D., 1985, *Lord Arundel and His Circle*, New Haven and London, Yale University Press

Hunt, J., 1985 'Curiosities to adorn cabinets and gardens', in Impey, O. and MacGregor, A., 193–203

Hunter, M., 1985, 'The Cabinet Institutionalised', in Impey, O. and Macgregor, A., 159–68

Hunter, M., 1989, 'Between Cabinet of Curiosities and Research Collection: The history of the Royal Society's Repository', in *Establishing the New Science: the Experience of the Early Royal Society*, Woodbridge, Suffolk, Boydell Press

Hutton, W., 1785, *Journey to London*, London

Impey, O. and Macgregor, A. (edsʃ), 1985, *The Origins of Museums: the Cabinet of Curiosities in sixteenth and seventeenth century Europe*, Oxford, Clarendon Press

Jenkins, I., 1992, *Archaeologists and Aesthetes in the Sculpture Galleries of the British Museum 1800–1939*, London, British Museum Press

Jenkins, I. and Sloan, K., 1996, *Vases and Volcanoes, Sir William Hamilton and his Collection*, London, British Museum Press

Jobert, L., 1697, *The Knowledge of Medals*, London

Kaeppler, A., 1978a, *Cook Voyage Artifacts*, Honolulu, Bishop Bernice Museum

Kaeppler, A., 1978b, *Artificial Curiosities: Being an Exposition of Native Manufactures Collected on the Three Pacific Voyages of Captain James Cook RN*, Honolulu, Bishop Bernice Museum Special Publication 65

Kaeppler, A., 1979, 'Tracing the History of Hawaiian Cook Voyage Artifacts in the Museum of Mankind', *British Museum Yearbook*, 3, 1979: 167–86

Kelly, A., 1990, *Mrs Coade's Stone*, London

Ketton-Cremer, R., 1964, *Horace Walpole*, 3rd edition, London

King, J., 1994, 'Vancouver's ethnography: a preliminary description of five inventories from the voyage of 1791–95', *Journal of History of Collections*, 6, 1: 35–56

King, J., 1996, 'New Evidence for the Contents of the Leverian Collection', *Journal of History of Collections*, 8, 2: 167–86

Kinner, C., 1648, *A Continuation of Mr J.A. Comenius' school endeavours*, London

Knight, D., 1981, *Ordering the World*, London, Burnett Books

Knowlson, J., 1975, *Universal Language schemes in England and France 1600–1800*, Toronto and Buffalo, University of Toronto Press

Kuhn, T.S., 1977, 'Mathematical versus Experimental Traditions in the Development of Physical Sciences' in *Essential Tension*, University of Chicago Press: 31–65

Landsdown, Marquis of (ed.), 1928, *The Petty–Southwell correspondence, 1676–1687*, London, Constable & Co.

Lang, W., 1939, 'Mary Anning (1799–1847) and the Pioneer Geologists of Lyme', *Proceedings of the Dorset Natural History and Archaeological Society*, 60: 142–64

Lang, W., 1959, 'Portraits of Mary Anning and Other Items', *Proceedings of the Dorset Natural History and Archaeological Society*, 81: 89–91

Larson, J., 1971, *Reason and Experience: The Representation of the Natural Order in the Work of Carl Linné*, Berkeley and Los Angeles, University of California Press

Lavendar, T., 1609, *The Travels of Certaine Englishmen into Africa, Asia, Troy*, London

Lawson, J., 1709, *A New Voyage to Carolina*, London

Lees-Milne, J., 1976, *William Beckford*, Tisbury, Wiltshire, Compton Russell

LeFevre, N., 1670, *A Complete body of chemistry*, London

Leith-Ross, P., 1984, *The John Tradescants: Gardeners to the Rose and Lilly Queen*, Bristol, P. Owen

Levine, J., 1977, *Dr Woodward's Shield: Science and Satire in Augustan England*, Berkeley, University of California Press

Ley, W., 1968, *Dawn of Zoology*, Englewood Cliffs, NJ

Lightbown, R., 1989, 'Charles I and the Tradition of European Princely Collecting' in MacGregor, A. (ed.), *The Late King's Goods*, London and Oxford, A. McAlpine

Lockhart, J., 1900, *Memoirs of Sir Walter Scott*, Vols 1–3, Edinburgh

Lyte, C., 1980, *Sir Joseph Banks*, Newton Abbot, David & Charles

MacGregor, A., 1983, *Tradescant's Rarities*, Oxford, Clarendon Press

MacGregor, A., 1985, 'The Cabinet of Curiosities in seventeenth century Britain' in Impey and MacGregor (eds), 147–59

MacGregor, A.G. and Turner, A.J., 1986, 'The Ashmolean Museum' in Sutherland, L.S. and Mitchell, L.G. (eds), *The Eighteenth Century* in Aston, T.H. (gen. ed.), *The History of the University of Oxford*, Vol. 5, Oxford, Clarendon Press

MacGregor, A. (ed.), 1994, *Sir Hans Sloane: Collector, Scientist, Antiquary, Founding Father of the British Museum*, London, British Museum Press in association with Alistair McAlpine

Mahmoud, F. (ed.), 1960, *William Beckford of Fonthill 1760–1844, Bicentenary Essays*, Cairo, Tsoumas and Co

Martyn, T., 1766, *The English Conoisseur: containing an account of whatever is curious in Painting and Scripture etc. in the Palaces and Seats of the nobility and Principal gentry of England both in Town and Country*, London

Menzhausen, J., 1985, 'Elector Augustus's Kunstkammer: an analysis of the inventory of 1587', in Impey, O. and MacGregor, A., 69–75

Meteyard, E., 1865–6, *The Life of Josiah Wedgewood*, Vols 1, 2, London

Millar, O., 1960, *Abraham van der Poort's Catalogue of the Collection of Charles I*, Walpole Society, 37, University of Glasgow Press

Millar, P., 1972 (ed.), *The Inventories and Valuation of the King's Goods 1649–1651*, Walpole Society, 43, University of Glasgow Press

Mirrless, H., 1962, *A Fly in Amber, Being an extravagant biography of Sir Robert Bruce Cotton*, London, Faber & Faber

Morris, I., 1994 (ed.), *Classical Greece: Ancient Histories and Modern Archaeologies*, Cambridge University Press

Morrison, A., 1893–94, *A Catalogue of the Collection of autograph letters and historical documents formed between 1865 and 1882 by A. Morrison. The Hamilton and Nelson Papers*, Vols I and II. Combined and annotated under the direction of A.W. Thibidean, London

Mullen, A., 1682, *An Anatomical Account of the Elephant Accidentally Burnt in Dublin ... Sent in a letter to Sir Will. Petty, Fellow of the Royal Society*, London

Mullens, W., 1917–1918 'Some Museums of Old London, 11. William Bullock's London Museum', *Museums Journal*, 17: 51–5, 132–7, 180–87

Murray, D., 1904, *Museums, and their History and their Use*, Vols 1–3, Glasgow, James Maclehose & Sons

Nicholson, J., 1987, 'Tinsel, Terracotta or Tantric: Representing Indian Reality in Museums' in Carruthers, A. (ed.), 1987, *Bias in Museums: Museums Professionals Group Transactions*, 22: 26–31

Norman, A., 1963, 'Arms and Armour at Abbotsford', *Apollo*, 76: 525–9

Oldroyd, D.R., 1987, 'Some Writings of Robert Hooke on Procedures for the Prosecution of Scientific Enquiries', *Notes and Records of the Royal Society of London*: 41

Olmi, G., 1985, 'Italian Cabinets of the sixteenth and seventeenth centuries', in Impey and MacGregor: 5–16

Ovenell, R.F., 1986, *The Ashmolean Museum 1683–1894*, Oxford, Clarendon Press

Palliser, D. and M., 1979, *York as they saw it*, York

Parkes, J., 1925, *Travel in England in the seventeenth century*, London, H. Milford

Peachman, H., 1634, *The compleat gentleman. Fashioning him absolut, in the most necessary and commendable qualities concerning minde or body that may be required in a noble gentleman*, London

Pearce, S., 1973, *Arts of Polynesia*, Exeter City Museum

Perez-Ramos, A., 1988, *Francis Bacon's Idea of Science and the Maker's Knowledge Tradition*, Oxford, Clarendon Press

Petiver, J., 1698, 'An Account of some Indian Plants, &c.', *Philosophical Transactions*, 20: 57–63

Petiver, J., 1769, 'Brief Directions for the Easie Making and Preseving collections of all natural Curiosities' in his *Opera, historiam naturalem spectantia; or gazophyl. Containing siveral 1000 figures of birds, beasts, reptiles, insects, fish, beelets, moths, flies, shells, corals, fossils, minerals, stones, fungusses, mosses, plants &c. from all nations, on 156 copperplates*, London, 1767

Plot, R., 1677, *The natural history of Oxford-shire, being an essay toward the natural history of England*, London

Popham, A.E., 1936, 'The Resta Collection', *Old Master Drawings*, 11, 41, June 1936: 1–19, Plates 1–18

Potts, A., 1994, *Flesh and the Ideal: Winckelmann and the Origins of Art History*, New Haven, Yale University Press

Praz, M., 1986, 'Introduction' in Fairclough, 1986: 7–33

Price, D., 1989, 'John Woodward and a surviving British Geological Collection from the Early Eighteenth Century.' *Journal of the History of Collections*, 1, 1: 79–85

Proudfoot, C. and Watkin, D., 1972a 'A Pioneer of English Neo-Classicism', *Country Life*, CL1, No. 3095: 918–21

Proudfoot, C. and Watkin, C., 1972b, 'The Furniture of C.H. Tatham', *Country Life*, CL1, No. 3912: 1481–6

Quarrel, W.H. and Mare M. (trans. and ed.), 1934, 'London in 1710' from *The Travels of Zacharias Conrad von Uffenbach*, London, Faber and Faber

Quiccheberg, S., 1565, *Inscriptiones Vel Tituli Theatri Amplissimi* ... , Munich

Raby, J., 1985, 'Exotica from Islam', in Impey and MacGregor: 251–9

Redford, G., 1888, *Art Sales*, Vols 1–11, London

Richardson, R., 1835, *Extracts from the Literary and Scientific Correspondence of Richard Richardson*, Yarmouth

Rigby, D. and E., 1944, *Lock, Stock and Barrel: The Story of Collecting*, Philadelphia, S.B. Lippincott

Rossi, P., 1984, 'Universal Languages, Classifications and Nomenciatures in the Seventeenth Century', *History and Philosophy of the Life Sciences*, 6

Salmon, F., 1998, 'Charles Heathcote Tatham and the Accademia di S Luca, Rome', *Burlington Magazine*, February 1998: 85–92

Salmon, V., 1979, *The Study of Language in seventeenth century England*, Amsterdam, Benjamins

Scheurleer, P., 1996, 'Rich remains from social anthropological fieldwork in eighteenth century India', *Journal of the History of Collections*, 8, 1: 71–92

Schiebinger, L., 1991, 'The Private Life of Plants: Sexual Politics in Carl Linnaeus and Erasmus Darwin' in Benjamin, 1991: 121–43

Schiebinger, L., 1993, 'Why Mammals are called Mammals: Gender Politics in Eighteenth-Century Natural History', *American Historical Review*, 98: 382–411

Scott, Sir W., 1816, *The Antiquary*, Edinburgh

Seelig, L., 1985, 'The Munich Kunstkammer, 1565–1807', in Impey and MacGregor: 76–90

Shanks, M., 1996, *Classical Archaeology of Greece: Experiences of the Discipline*, London, Routledge

Sharp, L.G., 1977, 'Sir William Petty and some Aspects of Seventeenth Century Natural Philosophy', DPhil, Oxford University

Sharpe, K., 1979, *Sir Robert Cotton*, Oxford University Press

Sheraton, T., 1803, *The Cabinet Dictionary*, London

Simcock, A.V., 1984, *The Ashmolean Museum and Oxford Science 1683–1983*, Oxford, Museum of History of Science

Simpson, F., 1950, 'The English Connoisseur and his Sources', *Burlington Magazine*, XLIII

Sitwell, E., 1936, *English Eccentrics*, London, Faber & Faber

Sloane, H., 1699, 'An account of a China cabinet, filled with several instruments, fruits, &c used in China: sent to the Royal Society by Mr Buckly, chief Surgeon at Fort St George', *Philosophical Transactions*, 20: 20–25

Sloane, H., 1707, *A Voyage to the Islands of Madeira, Barbados*, London

Smailes, H., 1991, 'A History of the Statue Gallery at the Trustees' Academy in Edinburgh and the acquisition of the Albacini Casts in 1838', *Journal of History of Collections*, 3, 2: 121–4

Smith, A.H., 1916, 'Lord Elgin and his Collection', *Journal of Hellenic Studies*, 36: 163–372

Smith, F.F., 1962, *The Historical Revolution*, London, Columbia University Press

Smith, V., 1991, *A History of Fine Art in India and Ceylon*, Oxford University Press

Soane, Sir J., 1835, *Description of the House and Museum on the North Side of Lincoln's Inn Fields with Graphic Illustrations and Incidental Details*, London

Soane, Sir J., 1844, *General Description of Sir John Soane's Museum with Brief Notes of the More Interesting Works of Art Therein*, 2nd edition, London

Southworth, E., 1992, 'The Ince Blundell Collection: collecting behaviour in the eighteenth century', *Journal of History of Collections*, 4, 1: 219–34

Spamer, E., Bogan, A. and Torrens, H., 1989, 'Recovery of the Ethelred Benett Collection of Fossils mostly from the Jurassic-Cretaceous Strata of Wiltshire, England', *Proceedings of the Academy of Natural Sciences of Philadelphia*, 141: 115–80

Spedding, J., Ellis, R. and Heath, D. (eds), 1890, *The Works of Francis Bacon*, Vols 1–8, London

Sprat, T., 1667, *The History of the Royal Society*, London

Springell, F.C., 1963, *Connoisseur and diplomat*, Maggs Brothers, London

Stafleu, F., 1971, *Linnaeus and the Linnaeans: The Spreading of their ideas in Systematic Botany 1735–1789*, Utrecht, A. Oosthoek

Stearns, R.P., 1952, 'James Petiver, promoter of natural science', *American Antiquarian Society Proceedings*, 62, 243–365

Stearns, R.P., 1970, *Science in the British Colonies of America*, Urbana, Chicago, and London, University of Illinois Press

Stearns, R.P., 1980, 'John Winthrop (1681–1757) and his Gifts to the Royal Society', *Publications of the Colonial Society of Massachusetts: Transactions*, 1952–6, 42

Stone, L., 1964, 'The Educational Revolution in England', *Past and Present*, 28: 41–80

Stoye, J.W., 1952, *English Travellers Abroad 1604–67*, London

Strange, J., 1779, 'An Account of some remains of Roman and other Antiquities in and near the Town of Brecknock, in South Wales', *Archaeologia*, 1779: 294–306

Sturdy, D. and Henig, M. [n.d.], *The Gentle Traveller: John Bargrave, Canon of Canterbury, and his collection*, Oxford, Ashmolean Museum

Summerson, J., 1982, 'Union of the Arts: Sir John Soane's Museum-House', *Lotus International*, 25: 64–75

Thoresby, R., 1715, *Ducatus Leodiensis*, London

Thornton, P. and Dorey, H., (eds), 1992, *A Miscellany of Objects from Sir John Soane's Museum*, London, Sir John Soane's Museum

Tischbein, J.H.W., 1793– after 1803, *Collection of Engravings from Ancient Vases Discovered in the Kingdom of the Two Sicillies between 1789 and 1790*, Vols 1–5, Naples

Torrens, H., 1985, 'Women in Geology 2, Ethelred Benett', *Open Earth*, 21: 12–13

Trease, G., 1967, *The Grand Tour*, Chicago, Rivehart & Winson

Turnbull, G.H., 1947, *Hartlib, Dury and Comenius*, London, University Press of Liverpool

Vale, M., 1977, *The Gentleman's Recreations*, London, Trowbridge & Esher

Vaughan, G., 1991, 'Albacini and his English patrons', *Journal of History of Collections*, 3, 2: 183–98

Vines, G., 'The Bone Ranger', *The Guardian*, 19 October 1992, Science: 18–19

von Schlosser, J., 1978, *Die Kunst- und Wunderkammem der Spätrenaissance. Eir Beitrag zur Geschichte des Sammelwesens*, Leipzig, Klinkhardt & Biermann

Waagen, G., 1838, *Works of Art and Artists in England*, Vols 1–3, London

Waller, R., 1789, General Index to the Journal, Register and Letter Books of the Royal Society (Royal Society Archives)

Waller, R. (ed.), 1705, *The posthumous works of Robert Hooke ... containing his Cutlerian lectures, and other discourses, read at the meetings of the illustrious Royal Society ...* , London

Watson, F., 1909, *The beginnings of the Teaching of Modern Subjects in England*, London, Sir I. Pitman

Webster, C., 1970, *Samuel Hartlib and the Advancement of Learning*, London, Cambridge University Press

Webster, C., 1975, *The Great Instauration: Science, Medicine and Reform 1626–1660*, London, Duckworth

Wilkins, J., 1668, *An essay towards a real character and philosophical language*, London

Williams, C. (ed.), 1937, *Thomas Platter's 'Travels in England' 1599, rendered into English from the German, and with Introductory Matter*, London, Cape

Williams, N., 1989, *The Breaking and Re-Making of the Portland Vase*, London, British Museum Publications

Willis, J., 1661, *Mnemonic, or the Art of Memory*, London

Wills, G., 1971, *English furniture 1550–1760*, Enfield, Guiness Superlatives Ltd

Wilson, C.H., 1837, *Descriptive Catalogue of the casts from Antique Statues in the Trustees' Academy*, Edinburgh

Wimberley, I.C., 1928, *Folklore in the English and Scottish Ballads*, New York, Dover Publications

Winckelmann, J., 1770, *Critical Account of the Situation and Destruction by the first eruptions of Mount Versuvius of Herculaneum, Pompeii and Stabia*, London, Carham & Newberry

Wisner, D., 1996, 'Jean Naigeon at the Dépôt de Nesle: a collector and culture-broker in the First French Republic', *Journal of the History of Collections*, 8, 2: 155–66

Witlin, A., 1949, *The Museum: its History and its Tasks in Education*, London, Routledge & Kegan Paul

Witlin, A., 1970, *Museums: in Search of a Usable Future*, Cambridge, Massachusetts, MIT Press

Wood, R., 1753, *The Ruins of Palmyra, otherwise Tedmor in the Desart*, London

Woodward, J., 1695, *An Essay Towards a Natural History of the Earth*, London

Woodward, J., 1728a, *Fossils of all kinds, digested into a Method*, London

Woodward, J., 1728b, 'Letter to Sir Isaac Newton', in *Fossils of all Kinds, Digested into a Method*, London

Woodward, J., 1729, *An Attempt towards the Natural History of the Fossils of England ...* , Vol. 2, London

Worsley, R., 1782, *The Trial, with the whole of evidence between the Right Hon. Sir Richard Worsley Bart and George Maurice Bissett Esq, defendant, for criminal conversation with the plaintiff's wife on Thursday the 21st of February*, Cr. Kearsley, London

Worsley, R., 1794, *Museum Worseyanum: or, a collection of antique basso relievos, bustos, statues and gems, with views of places in the Levant taken on the spot in the year MDCCLXXXV, VI and VII*, London, Shakespear Press

Yates, F., 1966, *The Art of Memory*, London, Routledge & Kegan Paul

Young, R.F. (ed.), 1932, *Comenius in England*, London, Oxford University Press

Index

William V of Orange 263
Willis, John 87
Willisel, Thomas 94
Willughby, Francis 66
Wilson, Andrew 234
Wilson, C.H. 233
Wilson, T.B. 183
Wiltshire, Miss Benett's collection of
fossils in Wiltshire 183–5
Winckelmann, Johann 195–6, 218
antiquities of Herculaneum and Pompeii
and 196–9
Windus, Thomas 142, 143, 144–5, 146
Winthrop, Adam 68, 71
Winthrop, John, report on American
curiosities 67–71
Wishcombe, Jonas 189
Woide, Mr 176, 178
Wood, Robert 214

on classical architecture and sculpture
214–17
Woodward, John 77, 111, 113
classification of fossils 114–17
Woodward, Samuel 184
Wooton, Edward Lord 50
Worsley, Richard 211
collection on Grand Tour 211–13
Worsley, Robert 211
Wyatt, James 299

Yates, Frances 3, 87
York
Castle Museum 297
exhibition in County Gaol 297–8
Young, R.F. 47

Zante/Zakynthos 239, 241
Zenobia of Palmyra, Queen 214

WITHDRAWN

WITHDRAWN